Beyond Words

Beyond Words

What Animals Think and Feel

CARL SAFINA

A JOHN MACRAE BOOK

HENRY HOLT AND COMPANY   NEW YORK

Henry Holt and Company, LLC
Publishers since 1866
175 Fifth Avenue
New York, New York 10010
www.henryholt.com

Henry Holt® and ® are registered trademarks of
Henry Holt and Company, LLC.

Grateful acknowledgment is made for permission to reprint excerpts from the
following copyrighted works:
From *Elephantoms* by Lyall Watson. Copyright © 2002 by Lyall Watson.
Used by permission of W. W. Norton & Company, Inc.

"Shackleton's Decision" from *Moving the Piano* by Faith Shearin.
Copyright © 2011 by Faith Shearin. Used by permission of Stephen F. Austin University Press.

From "Dear Elephant, Sir" by Romain Gary in *Life* magazine (December 22, 1967).

Library of Congress Cataloging-in-Publication Data

Safina, Carl, 1955–.
Beyond words : what animals think and feel / Carl Safina.—First edition.
pages   cm
"A John Macrae Book."
Includes bibliographical references and index.
ISBN 978-0-8050-9888-4 (hardcover)—ISBN 978-0-8050-9889-1 (electronic book)
1. Animal psychology.   2. Animal behavior.   3. Elephants—Psychology.
4. Wolves—Psychology.   5. Whales—Psychology.   6. Psychology, Comparative.
I. Title.
QL785.S14 2015 591.56—dc23

2014045385

Henry Holt books are available for special promotions and
premiums. For details contact: Director, Special Markets.

First Edition 2015

Maps by Jon Luoma
Orca graphic courtesy of OCAL
Designed by Kelly S. Too

Printed in the United States of America

1 3 5 7 9 10 8 6 4 2

For the people in these pages who watch and truly listen,
who tell us what they are hearing in other voices that share our air,
and in the silence

I thought of the long ages of the past during which the successive generations of these things of beauty had run their course . . . with no intelligent eye to gaze upon their loveliness, to all appearances such a wanton waste of beauty. . . . This consideration must surely tell us that all living things were not made for man. . . . Their happiness and enjoyments, their loves and hates, their struggles for existence, their vigorous life and early death, would seem to be immediately related to their own well-being and perpetuation alone.

—Alfred Russel Wallace, *The Malay Archipelago*, 1869

We patronize them for their incompleteness, for their tragic fate of having taken form so far below ourselves. And therein we err, and greatly err. For the animal shall not be measured by man. In a world older and more complete than ours they move finished and complete, gifted with extensions of the senses we have lost or never attained, living by voices we shall never hear. They are not brethren, they are not underlings; they are other nations, caught with ourselves in the net of life and time, fellow prisoners of the splendour and travail of the earth.

—Henry Beston, *The Outermost House*, 1928

CONTENTS

Beyond Words

Into the Mind Field

———•———

Ask now the beasts, and they shall teach thee; and the fowls of the air, and they shall tell thee: Or speak to the earth, and it shall teach thee: and the fishes of the sea shall declare unto thee.

—Job 12:7–8, King James Version

Another big group of dolphins had just surfaced alongside our moving vessel—leaping and splashing and calling mysteriously back and forth in their squeally, whistly way, with many babies swift alongside their mothers. And this time, confined to just the surface of such deep and lovely lives, I was becoming unsatisfied. I wanted to know what they were experiencing, and why to us they feel so compelling and so—*close*. This time I allowed myself to ask them the question that is forbidden fruit: *Who* are you? Science usually steers firmly from questions about the inner lives of animals. Surely they have inner lives of some sort. But like a child who is admonished that what they really want to ask is impolite, a young scientist is taught that the animal mind—if there *is* such—is unknowable. Permissible questions are "it" questions: about where it lives, what it eats, what it does when danger threatens, how it breeds. But *always* forbidden is the one question that might open the door: Who?

There are reasons to avoid so fraught an inquiry. But the reason we least acknowledge is that the barrier between humans and animals is artificial, because humans *are* animals. And now, watching these dolphins, I was tired of being so artificially polite; I wanted more intimacy.

I felt time slipping for both of us, and I did not want to risk having to say good-bye and realizing that I'd never really said hello. During the cruise I'd been reading about elephants, and elephant minds were on my own mind as I wondered about the dolphins and watched them pacing fluidly and freely in their ocean realm. When a poacher kills an elephant, he doesn't just kill the elephant who dies. The family may lose the crucial memory of their elder matriarch, who knew where to travel during the very toughest years of drought to reach the food and water that would allow them to continue living. Thus one bullet may, years later, bring more deaths. Watching dolphins while thinking of elephants, what I realized is: when others recognize and depend on certain individuals, when a death makes the difference for individuals who *survive,* when relationships define us, we have traveled across a certain blurry boundary in the history of life on Earth—"it" has become "who."

"Who" animals know *who* they are; they know who their family and friends are. They know their enemies. They make strategic alliances and cope with chronic rivalries. They aspire to higher rank and wait for their chance to challenge the existing order. Their status affects their offspring's prospects. Their life follows the arc of a career. Personal relationships define them. Sound familiar? Of course. "They" includes us. But a vivid, familiar life is not the domain of humans alone.

We look at the world through our own eyes, naturally. But by looking from the inside out, we see an inside-out world. This book takes the perspective of the world outside us—a world in which humans are not the measure of all things, a human race among other races. In our estrangement from nature we have severed our sense of the community of life and lost touch with the experience of other animals. And because everything about life occurs along a sliding scale, understanding the *human* animal becomes easier in context, seeing our human thread woven into the living web among the strands of so many others.

I'd intended to take a bit of a break from my usual writing about conservation issues, to circle back to my first love: simply seeing what animals do, and asking why they do it. I traveled to observe some of the most protected creatures in the world—elephants of Amboseli in Kenya, wolves of Yellowstone in the United States, and killer whales in the waters of the

Pacific Northwest—yet in each place I found the animals feeling human pressures that directly affect what they do, where they go, how long they live, and how their families fare. So in this book we encounter the minds of other animals *and* we listen—to what they need us to hear. The story that tells itself is not just what's at stake but *who* is at stake.

The greatest realization is that all life is one. I was seven years old when my father and I fixed up a small shed in our Brooklyn yard and got some homing pigeons. Watching how they built nests in their cubbyholes, seeing them courting, arguing, caring for their babies, flying off and faithfully returning, how they needed food, water, a home, and one another, I realized that they lived in their apartments just as we lived in ours. Just like us, but in a different way. Over my lifetime, living with, studying, and working with many other animals in their world and ours has only broadened and deepened—and reaffirmed—my impression of our shared life. That's the impression I'll endeavor to share with you in the pages that follow.

PART ONE

Trumpets of Elephants

Delicate and mighty, awesome and enchanted, commanding the silence ordinarily reserved for mountain peaks, great fires, and the sea.

—Peter Matthiessen, *The Tree Where Man Was Born*

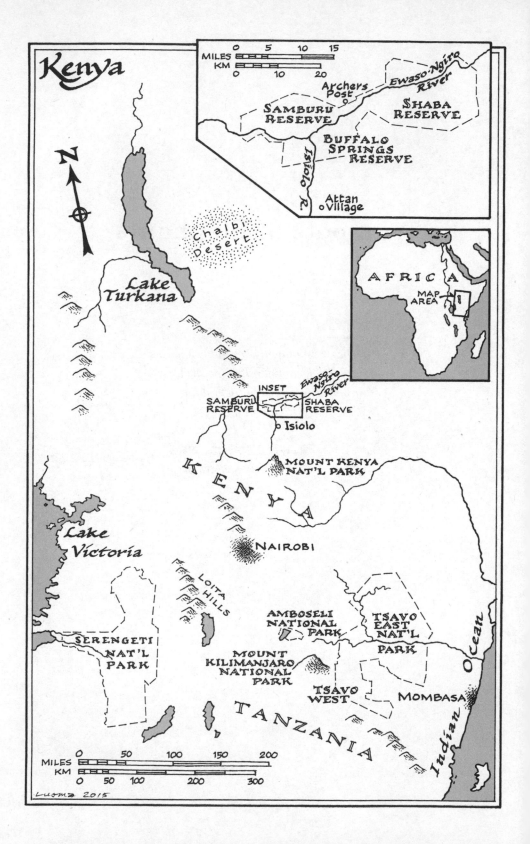

Kenya

MILES 0 5 10 15
KM 0 10 20

Ewaso-Ngiro River

Archers Post

SAMBURU RESERVE

SHABA RESERVE

BUFFALO SPRINGS RESERVE

Isiolo R.

Attan Village

Chalbi Desert

Lake Turkana

N

AFRICA

MAP AREA

Ewaso-Ngiro River

INSET

SAMBURU RESERVE

SHABA RESERVE

Isiolo

KENYA

MOUNT KENYA NAT'L PARK

Lake Victoria

NAIROBI

Loita Hills

AMBOSELI NATIONAL PARK

TSAVO EAST NAT'L PARK

SERENGETI NAT'L PARK

MOUNT KILIMANJARO NATIONAL PARK

TSAVO WEST

MOMBASA

Indian Ocean

TANZANIA

MILES 0 50 100 150 200
KM 0 50 100 200 300

Luoma 2015

Finally I saw that the very land itself had risen, that the sunbaked land had taken form as something vast and alive and was in motion. The land walked as multitudes, their strides so utterly of the earth that they seemed the source of the very dust. The cloud they raised engulfed us, seeped into every pore, coated our teeth, sifted into our minds. Both flesh and metaphor. That big.

And you could see their heads, like warriors' shields. Their great breaths, gushing in and out, resonant in the halls of their lungs. The skin as they moved, wrinkled with time and wear, batiked with the walk of ages, as if they lived within the creased maps of the lives they'd traveled. Travelers across landscapes, and through timescapes. The skin moving like swishing corduroy, textured and rough but sensitive to the slightest touch. The grind of their cobblestone molars as, sheaf by sheaf and mouthful by mouthful, they acquired the world. All the while uttering the contented purring of mounds of memories.

Their rumbles rolled through the air like distant thunder approaching, vibrating through the undulating ground and the roots of trees, rallying families and friends from the hills and rivers, sending among themselves greetings and recognitions and news of where they had been; sending to us a sign of something coming.

A mind moves a mountainous mass of muscle and bone, the brown eyes light a landscape, and one elephant rumbles in. See her squared brow, trace the tracks of snake-sized blood vessels. Heralded by her own trumpet, applauded by her own clapping ears, she strikes us as timeless and a bit sublime, aware and deliberative, peaceful and nurturing and deadly

dangerous as needs arise. Wise only within the confines of her capabilities, like us. Vulnerable. As we all are.

Watch. Simply listen. They will not speak to us, but to one another they
say much. Some of it, we hear. The rest is beyond words. I want to listen,
to open to the possibilities.

Disproportioned ears flapping. Tough dust-crusted hide. Bizarre pro-
truding teeth the size of human legs astride the world's most phallic nose.
Such gargoyle grotesqueness should strike us as hideous. Yet in them we
perceive a vast intangible beauty, at times so intense it fells us. We sense
much more, much deeper. We can feel that their march across the landscape is *intentional*. We cannot deny; they are going to a place they have
in mind.

That's where we're headed now.

The Big Question

———•———

"It was the worst year of my life," Cynthia Moss is saying over breakfast. "All the elephants over fifty years old died, except Barbara and Deborah. Most over forty died. So it's particularly amazing that Alison, Agatha, and Amelia have survived."

Alison, now fifty-one years old, is right *there,* in that clump of palms—see? Forty years ago, Cynthia Moss arrived in Kenya determined to learn the lives of elephants. The first elephant family she saw she named the "AA" family, and she named one of those elephants Alison. And there she is. Right there, vacuuming up fallen palm fruits. Astonishing.

With much luck and decent rainfall, Alison might survive another decade. And there is Agatha, forty-four years old. And this one coming closer now is Amelia, also forty-four.

Amelia continues approaching, until, rather alarmingly, she is looming so hugely in front of our vehicle that I reflexively lean inward. Cynthia leans out and talks to her in soothing tones. Amelia, practically alongside now, simply towers as she grinds palm fronds, rumbles softly, and blinks.

In the light of this egg-yolk dawn, the landscape seems an eternal ocean of grass rolling toward the base of Africa's greatest mountain, whose blue head is crowned by snow and wreathed in clouds. Through gravity-fed springs, Kilimanjaro acts like a giant water cooler, creating two miles-long marshes that make this place magnetic for wildlife and for pastoralist herders. Amboseli National Park got its name from a Maa word that refers to the ancient shallow lake bed—half the park—that seasonally glitters with the sparkle of wetness. The marshes expand and contract depending on the rains. But if the rains fail, panes of water dry to pans of dust. And then all bets are off. Just four years ago, a drought of extremes shook this place to its core.

Through times lush and calamitous, through these decades, Cynthia and these three elephants have maintained their presence, urging themselves across this landscape. Cynthia helped pioneer the deceptively complex task of simply seeing elephants doing elephant things. Longer than any other human being ever has, Cynthia has watched some of the same individual elephants living their lives.

I was expecting that, after four decades, the famous researcher might be a bit field-weary. But I found in Cynthia Moss a young woman in her early seventies, of bright blue eyes and startling bubbliness. A bit pixie-ish, actually. A *Newsweek* magazine writer during the 1960s, Cynthia decided, after her first visit to Africa, to chuck New York and all things familiar. She'd fallen in love with Amboseli. It's easy to see why.

Perhaps too easy. The great plain of mirages and heat waves conveys the illusion that Amboseli National Park is big. It is too small. You can easily drive across it in well under an hour. Amboseli is a postcard that Africa once mailed to itself and now keeps in a drawer marked "Parks and Reserves." Kilimanjaro, not even in the same nation, stands across an imaginary line in a place called Tanzania. The mountain and the elephants know that it is one true country. But the 150-square-mile park serves as a central watering hole for the surrounding three thousand square miles. Amboseli elephants use an area roughly twenty times larger than the park itself. As do cattle- and goat-grazing Maasai people. The only year-round water is here. The outer lands are too dry to water them. The park is too small to feed them.

"To survive the drought," Cynthia is explaining, "different families tried different strategies. Some tried to stay close to the swamp. But they did very badly as it dried. Some went far north, many for the first time in their lives. They did better. Out of fifty-eight families, only one family did not lose anybody." One family lost seven adult females and thirteen youngsters. "Usually if an elephant goes down, the family gathers around and tries to lift it. In the drought, they had no energy. Watching them dying, seeing them on the ground in agony—"

One in four of Amboseli's elephants—four hundred out of a population of sixteen hundred—perished. Nearly every nursing baby died. About 80 percent of the zebras and wildebeests died, nearly all of the Maasai's cattle; even people died.

So when the rain returned, the surviving female elephants bereft of babies all cycled into estrus at about the same time. Result: the biggest baby boom in Cynthia's forty-year history here, about 250 little elephants born in the last two years. This is a sweet spot in time to be born an elephant in Amboseli. Lush vegetation, plenty of grass—and little competition. Water makes elephants. And water makes elephants happy.

Several happy elephants are sloshing through an emerald spring under ample palm shade. It's a little patch of paradise. With their bouncy, rubbery little trunks, the babies seem to transit the outer orbits of innocence.

"Look how fat *that* baby is," I say. The fifteen-month-old looks like a ball of butter. Four adults and three little babies are wallowing in one muddy pool, spraying water over their backs with their trunks, then sprawling on the bank. As a little one melts in pleasure, I notice the muscles around the trunk relaxing, eyes half-closing. An adolescent named Alfre lies down to rest. But three youngsters pile on, stepping on Alfre's ear. *Oomph*. The fun softens to a snooze, with babies lying asleep on their sides, adults standing protectively over them, the adults' bodies touching one another's as they doze. Feel how calm they are, knowing their family is safe here now. It's soothing just to watch.

Many people fantasize that if they won the lottery, they would quit their job and immerse themselves in leisure, play, family, parenthood, occasional thrilling sex; they'd eat when they were hungry and sleep whenever they felt sleepy. Many people, if they won the lottery and got rich quick, would want to live like elephants.

The elephants seem happy. But when elephants seem happy to us, do they really feel happy? My inner scientist wants proof.

"Elephants experience joy," Cynthia says. "It may not be human joy. But it is joy."

Elephants act joyful in the same situations that make us joyful: familiar "friends" and family, lush food and drink. So we assume they feel the way we feel. But beware of assumptions! For centuries, people's assumptions about other animals have ranged from believing that animals cast spells on people to believing that they are aware of nothing and can't even feel pain. Observe what an animal does, scientists advise, but speculation about mental experiences is meaningless, a waste of time.

Speculation about animals' mental experiences happens to be the main quest of this book. The tricky task ahead: to go only where evidence, logic, and science lead. And, to get it right.

Cynthia's free-living colleagues seem wise. They seem youthful, playful. Powerful, majestic. Innocent. All these things, they are. Inoffensive. But of all the animals, they are the ones who can wage sustained resistance to human persecution with deadly force. As we do, they strive to survive and to keep their children safe. I guess I am here because I am ready to learn, ready to ask, How are they like us? What do they teach us about ourselves?

What I don't see coming is: I have the question almost exactly backward.

⤙

Cynthia Moss is most at home in her Amboseli field camp. The camp, nestled cozily in a clearing ringed by palms, features a small cook shack and half a dozen large tents, each with a proper bed and a bit of furniture. On a recent morning, tea was late. The researcher who unzipped her tent flap to go and inquire about the tea's progress found a lion dozing on the cook shack's step, and a very awake cook behind the door.

Today the tea is on time, and over toast I have, finally, gotten round to asking Cynthia what I think is the Big Question. "What has a lifetime of watching elephants," I ask, "taught you about humanity?" I glance to make sure my recorder's light is on, then settle back a bit. Forty years of insight; this will be good.

Cynthia Moss, however, gently deflects my question. "I think of them as elephants," she says. "I'm *interested* in them as elephants. Comparing elephants to people—I don't find it helpful. I find it much more interesting trying to understand an animal as itself. How does a bird like a crow, say, with so small a brain, make the amazing decisions it makes? Comparing it to a three-year-old human child—that doesn't interest me."

Cynthia's mild objection to my question comes so unexpectedly that at first I don't fully grasp it. Then I am stunned.

As a lifelong student of animal behavior, I'd long ago concluded that many social animals—certainly birds and mammals—are fundamentally like us. I've come here to see how elephants are "like us." I am *writing this book* about how other animals are "like us." But I'd just gotten a major course correction. It took a few moments—in fact, it took days—but, like an intravenous drip, it seeped in.

Cynthia's enormous little comment implied that humans are not the measure of all things. Cynthia is traveling a higher road.

Cynthia's comment hit Reset, not just on my question but on my thinking. I'd somehow assumed that my quest was to let the animals show how much they are like us. My task now—a much harder task, a much deeper task—would be to endeavor to see *who* animals simply *are*—like us or not.

～

The elephants we're watching are nimbly pulling grass and brush with their trunks, rhythmically stuffing tufts and wads into their cheeks, their massive molars mightily mashing away. Thorns that can puncture a tire, palm fruits, bundles of grass—it all goes in. I once stroked a captive elephant's tongue. So soft. I don't understand how their tongues and stomachs can handle those thorns.

What I see: elephants, eating. But those words cast, as all words do, the loosest lasso around reality. We are watching "elephants," true, yet I realize with embarrassment that I know nothing about their lives.

But Cynthia does. "When you look at a group of anything—lions, zebras, elephants," Cynthia explains, "you're seeing just two flat dimensions. But once you know them individually, their personalities, who their mother was, who their kids are, it adds new dimensions." One elephant in a family might seem regal, dignified, gentle. Another will strike you as shy. Another as a bully who will be pushy to get food in sparse times; another as reserved; another as "flamboyantly" playful.

"The realization of how complex they are took me about twenty years," Cynthia continues. "Over the period that we were following Echo's family—she was about forty-five years old at the time—I saw that Enid was incredibly loyal to her, Eliot was the playful one, Eudora was flaky, Edwina was unpopular, and so on. And slowly I realized that I'd begun knowing what would happen next. I was taking my cues from Echo herself. I was understanding her leadership—as her family was understanding it!"

I look at the elephants.

Cynthia adds, "It made me realize how totally super aware they are of what we're doing."

Super aware? They seem oblivious.

"Elephants don't *seem* aware of details," Cynthia explains, "until something familiar changes." One day a cameraman working with Cynthia decided that for a different angle, he'd position himself *underneath* the research vehicle. The oncoming elephants, who usually just passed by the vehicle, immediately noticed, stopped, and stared. Why was a human under the car? A male named Mr. Nick snaked his slithering, sniffing trunk under there to investigate. He was not aggressive and did not try to pull the man out; he was just curious. Another day, when the vehicle appeared with a special door designed for filming, elephants came exploring, actually touching the new door with their trunks.

Trunks are strangely familiar, familiarly strange things. Extremely sensitive and unimaginably strong, they can pick up an egg without breaking it—or kill you with an easy smack. An elephant's trunk terminates in two almost fingery tips, like a hand in a mitten. The way elephants use their trunks helps make them seem familiar, like one-armed people, hiding their hideous nose in plain sight and affecting its transformation. Can we ever get over how strangely wonderful, how wonderfully beautiful? Segmented like the tree trunks of the palms under which they sometimes rest, the trunk is an elephant's Swiss Army knife. Rounded on the outer edge, flattened on the inner, a great mine-sweeping, water-hosing, mud-flinging, dust-deviling, air-testing, food-gathering, friend-greeting, infant-rescuing, baby-reassuring caterpillar of a nose. "It has double hoses for sucking in and spraying out water or dust," wrote Oria Douglas-Hamilton. Journalist Caitrin Nicol adds that a trunk does "what a person would rely on a combination of eyes, nose, hands, and machinery to do." Yoshihito Niimura of the University of Tokyo offers: "Imagine having a nose on the palm of your hand. Every time you touch something, you smell it."

· · ·

They're firmly wrapping those wondrous noses around sheaves of grass, and when the soil is reluctant to surrender the clumps, they give a little kick to break them. The food is freed and lifted. Sometimes they shake soil from roots. The eating is slow, relaxed. Often they slightly swing the trunk for a little momentum in pitching the next mouthful into their triangular jaw. Sometimes they pause for a moment, seeming thoughtful. Perhaps they're just stopping to listen, monitoring indicators of their children's well-being, family safety, and possible danger.

I'd love to know how much overlap there is right now between what I am sensing and what the nearest elephant is sensing. Our input channels are similar: sight, scent, sound, touch, taste; what these senses bring to our attention must broadly overlap. We can see the same hyenas, say, as do the elephants and hear the same lions. But we, like most other primates, are very visual; elephants, like most other mammals, have an acute sense of smell. Their hearing is excellent, too.

I'm sure the elephants here are sensing much more than I; this is their home, and they have a history here. I can't tell what's going on in their heads. Nor can I tell what Cynthia's thinking as, quietly and intently, she observes.

The Same Basic Brain

—•—

Four rounded babies are following their massive mothers across a broad, sweet-smelling grassland. The adults, striding with deliberate purpose as though keeping an appointment, are nodding toward the wide, wet marsh where about a hundred of their compatriots are mingling. Families commute daily between sleeping areas in brush-thicketed hills and the marshes. For many it's ten miles (fifteen kilometers) round-trip. Between here and there and sun to sun, a lot can happen.

Our job: travel around in the morning, finding them as they're coming in; see who's where. The idea is simple, but there are dozens of families, hundreds of elephants.

"You have to know *everyone*. Yes!," Katito Sayialel is saying. Her lilting accent is as clear and light as this African morning. A native Maasai, tall and capable, Katito has been studying free-living elephants with Cynthia Moss for more than two decades.

How many is "everyone"?

"I can recognize all the adult females. So," Katito considers, "nine hundred to one thousand. Say nine hundred. Yes."

Recognizing hundreds and hundreds of elephants on sight? *How* is this possible? Some she knows by marks: the position of a hole in an ear, for instance. But many, she just glances at. They're that familiar, like your friends are.

When they're all mingling, you can't afford to say, "Wait a minute; who was *that*?" Elephants themselves recognize hundreds of individuals.

They live in vast social networks of families and friendships. That's why they're famous for their memory. They certainly recognize Katito.

"When I first arrived here," Katito recalls, "they heard my voice and knew I was a new person. They came to smell me. Now they know me."

Vicki Fishlock is here, too. A blue-eyed Brit in her early thirties, Vicki studied gorillas and elephants in the Republic of the Congo before bringing her doctoral diploma here to work with Cynthia. She's been here for a couple of years and has no plans to go anywhere else if she can help it. Usually Katito takes attendance and rolls on. Vicki stays and watches behavior. Today we're out on a bit of a jaunt; they're kindly orienting me.

Just outside the high "elephant grass," five adults and their four young babies are selecting a shorter and far less abundant grass. It's more work; it must taste better. They haven't read a treatise on the nutritional content of grass. In a sense, their subconscious tells them what to do by rewarding them with pleasure for making the richer choice. It works the same for us—that's why sugar and fat taste so good.

The grazing elephants trail a train of egrets and an orbiting galaxy of swirling swallows. The birds rely on elephants to stir up insects as, like great gray ships, they plow through the grassy sea. Light shifts on their wide, rolling backs like sun on ocean waves. Sounds of ripping, chewing. Flap of ear. Plop of dung. The buzz of flies and swoosh of swatting tails. Soft tom-tom footfalls. And, mostly, the quiet ways of ample beasts. Wordlessly they speak of a time before human breath. They get on with their lives, ignoring us.

"They're not ignoring us," Vicki corrects. "They have an expectation of politeness, and we're fulfilling it. So they're not paying us any mind."

"They weren't always like this to me," she adds. "When I started, they were used to vehicles snapping a few pictures and moving along. They were not wildly happy about me just sitting and watching them for long periods. They expect you to behave a certain way. If you don't, they will let you know that they notice. Not in a threatening way. You might get a head shake and a look like, 'What's *your* problem?'"

Through hummocks and the bush, in our vehicle we amble with them. An elephant named Tecla, walking just a few yards ahead to our right, suddenly turns, trumpets, and generally objects to us. To our left, a young elephant wheels and screams.

"Sorry, sorry, sorry," Katito says to Tecla. She brakes to a stop, turning off the ignition. It appears to me that we have separated this mother from her baby. But Tecla is not the mother. Another female, whose two breasts are full of milk, runs over, cutting just in front of us. *This one* is actually the mother. Basically Tecla was communicating, "The humans are getting between you and your baby; come and *do* something."

"Elephants, they are like human beings," offers Katito. "Very intelligent. I like their characters. I like the way they behave and hold their family, the way they protect. Yes."

Like human beings? In some fundamental ways we seem—we *are*—so similar. But I can see Cynthia wagging a finger of caution, reminding me that elephants are not us; they are themselves.

Mother rejoins baby, restoring order. We slowly proceed. When one individual knows another's relationship to a third—as Tecla knows who the baby's mother is—it's called "understanding third-party relationships." Primates understand third-party relationships too, and so do wolves, hyenas, dolphins, birds of the crow family, and at least some parrots. A parrot, say, can act jealous of its keeper's spouse. When the vervet monkeys that are common around camp hear an infant's distress call, they instantly look to the infant's mother. They know exactly who they *and everyone else* are. They understand precisely who is important to whom. When free-living dolphin mothers want young ones to stop interacting with humans, the mothers sometimes direct a tail slap at the *human* who has the baby's attention, signaling, in effect, "End the game; I need my child's attention." When the dawdling youngsters are interacting with dolphin researcher Denise Herzing's graduate assistants, their mothers occasionally direct these—what could we call them: reprimands?—at *Herzing herself*. This shows that the dolphins understand that Dr. Herzing is the leader of all the humans in the water. For free-living creatures to perceive rank-order in humans—just astonishing.

"What I find most amazing about it," Vicki sums up, "is that we *can* understand each other. We learn the elephants' invisible boundaries. We can sense when it's time to say, 'I don't want to push her.' Words like 'irritated,' 'happy' or 'sad' or 'tense'—they really *do* capture what that elephant is experiencing. We have a shared experience because," she adds with a twinkle, "we've all got the same basic brain."

• • •

I look at these elephants, so relaxed about us that they're passing within a couple of paces of our vehicle. Vicki says, "This is one of the greatest privileges, moving along with elephants who are okay with you being here. These guys all go into Tanzania, where there are poachers everywhere. But here—." Vicki talks to them in soothing tones, saying, "Hello, darling" and "Aren't *you* a sweet girl." Vicki recalls that after the famed Echo's death, her family went away for three months under the leadership of Echo's daughter Enid. "And when they returned, I started saying things like 'Hello, I missed you—' And suddenly Enid's head *swept* up, and she gave this *huge* rumble; her ears were flapping and they all came around, close enough that I could have touched them, and the glands on all their faces were streaming with emotion. That's trust. I felt as though," Vicki says fondly, "I was getting an elephant hug."

⌒

Once, I was watching elephants with another scientist in another African reserve. Several adult elephants were resting with their young in the shade of a palm, fanning their ears in the heat. The scientist opined that the elephants we were watching "might simply be moving to and away from heat gradients, without experiencing anything at all." He declared, "I have no way of knowing whether that elephant is any more conscious than this bush."

No way of knowing? For starters, a bush behaves quite differently from an elephant. The bush shows no sign of having a mental experience, of showing emotions, of making decisions, of protecting its offspring. On the other hand, humans and elephants have nearly identical nervous and hormonal systems, senses, milk for our babies; we both show fear and aggression appropriate to the moment. Insisting that an elephant might be no more conscious than a bush isn't a better explanation for the elephants' behavior than concluding that an elephant is aware of what's going on around it. My colleague thought he was being an objective scientist. Quite the opposite; he was forcing himself to ignore the evidence. That's not scientific—at all. Science is about evidence.

. . .

At issue, here, is: Who are we here with? What kinds of minds populate this world?

This is hazardous terrain. We won't assume that other animals are or aren't conscious. We'll look at evidence and go where it leads. It's too easy to assume *wrongly*, then carry those assumptions around for, say, centuries.

In the fifth century B.C.E., the Greek philosopher Protagoras pronounced, "Man is the measure of all things." In other words, we feel entitled to ask the world, "What good are you?" We assume that we are the world's standard, that all things should be compared to us. Such an assumption makes us overlook a lot. Abilities said to "make us human"—empathy, communication, grief, toolmaking, and so on—all exist to varying degrees among other minds sharing the world with us. Animals with backbones (fishes, amphibians, reptiles, birds, and mammals) all share the same basic skeleton, organs, nervous systems, hormones, and behaviors. Just as different models of automobiles each have an engine, drive train, four wheels, doors, and seats, we differ mainly in terms of our outside contours and a few internal tweaks. But like naïve car buyers, most people see only animals' varied exteriors.

We say "humans and animals" as though life falls into just two categories: us and all of them. Yet we've trained elephants to haul logs from forests; in laboratories we've run rats through mazes to study learning, let pigeons tap targets to teach us Psychology 101; we study flies to learn how our DNA works, give monkeys infectious diseases to develop cures for humans; in our homes and cities, dogs have become the guiding protectors for humans who see only by the light of their four-legged companions' eyes. Throughout all this intimacy, we maintain a certain insecure insistence that "animals" are not like us—though we are animals. Could any relationship be more fundamentally miscomprehended?

To understand elephants we must delve into topics like consciousness, awareness, intelligence, and emotion. When we do, we realize with dismay that there aren't standard definitions. The same words mean different things. Philosophers, psychologists, ecologists, and neurologists are the blind men all feeling and describing different parts of the same proverbial elephant. But, silver lining: their lack of agreement frees us to walk out of the academic bar brawls into clearer air and a wider view, and do a little of our own thinking.

So let's start by defining consciousness. The standard we'll use is: Consciousness is *the thing that feels like something*. That simple definition comes from Christof Koch, who heads the Allen Institute for Brain Science, in Seattle. Cut your leg, that's physical. If the cut hurts, you're conscious. The part of you that knows that the cut hurts, that feels and thinks, is your *mind*. Relatedly, the ability to feel sensations is called *sentience*. The sentience of humans, elephants, beetles, clams, jellyfish, and trees ranges on a sliding scale, from complex in people to seemingly none in plants. *Cognition* refers to the capacity to perceive and acquire knowledge and understanding. *Thought* is the process of considering something that's been perceived. Like everything about living things, thought also happens on a wide-ranging sliding scale; thinking can take the form of a jaguar assessing how to approach a wary peccary from directly behind, an archer aiming at a target, or a person considering a proposal of marriage. Sentience, cognition, and thinking are overlapping processes of conscious minds.

Consciousness is a bit overrated. Heartbeat, breathing, digestion, metabolism, immune responses, healing of cuts and fractures, internal timers, sexual cycling, pregnancy, growth—all function without consciousness. Under general anesthesia we remain very much alive though not conscious. And during sleep our unconscious brains are working hard, cleansing, sorting, rejuvenating. Your body is run by a competent staff that's been on the job since before the company acquired consciousness. Too bad you can't personally meet your team.

We might imagine consciousness as the computer screen we see and interact with, one run by software codes that we can't detect and don't have a clue about. Most of the brain runs in the dark. As science author and former *Rolling Stone* magazine editor Tim Ferris wrote, "One's mind neither controls nor comprehends most of what's going on in one's brain."

Why be conscious at all? Trees and jellyfish do just fine, yet may not experience sensations. Consciousness seems necessary when we must judge things, plan, and make decisions.

How does consciousness—elephant, human, whatever—arise in the mush of our physical cells and the mesh of their electrical and chemical impulses?

How does a brain create a mind? No one knows how nerve cells, also called neurons, create consciousness. What we know: consciousness can be affected by brain damage. So consciousness does happen in the brain. As Nobel Prize–winning mind-brain scientist Eric R. Kandel wrote in 2013, "Our mind is a set of operations carried out by our brain." Consciousness seems to somehow result from, and depend on, neurons networking.

How many networked neurons are needed? No one knows where the most rudimentary consciousness lurks. Jellyfish, probably not conscious; worms, maybe so. With about one million brain cells, honeybees recognize patterns, scents, and colors in flowers and remember their locations. The bees' "waggle dance" communicates to their fellow hivemates the direction, distance, and richness of nectar they've found. Bees "show superb expertise," says famed neurologist Oliver Sacks. Honeybees will interrupt a colleague's waggle dance if they've experienced trouble at the same flower source, such as a brush with a predator like a spider. Honeybees subjected by researchers to simulated attack show, said researchers, "the same hallmarks of negative emotions that we find in humans." Even more intriguingly, honeybee brains contain the same "thrill-seeker" hormones that in human brains drive some people to consistently seek novelty. *If* those hormones do deliver some tingle of pleasure or motivation to the bees, it means bees are conscious. Certain highly social wasps can recognize individuals by their faces, something previously believed the sole domain of a few elite mammals. "It is increasingly evident," says Sacks, "that insects can remember, learn, think, and communicate in quite rich and unexpected ways."

Can elephants, insects, or any other creature really be *conscious* without the big wrinkly cerebral cortex where human thinking happens? Turns out, yes; even humans can be. A thirty-year-old man named Roger lost about 95 percent of his cortex to a brain infection. Roger can't remember the decade before the infection, can't taste or smell, and has great difficulty forming new memories. Yet he knows who he is, recognizes himself in a mirror and in photographs, and generally acts normal around people. He can use humor and can feel embarrassed. All with a brain that does not resemble a human brain.

The common human notion that humans alone experience consciousness is backward. Human senses have evidently dulled during civilization. Many animals are superhumanly alert—just watch these elephants when anything changes—their detection equipment exquisitely tuned for the merest crackle of danger or whiff of opportunity. In 2012, scientists drafting the Cambridge Declaration on Consciousness concluded that "all mammals and birds, and many other creatures, including octopuses," have nervous systems capable of consciousness. (Octopuses use tools and solve problems as skillfully as do most apes—and they're *mollusks*.) Science is confirming the obvious: other animals hear, see, and smell with their ears, eyes, and noses; are frightened when they have reason for fright and feel happy when they appear happy.

As Christof Koch writes, "Whatever consciousness is . . . dogs, birds, and legions of other species have it. . . . They, too, experience life."

My dog Jude was sleeping on the rug, dreaming of running, his wrists flicking, when he let out a long, eerily muffled howl. Chula, my other dog, instantly piqued, trotted over to Jude. Jude startled awake and leapt to his feet barking loudly, just as a person wakes from a night terror with a vivid image and a scream, taking a few moments to get oriented.

Each line we attempt to draw crisply, as between elephants and humans, nature has already blurred with the smudgy brush of deep relation. But what about living things with *no* nervous system? That *is* a dividing line. Isn't it?

With no apparent nervous system, plants *make the same chemicals*—such as serotonin, dopamine, and glutamate—that serve as neurotransmitters and help create mood in animals, including humans. And plants have signaling systems that work basically as do animals', though slower. Michael Pollan observes, a bit metaphorically, that "plants speak in a chemical vocabulary we can't directly perceive or comprehend." That's not to say that plants experience sensations, necessarily, but they do some intriguing things. We detect chemicals by smell and taste; plants sense and respond to chemicals in air, soil, and on themselves. Plants' leaves turn to track the sun. Growing roots approaching an obstacle or toxin sometimes alter course *prior* to contact. Plants have reportedly responded to the *recorded* sound of a munching caterpillar by producing defensive chemicals. Plants attacked by insects and herbivores emit "distress" chemicals, causing adjacent leaves and neighboring plants to mount chemical defenses, and alerting insect-killing wasps to move in, blunting the attack. Flowers are plants' way of telling bees and other pollinators that nectar is ready.

But except for insectivorous and sensitive-leaved plants, most plants behave too slowly for the human eye. Gazing across a meadow, Pollan wrote, he "found it difficult to imagine the invisible chemical chatter, including the calls of distress, going on all around—or that these motionless plants were engaged in any kind of 'behavior' at all." Yet Charles Darwin concluded his book *The Power of Movement in Plants* by noting, "It is hardly an exaggeration to say that the tip of the radicle [root] . . . acts like the brain of one of the lower animals . . . receiving impression from the sense organs and directing the several movements." Granted, we are treading into a vast minefield of potential misinterpretation. Like Cynthia Moss with elephants, the late botanist Tim Plowman wasn't interested in comparing plants to people. He appreciated them as plants. "They can eat light," he said. "Isn't that enough?"

My main reason for getting into the weeds here is to realize that, compared to the strangeness of plants and the large differences between plants and animals, an elephant nursing her baby is so like us that she might as well be my sister.

Distinctly Human?

———•———

In grassy groves of sunlight, little baby elephants are trying to get the hang of their trunks, then seeking that reassuring nipple.

"Look at how friendly these two families are being," Vicki is saying. "Elin decided to move closer to the water, Eloise agreed, then she waited as the whole group moved up. They've obviously chosen to just spend time together today."

Obviously.

What causes elephant friendships? Certain young ones like the same games and always play together. Certain older individuals are "compatible," Vicki says, in "when they want to eat, when they want to sleep, where they like to go, what kinds of foods they like."

Compatible. Interesting. Difficult enough in humans.

The best answer to the question "Is an elephant conscious?" is that *all* the evidence indicates widespread consciousness. So the interesting question now is "What is consciousness like for other animals?" Consciousness might seem like a no-brainer to most pet lovers, but I can almost hear some people say, "Not so fast." Many researchers and science writers insist that we simply have no way to access the mental experience of animals. I understand where they're coming from. But I think they're mistaken. We now know more than we did.

Animal behavior is a young science. The simple fact that chickens establish a "pecking order" was not formally recognized until the 1920s. Also in the 1920s, Margaret Morse Nice first discovered that songbirds defend territories—and that's one of the most basic reasons they sing. To establish animal behavior as a science, the pioneering behaviorists of the mid-twentieth century, such as Konrad Lorenz, Niko Tinbergen, and Karl von Frisch, had to purge centuries of folklore and superstition (owls presage death, wolves are the devil's familiars) and fables that posed animals as caricatures of human impulses (grasshoppers are lazy, tortoises persistent, foxes tricky).

The new scientists were wonderful observers. They succeeded in stripping metaphorical projections that had built up on many animals like old coats of paint. Their approach: describe just what you see. They had to prove that watching animals could be objective work, and they did. For their studies of honeybee dance-language, fish courtship, and how baby geese "imprint" on the first moving object they see, von Frisch, Tinbergen, and Lorenz shared a Nobel Prize. The three curious naturalists must have felt euphoric.

But there was no scientific way to approach a question such as "What does an elephant feel when she nurses her baby?" There was nothing to go on. No one had watched free-living animals living their real lives. Brain science was in its infancy. So speculation about their feelings could only draw on our own feelings—leading ourselves in circles. The new scientists insisted on observation. Speculation was messy guessing that one had to avoid. We can observe *what* an elephant does. There's no way to know *how* the animal feels. So just observe how many minutes the elephant nurses its offspring. Even the noted elephant communication expert Joyce Poole has explained, "I was trained to view non-human animals as behaving in ways that don't necessarily involve any conscious thinking."

My own initiation into formal training included the classic directive: Do not attribute human mental experiences—thoughts or emotions—to other animals. (Doing so is called "anthropomorphism.") I appreciate that. We shouldn't assume that animals (or, for that matter, lovers, spouses, kids, or parents) "must be" thinking and feeling just as we would if we were them. They're not us.

But it wasn't that the question of animal thoughts and emotions awaited better data; it was that the whole subject became verboten. The observational approach hardened into a rigid mental straitjacket. Professional behaviorists could describe what they saw, period. Description—and *only* description—became "the" science of animal behavior. Wondering what feelings or thoughts might motivate behavioral acts became totally taboo. Radio blackout. You could say, "The elephant positioned herself between her calf and the hyena." But if you said, "The mother positioned herself to protect her baby from the hyena," *that* was out of bounds; it was anthropomorphic. We can't know the mother's intent. And this was stifling.

In establishing the study of behavior as a science, it had originally been helpful to make "anthropomorphism" a word that raised a red flag. But as lesser intellects followed the Nobel Prize–winning pioneers, "anthropomorphism" became a pirate flag. If the word was hoisted, an attack was imminent. You wouldn't get your work published. And in the academic realm of publish or perish, jobs were at stake.

Even the most informed, logical inferences about other animals' motivations, emotions, and awareness could wreck your professional prospects. The mere *question* could. In the 1970s, a book humbly titled *The Question of Animal Awareness* caused such an uproar that many behaviorists relegated its author, Donald Griffin, to the fringes of the profession. Griffin was no upstart; he'd been famous for decades as the luminary who'd solved the problem of how bats use sonar to navigate. So he was a bit of a genius, actually. But raising the Question was simply too much for many orthodox colleagues. Suggesting that other animals can feel *anything* wasn't just a conversation stopper; it was a career killer. In 1992, readers of the exclusive journal *Science* were warned by one academic writer that studying animal perceptions "isn't a project I'd recommend to anyone without tenure." It was no joke. Seriously.

By banning what was considered anthropomorphic, the behaviorists perpetuated the opposite error. They helped institutionalize the all-too-human notion that only humans are conscious and can feel anything. (The sense that everything revolves around us is called anthropo*centrism*.) Certainly, projecting feelings onto other animals can lead to us misunderstanding their motivations. But denying that they *have* any motivation *guarantees* that we'll misunderstand it.

Not *assuming* that other animals have thoughts and feelings was a good start for a new science. Insisting they did *not* was bad science. Peculiarly, many behaviorists—who are biologists—chose to overlook the core process of biology: each newer thing is a slight tweak on something older. Everything humans do and possess came from somewhere. Before humans could be assembled, evolution needed to have most of the parts in stock, and those parts were developed for earlier models. We inherited them.

Witness, for instance, the journey of jointed legs: from arthropod to quadruped to bipedal people. A frog's upper rear leg bone is a femur, no less than in a chicken, as in a child. Thus we trace a transformation from amphibian to flying bird to triathlete. A creature that sleeps is sleeping, species notwithstanding. One that sneezes is sneezing. Species differ—but are often not very different. Only humans have human minds. But believing that only humans have minds is like believing that because only humans have human skeletons, only humans have skeletons. Of course, we can see elephants' skeletons. We can't see their minds. But we can see their nervous systems, and we observe the workings of minds in the logic and limits of behaviors. From skeletons to brains, the principle is the same, and if we were to assume anything, it might be that minds, too, exist on a sliding scale.

That's not what happened. Professional animal behaviorists inserted a hard divider between the nervous system of the entire animal kingdom and one of its species: humans. Denying the possibility that any other animals have any thoughts or feelings reinforced what we all most want to hear: We are special. We are utterly different. Better. Best. (Talk about projecting!)

For decades, scientists who stepped out of bounds continued to face withering scorn from their colleagues. A few new revolutionaries who were *not* trained behaviorists—Jane Goodall being perhaps the first such pioneer—experienced just that. Goodall recalls that after her first studies of chimpanzees, when she later enrolled as a doctoral student at Cambridge, "It was a bit shocking to be told I'd done everything wrong. Everything. I shouldn't have given them names. I couldn't talk about their personalities, their minds or their feelings. Those are unique to us."

To this day, "anthropo"-phobia remains widespread among behavioral scientists and science writers who ape the outdated hypercaution of the orthodox behaviorists who trained them. We are *not* to attribute to other animals any emotions that humans have, they say to each other—and to their students, who parrot their rigidity and feel professional.

But what is a "human" emotion? When someone says you can't attribute human sensations to animals, they forget that human sensations *are* animal sensations. Inherited sensations, using inherited nervous systems.

Simply deciding that other animals can't have any emotions that humans feel is a cheap way to get a monopoly on all the world's feelings and motivations. People who've systematically watched or known animals realize the absurdity of this. But many others still don't. "The dilemma remains," author Caitrin Nicol noted as I was writing this book, "how to get an accurate understanding of the animals' nature and (if appropriate) emotions, without imposing on them assumptions born of a distinctly human understanding of the world."

But tell me, what "distinctly human understanding" hampers our understanding of other animals' emotions? Is it our sense of pleasure, pain, sexuality, hunger, frustration, self-preservation, defense, parental protection? Ours doesn't *prevent us* from understanding theirs; it helps us. But okay; doesn't that lead us right back to mistaken assumptions? Not if we incorporate all we've learned. Consider romantic love. It is obvious that elephants, with their matriarchal families, wandering males, absence of male-female pair bonds, and no male care of young, don't have romantic love. And because it's so, elephant researchers don't make that mistake. Thus, evidence and logic can be trustworthy guides. In fact, one term for evidence+logic is: "science."

We never seem to doubt that an animal acting hungry feels hungry. What reason is there to disbelieve that an elephant who seems happy is happy? We recognize hunger and thirst while animals are eating and drinking, exhaustion when they tire, but deny them joy and happiness as they're playing with their children and their families. The science of animal behavior has long operated with that bias—and that's unscientific. In science, the simplest interpretation of evidence is often the best. When elephants seem joyous in joyful contexts, joy is the simplest interpretation of the evidence. Their brains are similar to ours, they make the same hormones involved in human emotions—and that's evidence, too. So let's not assume. But let's not bury evidence.

When a dog is scratching the door, some humans would insist that we *cannot know* whether the dog "wants" to go out. (Meanwhile, of course, your dog is thinking, "Hellooo—let me out; I don't want to pee in the house.") Obviously, the dog *wants* to go out. And if you insist on ignoring the evidence, have a mop handy.

Elephants form deep social bonds developed through deep time. Parental care, satisfaction, friendship, compassion, and grief didn't just suddenly appear with the emergence of modern humans. All began their journey in pre-human beings. Our brain's provenance is inseparable from other species' brains in the long cauldron of living time. And thus, so is our mind.

Deep and Ancient Circuits

———•———

How might we discern an elephant's or a mouse's sense of the world? Elephants and mice might not tell us what they're thinking. But their brains can. Brain scans show that core emotions of sadness, happiness, rage, or fear, and motivational feelings of hunger and thirst, are generated in "deep and very ancient circuits of the brain," says the noted neurologist Jaak Panksepp.

Researchers in labs can now trigger many emotional responses by direct electrical stimulation of the brain systems of animals. Rage, for example, gets produced in the *same parts* of the brains of a cat and a human.

Further evidence of shared experience: Rats can become addicted to the same euphoria-producing drugs that humans get addicted to. Dogs with compulsive behaviors show the same brain abnormalities as humans with obsessive-compulsive disorder; they respond to the same medications. It's the same disease. Under stress, other animals' blood carries the same hormones that the blood of stressed-out humans does. Crayfish hid for extended periods after getting mild electrical shocks and showed elevated levels of serotonin—evidence of clinical anxiety. When researchers gave the same crayfish a drug commonly used to treat humans suffering from anxiety—chlordiazepoxide—they resumed normal crayfish activities and explorations. The researchers wrote, "Our results demonstrate that crayfish exhibit a form of anxiety similar to that described in vertebrates."

Having subjected crabs and lobsters to worse treatment than mild electric shocks, I find this discomfiting. Perhaps try the pasta. Anxiety in many species apparently shares ancient chemical systems largely unchanged during evolution. Makes sense; being afraid of venturing out while danger is lurking has obvious survival value for all kinds of animals.

Complex animals have inherited *very ancient* emotional systems. The genes that direct our own bodies to create the mood-making brain hormones oxytocin and vasopressin, for instance, date back at least seven hundred *million* years. They "likely arose when animals became mobile and started to make experience-based decisions," wrote researchers.

"When a worm is suddenly illuminated," Darwin wrote, it "dashes like a rabbit into its burrow." But if you keep scaring it, the worm stops withdrawing. Such apparent learning suggested to Darwin "the presence of a mind of some kind." Watching as worms evaluated the suitability of objects for plugging their burrows, Darwin offered the idea that worms "deserve to be called intelligent, for they then act in nearly the same manner as a man under similar circumstances."

Ridiculous? Consider this: "The same neural mechanisms are at work in worms and humans," wrote S. W. Emmons in a 2012 article with the intriguing title "The Mood of a Worm." He's referring to the tiny one-millimeter-long *C. elegans*—the elegant nematode. Here's the thing: the worm has nearly the same suite of genes that underlie the nervous systems of humans, giving the worms "connectivity patterns also found in the human brain." *C. elegans* has just 302 nerve cells. (Humans have roughly 100 billion.) Yet *C. elegans* produces a motivating chemical similar to oxytocin, called nematocin, and its function is familiar. It makes the worms seek sex. Mutant males lacking it spend less time looking for a mate, take longer to recognize one, then initiate copulation more slowly "and execute poorly." Poor worm! Emmons, who is a professor at the Albert Einstein College of Medicine, leaves us with this insight: "Just as today's major roads and highways may once have been ancient trails, biological systems can retain essential features derived from their origins." He cautions, "It is a mistake to consider small invertebrates as primitive."

Oxytocin drives bonding, and it makes elephants and many other species act social or sexual. Block the hormone; many mammals and birds lose interest in socializing, pairing, nesting, and contact. Oxytocin and opioid hormones create sensations of pleasure and social comfort in many species, including humans. Given a sniff of oxytocin, human fathers get more playful with their babies, increase eye-to-eye gazing, and show greater interest in the child. This is the chemistry of bonding.

When we do something that we know is a bad idea, it's often because hormone-flooded ancient parts of our own brains disable our intellectual override switch. Hormones can unlock—for instance—the cages that contain deep sexual feelings, setting loose behaviors we become power-less to resist, leaving rationality bound and gagged while emotions hijack our minds. Sex is often so risky and costly that we might never repro-duce if our brains weren't chemically sparking urges for obtaining our next fix. It sounds quite animal, doesn't it? And it feels that way—because it is. It so deliciously, so frighteningly is.

In 1883, George John Romanes recognized that "with nerve-tissue in a jelly-fish, an oyster, an insect, a bird, or a man, we have no difficulty in recognizing its structural units as everywhere more or less similar." Sigmund Freud observed that the nerve cells in a crayfish were basically the same as the nerves in human beings. Freud grasped that the nerve cell is *the* signaling unit of the animal nervous system. As Oliver Sacks explains, neurons "are essentially the same from the most primitive animal life to the most advanced. It is their number and organization that differ."

So when Vicki said, "We all have the same basic brain," she almost lit-erally opened a can of worms.

Uncertainty, anxiety, worry, pain, fear, terror, defiance, defensiveness, protectiveness, anger, disdain, rage, hatred, distrust, disappointment, reas-surance, patience, persistence, interest, affection, surprise, happiness, delight, joy, exuberance, sadness, depression, remorse, guilt, shame, grief, awe, won-der, curiosity, humor, playfulness, tenderness, lust, longing, love, jealousy, loyalty, compassion, altruism, pride, vanity, shyness, calm, relief, disgust, gratitude, abhorrence, hope, modesty, sorrow, frustration, fairness—Is it possible that humans *alone* feel *all* these things, that elephants and other animals feel *none* of them? I don't think so. If we deny the possibility that they have feelings, and they actually *do* have feelings, we'd have been wrong. I think we've been wrong in exactly that way. I'm not suggesting that humans and elephants have *all* the same emotions. Self-loathing seems uniquely human.

So we needn't be so fearful that we mistakenly project the emotion of, say, fear when elephants seem afraid. Certain seabird and seal species have lived for millions of years on oceanic islands hundreds of miles from continental shores. Safely distanced from continental predators in miles and in time, the seabirds and seals lack the *ability* to fear them. They cannot acquire needed fear when rats, cats, dogs, and people arrive by boat. They did not fly or run as people clubbed them by the millions for their feathers or fur.

On the other hand, continental animals with a long history of being hunted by humans, fully capable of fear, relax in places safe from hunting, such as national parks. In suburban neighborhoods, animals that are usually shy—ducks, geese, deer, turkeys, and coyotes—can be calculatedly brazen. In African parks, cheetahs sometimes even hop up on vehicles full of tourists for a more commanding view of potential prey. Elephants can be fearful, aggressive, or nonchalant around humans, depending on what they've learned to expect. My point: rather than mistakenly attributing emotions that they do not experience, we have made a larger mistake by denying emotions that other animals do experience.

So, do other animals have human emotions? Yes, they do. Do humans have animal emotions? Yes; they're largely the same. Fear, aggression, well-being, anxiety, and pleasure are the emotions of shared brain structures and shared chemistries, originated in shared ancestry. They are the shared feelings of a shared world. An elephant approaches water anticipating the relief of refreshment and the pleasures of mud. When my puppy rolls on her back to prompt me to rub her belly—again—it's because she anticipates the soothing experience of our warm contact. Even when my dogs aren't hungry, they always enjoy a treat. They *enjoy* a treat.

The problem isn't "imposing . . . a distinctly human understanding of the world." The problem is imposing a distinctly human *mis*understanding. Our deepest insight into the living world: all life is one. Their cells are our cells, their body is our body, their skeleton our skeleton, their heart, lungs, blood, ours. If we impose *that* distinctly human under-standing, we've taken one giant stride in seeing, truly, each species within the vast living venture. Each is a distinction on a continuum, like notes on a violin's fingerboard. There for the finding. Fretless. No abrupt breaks. And quite a symphony.

We Are Family

———•———

In the late 1960s, a few years before Cynthia Moss arrived in Kenya, another towering pioneer of behavior, Iain Douglas-Hamilton, first realized that the basic unit of elephant society is a female and her children. Forty years later, Iain resonantly recalled for me the extraordinary impression this made on him at a time when everyone had assumed that males led everything in the world. "When I first realized that elephants were organized by families headed by a matriarch," Iain told me, "I saw in them an undaunted female intelligence." (Much more recently, a man named Dhruba Das, who trains Indian villagers to reduce human-elephant conflict, has commented, "It's more like wisdom. They can sense things. They know what to do. They'll take whatever a situation offers them and use it to their best advantage.")

An older female, her sisters, their adult daughters, and all their children live together. The family is the foundation for shared infant care and child rearing.

Usually the oldest female serves as the prime holder of living history and knowledge. This "matriarch" makes decisions about where the family will go, when, and for how long. She serves as the family's rallying point and chief protector, and her personality—whether calm, nervous, firm, indecisive, or bold—sets the whole family's tone. While a matriarch is alive, her daughters are very unlikely to strike out on their own, even temporarily.

Elephants live their lives in relationships that radiate into wide, layered social networks. Two or more families having special friendly affinity for each other are called a "bond group." Bond groups might be made up of relatives, a former family that has split into two, simply friends, or any combination. Adolescent males leave their families to socialize with other males, doing considerably more wandering.

"See this one, trailing behind?" Vicki points to a rather small elephant following several others at a distance, across a span of short grass. "That's Emmett, a fourteen-year-old boy." He has left his family—and perhaps been encouraged to leave—because of his age. "He just keeps following different families." It's a tough transition. He looks like he feels lonely. I wonder if he feels rejected. He'll follow families until he learns how to be on his own among other males. Adult males live in groups or wander among and between families, searching for the thing that interests all males.

Males grow faster than females and continue growing for twice as long; they can end up twice as heavy. Females reach nearly full body size at around twenty-five years old, eight feet at the shoulder, and can continue bulking to around six thousand pounds. As males continue growing they can reach eleven to twelve feet at the shoulder; the largest can weigh twelve thousand pounds.

Growing numbers or a matriarch's death can cause families to slowly split up. On the other hand, fragmented families sometimes merge. Their splitting and merging is called "fission-fusion." Because elephants, like humans, live in fission-fusion groups, a striking thing about them is that what they're doing makes sense to us. Many of the most complicated societies, including ours, apes', wolves', and certain whales', are also fission-fusion.

Whether families split or merge is really about personalities. "I *can* tell you," Vicki adds, "that the most important thing for an elephant family is: 'We're all together.' I can also tell you, I've *never* seen, or even heard of, an elephant family simply breaking down for no clear reason."

Vicki has studied why forest elephants in central Africa gather in particular forest clearings. "At the start, I had all these very nice, logical theories like: finding mates, or special minerals in the soil," Vicki says. "I found no evidence—at all—for them." Her conclusion: elephants go to certain spots because other elephants go there. "No better reason. They do things because"—she shrugs—"they just *want* to." A major rule of elephant society is that individual personalities trump rules. Things happen simply because somebody likes somebody else and they want to hang out. "They may be on their way to one area, then they hear another family they recognize and it's like, 'Oh, I haven't seen so-and-so for a while, let's go over and join them.'" Particular females can stay friends for sixty years. "The fundamental truth of elephants," Vicki sums up, "is that elephants like being with other elephants. It gives them benefits, but they just find it satisfying."

Elephants seem better than apes—even humans—at keeping immediate track of a large number of individuals. Their recognition ability exceeds primates' (except perhaps a few of the elephant researchers!). Each elephant in Amboseli probably knows every other adult in the population. When researchers played the recorded call of an absent family member or bond-group member, elephants returned the call and moved toward the sound. Played a recording of an elephant outside their bond group, they didn't react noticeably. But when played calls of total strangers, they bunched defensively, raising their trunks to smell.

"Intelligent, social, emotional, personable, imitative, respectful of ancestors, playful, self-aware, compassionate—these are qualities that would gain most of us membership to an exclusive club," wrote Cynthia Moss along with Joyce Poole and several colleagues. "They also describe elephants." Elephants "deserve our respect in the same way that human life deserves respect," wrote Iain Douglas-Hamilton, the founding father of elephant behavior research. Nice words—but surely elephants must get ruthless when things get rough. Dry seasons confront elephants with the need to compete for disappearing food and water. Yet—. "Even in times of distress and danger," writes Iain, elephants "behave with exceptional tolerance to their own kind, and hold fast to their family ties."

Unlike many primates, elephants seldom try to assert a bid for increased dominance or attempt to acquire higher status. Status seeking isn't really a big part of elephant society. In elephants, status comes with age, as though what elephants most respect is experience. Even during hard times, dominance is nuanced, asserted in subtle gestures and sounds, reinforcing expectations, acknowledged with very little squabbling within families.

> Nature's great master-peece, an Elephant,
> The onely harmlesse great thing; the giant
> Of beasts . . .
> And foe to none, suspects no enemies.
>
> —John Donne, 1612

There *are* exceptions to elephants' typical peaceability. In droughts when food gets scarce, a family's size can affect its dominance, partly determining access to food and water and how well it survives. Again individual personality matters. The matriarch Slit Ear was so aggressive toward other families on behalf of her own that Cynthia Moss remembers her as "a real bitch. But . . . spirited!"

<hr>

"When a family is big," Vicki is saying, "it means they have a strong matriarch that everyone likes to follow." Elephants respect their elders with good reason: survival can depend on an individual who learned a key bit of information decades earlier. Old females also have the most extensive knowledge of the voices and calls of individuals in other family groups, the biggest social lists. In fact, the experience that comes with age matters in everything about elephant society. Elephants are famous for memory because there's a lot to remember.

"So for instance," Vicki relates, "an experienced leader could in effect decide, 'We'll be going up those slopes, because I remember there's water there at this time of year and some grass I know about.'" Desert-living elephants visit water sources as much as forty miles (sixty-five kilometers) apart and, doing so, can cover about four hundred miles (650 kilometers) in five months. They sometimes travel hundreds of miles, along routes not used for many years, to arrive at water sources just after the onset of rains. Do they detect distant thunder rumbling through the earth and turn toward it? How much is memory? They need to know where they're going. And a lot depends on making the right decisions.

"There's better survival in families with matriarchs older than thirty-five," Vicki explains. Elephants seem to know this. Some families follow *other* families having older matriarchs. So older matriarchs tend to lead larger, dominant families; success literally breeds success. The oldest Amboseli female known to have given birth was sixty-four years old. However, they generally have fewer babies after around age fifty-five, entering a sort of grandmothering wise-elder leadership role, helping younger ones survive. Elephants have six sets of teeth during their lifetime. The final set appears when they are about thirty years old and can last until they're into their sixties. Eventually their teeth wear down to the gums; when elderly elephants cannot feed properly, they die. And by the time a matriarch dies of natural causes, she usually has mature daughters who themselves have gained sufficient knowledge to competently lead their family. In humans, wielding knowledge to survive new existential challenges is sometimes called "wisdom."

So an elephant isn't just flesh; it is a deep store of knowledge needed for survival. All it takes for that kind of knowledge to continue succeeding is for the world not to change too much over the decades of a life. And for many thousands of years, that worked.

However, elder matriarchs' big tusks make them poachers' preferred targets. Elephants are dying younger. Killing elders decades prematurely leaves their family members unprepared. Their matriarch's death triggers, first, devastating psychological consequences. Some families disintegrate. Elephants have extraordinarily close care bonds with their young, and breaking them causes intense suffering. Babies orphaned at under two years of age die soon; orphans under ten die young. If they still need milk, they are almost always out of luck. Any family member with milk has her own nursing child, and an elephant can't produce enough milk for two growing elephants. Rarely, a newly orphaned infant happens to meet a nursing mother who has just lost her own child and is feeling adoptive. Older orphans sometimes wander in bunched-up, leaderless groups. Survivors, carrying traumatic memories, become fearful and sometimes more aggressive toward humans—which spurs human antagonism toward elephants.

"Here's someone feeling a little silly," Vicki says, pointing. "See her with that loose walk and her trunk swaying?"

I *do*.

"One day when I was new here," Vicki recalls, "Norah and I were watching and suddenly everyone started running around and trumpeting. I was like, 'What the hell just happened?' Norah said, 'Oh they're just being silly.'

"I thought, '*Silly?*' And the next thing I know, a full-grown female comes along walking on her knees and throwing her head around, acting just daffy. They were just happy. They were like, 'Yaaay!' Everyone says how smart they are. But they can be ridiculous, too. If a young male doesn't have a friend around, sometimes he'll make a little mock charge at us, then back up or twirl around. I actually had one male kneel down right in front of the car and throw zebra bones at me, trying to get me to play with him.

"In wet times, they're happy and jaunty. The rain makes them feel good. I'm just realizing that when I got here, the elephants were still feeling somber from the drought. Now they're coming out of it. You see more nice, positive interactions, or just funny behavior. I'm also seeing how they're being transformed by all these babies. These females seeing their babies tumbling and playing and sleeping; it stimulates a sense of well-being that everything's okay with the family because, well—babies are *great*."

Motherhood Happens

———

The babies are so fat they seem overindulged. A close-crossing elephant fills our windshield and Vicki observes, "Look at this mama with her enormous breasts; they properly *bounce* when she walks. Plenty of milk for her baby." Plenty means roughly five gallons (twenty liters) daily. Young ones can get suckled for up to five years, and when they first sprout little tusks, I'm guessing their mothers endure some discomfort.

In motherhood as in matriarchs, experience carries consequences. "Females can breed when they're thirteen," Vicki observes, "but a teenage mother is more likely to get into difficulties than a twenty-year-old." Young mothers might go into cold water that chills the baby. They may take their offspring over terrain they can't handle. They might simply not know how to be a mother. When seventeen-year-old Tallulah had her first baby, she acted upset, confused, and generally inept. She didn't have the experience to direct the baby to her nipples and then stand quietly with her leg forward to lower the breast so the little one could suckle. When it almost latched its mouth onto a nipple, it promptly got bumped in the nose and knocked over. Then Tallulah did not know how to pry the youngster up. Eventually, she did figure out what to do.

By contrast, Deborah, approximately forty-seven years old and having given birth several times, was relaxed and competent from the moment her newest baby was born. The baby fell down five times in the first half hour, but Deborah carefully got it up by gently putting a foot under it and steadying it with her trunk. In an hour and a half it found Deborah's nipples and sucked vigorously for over two minutes, while Deborah stood quietly with her leg well forward so her newborn could nurse. Vicki emphasizes this point: "The older ones are *fantastic* mothers. They're super chill, and they often have loads of helpers by that age."

She seems to consider something for a moment, then adds, "The timeline of their lives mirrors ours. In their twenties you see them forcing their role a bit. In their thirties, settling in and settling down. By the time they're fifty, sixty, they know what's going on and they're relaxed in their role."

At birth, an elephant weighs 260 pounds and stands just short of three feet. Most mammals are born with brains weighing 90 percent of their adult weight. Elephants' brains at birth weigh 35 percent of their adult weight. Humans: 25 percent. Elephant brains, like human brains, do most of their development after birth.

"They're born knowing how to suckle and follow their mother—that's about all," Vicki says. A newborn el-infant can soon walk but otherwise is nearly helpless. In its first week, it can hardly see. For its first months, the baby sticks within range of its mother's touch, often in actual physical contact with mama. Mother, meanwhile, frequently makes soft, humming sounds to her infant, saying, in effect, "Here I am; I'm right here."

As it wobbles behind, the baby frequently trips on roots or gets trapped in high grass. Extraction from such predicaments is often performed by attentive adolescent cousins. When the baby falls or gets stuck, or is pushed or bullied at all, it makes a squeaky-door cry—*loud*—that brings an immediate response. Young females rush so avidly to a baby's aid that they often get in the way of its own mother. Experienced mothers often simply let the younger females deal with it. If a baby falls, all the females run over and make sure it's okay, uttering a special vocalization that helps provide deep reassurance.

The littlest babies reach out to any adult. Aunts and grandmothers are important babysitters, and the experienced mother will be calm as long as she sees to it that her child is with a suitable adult female. Young elephants usually remain within one body length of a family member for the first five years of life. Elephants have to *learn* everything about how to be an elephant from other elephants, who protect them. Friendly, supportive contacts between young and adult elephants are normal and frequent; aggression toward youngsters, rare. Babies can learn to manipulate the attention, and may become a bit spoiled. Distress calls from babies are so frequent, researchers often get the impression that the youngster isn't really in trouble.

The newborn's trunk is its main conduit to the world—constantly reaching, sniffing, feeling. But its trunk is also the baby's most perplexing dilemma. Little trunks are rubbery, not-quite-under-control appendages. Babies must learn trunk management. They often experiment by swinging or tossing or whirling it around, seeing what this thing can do. Sometimes they step on their own trunk and trip. Often they suck their trunk for comfort, the same way a human child sucks its thumb.

From the first week, they start trying to pick up things. Little elephants show lots of concentration while working to master such tasks as picking up sticks. Young elephants start trying to eat at about three months of age. A youngster might twirl and twirl its trunk around a single blade of grass, finally grasp it, drop it, and have a hard time getting it back, then simply place the grass blade atop its head. Sometimes they dispense with the troublesome trunk and just kneel down and bite the grass they want to sample. They often do the same to drink water. It takes young elephants about five months to master their nasal irrigation system.

I'm watching an eight-month-old trying to pull up some grass. It reminds me of someone learning to use chopsticks; the food won't cooperate. Half the grass falls back to the ground. She looks to her mother, who pulls a sheaf of grass and eats it as if making sure her babe is watching. Often, babies reach into the mouths of family members, taking a bit of what they're eating, learning the scents and tastes of vegetation that is good.

Right now several families, about 130 elephants total, are together in a patch of vegetation that smells like sage, including many babies and many following males. One male puts his trunk in a female's mouth; it's an intimate gesture between elephants who trust each other.

Around them all orbit thousands of swallows, zooming after flying insects disturbed by the herd. The elephants proceed to a broad plain of thick, short grass. On that plain, white egrets trail them but the swallows leave them. The insects of short grass must be different.

The sight, the smells, the peaceable masses of interwoven lives and times, the layered rhythms and the meter of the moment, the promise of youth and such obvious contentment and happiness—it's a scene as sublime as anything there is.

. . .

Here's a family called the "Zs." Vicki, who has caught the contagion of the overall good mood, appraises them: "They're a short little family." She says some of the families have certain traits; for example, "Some tend to have big ears." (Don't they all? They're *elephants*.) Some look rounder.

An adult comes by and shakes her head, expressing a bit of annoyance at us for being here. In a soothing voice, Vicki coos, "Look at you, you little short-ass." Family resemblances aren't just physical; members of families *act* similarly. "Because they learn from each other hugely, they learn each others' habits," Vicki says. During what part of the day does this family go to drink? Which wetland do they drink at? Those are things they learn from their family as babies. Those things become family traditions.

We come upon three big males. One, Vronski, loves fighting. Even some males who are older defer to him. Vronski happens to be in the period of intensified sexual appetite and aggressiveness unique to large, higher-ranking males in their thirties or older. It's called "musth," and it lasts several months. Males in musth are big, aggressive competitors with other males. Male elephants in musth are a little like male deer in rut. But deer all come into breeding readiness at the same time. With elephants, each individual male comes into musth at about the same time each year, but musth occurs at different times for different males. It's an unusual, rather admirable system that makes life easier for females and less violent for males. (It's a better system than, say, that of impalas or seals, in which dominant males defend their harems through such constant fighting that, after a relatively short spell at the top, they get worn down, injured, and deposed, and then their life is basically over.) The biggest, oldest males get the best of the time-share after the rains, when the most females are in estrus, fertile and receptive.

Vicki explains, "Males are usually playful and very sweet with each other, actually. They're not really competitors. Unless there's an estrus female around, there's nothing to contest. Males of fifteen or twenty are interested in females, but there isn't much competition between a twenty-year-old male and a fifty-year-old male weighing double." Musth males are bossy and aggressive, with quadrupled testosterone levels. And because females greatly prefer musth males, that pretty much precludes flirting from young males. Younger males must wait until they are at least thirty years old before their first musth and their first real sexual experience.

Older males exert a suppressive hormonal effect on younger males, enhancing the overall decorum in a population. When several orphaned males were all sent to one park in South Africa where no older males were around to suppress their raging testosterone, they started killing rhinos. Unheard of. "For an elephant," adds Vicki, "losing its family is *so* abnormal. I think that those rhino-killing orphans basically had post-traumatic stress disorder. It would be ridiculous to assume that losing their family doesn't profoundly affect them." The authorities shipped in two big males, each around forty years old, and the problem stopped.

Besides Vronski, there's another male here, a stranger, also in musth. That complicates things. Vicki doesn't know who he is, his disposition, or his history with humans. He turns to face us.

"Around musth bulls," Vicki says as she reaches for the ignition, "I always have my car in gear and my hand on the key. If you don't have your escape route, you'd better make one."

In another research camp I saw a vehicle that had been crushed by the *loser* of a fight between two males in musth. Displaced aggression. The occupants were lucky to sneak off with their lives.

"When they *really* want to get at you," Vicki warns, "they just come, no preliminaries. If there's a lot of head shaking, that's bluff. Then you're safer. If I don't know a big male, like this one, I'm always wondering, 'Are you thinking of having a go at us?'"

He moves closer, until he is alongside a substantial tree. Then he begins rubbing his rump on the bark. Vicki relaxes, saying to him, "Ah, a good ass scratch sorts everything out, eh, buddy?" He half-closes his eyes, and Vicki narrates: "Ooh, hits the spot."

A female elephant comes into her first period of sexual fertility and receptiveness, called estrus, at around age eleven. Estrus usually lasts for three or four days. Almost every time she goes into estrus, she'll conceive, be pregnant for two years, nurse her baby for two years, then again cycle into estrus. Four years after her last birth, she'll give birth again.

In other words, each adult female will receive male suitors for only about four days every four years. The rareness and urgency creates high excitement. Males in musth walk around visiting different families, streaming fluid from the glands at their temples. In both sexes, those glands stream whenever there is intensified emotion or excitement of any kind—a little like having sweating armpits on the side of your face, I guess. (Researchers call them temporal glands, a seeming misnomer because the English word "temporal" means having to do with time. I think of them as "temple glands.")

Musth males also constantly dribble pungent urine, which broadcasts their elevated sexualized status, and their penis appears greenish. Cynthia Moss and Joyce Poole figured all of this out for African elephants in the 1970s. At first they thought the males were sick; they called the whole event "green penis disease." That's how little we knew about elephants, and how recently we've learned the most basic things.

So the musth males all go around sniffing the air and sniffing the herds for estrus females. They walk up to adult females, and instead of saying, "What's your sign?," they touch their trunk tip to her vulva, have a sniff, and, often, put the trunk into their mouth to test the taste. This forward familiarity disturbs the ladies not in the least; they take it literally in stride, walking or feeding the whole time as if nothing is going on. Elephants are in many ways like humans, but there are limits to the comparison. Or, at least, to the etiquette. If a female is in estrus, various males will follow her and her family. When a male in musth arrives, he will haze away all rivals and guard the estrus female. She will seem to be quite attracted to the musth male.

Now, as the huge unknown male comes swaggering in among several families surrounding us, I see just how *big* males get compared to females. "Wow," Vicki offers, "he's a monster." That female behind him is full-grown and twenty-five years old. He seems twice her size. "Oh, look—she's going over and greeting him." They rumble and briefly wrap trunks. Her baby appears too young for her to be cycling again. But he's warding off another big male. Then he pauses, just standing there with an almost exaggerated nonchalance, his gigantic trunk draped over a massive tusk. "It's to show females, 'I'm not so scary; look how relaxed and casual I am.' We actually call it 'being casual,'" Vicki tells me.

"It's always a soap opera," she adds. "You get caught up in their lives. Who's going to mate whom? What's Vronski going to do?"

Avoiding fighting is very important. If they actually fight, "that's as much as six tons each, going straight at each other at thirty miles an hour with these two massive sharp poles on the front. That's damage." Cynthia Moss once watched two evenly matched males in musth spend fully ten hours and twenty minutes in one continual fight, without relaxing. They physically clashed just three times, violently locking tusks and trying to twist each other off balance. They spent all the other hours constantly circling each other, moving closer and farther, vocalizing, and tearing up bushes and trees as an intimidation tactic. At one point, one combatant put his front feet on a dead log to make himself appear taller. Eventually the younger titan ran away.

Two groups, about half a mile apart, are heading for the marsh and for each other. "I would just like to fully share that world for five minutes," Vicki says a little dreamily. Meanwhile, Duke, around fourteen years old, comes to within fifteen feet of me with his trunk extended, sniffing the new human. Just for show, he objects mildly, turning away and then wheeling and sweeping his head up, slapping ears against body and facing us with ears out, then shaking his head haughtily and swinging his trunk impressively. Looking at me with his brown eyes, confronting us so closely with his creased and wrinkled nose hose and the living leather of his fanning ears, he appears magnificent in every detail and—as far as threatening—not at all convincing.

He could, of course, crush us but has no such intention; he's just showing off in a teenage male way. That comes across. He's showing that he's big enough to be taken seriously. But he's not terribly confident and is trying out his role. He's confident enough in *us* to be focusing some attention on us, yet he isn't threatened by us, isn't really agitated, isn't frightened, doesn't intend to harm us. I know what he's doing. He's expressing, and I'm understanding. He is sending a message, and I'm receiving it. In other words—by formal definition—we're communicating.

Do Elephants Love Their Babies?

———————

The two converging groups are each part of the family called the FBs. All mothers are keeping in physical contact with their babies by touching them with their tails. Right now Felicity is with her daughters and two unrelated females—Flame and Flossie, who are sisters. Fanny is leading her young ones, her niece Feretia, and her great-niece Felicia. Vicki tells me that Fanny is very level but not hugely affectionate with her young ones. By contrast, Felicity and her offspring are always touching one another.

Fanny's group joins Felicity's. In elephant families, it doesn't just matter *what* you are—it doesn't just matter that you're female and forty-eight years old. "It matters that you're Felicity from the FB family, and you're forty-eight years old," Vicki explains. It matters *who* you are. They have lives, and they matter to one another. That's really the whole point.

Felicity knows that this area they've just covered is safe. Her family feels secure at the moment because Felicity's got their back. Often a matriarch will lead from the rear of the group. But when she stops, everyone stops. They're listening to her even when she's behind. They know right where she is.

A researcher named Lucy Bates collected some urine when a particular elephant in the back of the group she was studying stopped to pee. Then, as the family was moving along, she laid down the urine ahead of them. When they encountered fresh urine from an elephant they knew was behind them, they seemed truly baffled, as though thinking, "Wait a minute—how'd she pass us? She's back behind us, but—" This shows, Bates concluded, "that elephants are able to hold in mind and regularly update information about the locations" of family members.

When something scary happens up ahead, the family will rush back to Felicity. If there's something dangerous, like a lion or buffalo, she may choose to retreat or have the family charge and drive them off.

"That decision is up to her," Vicki tells me. Right now, Vicki observes, "Everyone feels safe and secure, everyone's relaxed; kids are playing. Nobody's worried about anything.

"So, Felicity's an unusually good matriarch. If you have a matriarch who's a suspicious, high-stress type, everybody's always being vigilant, always listening for danger. Elephants like that continually have elevated levels of the stress hormone cortisol in their blood; that is not good for metabolism." Vicki says to the elephants, "So it pays to be chilled out, doesn't it, guys?"

Everyone assents by calmly continuing what they are doing.

Felicity's tiny baby is about fifty yards away from her mother, up here near us with the rest of the family. She's a particularly confident little elephant. Her big sister is right next to her. Suddenly she runs back to her mother.

"It's a bit of a game," Vicki interprets. "Like, 'Look, I'm over here, and I'm okay!'" She's having fun, ears out, waving her little trunk around, charging an egret. It looks like the *kind* of charge an adult might use to scare off a lion. Part of the family's role is allowing youngsters to explore and learn through their own experiences. Male youngsters tend to play pushing contests against each other. Females tend to play "I'm chasing enemies." Felicity's baby charges a couple more egrets. "But you also have to teach them to respond to danger."

Even full-sized adults sometimes play games against *imaginary* enemies. They might start running through tall grass, thrashing it, the kind of behavior they might actually use to chase away lions. "But the elephants are playing," declares Vicki. "They know there are no lions."

But—if elephants act like there are lions and there are no lions, isn't it possible they're just making a mistake or being extra careful?

"It's easy to tell," Vicki explains. A serious elephant faced with a real threat pays steady attention. Playing elephants run in a loose and "floppy" way, shaking their heads to let their ears and trunk flap and flop around.

"They are not making mistakes or giving false alarms. They're running around as if highly alarmed but doing what we call 'play-trumpeting.' They all know they're playing."

When doing serious things in non-serious moments—staring over their tusks at imagined enemies in the *wide-eyed* display or shaking their heads before charging and running away in mock fright, in faked fear—playing elephants often seem to be going just for the humor value. And they're all in on the game. Such blatant silliness must be—I am guessing—as close to hilarity as an elephant perceives; the elephants must be cracking themselves up. Clearly, they're having fun. "Sometimes they put bushes on their heads and just look at you like that," Vicki says. "Ridiculous."

Fanny's little one flares her ears at us, sizing us up, deciding whether we're now the enemy. She pulls herself up to full height and kind of looks down her nose at us. "We call that posture 'stand tall,'" Vicki explains. The little one seems to decide we're either okay or too big to mess with. In a few moments she's under her sister's chin, deciding whether to charge a grouse-like bird called a yellow-necked francolin.

The scene is so moving, so filled with beautiful innocence. But their lives are not always this perfect. No lives are.

Flanna's ear has a big triangle missing, where a spear went through it. One of these elephants lacks a tail. Hyenas sometimes bite off an elephant's tail while she is giving birth. Hyenas will also seize a baby if they can. Lions can kill smaller elephants. The joys and the dangers are both very real, and these babies, running around just having fun, are as naïve as they are vulnerable. They have to be *taught* to fear lions.

Felicity has been leading from the rear but has slowed and dropped even farther behind, as if something is up. Suddenly she wheels, and a hyena peeks out from behind a bush. Felicity stares. Its cover blown, the hyena saunters off.

"So, see—" says Vicki rather proudly. "Felicity is *such* a good matriarch." Some elephants are born leaders, some have leadership thrust upon them, and some shirk it. Echo's sister Ella is much older than everyone else in her family; she should be the matriarch. But she prefers spending time with her daughters and grandkids. She can't be bothered with the other two dozen or more members of the family. "I'm convinced that when she hears them call," says Vicki, who has extensively observed her, "she chooses not to answer." Some females are really motivated to protect and look after everyone. But Ella is not motivated to be a leader.

The sun is levitating. The equatorial heat begins hurrying the elephants toward the quenching wetland. Mothers are positioning their babies on their shady side.

We follow along, keeping pace in elephant time. Around many kinds of animals, I often feel the way I feel around people from other cultures who live in my community. I am not going to step into their life, and they are not going to step into mine. Our backgrounds prevent us from being interchangeable. At the post office I see people who share my time and place yet live different lives. But we understand some things about each other. We know we are basically the same. We value our own lives more because we must. But we are moral equals.

I don't mean to imply that I value the life of a fish or a bird the same way I value a human life, but their presence in the world has as much validity as does our presence. Perhaps more: they were here first; they are foundational to us. They take only what they need. They are compatible with the life around them. On their watch, the world lasted. They are not the same as us, but they experience their lives vividly; they burn brightly. We've taken much of what they need, dimming their candle. They enliven the world, and beautifully.

There's a little commotion up ahead. "See Felicity pushing off that male?"

It isn't easy for me to discern in the swirl of gray bodies and dust.

"She wants to break up this bunch of males because they're holding up her family," Vicki explains.

One of the young males starts doing a rocking, exaggerated walk, coming up behind Felicity. She knows him well. He hangs around with the family quite a lot. He's testing his dominance, trying to push her off a bit.

She turns around and threatens him.

He backs away, then seems to realize that at age twenty he's now as big as she is. He advances. Felicity seems just a bit intimidated. Though she doesn't press the issue, she pivots away; she's confident enough to turn her back on him.

Older females don't like these young males, explains Vicki. They tend to get in the way, "and they're a little too dramatic at times. Females with

young ones don't need the distraction these males create. If they are sparring, they can knock into babies. They just generally get on females' nerves."
So: he was disturbing the peace a little bit, and she was trying to discipline him; then he reminded her that he might be only twenty, but size
matters. "I'm surprised she took that," Vicki comments. "Some females
would have followed through."

And some males might have behaved better. One day, Cynthia saw a
young male she called Tom seeming to figure out how to deal with the
issue of being bigger than the other children in his family's bond group.
He'd just lain down to rest when a youngster named Tao spotted him, ran
over, and started climbing on him. Tom wiggled and kicked, and when
he kicked a bit too hard, Tao ran to her mother, Tallulah, in alarm. Tom
followed and then simply lay down flat beside Tao, as if inviting her to
climb onto him again, which Tao immediately did. Cynthia also saw a
large adult male drop to his front knees with his rear legs out behind him
to encourage a much smaller male to come and play. As soon as he low-
ered himself, the smaller male trotted right over. The larger male had convinced the smaller male that he'd be a safe sparring partner. And that
seemed to be his intention.

Felicity turns to us. Resplendent, dignified. About to enter the marsh, she's
stopped to let her child nurse. Females nursing babies need water daily.
But, Vicki is explaining, "elephants like to top off their calves before entering the wetland for the day, because it's not easy to nurse if they're up to
their bellies in water."

Consider the forethought. Premeditated, situational nursing.

So back to a question I'd asked earlier. Does an elephant nurse her baby
because of instinct or because of love? Is love instinctive? Or does nursing
merely satisfy some minor urge, as does scratching?

Raising young requires a heavy parental investment and the sharing
of food. Parents must get some good feeling in exchange. If a mother
derived no pleasure from doing a necessary task that was difficult or
involved delaying gratifications like eating or drinking, what would motivate her to take care of her baby?

In *When Elephants Weep*, Jeffrey Moussaieff Masson and Susan McCarthy wrote that when wondering whether a mother ape loves her baby, we
might equally wonder whether it is possible to know if the people down

the street love their baby. "They may *say* they love their baby, but how do we know they are telling the truth? Ultimately we cannot know exactly what other people mean when they speak of love."

An ape who feeds and cradles, tickles and defends her baby, or the mother brown bear I saw run with her triplets from the sight of a potentially dangerous male a mile away, is certainly acting out of instinct. Certainly, right? And is a new human mother, presented with her new baby, not feeling "instinctual" surges and urges? Of course she is. We all do.

When we feel love for our own babies, it's instinctive, not intellectual. Situations produce hormones, and hormones produce feelings. It might be as automatic as the letdown of milk—but we feel it as love. Love is a feeling. It motivates behaviors such as feeding and protection. There is no shame in that, no shame in reveling in the glory of love that springs from deep and ancient wells within our cells. Indeed, it is best not to intellectualize too thoroughly about the lovability of a newborn. Better just to cherish. The override of instinct over intellect has conceived many a baby in the first place.

In one sense, love is a name for a feeling that evolution uses to trick us into performing risky, costly behaviors such as child rearing and the defense of our mates and children. A purely rational calculation of our own welfare would make us avoid such risk and expense. Love helps commit us to them. The capacity for love evolved because emotional bonding and parental care increase reproduction. That doesn't mean love is not profound. It only means that love grows from a deep tangle of roots. And as you know, it can feel that way.

If an animal comes to lick you and lie next to you, you assume it "loves" you. And I think that's a pretty reasonable conclusion, especially considering the enormous range of emotions that we label with the word "love." Romantic love, parental love, infantile love, love of community, of country, love of food, of chocolate, love of books and education, of sports, the arts . . . The word "love" is a catchall for many different positive emotions. Emotions that motivate us to erase a distance, to protect, to care for things, to participate, to stay; it's hard to know what humans won't reference with the word "love." We say we love ice cream, a certain movie, practical boats and impractical shoes, or a summer day. Some people love fighting. If we allow ourselves to be so sloppy with such a seemingly crucial word, then one conclusion is almost inescapable: other animals love.

The more interesting question is: Which animals, what do they love, and in what way? How do they experience it—what positive, gap-closing emotions do they feel?

Felicity's baby disengages, with milk dribbling from its chin, and ambles floppily around, smacking its lips. Life is good near Mommy's nipples. But several slightly older youngsters, near weaning, trumpet peals of protest as their milk-depleted mothers deny them their accustomed chance to suck before moving into the water. Sometimes when blocked from nursing, a young elephant throws terrible tantrums. Vicki's seen it more than once.

"They *scream*, like, 'What do you *mean* I can't have any more!'" Vicki saw one near-weaning baby trying again and again to suckle from a mother who wanted a break. All a mother has to do is move her foreleg back to block the baby's access to the breast, and she kept doing that. "He got so upset, pushing her, poking her and tusking her, and finally it was like, '*Ooh*, I *hate* you!'—and he stuck his trunk *into* her anus. I guess he thought that would really get her attention. And then he turned around and kicked her. And I thought, 'You little *horror!*'"

Emotions occur along a seamless range; the words for them are like the points on a circular compass, radiating in different directions to differing degrees. "Happy," "sad," "fear," and "love" are the north, south, west, and east of our emotional range and bearing. Perhaps "beauty" lies toward the northeast, between "happy" and "love." What is the emotional response of a bird to the intricately patterned new plumage of a worthy mate or the dance of a courting suitor? In similar circumstances, we dance when courting. We sense mere patterned light as beauty. And we are drawn. At Gombe Stream National Park in Tanzania, a researcher watched two adult male chimpanzees separately climb to the top of a ridge at sunset. There they noticed and greeted each other, clasped hands, sat down together, and watched the sun descend. Another researcher wrote of a free-living chimpanzee gazing for fifteen minutes at an especially striking sunset. If they really are admiring the sunset, it's probably for no deeper reason than that it looks pretty to them. Same as us. Perhaps they feel a sense of wonder, that raw material for the question to which humans hammered the answer of religion. One difference is that they can't pour themselves a glass of wine and make a toast. Neither could most people that have ever lived.

Among life's great mysteries is that many different beings seem drawn to similar beauties. In the jungle, Jared Diamond encountered a woven, circular hut eight feet in diameter and four feet high, with a doorway large enough for a child to enter and sit inside. In front of the hut was a lawn of green moss, clean except for hundreds of natural objects placed intentionally as decorations. Similarly colored decorations were together, such as red fruits next to red leaves, and yellow, purple, black, and a few green items in other locations. All blue objects were inside the hut, red ones outside. He had found a bowerbird's courtship pavilion, or "bower." When Diamond tested the males' aesthetic finickiness by moving decorations, the bower owner restored them to their original places. Diamond described his emotional response with the word "beautiful." The bower's proprietor expressed some definite opinions. When Diamond put out poker chips of various colors, "the hated white chips were heaved off into the jungle, the beloved blue ones stacked inside the hut, and the red ones stacked on the lawn next to red leaves and fruits." The whole thing had been created strictly to impress females (it was neither shelter nor nest), so while looks aren't everything, sometimes they are.

When animals create something we perceive as beautiful, does it indicate a shared aesthetic sense? I've seen an orangutan string and wear a bead necklace that no one taught her to make. The topic of aesthetics raises the oft-asked question "Why do birds sing?" Diamond writes, "It is suspicious that they sing mainly during the breeding season. Hence they are probably not singing just for aesthetic pleasure." Agreed, not *just* for pleasure. But how many human songs are love songs? And isn't the bulk of popular music most enthusiastically heard and sung by humans who are sexually mature and not yet married—in other words, in their own mating season? Our music isn't purely aesthetic; it, too, serves social functions. Flowers and bird courtship colors and the patterns of reef fishes—all are mainly utilitarian but also highly attractive; their functional effectiveness depends on a widely perceived aesthetic.

Flowers' appearance and fragrance's only *purpose* is to attract pollinators (mainly insects, at that, plus hummingbirds and honeycreepers and specialized bats). There is scant utilitarian reason why humans should also find the sight of flowers and their perfume any more attractive than the sight of fallen leaves. Yet we perceive flowers as so beautiful that we equate their beauty with the appreciation of life itself, advising friends to "stop to smell the roses," offering them in courtship, bestowing them at funerals. Birds bejeweled in extravagant plumage whose purpose is to attract mates—hummingbirds, wood warblers, birds of paradise, long-plumed egrets—we perceive as beautiful. So beautiful, in fact, that for ages humans have worn birds' dead body parts in order to steal the same attractive colors and patterns that birds see in one another. Fishes of warm coral reefs dazzle us with pageantry as their body markings signal to one another who to school with and mate with. As brains elaborated from a bee's pleasure in a field of flowers, to our inner fish, to a bird's delight in dance, and to our own—have our brains retained aesthetic roots that arose in insects? If so, the insects' gift to us cannot possibly be repaid, except perhaps as reverence for the little elders at our feet and flitting among the flowers of our gardens. Regardless of who gets our thanks for the honor, there is no more wondrous fact than that we are kin, bee and bird of paradise—and great elephant—stardust, all.

Elephant Empathy

All the elephants in view are now busy drinking and feeding. Vicki points to another female nursing her baby. A few months ago, that infant fell into a well as deep as he is tall, and when Vicki went to help rescue him, this mother was there, upset. "She frantically objected to us using the vehicle to get her away from the well. But we had to; it would have been just too terrifying for her to see us roping up and pulling on her baby. I didn't want her to think I was being indecisive with her, so I was being as obnoxious as I knew how, screaming at her. She almost sat on the fender. It was all very stressful and very extreme. She stayed nearby, and as soon as we reunited her with her baby, she just suckled him and she wasn't upset with us. I think she understood that we'd intended to help."

I've seen the video of that incident, and the thing that astonishes me is that here you have this, yes, frantic mother being chased away, and she objects by *turning her back* to the vehicle and attempting to stop it by sitting on it, rather than charging. She has no malice. She does not want to hurt the people who are being so rude. She is clearly not defending her vulnerable child against Vicki and the other humans; she doesn't view them as a threat. She just wants to stay with her baby. She does eventually agree, one might say, to leave. And when the baby is tied to the bumper and dragged up out of the well, the baby knows exactly which way to run— the mother must be calling the whole time—and they run to each other and the reunion is immediate.

Elephants understand cooperation. They cooperate with one another, aiding individuals trapped in muddy riverbanks, helping to retrieve babies, or raising an injured or fallen comrade. They sometimes stand on either side of an elephant hit with a tranquilizer dart, for instance, attempting to hold her up. Once, Cynthia Moss saw a baby elephant fall into a small, steep-sided water hole. The mother elephant and the baby's aunt could not lift the baby out, so the elephants started digging out one side of the hole, and made a ramp. With that bit of problem solving, they saved their baby.

Another time, a young mother named Cherie, wanting to rejoin the rest of her family, tried several times to cross the dangerously high-running river in Kenya's Samburu National Reserve. In one disastrous attempt, the waters swept away her three-month-old baby. Cherie pursued her through the rough and rapid water, caught up with her, then guided her to calm water on the far bank. The infant must have inhaled a lot of water, though, or perhaps gone hypothermic; it reached the shore looking very distressed, and in a little while, it died. In Burma, one J. H. Williams witnessed an elephant that was swept with her young one into a swollen river: "She pinned the calf with her head and trunk against the rocky bank. Then with a really gigantic effort she picked it up in her trunk and reared up until she was half standing on her hind legs so as to be able to place it on a narrow shelf of rock five feet above the flood level. Having accomplished this, she fell back into the raging torrent and she herself went away like a cork." But half an hour later, as the terrified youngster still shivered in the same spot, Williams heard a mighty roar, "the grandest sounds of a mother's love." Running back along the bank, she retrieved her baby.

Normally, little elephants aren't allowed to get lost. Mothers keep them in sight. No child gets left behind. The matriarch usually paces the herd's travel to make sure the young ones get a chance to rest.

In 1990, here in Amboseli, the famed Echo gave birth to a baby who could not straighten his forelegs, could barely nurse. He shuffled painfully slowly on his wrists, frequently collapsing. Researchers were convinced that his wrists would abrade and get infected, that he could not survive; they wondered whether it would be humane to shorten his misery. True to the nature of their kind, Echo and her family remained persistent, raising him when he fell over. Echo's eight-year-old daughter, Enid, also prodded the infant at times, in an attempt to raise him, but Echo slowly and carefully pushed Enid off, and as they stood over the baby, Enid frequently reached her trunk to Echo's mouth, seemingly seeking reassurance. For three days, as the exhausted infant hobbled along, Echo and Enid slowed their pace to his disabilities, continually turning to watch the little one's progress, waiting as he caught up from behind. On the third day, he leaned back until he could put his bent front soles on the ground, then "carefully and ever so slowly he transferred his weight back towards the front end of his body and simultaneously straightened all four legs." And though he fell several times, by day four he was walking well and never looked back. His family's persistence—which in humans facing a similar situation we might call faith—had saved him.

"A few days ago," Vicki mentions as we amble along, "Eclipse was suddenly running around, calling, seeming frantic." The family, at that point, was strung out over about 250 yards, with the kids well up ahead with some females. "I think her son was with his friends and just didn't answer her," Vicki speculates. "She was *so* agitated." Then she found him—and everything was fine. Cynthia Moss tells of a one-year-old male who got so absorbed playing with several age-mates from another family that he didn't notice that his family had moved off. Neither did they realize that they'd left him. Suddenly he panicked and screamed the deep "lost baby" cry. Several females in his family immediately came back for him, and he ran at full speed toward them.

While small babies usually get retrieved quickly, adolescents can become so busy socializing that they get truly separated from their families. "Getting lost like that is *really* scary for them," Vicki tells me. On windy evenings when it's harder for them to hear, she's seen elephants rushing in one direction, calling and then listening, then rushing off in another direction. "Sometimes you wish you could say, 'Go farther *that* way.'" As good as they are at keeping tabs, even older elephants can get separated, also usually when it's very windy and they can't hear one another. Then they act lost and frightened, rushing around and calling. Reunions can be emotional. "They act like, 'That was the worst thing *everrr*,'" Vicki says, poking fun at elephant melodrama.

It would be a stretch to think that lost elephants acting frantic *don't* feel anxiety. Elephants are not very expressive with their faces, but,

Vicki says, "They have what we call 'worried face,' 'suspicious face,' 'lost face'—I'm not even sure what I'm cuing in to, but they do have readable facial expressions."

Lone animals are much more vulnerable to predators. Lost elephants, like us, don't feel comfortable being alone in the wilderness. Being near others soothes them.

That shouldn't surprise us; humans came of age in the same wilderness. Human and elephant minds emerged while we maneuvered through the same landscape with the same challenges, timing our days by the arc of the same sun and our nights by the roars and whoops of the same dangers. We needed to know the same things they know. We seem in sync because fundamentally we are compatriots.

Here's a two-year-old youngster whose mother is not present. This little guy is streaming from his temple glands, a sign of stress. His mother might be in estrus and off with a male somewhere. Younger mothers get distracted by attractive guys. We hope it's no worse than that.

One day, Katito saw an elephant walking with a spear stuck in her. Katito went for help. Returning with a veterinarian who'd come to administer a dart filled with antibiotics and painkillers, they saw that another elephant was with the wounded one—and that the wounded one no longer had the spear in her. No one had ever heard of an elephant removing a spear from another elephant; it must have fallen out. But when the veterinarian's dart hit the wounded elephant, the friend moved in and pulled out the dart. Researchers once saw an elephant pluck up some food and place it into the mouth of another whose trunk was badly injured. "Elephants show empathy," Amboseli researchers Richard Byrne and Lucy Bates state plainly. They aid the ailing. They *help* one another.

More mysteriously, elephants sometimes help people. George Adamson, who helped raise the famous lion Elsa of the book *Born Free,* knew an elderly, half-blind Turkana woman who'd wandered off a path; nightfall caused her to lie down under a tree. She woke in the middle of the night to see an elephant towering over her, sniffing up and down with its trunk. She was paralyzed by fear. Other elephants gathered, and they soon began breaking branches and covering her. The next morning, her faint cries attracted a herder, who released her from the cage of branches. Had the elephants mistaken her for dead and attempted to bury her? That would have been strange enough. Had they sensed her helplessness and, in empathy and perhaps even compassion, enclosed her in protection from hyenas and leopards? That would have been stranger still. In *Coming of Age with Elephants,* Joyce Poole tells of a herder whose leg was broken in an accidental confrontation with a matriarch. Discovered under a tree along with an aggressive elephant, the herder frantically signaled the search party not to shoot. Later he explained that after striking him, the matriarch had realized that he could not walk and, using her trunk and front feet, had gently moved him a short distance and propped him under the shade of the tree. Occasionally touching him with her trunk, she'd guarded him through the night, though her family left her behind.

Empathy seems quite special. Many believe that empathy "makes us human." Fear, on the other hand, might be the oldest, most widespread emotion. So it's surprising to learn this: fear and empathy are tightly related, and fear is a kind of empathy. Empathy is the ability to match the emotional state of another. When a flock of birds suddenly flies off because one of them startles, the spread of emotion is called "emotional contagion." Infant crying works by emotional contagion, spreading distress to the parent. Picking up on another's distress or alarm requires your brain to match their emotion. That's empathy. When your companion's fear gets you scared, that's empathy. They yawn and you yawn—empathy. Empathy's roots go all the way back to contagious fear. Yes, empathy is special; it just happens to be common. (Many people on the autism spectrum have an impaired ability for "reading" the emotions of others.)

In a recent study, one-year-old children, dogs, and cats *all* attempted to comfort "distressed" family members—who acted like they were sobbing, pained, or choking—by, for example, putting their head in the upset person's lap. Humans and apes who view emotionally charged images respond with similar changes in brain and peripheral skin temperature. People's expressions respond to differing pictures of people shown so briefly that the subjects can't consciously perceive the image. Conclusion:

empathy is automatic. No thinking needed. The brain automatically creates the mood match, then makes you aware of the emotion.

In play, animals have to know that the individual chasing and attacking them is not serious. Empathy. You have to understand the invitation to play. Empathy. You have to be skilled in the give-and-take alternation of vulnerability and harmless aggression. I see this daily in my dogs Chula and Jude, who play very vigorously with lots of bared teeth and growling but take turns "handicapping" themselves by rolling over or play-crouching, then licking. They're best friends forever, and they know and trust each other.

Dancing, singing, or worshipping together, going with friends to plays and concerts—bodies move in synchrony as minds mimic what we see in others, each producing an approximation but never truly *sharing* one sensation because we feel only within our own individual mind. This gets us as close as we can to being united. We cannot see with another the color red, or experience another's taste of bean soup, or their perception of Led Zeppelin's "Kashmir." But empathy lets us instantaneously compare experiences and create a facsimile. It's an illusion that works to show to our friends and lovers, "This is how I feel." Our brains gift us the rush of saying, "Really? Me, too!" That's about all there is. And it's the best there is. It's miraculous.

We often use "empathy" interchangeably with "sympathy" or "compassion." But I'd like to distinguish a scale of feeling for others. *Empathy* is a mood-matching sense of a shared feeling. I'm frightened if you're frightened; happy when you're happy; sad when you are sad. *Sympathy* is concern for another who is distressed. It's a bit detached; your feeling might not match the other's emotion—"I am sorry to hear of your great-grandmother's passing." You don't share their sadness, but you sympathize. *Compassion* is sympathy plus motivation to act: "Seeing you in such pain makes me want to help." You buy a sandwich for a homeless person or sign a petition to help save whales. Of course, the words "empathy," "sympathy," and "compassion" label interwoven feelings. But if compassion is a desire to act toward easing another's suffering, an elephant who protects a lost old woman feels—and wields—the full range from empathy to sympathy to compassion in action.

Jane Goodall, noting that chimpanzees and bonobos (pronounced buh-NO-bos) cannot swim, tells us that in zoos with moats, they have sometimes made "heroic efforts" to save companions from drowning. One adult male drowned trying to rescue a small infant who'd fallen into the water. Once, after a moat was drained and cleaned, the keepers turned on the water to refill it. Suddenly the group's senior male came to the window, screaming and frantically waving his arms to get their attention. Several young bonobos had entered the dry moat and now couldn't get themselves out. They would have drowned. The old male himself pulled the smallest to safety.

Rats will free cagemates restrained in a container. Even if there is chocolate in an adjacent container, they will free the prisoner *first,* then share the treat. Thus, rat empathy moves to sympathy, compassion, and an altruistic act. Because helping others can pay off later, our brain gives itself a shot of oxytocin to reward us for being nice. That's why, when we do good, we *feel* good. Altruism among friends is like buying insurance. It's better to pay the premium even if you think you'll never need the protection, because you might, in fact, need it. If you're a rat, a rat you've freed might come in handy later. If a predator attacks, having a companion halves your chances of being eaten, and the companion doubles the chance that the predator will be noticed and its attack thwarted.

But not everything is utility. Kindness sometimes spills into the transcendent, reaching across species. In an English zoo, a bonobo captured a starling. When a keeper urged her to release it, she climbed to the top of the highest tree, wrapped her legs around the trunk so she could use both hands, carefully spread the bird's wings, then hurled the starling skyward. She understood the situation, and knew a little about birds. I wonder whether she imagined what it might be like to fly.

The precise why and wherefore of elephants' feelings of empathy and compassion remain in the realm of mystery. We may not know exactly what elephants are feeling, but *they* do. Or perhaps they don't. Perhaps elephants, too, are searching for some deeper comprehension of life and death that eludes them, as it does us. Perhaps we are not alone in bursting the confines of reason and logic with a large enough mind to ponder imponderables. Perhaps like us, they simply wonder. If so, there must be others who wonder, too.

I wonder. Many other animals are curious, and human curiosity is a precursor to wonder, which is a precursor to spirituality, which is a precursor to science. Science seeks to find out what's really going on. And science's searching is everlasting wonder.

Good Grief

───

Cynthia Moss had been there when the family finally returned. Teresia came back minus half a tusk; perhaps it had been shattered by a bullet or had cracked as she was attempting to lift a family member who'd buckled. Trista was missing. Wendy was missing. Tania had three badly infected gun wounds: left shoulder, behind her left ear, and on her rump. She kept dusting and feeling her wounds with her trunk. Her breasts were shriveled, but her youngest son, still nursing age, was vigorous. He'd quickly learned to eat.

Cynthia was about to leave when Tania walked right up to her Land Rover window and stood there just looking at her. Touched and disturbed, Cynthia felt that Tania was trying to communicate her distress. There was nothing that Cynthia could do.

Tania recovered, and her son survived. Wendy's orphan survived in the protective company of her aunt Willa. Teresia lived to be about sixty-two years old.

Since Teresia's birth, around 1922, the world had changed. During her lifetime it had filled with people and new machines. She lived through, but knew nothing of, the Great Depression, World War II, Nazi camps, and Hiroshima; nor was she aware of the horrors of Burma, Korea, Cambodia, Vietnam; nor the incomprehensible Apollo missions to the same moon by whose light she traveled; nor the swing era, jazz, or rock and roll; the civil rights movement passed her by, and the women's movement, and *Silent Spring* and the environmental movement. She spent the Cold War in the warmth of tropic sunshine and took no note of Nelson Mandela's struggles to liberate the humans of a country that had killed nearly all its elephants. On the time line of the world, her life overlapped all these things. She moved to an older, more constant rhythm. She was the oldest individual in the population when three Maasai spears struck her. The wounds went septic; about two weeks later the infections killed her.

Few elephants nowadays live as long as did Teresia. To survive now, many elephants must abandon exactly the learned traditions and knowledge—the cultures—that have kept them alive: ancient migration routes and centuries-old, handed-down paths to known reserves of food and water, reserves that themselves are vanishing as people occupy and replace them.

Teresia experienced childhood in a world with more room. "There were many bright-green, sun-filled days," Cynthia recalled, "with Teresia and the other youngsters . . . racing about, beating through bushes and tall grass, heads up, ears out, eyes open wide glinting with mischief . . . letting forth wild, pulsating play trumpets." Of course, there were the bad days too, droughts and deaths. But that's life; it can last like that, bad times notwithstanding, for a million years or more. Now, though, an elephant's chance of being killed by a human is greater than their risk of death from any other cause.

Elephants die; we all do. To elephants and some others, it matters who has died. It's why they are "who" animals. The importance of memory, learning, and leadership is why individuals matter. And so, a death matters to the survivors.

A researcher once played a recording of an elephant who had died. The sound emanated from a speaker hidden in a thicket. The family went wild calling, looking all around. The dead elephant's daughter called for days afterward. The researchers never again did such a thing.

Elephants' response to death has been called "probably the strangest thing about them." They almost always react to a dead elephant's remains. Occasionally they react to a human's. The remains of other species, they ignore.

Joyce Poole writes, "It is their silence that is most unsettling. The only sound is the slow blowing of air out of their trunks as they investigate their dead companion. It's as if even the birds have stopped singing." Vicki has seen it herself; she says it is "heart-stoppingly sad." The elephants cautiously extend their trunks, touching the body gently, as if obtaining information. They run their trunk tips along the lower jaw and the tusks and the teeth: the parts that would have been most familiar in life and most touched during greetings—the most individually recognizable parts.

Cynthia told me of a wonderful matriarch named Big Tuskless. She died of natural causes, and a few weeks later Cynthia brought her jawbone to the research camp to determine her age at death. A few days after that, her family passed through the camp. There are several dozen elephant jaws on the ground in the camp, but the family detoured right to hers. They spent some time with it. They all touched it. And then all moved on, except one. After the others left, one stayed for a long time, stroking Big Tuskless's jaw with his trunk, fondling it, turning it. He was Butch, Big Tuskless's seven-year-old son. Was he remembering his mother's face, imagining her scent, hearing her voice, thinking about her touch?

Nowadays humans immediately cart off every tusk. But in 1957, David Sheldrick wrote that elephants have "a strange habit of removing tusks from their dead comrades." He noted "many instances" when elephants carried tusks weighing as much as a hundred pounds up to half a mile away. Iain Douglas-Hamilton once moved part of an elephant shot by a farmer to a different location. Soon a familiar family came along. When they caught the scent, they wheeled around and cautiously approached the body, drawing nearer with their trunks waving up and down, their ears half forward. Each seemed reluctant to be first to reach the bones. They advanced in a tight huddle, then began their detailed sniffing and close examination of the tusks. Some bones they rocked and gently rolled with their feet. Others, they clonked together. Some they tasted. Several individuals in turn rolled the skull. Soon all the elephants were investigating, many carrying bones away. George Adamson once shot a male elephant who had chased an official around his own garden. Local people butchered the animal for meat, then moved the carcass half a mile away. That night, elephants returned a shoulder blade and leg bone to exactly the spot where the elephant had fallen.

Elephants sometimes cover dead elephants with soil and vegetation, making them, I think, the only other animals who perform simple burials. Elephants have done the same with humans on several recorded occasions. When sport hunters shot a large male elephant, his companions surrounded his carcass. The hunters returned hours later to find that the others had not only covered their dead comrade with soil and leaves but had plastered his large head wound with mud.

Do elephants have a *concept* of death? Do they *anticipate* death? One day a few years ago, in Kenya's beautiful Samburu National Reserve, a matriarch named Eleanor, ailing, collapsed. Another matriarch, Grace, rapidly approached her with facial glands streaming from emotion. Grace lifted Eleanor back fully onto her feet. But Eleanor soon collapsed again. Grace appeared very stressed, and continued trying to lift Eleanor. No success. Grace stayed with Eleanor as night fell. During the night, Eleanor died. The next day an elephant named Maui started rocking Eleanor's body with her foot. During the third day, Eleanor's body was attended by her own family, by another family, and by Eleanor's closest friend, Maya, and again Grace was there. On the fifth day, Maya spent an hour and a half with Eleanor's body. A week after her death, Eleanor's family returned and spent half an hour with her. Recalling this to me, Iain Douglas-Hamilton used the word "grief."

Do elephants really grieve? And can we really know? After a young elephant dies, its mother sometimes acts depressed for many days, slowly trailing far behind her family. When a female named Tonie gave birth to a stillborn baby, she stayed with her dead child for four days, alone in the heat, guarding it from the lions who wanted it. Eventually, she moved on.

Elephants sometimes carry sick or dead babies on their tusks. An Amboseli elephant transported a prematurely born, dying baby about five hundred yards into the cool seclusion of a grove of thick palms. Similarly, people have seen apes, baboons, and dolphins keep their dead babies with them for days. But is the mother really sad? Or is she simply carrying an infant she would be carrying if it were alive? Answer: elephants and dolphins never carry healthy youngsters. It's different.

In September 2010 off San Juan Island, Washington, people watched a killer whale push a dead newborn for six hours. If this whale understood death purely rationally, she should have just left it. But humans don't simply leave dead babies, either. For us there is a concept of death, and also a feeling of grief. Our bonds are strong. We don't want to let go. Their bonds, too, are strong. Perhaps they, too, don't want to let go.

A few years ago on Long Island, a nursing-age young humpback whale, somehow ailing and alone, still alive, washed into the surf at Easthampton. Marge Winski, the lighthouse keeper at Montauk, fifteen miles away, told me that the night after the young humpback drifted ashore, she heard "incredibly mournful whale sounds," as if from a searching mother. When a free-living Atlantic spotted dolphin named Luna got permanently separated from her days-old infant in murky water in the presence of a large tiger shark, Denise Herzing wrote, "I had never heard a mother more vocally distressed." When a captive dolphin named Spock suddenly died, his inseparable companion looked bewildered and lay lethargically on the bottom of her pool for days, rising only to breathe. After nearly a week she resumed eating and began socializing. Maddalena Bearzi writes, "A grieving dolphin mother may seek seclusion, away from her group, but in this time of grief, she might be visited by a group of her peers, perhaps coming to check on her, as we humans often do when someone we know is bereaved."

So: *Do* other animals really grieve? To continue this discussion with intelligence and clarity, we need a more scientific definition of grief. Anthropologist Barbara J. King provides one. To qualify as grieving, surviving individuals who knew the deceased must alter their behavioral routine. They might eat or sleep less, or act listless, or agitated. They might attend their friend's corpse. King's definition of grief is quite useful. Yet science thrives best on things that can be measured. Sadness is not a pound lighter than grief, and mourning isn't two yards shorter than happiness. In humans these emotions grade, and sometimes come and go. And they seem to grade in non-humans, too. A person might miss several days of work following the death of a parent or sibling; mourners might attend a wake for a day or two; and an elephant family might for several days return to the body of the deceased. Later, the humans might visit the grave. Ditto the elephants. The trajectory of human lives may be permanently altered by the death of a key family member. Ditto, again, elephants, apes . . .

In a zoo in Philadelphia in the 1870s lived two inseparable chimpanzees. "After the death of the female," the keeper wrote, "the remaining one made many attempts to rouse her, and when he found this to be impossible his rage and grief were painful to witness. . . . The ordinary yell of rage . . . finally changed to a cry which the keeper of the animals assures me he had never heard before . . . *hah-ah-ah-ah-ah*, uttered somewhat under the breath, and with a plaintive sound like a moan. . . . He cried for the rest of the day. The day following, he sat still most of the time and moaned continuously." More than a century later at the Yerkes Research Center, a chimpanzee named Amos remained in his nest while the others went outside. The others kept returning indoors to check on Amos. A female named Daisy gently groomed the soft spot behind his ears and stuffed soft bedding behind his back as a nurse might arrange a patient's pillows. Amos died the next day. For days afterward the others acted subdued, eating little. Two male chimpanzees in Uganda had for years been inseparable allies. When one died, the other, who'd been sociable and high-ranking, "just didn't want to be with anybody for several weeks," said researcher John Mitani. "He seemed to go into mourning."

Patricia Wright studies Madagascar's primates, called lemurs (pronounced LEE-murz). Pat says that when a lemur dies, "For the whole family, it's a tragedy." She detailed for me what she observed after a catlike mongoose called a fossa killed a sifaka lemur: "After the fossa left, the family returned. His mate gave the 'lost' call over and over. When sifakas are really *lost* they give it less often and it's higher and more energetic. But this was a low whistle, mournful, haunting, over and over." The other members of the group, all sons and daughters of the dead male, also gave "lost" calls while viewing the corpse from just above it, in tree branches fifteen to thirty feet off the ground. Over five days, the lemurs returned to the body fourteen times.

Professor and behavioral ecologist Joanna Burger's Amazon parrot, Tiko, used to spend time in the company of Joanna's mother-in-law while she was living with them during her last year of life. During the elder woman's final month, Tiko would try to prevent the hospice people from touching her. If they merely wanted to take her temperature, he'd attack them; he had to be moved to his room while they were there. In her last week, Tiko spent the days sitting by her head as she lay there sick, guarding her. "He barely wanted to leave to eat," Joanna explained. The night the woman died, after her body was removed from the house, Joanna says, "Tiko spent a lot of the night screaming from his room, where he'd *never before* made a sound at night, no matter what was going on downstairs." For months, Tiko would spend hours on the bed that his elderly human acquaintance had used.

· · ·

Grief is not just a response to death. Sometimes people we know die but we don't grieve. Sometimes people we love decide to walk out of our lives, and though they remain alive, we grieve. We simply terribly miss them. Knowing them changed our lives, and losing them changes our lives. Grief isn't solely about life or death; it's mostly about loss of companionship, loss of presence. Barbara J. King says that when two or more animals have shared a life, "Grief results from love lost."

Is "love" *really* the right word? If an elephant sees her sister and calls to maintain contact, or a parrot sees its mate and wants to be nearer, some *feeling* of the bond makes it seek closeness. One word we use for the *feeling* behind our desire for closeness is "love." Elephants and birds don't feel their love for one another the way I feel my love, but the same is true of my own friends, my mother, my wife, my stepdaughter, and my next-door neighbors. Love isn't one thing, and human love isn't all identical in quality or intensity. But I believe that the word that labels ours also labels theirs. Love, as they say, is many splendored. "Love" probably *is* the right word.

Various non-humans do *not* seem to miss dead companions and family members—but is that because they don't, or because we're not watching, or because we miss the signs? Who can watch a gull or a mongoose until its mate dies and then observe it for weeks afterward? (Or in the case of albatrosses, the *years* before they court and bond with another mate?) Stories of grief in free-living creatures are rare and anecdotal, because natural death is seldom seen. Most of the world does its living and dying away from human eyes. Pet owners, on the other hand, have many stories of cats who wail and remain lethargic for weeks, of depressed bunnies, of a dog who visits a companion's grave or continues going to the train station daily for years to await a deceased person's return, and on and on. A friend tells me that when one of her two bearded dragon lizards died, the survivor hardly moved for a couple of weeks, then resumed a more normal level of activity. Is it possible that even a lizard might miss a companion?

I have almost never observed what happens when another animal loses its mate. But my wife and I had two ducks, raised together since duckling-hood, who lived with our four chickens. The birds often wandered our yard together, but the ducks were inseparable. They bathed together and, in season, mated. One day, both ducks suddenly fell ill. A day later, the drake, Duck Ellington, died. Our female (Thelonius Duck, a.k.a. Beeper) recovered. But for days she wandered the yard, the ivy beds, the bushes, calling and searching. Grief? Sorrow? She certainly missed her companion, her mate. Eventually she stopped searching and cast her lot fully with the chickens, becoming the odd duck. I am not sure how it felt to her, but she clearly missed him and had been trying to find him. And eventually she just had to get on with life—as we must. Individually such anecdotes are weak, prone to misinterpretation. Yet collectively—they add up.

As with humans, certain individuals take particular losses hard. In 1990, the killer whale matriarch Eve died in the Pacific Ocean off Canada, at age fifty-five. Her sons Top Notch and Foster circled Hanson Island, calling and calling. For the first time in their lives—Top Notch was thirty-three years old—their mother did not return their calls. The two brothers spent days visiting and revisiting the places their mother had been during the last days of her life. Faithfulness, longing. Grief. Dame Daphne Sheldrick, who has half a century's experience with orphan elephants, told me quite matter-of-factly, "An elephant can *die* of grief." She's seen it happen. Daphne says that from her fifty years of raising orphaned elephants, she has learned this: "To understand an elephant, one must be 'anthropomorphic,' because elephants are emotionally identical to ourselves. They grieve and mourn the loss of a loved one just as deeply as do we, and their capacity for love is humbling."

But even if we accept that they grieve, do they really grieve "just as deeply as do we"? Just how deeply do we grieve? Consider a human wake: A day or two of gathering. The grandkids and adult children present, the relatives, friends; the colleagues sharing a joke and business cards; the young woman whose black dress seems calculated to take one's mind off sadness; the hole that heals and the pain that never leaves. The lives changed, and those unaffected. What is "human grief"? There is no such thing. Like human love, human grief is many things, of differing intensities, in many minds. And not exclusively humans'.

Grief doesn't require understanding death. Humans certainly grieve, but they disagree on what death is. People learn widely varying traditional beliefs—in heaven, hell, karmic reincarnation, and other devices for keeping the deceased undead. The main thing humans seem to believe about death is: you never really die. A minority believe that we simply end, ceasing to exist. But most people find that notion inconceivable.

"I believe in life everlasting" are words I was taught to repeat in church. So when a chimpanzee or dolphin carries its dead baby, does it understand any less about death than does the pope? When an elephant fondles the bones of its dearly departed, does it understand more?

Fully *two years* after Teresia's death from being speared, Cynthia saw Tallulah, Theodora, and their younger family members "being silly"—floppy-running through bushes, pirouetting round with tails curled, plunging into water and amusing themselves by making waves and splashing. They had recovered from Teresia's death "and were once again," as Cynthia put it, "the sprightly, often whimsical elephants that I remembered and loved so much."

I Don't Know How You Say Good-bye

———•———

The ones we're observing move into the marsh, crashing through the tall grass and sloshing into the cooling wetness.

How do families decide where to go, and when? Vicki has watched this *very* carefully. "If someone in the family fancies going to a certain place, she stands at the edge of her group, facing the direction she wishes to travel." It's called a "Let's go" stance. Every minute or so, the elephant with an idea rumbles, "Let's go." It's a proposal: "I want to go this way; let's go together." "Either they agree to go," says Vicki, "or they just won't move."

And if they don't move?

"If they don't move, the one that's wanting to move might come bouncing back to the family and initiate a big greeting to get support. Like, 'Hey! We're really great friends! Now I want to go—*there*.' So a greeting can be a strategy, as well."

Sometimes assent comes quickly. The matriarch makes a long, soft rumble, raises her ears and flaps them against her neck and shoulders like a hand clap, and the family sets off as if this was the signal they had all been waiting for. Other times, discussions can go on for hours.

"They know what lies ahead," Vicki explains. "If a big, dominant family happens to be where you wanted to go, you just avoid the hassle by going someplace else. Sometimes it's obvious. Other times, I can't explain why they're doing what they're doing."

Vicki pauses to say, "Hello, Amelia." Then, to me: "That female who's moving and flapping her ears? That's Jolene, the JAs' matriarch. And—" Vicki looks through her binoculars at a female farther into the marsh and tall grass. "Yeah, okay, so that's Yvonne."

So: here we have the AAs, YAs, and JAs. AAs are friends with JAs; YAs are also friends with JAs. They're all going to greet one another. Vicki translates, "They're not just saying, 'Oh, hello.' It's more like, 'This is me and this is you—and we're friends, and we're here.'"

The greeting is drawing all the individuals in, pooling their feelings and relationships.

Researcher Joyce Poole calls this a "bonding ceremony." The participants are signaling to one another and to distant listeners that they "are members of a supportive unit," Poole has written, "and that together they form a united front."

"Want to know whether elephants are good friends or close relatives?" Vicki asks rhetorically. "Watch their greetings." The more intense and excited the greeting, the more important the relationships. During high social excitement, elephants often suddenly and dramatically grasp each other's trunks, press their bodies against one another; there's trumpeting, rumbles, trunks reached toward faces or into another's mouth, ear flapping, tusk clicking—. You know "excited" when you see it.

Elephants use well over one hundred ritual gestures to communicate in various contexts, with context helping convey the meaning. An ambivalent or apprehensive elephant may stand listening and watching, twisting the tip of their trunk back and forth; they may touch their own face, mouth, ear, trunk, apparently for reassurance, like a person touching their cheek or putting a hand to their chin. Near-constant calling emphasizes the family unit, reinforcing bonds, reconciling differences, defending associates, forming coalitions, coordinating movements, and maintaining contact. Elephants use their familiar mammalian larynx or "voice box" for making some calls, their trumpeting trunk for others.

And when elephants have had a problem with each other, they may reconcile with the help of a mediator. Researchers write, "Typically a third party, such as the matriarch or a close associate of the aggrieved individual, initiates the reconciliation. She approaches the conflicting elephants . . . and, while standing head to head, rumbles while head-raising and ear-lifting and reaching toward the other with an outstretched trunk in an affiliative gesture."

. . .

Vicki's a bit disappointed on my behalf at the energy level in this partic-ular greeting ceremony. "If the EBs were over here, it would have been *huge* and full of excitement and trumpeting, lots of body rubs, touching—. We call them the Italian family because they're just *hugely* demonstrative. This was a very muted join-up."

The JAs, a small family, have reason to be muted. "They used to be led by a very beautiful matriarch," Vicki explains. "She died after get-ting speared. Their next matriarch died during the drought." With their elders gone, the survivors seem diminished emotionally. For "who" animals, death matters most, in a sense, to those who survive.

Most of the family is hidden behind the bushes. The close one now is Jamila. That next one, who's just put a trunkful of grass on his head, is Jeremy, age nine. If you look just right of him, that female whose tusks touch at the tips is Jolene, their current matriarch. Next to her is Jean; she just lost a pregnancy. That female with the very upcurved tusks—that's Jody. Jolene's earned a reputation as a matriarch very sensitive to family needs, calm, quick to offer reassurance, leading by example. "They're a very sweet family with each other, very cohesive, very affectionate. One of my favorite families," Vicki says with evident fondness.

And they're one of the most surprising: genetic tests show that Jolene, Jamila, and Jody aren't closely related. "They are friends who func-tion as a family, emotionally very close, always together; there's always a lot of body touching, rubbing—. Oh look: Jamila is greeting the calf. 'Hello, we're all here.'"

Jolene must have just been talking with Jetta, the female stuffing her face in front of Jody now; they are both streaming from their temple glands.

Jody is holding her ears out. "That means she's listening," Vicki explains. "And see that small ear flap she just did? They're talking back and forth."

I am wondering why I can't hear them.

Vicki starts telling me, a bit spookily. "Often, we can't hear them, and yet we'll say, 'I feel there are elephants around' or 'I can't feel any elephants.' We all can sense whether there are elephants nearby, and we don't know why. Something very subtle that we're cuing to, not even aware of. I think we're feeling their subsonic calls and are not conscious of it."

Elephant song spans ten octaves, from subsonic rumbles to trumpets, about 8 hertz to around 10,000 hertz. Studies with instruments that can shift very low sounds up into the range of human hearing show that if elephants are excited enough to be streaming from their temple glands, they're also vocalizing. It's just that, often, their rumbles, though loud, are too low-frequency for humans to hear.

Elephants' low-frequency rumbles create waves not only through the air but also across *the ground*. Elephants can hear rumbles inaudible to humans over distances of several miles. Their great sensitivity to low frequencies derives through ear structure, bone conduction, and special nerve endings that make their toes, feet, and trunk tip extremely sensitive to vibration. So part of elephant vocal communication is sent through the ground and received through their feet. (Their ability to detect ground-traveling vibrations might account for stories of elephants running uphill before humans spotted an oncoming tsunami.)

When you do hear an elephant rumbling, you're just catching the top frequency of a vertical wall of sound they're making, like hearing only the higher notes of a complex chord. To put it visually: if the sound were a house, you'd be hearing just the attic of a call that contains a finished basement. Elephants create different *kinds* of rumbles with varying sonic structures. Rumbles during tense encounters have different amplitude, frequency, and duration from rumbles uttered during peaceful amity. Saying simply that elephants rumble is a little like saying that humans laugh. We have different laughs for different contexts and intensities, from polite chuckles to sarcastic sneers to belly laughs. Same with rumbles: different kinds.

"A lot of what they're saying is below human hearing," Vicki relates, "but you can see them pause, and you see little postures, subtle little things. You can sometimes see the forehead wrinkle as they call. If you're right next to them, you certainly *can* feel them in your solar plexus, right in your chest; it goes right through you."

What—if anything—*are* they saying? "Communication" is a message from a sender that is understood by a receiver. Surprisingly, communication does not always require consciousness. A flower is a plant's way of communicating information to bees and other pollinators. The world is full of electronic impulses, chemicals, visual cues, and motions that convey information. It's not language in the human sense, but it is effective crucial messaging. An elephant, though, is not a bush; animal communication is often two-way. When my dog Jude puts his snout over my keyboard and with his nose types me a note—such as "deqwwsaa"—then turns sideways and wags his tail, we both know he means: "I was just thinking that it would feel good if you scratch my rump."

Words are only one part of communication. The world sparkles with silent sentiments, all in their quiet ways signifying sentient somethings. From crustaceans and insects and octopuses on up, millions of species communicate using scents, gestures, postures, hormones and pheromones, touch, glances, *and* sounds. The living world almost shimmers with instant messages and long-distance calls. In the ocean, the great whales can hear one another calling through hundreds of miles of seawater. Many fish grunt invitations and RSVPs to one another. Snapping shrimp make their undersea places crackle. A lot is going on. We've hardly attempted to study how other animals use and perceive one another's vocal arrays, scent palettes, and gestural vocabularies.

For centuries, the fact that other animals don't converse the way humans do has been interpreted as evidence of empty minds. Of course, that helps justify what we do to them. If they can't think, there's no need to care what they think. So before we can get to communication, we need to unbraid the tangled topics of communication, thinking, and cruelty.

In the 1600s, René Descartes jumbled up communication, consciousness, thought, human superiority, and religion. He asserted, incorrectly, "The reason animals do not speak as we do is not that they lack the organs but that they have no thoughts." He added, illogically, "If they thought as we do, they would have an immortal soul like us."

Voltaire disdainfully called out Descartes's contradictions of logic, even referring to him and his followers as "barbarians": "What a pitiful, what a sorry thing to have said that animals are machines bereft of understanding and feeling," wrote Voltaire. He continued:

Is it because I speak to you, that you judge that I have feeling, memory, ideas? Well, I do not speak to you; you see me going home looking disconsolate, seeking a paper anxiously, opening the desk where I remember having shut it, finding it, reading it joyfully. You judge that I have experienced the feeling of distress and that of pleasure, that I have memory and understanding. Bring the same judgment to bear on this dog which has lost its master, which has sought him on every road with sorrowful cries, which enters the house agitated, uneasy, which goes down the stairs, up the stairs, from room to room, which at last finds in his study the master it loves, and which shows him its joy by its cries of delight, by its leaps, by its caresses. Barbarians seize this dog, which in friendship surpasses man so prodigiously; they nail it on a table, and they dissect it alive in order to show the mesenteric veins. You discover in it all the same organs of feeling that are in yourself. Answer me, machinist, has nature arranged all the means of feeling in this animal, so that it may not feel? Has it nerves in order to be impassible? Do not suppose this impertinent contradiction in nature.

During the live dissections, or "vivisections" of his pre-anesthesia time, Descartes's ideas were used to discount the dogs' and others' cries of suffering. Is a conscious, feeling non-human just too awful to accept? Why did Descartes need to assert human superiority in terms that justified causing suffering to other animals? I think the answer is precisely that the terms did just that. Others objected. "The question is not, Can they *reason*? nor, Can they *talk*? but, Can they *suffer*?" challenged Jeremy Bentham succinctly in 1789. "Every one has heard of the dog suffering under vivisection, who licked the hand of the operator," wrote Charles Darwin in *The Descent of Man*. "This man, unless the operation was fully justified by an increase of our knowledge, or unless he had a heart of stone, must have felt remorse to the last hour of his life." Darwin jotted in his notebook this searing one-liner: "Animals, whom we have made our slaves, we do not like to consider our equal."

Sometimes it seems that humans do think but do not deeply feel. It would be disturbing if a pig screamed, "I am in terror! Don't kill me!" This, of course, is exactly what a pig says as it's being killed. It can't speak English, but neither can many people in France. Every other animal I've known seems as interested in living as any human. In fact, many humans seem less interested. Self-destructive behavior, for instance, seems distinctly human. Depression-related suicide appears nonexistent in free-living animals. Most animals do everything they can to stay alive.

Let's reconsider communication. When someone insists that we cannot know another species' thoughts because we can't talk to them, there is a large dollop of truth here. It's difficult to know exactly what they're feeling. We can't even talk to our parents at times, or our spouses or children. And often we ourselves "can't say what we mean," "can't express what we feel," "can't find the words."

We can't ask a creature to tell us, but we can observe behavior, ask sensible questions, create some good experiments, and come to a better understanding. Einstein did this with the universe. He learned a few things. Newton did it with physics. Darwin with the tree of life. Galileo didn't complain to his friends that the planets wouldn't talk to him. And despite the astronomical distances planets travel, nothing about their behavior gave anyone the impression that planets think or feel. Animals, though, give that impression—while they are thinking and feeling. Yet because we cannot converse with other animals, animal behaviorists threw up their hands, saying we can't know if they think or feel, and we should assume they cannot. Human behaviorists—Freud comes to mind—suffer no such self-straitjacketing. They try to tell you what you don't realize you are thinking. What you are *feeling* that you haven't verbalized. This double standard is peculiar, don't you think? On the one hand, you have professionals saying that we can't know whether other animals think because they're not using words, yet different professionals say that words can't explain what *humans* really think.

Words are at best a loose cargo net of labels that we throw over our wild and woolly perceptions, hoping to catch and observe some of our thoughts and feelings. Words are sketches of the real thing, and some sketches capture a better likeness than others. Can you describe the *feeling* of an itch without the label "itch"? Neither can a dog, but the dog scratches, so we know it, too, itches. Can you describe the wetness of water? Or how love feels, or sadness, or the smell of snow or how an apple tastes—? No words equal the experience.

Speech is a slippery grip for measuring thoughts. People might lie. We sometimes ignore what someone is saying and use body language as a more truthful guide to what they're *really* feeling. Sometimes words fail us. And the fact that we learn different languages shows that words are rather arbitrary: that authentic thoughts arise first; then we paste words onto them. Words interpret thoughts. Thoughts come first.

Strangely, a human brain gets active several seconds before the person becomes aware of the thought. Much happens before words flow. Looking around a room, you don't say to yourself, "My refrigerator, the sink, my love." A photo of a loved one is worth a thousand words—and doesn't need any. Instant and wordless, it says all. The fewer words, the more directly you experience. After a dog has been scolded, they understand when a mere touch says, "We're still friends—let's move on." For some huge things, words are optional. "I love you" is enough said, and more reliable if silently shown. A gesture often says it. The other animals know it. And so do we. If you hit a rough spot with your honey and words are failing, you can say it with flowers. And visual arts, music, and dance continue ancestral conversations when words cease.

Watch elephants communicating, and they seem masters of subtlety. But we have no nuanced vocabulary for translation. We have only clumsy categorizations. Elephants use what researchers call—for lack of better words—snorts, barks, roars, grunts, cries, and squeaks. But to the actual authors and receivers of those sounds—the elephants themselves—their intent must be as clear and familiar as human words are to us humans.

Turn the tables. An elephant hears human speech as we hear people speaking a foreign language. Imagine describing, say, Vietnamese by categorizing the *types of sounds* involved. You'd never decode it.

But translating elephant language into Vietnamese or English: that's tricky. No one can argue with the statement "The elephant rumbled." The description is safe. But many would object to concluding, "The elephant said 'Hello.'" Yet without an interpretation and a *translation,* we won't understand what they are communicating. For half a century, the study of animal communication has been stalled at description; translation is where it needs to go.

A recent state-of-the art description of elephant vocalization by Dr. Joyce Poole of ElephantVoices shows how difficult it is to convey the nature of elephant calls in human terms. Here Dr. Poole discusses elephant rumbles:

> *Estrous-rumbles, greeting-rumbles/bonding-rumbles, mating-pandemonium,* and *roaring-rumbles* (heard when elephants are mobbing predators) are all marked during the peak of excitement by increased amplitude, increased noise, and increased modulation, with energy distributed in the upper harmonics (rather than in the second harmonic as in most rumbles), with calls becoming softer, less modulated, and less noisy with time. . . . *Greeting-rumbles* or *bonding-rumbles,* in particular, show an extreme range in the frequency contour of calls. They may be flat, slightly arched, highly arched, bimodal, multimodal, skewed left or right.

Poole's observations are detailed. But imagine trying to understand a human greeting if it was described the way Poole describes an elephant greeting: "Within a single Greeting-Ceremony, arched, skewed, arched with a wiggly contour, bimodal, bimodal and skewed, and multi-modal *rumbles* occur."

After rumbles, Poole moves to roars, writing, "The sound quality of *roaring* calls is highly variable and might be described as squealing like a pig, screeching, roaring, shouting, yelling, crying, and even crowing like a rooster."

Highly variable indeed. But, please: *You've watched them for thousands of hours, so don't be bashful; I'd like to know what you think they're actually saying with all that variability.*

"The variability of calling may simply reflect the intensity of excitement," she writes. "It may, alternatively, reveal additional information, such as a caller's signature or perhaps even reference to specific individuals."

In other words: they're talking, perhaps even calling each other by name. We don't yet know what they're saying. So far, we can't do much more than describe the physical characteristics of their sounds.

. . .

A researcher from another planet might describe the chattering sounds we humans make during our greeting displays like this: "Upright Earthlings' greetings may be low- or high-intensity. High-intensity greetings may involve high-decibel, high-frequency *shouts* and *screams*. Post-juveniles often perform the *touch-hands* display. Unlike the researchers from outer space, we'd summarize the same human greetings insightfully: "Greetings vary, sometimes full of excitement, sometimes rather formal. Friends might shriek with excitement when they see each other. Most adults shake hands when they meet." The researcher from another planet describes what it's seeing because it doesn't understand what's going on. We down-to-Earthlings can explain what's going on because we understand one another.

But when it comes to other animals, we harbor no vocabulary for *their* vocabulary other than the crudest words, like "rumble." How we *describe* how elephants talk determines how we *understand* their talking. You wouldn't say that a Spanish speaker "just gave the *ho-la* call"; you'd translate: "He just said 'hello' to her."

Because we're not elephants, their sounds don't yield easily to our ears or our alphabet. Imagine trying to write out, in *words,* Beethoven's Moonlight Sonata or John Coltrane's *A Love Supreme*. It can't be done. (Beethoven goes "da da da da da da da dada da"; Coltrane "emits highly variable shrieks, bellows, and squeals.") Imagine describing a sunset by listing the wavelength distributions of the colored light. Likewise, we don't have a notational system for elephants' sounds (or birds' songs, or dogs' barks, and on and on). For human speech we can simply write, "In Spanish, *hola* means hello." We can't write out elephant rumbles phonetically, then translate: "This call means 'Here's food'; this one means 'Where are you?'; this means 'Come mate with me'; this means, 'I'm lost—help!'" We don't have a good notation or a translation.

An exception is the rumble that researchers refer to as "Let's go." That label *is* also a translation. The bigger question, the true nut of it, is: Do elephants actually *mean* different things with different calls in different contexts? Even when we label the context—like "contact call," "little greeting," "musth chorus," and so on—it's a little like labeling our words "Hello, how are you doing?" as our "greeting call." It doesn't quite translate. When elephants utter a "greeting rumble," are the elephants saying "Hello" or "Get out of my way"? What do the elephants *mean*?

I Say Hello

————

African elephants have one particular alarm that appears to be their word for "Bees!" They run from the sound of buzzing bees, shaking their heads as they go. Elephants also run away shaking their heads if they merely hear a recording of elephants calling as they run from bees. They don't head-shake when played recorded voices of people. The head shake is reserved for bees, because they're trying to run away without getting angry bees into their ears and noses. Zoo elephants in the United States who've never been swarmed by African honeybees do not respond to the sound of bees. Older elephants in Africa respond directly, while younger ones look to their elders and copy their response. "They see that their mom treats them as dangerous," researcher Lucy King explained one day. "And that's one way they learn." A friend of mine saw impalas run away when they heard elephants scream at a pack of wild dogs; her guide said that impalas never run when elephants are screaming at people or each other. If true, that means elephants say some specific things that impalas understand.

Baby elephants "rumble," but they have two very different "words" that express contentment or annoyance. They respond to being comforted by going *Aauurrrr* and to being insulted—pushed, tusked, kicked, or denied their mother's breast—by going *Barooo*. Some rumbles by mothers have the immediate effect of bringing a wandering baby back to her side. It seems fair to interpret that as them saying, "Come here."

Elephants' interactions show that they understand what they're saying, whether it expresses fine-grained information, such as "Let's go," or simply conveys emotional intensity, what we might understand as tone of voice. "I'm getting *impatient*! Let's *go*!" Meaning often depends on context. Because the listener knows the context, they understand the message.

Some human speech is like that; meaning often depends on context and intensity. I can say, *"Hey!"* in a friendly or a sharp voice, and you understand whether I intend it as an amicable greeting or a threatening warning. To an elephant, a trumpeting elephant might sound like someone yelling, *"Hey!"* The finer meaning is intended by the sender, and understood by an experienced listener. That kind of coding and decoding is one of the things elephants do with their ten-pound, bread-loaf brains.

Not until 1967 did anyone realize that vervet monkeys—which are very common—have calls with distinct meanings. In other words: words. If a dangerous cat is detected, the alarm that's given makes everyone run up a tree. When a martial eagle or crowned eagle flies over, the alert monkey's two-syllable call causes the other monkeys to look skyward or run into thick groundcover (*not* up a tree). And they are astute bird-watchers; they don't respond to black-chested snake-eagles and white-backed vultures; those birds don't prey on vervets. A monkey who sees a dangerous snake gives a "chuttering" call that causes other vervets to stand up on their hind legs, scanning the ground for the reptile. All together, vervets of Amboseli have words for "leopard," "eagle," "snake," "baboon," "other predatory mammal," "unfamiliar human," "dominant monkey," "subordinate monkey," "watch other monkey," and "see rival troop." Until the age of six or seven months, vervets may respond incorrectly to alarm calls—for instance, jumping up a tree when the eagle alarm is sounded. Until age two, a young vervet may cry "eagle" for harmless birds overhead and "leopard" for small cats, too. Vervets acquire fully skilled pronunciation about halfway to puberty, a bit like humans.

Some other monkeys also have alarm calls that name specific threats. Titi, putty-nosed, and colobus monkeys, among others, provide additional information through the order of calls, not just the individual call components. (Surprisingly enough, so do some small birds, such as golden-winged warblers and European robins; one wonders who else.) Campbell's monkeys use the sequences of the calls—in a syntax-like way, where order changes meaning—to announce whether they actually see or just hear a predator. If the threat is far off, a Campbell's monkey will introduce the alarm call by a sort of adjectival modifier, a low-pitched "boom" that means, basically, "I see a distant leopard. Just be aware." Without the boom the alarm means, urgently, "Leopard—here!" Campbell's monkeys have three call sequences for leopards and four for crowned eagles. Diana monkeys respond to Campbell's monkeys' alarm calls; they can't afford to let a language barrier get in their way when the stakes are high. Gibbons ("lesser" apes of Southeast Asian forests) assemble at least seven different calls into songs. The songs repel intruding gibbons, attract mates, and warn of predators. Chimpanzees use nearly ninety different call combinations, along with log drumming, in specific contexts. A familiar female's "pant-hoot" may announce her arrival to the whole party, but she switches to a "pant-grunt" during her final approach to the dominant male. She might in effect say, "Greetings—now *I* am doing *this*." When one chimpanzee gets attacked by another, the victim may "tend to exaggerate" *if* there's a high-ranking individual within earshot who might interrupt the assault.

One morning in Trinidad, a naturalist at the Asa Wright lodge where my wife and I were staying said he heard a bird called a motmot uttering its alarm for "Snake!" Sure enough, we soon found the excited motmot up in some high branches, fluttering around—and occasionally nipping—a Cook's tree boa. Other birds understood well enough to come join the scold, depriving the stealthy snake of its element of surprise. If motmots have a word for "snake," the now-familiar question arises: What else are we missing? One hint: Tiko, Joanna Burger's Amazon parrot, gives different calls for a hawk, person, cat, or dog in the yard. "I know what is there," she tells me, "before I look."

Two elephants approaching each other give a soft, short greeting rumble. When human caretakers call an orphaned elephant's name, the one they've called often replies with this same greeting rumble. (In effect, the caretaker speaks English and the elephant replies in elephant.) Researchers say it means something like "Hello, it's good to be near you again" or, perhaps, "You are important to me."

In human language, "You are important to me" means something different from "Are you important to me?" The order of the words changes the meaning. That's syntax. Dolphin researcher Louis Herman noted, "Syntax is what tells us that a Venetian blind is not a blind Venetian." Many communication experts consider syntax to be the defining characteristic of true "language." They're probably right.

Herman, who studied captive dolphins in Hawaii, found that the dolphins understood the difference between "Get the ring from John and give it to Susan" and "Get the ring from Susan and give it to John." They understood syntax.

What most other animals don't have—and I think we can be pretty sure of this—is complex syntax. Complex syntax characterizes human language. Dolphins may use some simple syntax of their own in the wild. Some apes—especially bonobos—can learn to use some human syntax.

That means something very striking: it means that these creatures *have* these capacities to mentally manipulate parts of human syntax and respond appropriately. Trainers can coax it up and out in a form humans can detect—capabilities so similar to ours that we can understand each other.

It would make no sense for another animal to be capable of using syntax with a human if it didn't use syntax with others of its species or with itself. What makes sense is: we probably don't fully understand this yet.

Maybe they use syntax a little differently. Here's one possibility. Many animals have the ability to silently size things up, so that they recognize the difference between "If I attack you, I'll win," "If you attack me, I'll lose," and so on. Even fish must be able to understand the difference between "I'm big enough to eat you" and "You're big enough to eat me." In the complex social animals, where status depends largely on age and experience, perhaps there's a kind of syntax in the common evaluation "I can dominate her, but he can dominate me." Hundreds of social interactions rely on being able to evaluate those relationships correctly.

Imagine how many evaluations of the risks and benefits of social and strategic decisions an elephant or ape must make over decades! They must not only look before they leap, they must understand their likelihood of coming out on top. Their minds must be able to swap actors in different potential scenarios and judge likely outcomes. Does the picking and choosing and distinguishing show, in a sense, a kind of syntax of survival? Is *that* why their minds can learn, when among humans, that swapping the order of words alters their relationship? Perhaps that has something to do with it.

Right? Joyce Poole says that the placement of different trumpets amid different rumbles "can be viewed as a simple form of syntax." Elephants' different forms of trumpeting (seemingly every kind except Dixieland) convey the excitement and "importance" that elephants give an event. If syntax is about where the words appear in relation to one another, then context itself is a kind of syntax; meaning depends on *where* the individual is in relation to other elephants. When your dog is scratching the door, she doesn't need to give a soliloquy on desire; you just need to know which side of the door she's on.

So one might conclude: Humans can speak in sentences; others use phrases. The sentences "I would love to go for a walk around the pond. We'll meet some of those other dogs" could easily be reduced to the human words "Walk, pond; dogs." Or conveyed without words, by a nose at the door and a wagging tail. The idea gets communicated. It's basically the same thought, resulting in the same desired outcome, either way. Thousands of creatures survive in highly demanding environments, clearly signaling their intentions, without a single adverb or gerund.

We happen to be talkers. But most of what we jabber on about could be said in fewer words (as my editor emphasizes). Most days, we have few thoughts worth remembering. Most talk is so trivial it might be better left unsaid. Think of the words wasted. Professional counselors attempt to help walk us across bridges built over rushing rapids of failed words. The craft of war designates spears and bombs to do the speaking. Millions of words prove unable to close gaps between ethnic injustices, ideologies, religions; think of the United Nations, the climate talks, the "peace process."

Think of love, of the way truly important things can be communicated with open arms, fingertips, a smile—with no need of sentences, and without syntax. The silent power of true intent.

We've tended to be lazy about other animals' vocabularies. We say merely that dogs "bark" or "whine." That's like saying people "speak" or "scream" and leaving it at that. You can easily hear the difference between your dog barking to be let out and your dog barking at a stranger who has suddenly appeared at the same door. Even to us, the pitch, sound quality, and intensity of what the dog is saying are different, easily recognizable. Your dog understands, and lets you understand. When I'm in my writing room, I can tell by the barks whether Jude and Chula are barking at someone walking past, someone walking past with a dog, a delivery person, a squirrel they've treed, or each other, in play or in mock combat.

Yet of other animals' vocabulary, we remain almost tone-deaf. By veiling their vocal repertoire with our one-size-fits-all word—"bark," "rumble," "howl"—that doesn't actually fit all, we hobble our understanding of *their* understanding of what they mean.

Now look at how a conversation develops as two elephants or two groups approach each other. One begins uttering "contact calls." Translation: "I am here; where are you?" Another elephant hears this and responds with a sudden, abrupt lift of her head, followed by an explosive rumble that says, "It's me; I am over here."

Next, the initial caller's posture relaxes, as though she's thinking, "Okay; there you are." She may call back, as if confirming receipt of the answer. Nearby family members may chime in, calling back and forth. This can continue for hours as the animals converge.

The callers meet up. Now the conversation explodes, and their vocabulary changes into a series of intense, overlapping greeting rumbles. Next, the conversation shifts again, to softer rumbles that are structurally quite different. This part often continues for many minutes.

Even if elephants don't have a sophisticated syntax, they have a vocabulary. They wield a communication kit with dozens and dozens of gestures and sounds and combinations. Why don't we understand them better by now? It's been just a few decades since humans first attempted to study how other animals communicate, so short a time that the pioneers of elephant communication are still working. And only a handful of people in the world do this work.

Is it likely that, over the ages, elephants developed such a wide array of complex sounds and yet they are arbitrary, meaningless? It's unlikely. Their meaning might be limited, but understanding must sometimes mean the difference between life and death. If it didn't, their repertoire of gestures and their sound library would never have become so intricate.

. . .

Hauntingly, elephants communicate over very long distances. No one knows how they do it. Even though the low frequency of their rumbles pitches much of the calling too low for human hearing, those calls are loud (115 decibels, comparable to loud live rock music at 120 decibels). Loud enough that, in theory, elephants six miles away can hear such calls. We know that special receptors, called Pacinian corpuscles, in their feet help them pick up elephant rumbles traveling across the ground. Have they got another way of calling that penetrates even farther? Do they relay calls, like human drumming?

How do we explain certain remarkable stories about elephant communication? For instance: In a privately owned wildlife sanctuary in Zimbabwe lived some eighty well-known, very relaxed elephants who hung around a tourist lodge's artificial water holes. Officials ninety miles away in Hwange National Park decided to reduce the park's elephant densities by "culling" hundreds of elephants (using helicopters to herd elephants to waiting marksmen, who were instructed to kill whole families). On the day the distant slaughter started, the relaxed tourist-lodge elephants abruptly vanished. Several days later, they were found bunched together in the corner of the sanctuary farthest from Hwange. "Elephants are able to detect distress calls over large distances and are fully aware when their fellows are being killed," Cynthia Moss has said. Many researchers say that when elephants are being killed, they know very well what is going on. But how?

Similarly, perhaps, soon after the "elephant whisperer" Lawrence Anthony passed away, nearly two dozen elephants—whom he had rescued and given asylum on his enormous reserve—converged on his home in two groups on two consecutive days, and lingered for two days. They had reportedly not been there for a year. We understand that elephants can grieve. But grieve for a human? And how might elephants a twelve-hour walk away get a message that a certain man's heart has stopped? No one knows. My skeptical mind seeks more proof, better evidence: Are these stories entirely true?

After being bottle-fed for several years in a nursery adjacent to Nairobi National Park, elephant orphans rescued by the David Sheldrick Wildlife

Trust go to Tsavo National Park, where they join others who've been through the same process years earlier and are now free-living. There they begin a new life in the bush in a more normal, multi-aged elephant society. At the nursery, as I accompanied the exceptionally talented keeper Julius Shivegha on a bush walk with a group of orphans, he tried to explain, saying, "When they first arrive in Tsavo, they come and ask us, 'Where are we? Why have you brought us here?' Not in our language, but by the way they follow us everywhere. Later on, when they communicate with the others in that language of theirs, they come to understand everything." Daphne Sheldrick herself added, "The older ones know exactly where these orphans are coming from, because they've been through the nursery themselves."

If the older ones really *do* remember the orphanage and how they themselves got to Tsavo, if they understand what is happening to the new arrivals, it means they have their story in mind, and that they know that they have it. Skeptics who've seen the greetings at Tsavo tend to come away convinced that they have witnessed something inexplicable. The people who work with the orphans have no doubts. Drawing on decades of experience, Daphne Sheldrick insists that the elephants in Tsavo know when a new group of orphans is headed there in trucks on the road from Nairobi. She claims that free-living grown-ups come from the bush, ready to meet young new orphans when they arrive. She calls it "telepathy." I filed her claim in my mind's "unlikely stories" bin. But that bin gets cluttered; there are many "unlikely" stories about elephants.

It seems a common human assumption that each species has one set of calls—no dialects, no differing languages analogous to those among humans. An implicit assumption seems to be that their vocalizations are innate and don't have to be learned. Individuals taken from the wild as infants—as with zoo apes and circus elephants and killer whales—likely never learned important aspects of their own native ways of communicating with sound, gesture, context, nuance.

Many birds have regional dialects. Killer whales also have call vocabularies used exclusively by some groups and not shared by others. Differences like this are everywhere around us, but our discoveries about them are ongoing. We are still cataloging such behaviors and describing calls. Translating their communication, though, might turn out to be a difficult-to-reach itch. For now, what elephants are saying and understanding is more sophisticated than is our understanding of what elephants are saying.

Holding Back, Letting Go

———

"This," Vicki says enthusiastically, "is what I mean by a cohesive family!"

Having finished eating, the elephants gather closely, adults facing out, children in the middle. Jean is very slowly backing into Jolene, touching her. "See them all standing together now, leaning against each other, touching with tails, trunks—. This is perfect. Everyone's feeling really safe. They'll probably have a snooze now."

Babies sprawl abundantly, dozing peacefully within their tribe's safe-keeping. The adults just stand quietly. At least it seems quiet.

"All that ear flapping?" says Vicki. "That means they're talking." We can't hear them.

Lyall Watson describes finding himself in an extraordinarily poignant encounter on the cliffs of South Africa's seacoast while he was watching a whale:

> The sensation I was feeling on the clifftop was some sort of reverberation in the air itself. . . . The whale had submerged and I was still feeling something. The strange rhythm seemed now to be coming from behind me, from the land, so I turned to look across the gorge . . . where my heart stopped. . . .
>
> Standing there in the shade of the tree was an elephant . . . staring out to sea! . . . A female with a left tusk broken off near the base. . . . I knew who she was, who she had to be. I recognized her from a color photograph put out by the Department of Water Affairs and Forestry under the title

"The Last Remaining Knysna Elephant." This was the Matriarch herself. . . .

She was here because she no longer had anyone to talk to in the forest. She was standing here on the edge of the ocean because it was the next, nearest, and most powerful source of infrasound. The under-rumble of the surf would have been well within her range, a soothing balm for an animal used to being surrounded by low and comforting frequencies, by the lifesounds of a herd, and now this was the next-best thing.

My heart went out to her. The whole idea of this grandmother of many being alone for the first time in her life was tragic, conjuring up the vision of countless other old and lonely souls. But just as I was about to be consumed by helpless sorrow, something even more extraordinary took place. . . .

The throbbing was back in the air. I could feel it, and I began to understand why. The blue whale was on the surface again, pointed inshore, resting, her blowhole clearly visible. The Matriarch was here for the whale! The largest animal in the ocean and the largest living land animal were no more than a hundred yards apart, and I was convinced that they were communicating! In infrasound, in concert, sharing big brains and long lives, understanding the pain of high investment in a few precious offspring, aware of the importance and the pleasure of complex sociality, these rare and lovely great ladies were commiserating over the back fence of this rocky Cape shore, woman to woman, matriarch to matriarch, almost the last of their kind.

I turned, blinking away the tears, and left them to it. This was no place for a mere man. . . .

Early afternoon.

They were coming to this place, to this tall grass, all along. They will feed here for a while and then, because there's no water right here, go down to where those egrets are. There's water there. After they've had a good drink, they might make a big loop and come back here again later to feed some more. It will be a one-family-at-a-time choice as the adults decide when to drink and bathe.

When elephants are finally ready to make a significant move, everyone points in the same direction. But they do wait until the matriarch decides. "I've seen families cued up waiting for half an hour," comments Vicki, "waiting for the matriarch to signal, 'Okay.' "

And now they go. Makelele, eleven years old, walks with a deep limp. Five years ago he showed up with a broken right rear leg. It must have been agony, and it's healed at a horrible angle, almost as if his knee faces backward, shaping that leg like the hock on a horse. Yet he is here, surviving with a little help from his friends. "He's slow," Vicki acknowledges. "It's remarkable that he's managing, but his family seems to wait for him."

Another Amboseli elephant, named Tito, broke a leg when he was a year old, probably from falling into a garbage pit. He walked slowly and with great difficulty, seemingly in pain. His mother always waited for him; she never left him behind. He survived for just five years; Makelele is more than double that age so far.

Makelele's family travels a lot. They go twenty, twenty-five miles into Tanzania. "That's a *long* way," assesses Vicki. But he's obviously coping. He's still fat.

Makelele, in fact, will survive at least long enough to become independent from his family. I hope Makelele's bad leg remains the worst of his problems. With their own baby boom and the human population explosion and the ivory situation, it's both the best and worst of times for these elephants.

━

"You see all these good things in their lives," Cynthia Moss is telling me at breakfast. "Caring, loyalty, bonding, affiliation, cooperation—things we wish were in our lives." You see them helping babies and one another. And there are rare, extraordinary glimpses: the elephant feeding another who cannot use her trunk; an elephant attempting to feed another who has died. We've already seen how elephants have responded to helpless or injured humans. These and dozens of other gestures do not show that elephants are like us; they show that, not unlike us, elephants are aware of their relationships and have many ways of using their bodies, voices, scents, and minds to maintain, reinforce, and coordinate their social values.

. . .

Around 1980, one of the Amboseli lodges intentionally lured elephants in with food, as a tourist draw. Soon those elephants' innocent rummagings began doing damage to the lodge's trees and kitchen compound. People started to yell, throwing things at them, trying to scare them off—even hitting them with sticks and brooms. Any of those elephants could have fatally swatted a threatening human like an annoying mosquito. They had ample provocation to do so, and many opportunities.

"And yet," Cynthia says, "though I witnessed many interactions, Tuskless and the others always avoided hurting a person. One day Tania lost her temper and charged a woman tourist, who ran toward the lodge but fell on the lawn. Tania, only a few feet behind her, skidded to a halt and towered above her."

The elephant backed up, turned, and ambled back to her family. Any contact would likely have killed the woman. And yet—even though the woman had irritated her, Tania had expended such energy to avoid making contact that she'd left deep skid marks in the ground.

Why such restraint?

We assume that other animals cannot understand what might motivate a human, sometimes, to act with kindness. Likewise, we humans cannot understand why an elephant might forbear. Elephants seem to eschew fighting, and they have the social skills to assert themselves and show dominance without risking the violence that can bring harm to both sides.

At times we see restraint in other animals. Most of us have encountered an angry dog who did not attack. A sign-language-trained chimpanzee named Nim used the *signs* for "bite" and for "angry" instead of actually biting or attacking, and his anger would then diminish. Using the signs seemed to satisfy his need to express anger.

Elephants can plan revenge. Can they also intuit that harming humans brings future trouble? Had she harmed the woman, Tania surely would have lost her life. Did she treat the woman differently because she was indeed a human? It's difficult to imagine an elephant leaving skid marks to avoid harming, say, an annoying hyena.

Tuskless and Tania and their family (not to be confused with Butch's mother, Big Tuskless of the BBs) were regular visitors to Cynthia's camp. Cynthia had written that Tuskless was "smart, brave, inventive, and gutsy, and at the same time one of the sweetest-natured animals I have ever known. I can never become deeply angry with her, regardless of how badly she and the others sometimes behave." Describing her feelings for Tuskless as "love and admiration," Cynthia added, "They are still wild animals, but we accept each other and we do have some understanding of what is allowed and what is not."

But when an elephant tries to convey its sense of what is allowed, the human reaction usually ranges from panic to violence. On a January day in 1997, people complained to the Kenya Wildlife Service that a male—with tusks—had killed one of their cattle. The service arrived, found a family of females and their youngsters nearby, and chased them for more than two hours. When the harried matriarch finally turned to defend her family, they shot her, fatally. The matriarch was Tuskless.

Tuskless had appeared in over one hundred wildlife films; she was the most photographed elephant in Amboseli and had, Cynthia commented, created more wonder and joy for visitors than any single wild elephant anywhere in the world. "It hurts," she said, "more than I could ever have imagined."

Troubled Minds

———

In camp this morning, a new report is circulating, telling us that in the last ten years, poachers have killed *one hundred thousand* African elephants. That in the last ten years, central Africa has lost about 65 percent of its elephants, and they are everywhere dwindling.

The numbers numb me. The disparity between that cruelty and these kind and kindred creatures with whom I have fallen in love shatters my ability to think. It's an irrational number, impossible to reconcile with the world my mind inhabits.

Katito confirms the downward spiral. "In the early days we had many big bulls with big, big ivory. Now they are less. It does not compare."

Ivory, the darkest white thing. Killing is again up sharply all over Africa, back to where it was before the ivory ban of the early 1990s. Katito's opinion, which many share, is that—baby boom or not—it's going to be tough for elephants.

This park's border is porous—elephants walk in and out. Amboseli elephants leave, Kilimanjaro elephants arrive, they all wander into Tanzania and back, Tsavo males come over. Tsavo may be a national "park," but it's no picnic. Poachers kill elephants, rangers kill poachers, poachers kill rangers. Because patrols are improving and gunshots reveal location, poachers have gone back to poisoned arrows. In 2014, after two poison-arrow attacks three months apart on the largest living elephant in Kenya, a male named Satao, they got his two-hundred-pound tusks. Like an assassination.

But if there's such risk to them, why not just fence elephants in and people out?

"That's not nature conservation. That's gardening," Vicki asserts defiantly. "And we don't even know whether fenced parks can work long-term any more than can a zoo. We can't afford to lose more; we've lost too much already."

One Amboseli male went to Lake Natron, about eighty-five straight-line miles from here. These are real elephants, in other words. They live the way the world made them, the way they are made for the world. What's at stake is reality itself. But reality is slip-sliding away.

Many of these elephants must be thoroughly terrorized. A recent study shows that after losing a leader, the surviving elephants have elevated stress hormone levels for at least fifteen years, and give birth to fewer babies. Again we see how death affects the survivors.

After spending thirty years working with elephants in central Africa, biologist Richard Ruggiero, whom I knew in graduate school, says, "This is an animal that is somehow aware that something terrible is happening to it, a very sentient creature who really knows that there's a genocide going on."

"They know they're safer here," Vicki says. "If anything bad happens outside the park, they rush back into the park."

The ones that haven't fallen, she means.

Still inside the national park, we come to an overgrazed area. Domestic livestock have done this. Several young Maasai *morani*, whose roles are warriors and herders, walk with their cattle and goats. They're dressed in red *shukas*, still carrying traditional spears, clubs called *rungus*, and broad knives, or *simis*; their hair is drawn back in the traditional long braids and adorned with headbands decorated with metallic bangles.

Within their light stride is a dance with authority. They are allowed at certain times and in particular places to lead their cattle to water inside the park and, occasionally, to let them graze. They don't make the rules, so they both observe the laws and break them. The Maasai bring herds into the park for watering when their wells run dry, sometimes legally and other times not. They claim that the officials don't maintain their wells as promised. Another source of contention and tension.

Around here, the most important danger that elephants need to learn about is these local herding people: the Maasai. That's ironic. Part of the irony is that wildlife thrived across immense spans of landscape over centuries of Maasai occupation. Katito, who is Maasai, has reminded me that the Maasai do not eat wild meat; the wild ones are considered "God's cattle." That is why you can see wild animals on Maasai lands. And indeed, during my first trip to Africa, in the 1980s, I stayed with a Maasai friend and walked freely in the Loita Hills among zebras and gazelles and Maasai cattle, slept in a fire-lit dung hut, and greeted the mornings in a waking dream of Old Africa.

Fierce in fact and reputation, the Maasai did not tolerate poachers from outside and frequently blew their cover. Thus the Maasai kept poaching in check and Amboseli's elephants relatively safe—and relatively free to move—compared to elephants in many places.

The Maasai once occupied an area from what is now central Kenya six hundred miles southward to central Tanzania. In 1904, to make room for European settlers, the British colonial administration forced the Maasai into just 10 percent of their former lands, in two reserves. Then, in 1911, to make more room for European farmers, they herded the Maasai onto a single reserve. Farmers were not inclined to afford room to either tribal peoples or elephant families, treating both, in essence, as crop pests.

The Maasai had long coexisted with wildlife. Wildlife populations shrank and shriveled as Europeans took land and shot the animals. Then emerging European pressure to conserve wildlife focused on Maasai lands, which held the highest concentrations of free-living animals in Kenya. Savor the bitter irony. In the 1940s, the British began designating game reserves that excluded the Maasai, severing the people from the water sources that had been crucial to their existence. After the Maasai were prohibited livestock access to a central part of the Amboseli Game Reserve, in 1961, the Maasai began spearing elephants and rhinos in protest. For the Maasai, wildlife conservation has been a sinister legacy of colonial injustice.

And yet as pastoralists yield to farmers, and towns completely replace free-living animals and their lands, the Maasai herders seem less like the problem and more like the reason there is any wildlife here at all. It's because of the Maasai's traditional land stewardship that the park service makes so much money.

"Realize," Vicki says righteously, "eighty percent of the time, our elephants are out of the park on Maasai land. There are maybe forty rangers here. There are three thousand Maasai warriors."

Elephants must leave the park because it is much too small for them. Herders come into the park when their lands lack water. Outside, elephants run into herders. Inside, they also run into herders. The fearful symmetry of shared existence. The counter-tensioning of identical needs.

In Vicki's opinion, the future of elephants here depends on giving the Maasai the opportunity to continue their custodianship. That doesn't mean the Maasai relationship with elephants is always peaceful. During the forty-year tenure of this research project, Maasai spears have killed several hundred elephants.

The Maasai both revere and revile elephants. They believe that only humans and elephants have souls. In Maasai culture, brides leaving their home are told never to look back; a human bride did look back, and she became the first elephant. That's why elephant breasts look like human breasts. Traditionally, when the Maasai encounter the bones of a human or an elephant, they place grass on them to signal respect. This they do with no other animals.

For centuries, the Maasai's well-earned reputation for ferocity toward outsiders kept this land open and full of wildlife. The good news is, this place is still open and free. The bad news: even with no fences, other constrictions are closing in.

Much Maasai land has been subdivided. Now each Maasai owner has sixty acres. Outsiders are buying land from the Maasai. The sellers get the cash, but they are left with no way to make a living. Once off the land, they buy things like motorbikes, which require costly fuel and don't generate income as do cows. So, many people's living standards are plummeting. A patchwork of subdivisions with new owners is being developed for more agriculture and tourism. Lodges and farms, of course, will further erode habitat and block wildlife movements. It's a great system for making things go wrong.

The original Maasai culture had little use for the ivory business. Now the lack of opportunity combined with the promise of ivory money is too tempting for some. The word *moran*, usually translated as "warrior," refers to young men after their initiation into puberty; for a few years, they are traditionally both the defenders and the aggressors of their tribal communities—soldiers, basically. The increasing population creates a pool of young men with little to do. Here, elephants can become the billboards for protest and for lashing out. For reasons ranging from revenge to adolescent bravado to political protest, the Maasai sometimes hurt elephants.

Vicki starts telling me about an elephant named Ezra. "I'd had him come over in full musth and just walk up to the car and say hi. He was the *sweetest* male."

Guess where this story is headed.

"Forty-six years of walking in these hills. Never gave anyone any hassle. Wasn't a crop raider—"

As a political protest, some *morani* threw seven spears into him. "People followed him a long time, but he was so badly wounded there was nothing anyone could really do. He just bled and bled. Just—bled to death. *Every* time I pass the spot where I last saw him—"

A few moments pass in silence. I watch the elephants in the marsh doing their elephant things.

"It was about a lack of respect for their community," Vicki continues. "And I mean—they're right about that." What happened was, people said that a young boy had been killed by a buffalo, and a park official who went to assess a compensation payment implied that the family had killed their boy for the money. "Well, that got people very upset. That's just *really* insulting. I mean—. The Maasai are *nice* people. They love their children as much as anyone. Human lives *mean* something here." The official was not Maasai; this raised a larger issue of intertribal bias.

Last summer, Vicki saw three hundred *morani* come into the park looking for animals to spear in protest. "It was sickening to watch. And we were terrified because if those young men go out of control, there's nothing you can do." Enfranchisement, elephants. Disenfranchisement, dysfunction.

Above all else and with abundant reason, Amboseli elephants fear Maasai people. They will panic and run when they see or smell a Maasai half a mile away.

Elephants react differently to different *kinds* of humans. When researchers Richard Byrne and Lucy Bates presented Amboseli elephants with T-shirts worn by either the agricultural Kamba people, who rarely interact with elephants, or by the spear-wielding Maasai, or by the researchers themselves, the elephants showed fear only of the garments worn by the Maasai. Their smell—and their sense of recognition—is that good. And their fear of the Maasai is that strong.

Humans might not easily hear differences in elephant voices. But in addition to individually identifying at least a hundred or so other elephants by their voices, elephants can also distinguish human languages. A loudspeaker smells the same whether it's playing recordings of Maasai- or English-speaking people. When elephants heard recorded voices of researchers, Maasai herders, and Kamba farmers, they showed fear only of the Maasai voices.

When researchers played recorded sounds of Maasai cowbells to more than a dozen elephant families, the elephants immediately froze, then faced the speaker, then turned their heads from side to side to best pinpoint the sound's source, meanwhile evaluating the air with their trunks up. They moved closer together, then turned and retreated—usually by running—up to three hundred yards away, where they clumped closely together, with their young protected at the center of the family group. When researchers played recorded sounds of wildebeest, the elephants seldom even paused; not one turned in the direction of the sound. That's how well they understand their world.

Big brains aren't necessarily necessary for certain high-performance mental abilities. (Quoth the raven, for instance, its brain tiny, its mind amazing.) Nonetheless, elephants do have very large brains, even larger than expected proportional to body size, compared to most mammals. Elephant brains are simply bigger than any other land animals'. Elephants' pyramidal neurons—which help enable motor control, cognition, recognition, and other abilities—are larger than those in humans and are structured for many more connections. This may create elephants' high-functioning memory capacity and learning ability. And one of the things elephants have been learning and remembering is: humans are not alike, and certain humans are dangerous.

• • •

This elephant's trunk shows a newly healed spear wound. The mere thought is too painful.

"Looks better," Vicki assesses. It had been leaking fluid.

"Elephants sometimes kill people," Vicki reminds me. "Some elephants just *hate* people and will take any opportunity to hurt them."

I ask why.

"Something bad happened. I can't imagine that an elephant who hasn't had a negative interaction with humans would hate humans."

What proportion of the elephants here have experienced or seen human violence toward elephants?

"Hmm . . ." Vicki thinks about this. "Every member of the AAs over ten years old has experienced losing a family member to humans. And the AAs don't even really leave the park. The JAs also don't leave the park, but that big hole in Jackson's ear is from a spear. EBs, EAs—. Y'know, now that I think of it, every single family has experienced something negative and violent with humans."

That means they've witnessed an attack by people and have been involved in the panic. Some have felt the pain of injury.

And occasionally when elephants get a chance to turn the tables, they do. Though Maasai life is changing, many Maasai remain pastoralists whose living derives from cows. The elephant called Fenella was a cow killer. Fenella disappeared.

Why would elephants kill cows?

Elephants never kill donkeys. Donkeys are owned by women. And women never accompany their donkeys into the bush—husbands don't like that (not quite for reasons of their wives' safety, I surmise). So donkeys just roam on their own and return. Cows, however, get accompanied into the bush by men and boys. Some herders are boys nine, ten years old. They might not even see elephants in their path. Surprise is bad. In the dry season, the Maasai bring their cows to the last remaining bits of water. Tension flares as herders try pushing elephants from water holes.

So it seems that the men bring livestock into confrontation with elephants. Men are the flash point. If you're getting repeatedly harassed by humans whenever cows show up, you might learn to dislike cows. Sometimes an elephant registers its objection. And it may be answered with a flying spear. Which makes the elephants retaliate, killing more cows and more men. The revenge and reprisals cycled and simmered like a tribal war, with no solution.

Except money. Because to the Maasai, cows are money. Nowadays the Maasai around Amboseli can receive a "consolation" payment that handily takes elephants out of the revenge cycle. The goal is to harmonize the Maasai and the elephants. Now far fewer spears get thrown at these elephants. Where does the money come from? Gifts. Donate online.

Later in the day we encounter a large herd of elephants commuting up out of the swamp for the night, marching across plains lit in gold-slanted sunlight. As we sense and can plainly see, their major self-governing principle is simply "Live and let live." The elephants' way is humbler than ours. The elephants are like poor people, like tribal people. They demand less of the world. They take less from the world. They live in better resonance with the rest of their world.

While hundreds of other elephants plod across the dusty plains toward distant hills, one family, for whatever reason, is still blowing water and rolling in a deep, lushly vegetated spring-fed pool. Maybe they're having too much fun.

They submerge like hippos and spout like whales; they roll and splash and plow underwater with only their rumps showing. They periscope their trunks, snorkeling the air, moving along like black submarines.

After a while, they move single file to a farther bank and emerge shiny and wet like autos from a carwash. But one has not yet even gone in. She remains on the bank with her baby. Her baby is hesitant. The mother is patient. She is touching the water with her trunk but is waiting. Eventually the mother enters. The baby follows. The baby gets alongside her mother and wraps her trunk around her mother's tusk for support. Soon the water floats the baby, and the mother, with her trunk, guides her child along.

Ebony and Ivory

———•———

"I cannot tell them, 'This man is writing a book; be nice to him,'" Julius Shivegha is saying. "They will see you as a good person if you are a good person. If they love you, they will love you just for yourself."

The youngest reaches his tiny trunk up to Julius's mouth. Normally, a baby puts its trunk to its mother's mouth to learn, from food she is chewing, the scent of safe and nourishing plants. This query—"What are you eating?"—later becomes the elephants' trunk-to-mouth greeting, perhaps a bit similar to humans' kissing. Julius takes the little trunk, blowing into it playfully. The baby lets his trunk go completely limp, the elephant equivalent of a puppy rolling over so you can rub its belly. Julius obliges, rubbing his trunk vigorously between his palms, like a baker forming a piece of dough into a baguette.

This baby who's getting his trunk massaged was two weeks old when found alongside his fatally wounded mother. And there is one marked by a machete. And there is Quanza, sole survivor of her famously photographed Amboseli family. Because she was more than a year old at the time of the attack, Quanza's mind recorded an imprint of terror and confusion. "She is still very agitated," Julius says by way of explaining her tendency to shove her bantam weight around. "If they are mourning or grieving, you see that. When they are joyous and playing, you can tell."

All orphans of ivory, these luckier few have been rescued and brought here to the Sheldrick Trust, in Nairobi. Young enough to forgive us, they are thereby younger than I will ever again be. Yet this, too, is us: guiding them in the bush for their daily exercise, walking them through the hills and vales of a second chance.

In the 1960s, Iain Douglas-Hamilton found, in deep forest, a trail smoothly beaten down and at least twelve feet wide. It might have been thousands of years old. Elephant roads once connected the continent, water source to water source. When humans arose, we followed roads made by elephants across Africa, and when the time came for us to venture beyond, we probably traveled out, too, on elephant roads. Now most such ancient roads have fallen silent. Where elephants survive, they cling to islands of habitat cut off from other populations. For centuries now, they've been under siege.

At the dawn of the Roman Empire, elephants thoroughly inhabited Africa. From Mediterranean shores to the Cape of Good Hope and from the Indian Ocean to the Atlantic, except for the bleakest lozenge of the Sahara, elephants trod. Imagine, now, a giant eraser with an ivory grip. By a thousand years ago, elephants had already been wiped from North Africa. During the 1800s, southern Africa's elephants were splintered and isolated, and most pocketed populations got finished off in several wipes. East Africa's coastal elephants were swiped, too. Amazing disgrace. By 1900, the animal that never forgets was forgotten by most children born in West Africa. The 1970s and '80s brought the perfect storm of rising human densities, increasingly deadly weapons, escalating ivory prices, widening international markets, and worsening governments.

During the last two million years, about a dozen different elephant species wore grooves across varied parts of Earth. Tiny three-foot-high elephants once lived on the Mediterranean island of Malta, and a pygmy mammoth inhabited what are now California's Channel Islands. The komodo dragon of Indonesia likely evolved to prey on the pygmy elephants of two species that lived there before being exterminated by early human venturers. On continents, elephants outgrew predators, becoming so big that they didn't need to hide. Size served them well. But when the predator of predators lifted its knuckles from the dust, elephants *couldn't* hide easily. People learned to hunt elephants, and some got too good at it. In Czechoslovakia, a mammoth hunters' camp strategically placed at a pinch point between two mountain ranges accumulated the remains of nine hundred mammoths. The last mammoths died out in the Arctic only about four thousand years ago; Egyptians had already erected the Great Pyramids. In arctic Alaska I once saw an Inupiat girl carrying a small time-blackened mammoth tusk that had washed out of a riverbank. Though recent people of the Arctic can scarcely imagine a mammoth, they have never stopped coveting their ivory.

Whenever elephants met men, elephants fared badly. Syria's final elephants were exterminated by twenty-five hundred years ago. Elephants were gone from much of China literally before the year 1 and from much of Africa by the year 1000. Meanwhile, in India and southern Asia, elephants become the mounts of kings; tanks against forts, prisoners' executioners, and pincushions of arrows, driven mad in battle; elephants become logging trucks and bulldozers, and, as with other slaves, their forced labor requires beatings and abuse. Since Roman times, humans have reduced Africa's elephant population by perhaps 99 percent. African elephants are gone from 90 percent of the lands they roamed as recently as 1800, when, despite earlier losses, an estimated twenty-six million elephants still trod the continent. Now they number perhaps four hundred thousand. (The diminishment of Asian elephants over historic times is far worse.) The planet's menagerie has become like shards of broken glass; we're grinding the shards smaller and smaller.

Elephants' main message in a bottle: vulnerability. Roman elites demanded so much ivory that in the year 77 Pliny the Elder voiced alarm over dwindling elephant numbers in north Africa, "the demands of luxury having exhausted all those in our part of the world." For centuries, before the first firearms, the elephant populations of northern Africa withered. Then for over a thousand years, Arab traders sailed dhows along East Africa to barter for ivory and live-caught humans. By the 1400s, elephant numbers had shrunk along Africa's east coast. Ivory routes pierced hundreds of miles inland. Centuries later, the 1800s brought the Industrial Revolution, whose flywheels and gears and belt-driven machines turned out ivory hair combs, ivory toothpicks, buttons, billiard balls, shaving kits, cigarette cases, pot handles, telegraph keys, mirror frames, and millions of piano keyboards, for which hunters killed millions of elephants. For the new middle class, the precious became prosaic as ivory served as the plastic of its time.

The very word "ivory" distances and obscures its elephant source; ivory is a material and a color, like "jade" or "gold." It lends its name to selling soap advertised as "99 and 44/100ths percent pure," virginal. The word "ivory" accomplishes a linguistic dissociation not achieved by "rhino horn," "tiger bone," or "shark fin." It's not called "elephant tooth." Perhaps that is why ivory must be explained.

"The hollow of my hand was still ivory-full of Lolita," wrote Nabokov, "full of the feel of . . . that ivory-smooth, sliding sensation of her skin through the thin frock." Ivory freights sexual metaphors for white female tumes-cence, but for ebony-breasted women, ivory was just another avenue for torment. By the 1500s, Europeans had fully industrialized the commer-cialization of human beings, and for centuries slavery and ivory lived together in abject misery. Bringing ivory to ladies in parlors were traders trafficking in both tusks and humans. In tandem, Africa literally hemor-rhaged to supply ivory and slaves as elephant populations crumbled and slavers depopulated humans from vast areas. Reaching a village of any size eventually required a three-week trek inland. Captured humans marched captured ivory to coastal ports, where both were shipped. And the ivory was more valuable and better handled than the humans forced to carry it. On an 1844 trip to Zanzibar for his Salem, Massachusetts–based father, one Michael Shepard noted, "It is custom to buy a tooth of ivory and a slave to carry it to the sea shore." In the 1800s, tusks often weighed over eighty pounds each. (Now tusks average one-third that. The largest tusks ever recorded, from a gigantic elephant shot in 1898, by a slave, on the slopes of Kilimanjaro not far from Amboseli, weighed, as a pair, over 440 pounds. In a photo, each tusk, measuring over ten feet long, utterly dwarfs two men.)

The comprehensive cruelties defy comprehension. As late as 1882 (after slavery had been abolished or restricted in many countries) in what is now Tanzania, the British missionary Alfred J. Swann absorbed a gruesome sight: human beings chained together, their necks fastened into the forks of poles about six feet long, carrying elephant tusks. "The women, who were as numerous as the men, carried babies on their backs in addition to a tusk of ivory. . . . Feet and shoulders were a mass of open sores, made more painful by the swarms of flies which followed the

march and lived on the flowing blood . . . a picture of utter misery."
Aghast, wondering aloud "how any had survived the long tramp from
Upper Congo, at least 1,000 miles distant," he was assured by the headman, "Yes, numbers have died." Swann remarked that many now seemed
unfit to bear their cargo. The headman responded with a smile: "They
have no choice! They must go, or die!" He explained that the slavers killed
the sick, because, quite logically, "If we did not, others would pretend they
were ill in order to avoid carrying their loads. No! We never leave them
alive." But, queried Swann, if the women become too weak to carry both
their child and—? As though Swann's priorities seemed preposterous, the
headman replied, "We cannot leave valuable ivory on the road. *We spear
the child and make her burden lighter*. Ivory first."

Then the ivory and slaves were sailed to Zanzibar to be sold. The slaves,
noted Michael Shepard, were "discharged in the same manner as a load
of sheep . . . dead ones thrown overboard to drift down with the tide
and . . . the natives come with a pole and push them from the beach."

Eventually the slave ships furled sails for the final time. Ivory hunting
had already exterminated elephants from most of Africa. Ivory demand
continues, worse than ever. For several thousand years now, the ivory
business's *modus* is extermination. The story of elephants in our time is:
annihilation for ivory and compression by human expansion into "refuges." They are refugees. And because of ivory, there's no safety in refuges.
And because of human expansion, no refuge is safe long-term.

~

Three hundred miles north of Amboseli as the augur buzzard flies, the
great and timeless landscape of Samburu National Reserve begins at a taw-
dry town called Archer's Post. Those calling it home include a handful of
ivory-dealing criminals and a haze of desperately poor goat-herding
people, many living in hovels of bent-over saplings quilted with discarded
plastic sheets and flattened trash bags. Poverty numbing just to look at.
Certainly they have nothing they can afford to share with elephants or
anyone else. From the dawn of humans until just recently, Africa offered
space sufficient for coexistence. As human numbers surge, elephants lose
footholds. Many people lose everything else: opportunity, options, human
dignity—. Every depiction of Noah's ark shows elephants safely aboard

along with the humans. An apt metaphor; most animals of the world are awash in a rising sea of us. Poor people are in the same boat. Everyone I meet is friendly, the children alert, wide-eyed as puppies. Young Samburu men carrying a spear and a club and a large flat knife in their belts approach me so that they may break a dazzling smile and shake my hand with both of theirs. Some ask whether there are lions and elephants in my country, or inquire politely how many cattle I own (and are politely aghast at the puzzling poverty my answer indicates). They are in all ways like me, but the thing that has failed them is luck, and they are as unlikely to escape theirs as I am to forfeit mine.

Samburu, like Amboseli, is one of the few remaining places where elephants can live without being entirely dominated by one emotion: fear of humans. They can still live a full range of their emotional lives. But the fear is here, too. Too much of it.

In the afternoon, the air tastes of fine dust. It settles into everything, so that one of the things you share with elephants is being at all times lightly enveloped in this harsh, welcoming last-stand land.

Shifra Goldenberg downshifts to neutral, and as our dust clears she explains that here in Samburu, researchers' names for elephant families are "themes" rather than letters. So, for instance, this family moving along atop the riverbank is named after famous poets.

"This family's been heavily affected by the poaching," Shifra informs me. "All the older females are dead." Emily Dickinson, who'd lived to fifty-five years of age, is dead. Virginia Woolf, Sylvia Plath: dead. Alice Oswald is alive. Maya Angelou, dead—. Here, now, eleven living members are present and accounted for, but the family's current matriarch, Wendy Cope, is not here. Her four-year-old—also not here.

Wendy's previously been shot. Her two youngsters were shot. The wildlife veterinarian tranquilized and treated them. Wendy and one youngster recovered. The researchers and the elephants watched her other child endure two weeks of dying.

Wendy is wearing a collar for pinpointing her location. Two days ago, Wendy led her whole family about fifteen miles to Shaba National "Reserve," in quotes; Shaba has become dangerous for elephants. And not entirely safe for poachers. Not long ago, Kenya Wildlife Service rangers fatally shot two poachers. Now Wendy's family is back here without Wendy, and they seem upset, an unusual amount of streaming from their temple glands indicating that they are feeling much emotion. They're neither going to the water nor eating—just moving along above the riverbank.

Shifra calls Gilbert Sabinga at our Samburu camp. He tells us he'll try to access Wendy's collar signal. We wait. Shifra is a graduate student studying the effects of poaching on the social lives of elephant families. Gilbert works for Iain Douglas-Hamilton's Save the Elephants.

Collars tell of travels invisible. One male went 155 miles (250 kilometers) in four days, mainly through farmland, traveling only at night and hiding by day. He knew well, it seems, that he was transiting dangerous territory.

In the 1980s, when I was in my twenties, my childhood friend Richard Wagner, our Maasai friend Moses ole Kipelian, and I stumbled upon Samburu after a long and sometimes more dangerous than bargained for trip across the Chalbi Desert. Samburu seemed eternal, a true remnant of wildest Africa. With the sun already set, we hastily pitched our frail tent and lay all night listening to roaring lions, sleeping little. Outside the parks and reserves, we saw ample free-roaming herds of antelopes, zebras, giraffes . . .

Getting here was not a drive; it was an expedition. It's different now. From the goat-scorched country just south of this park, to the town of Isiolo, whose streets are thronged with more goats, trash, the aimless poor, and the overworked unemployed, continuing south to where once trotted gazelles and kudus and the golden shadows that followed them, the land now bears a coating of corn and bright yellow mustard fields, spanning the taut curves of cultivated hills. It would be as easy for elephants to live there now as to roam Iowa, whose own land-darkening bison and sun-blotting cloud-flocks of passenger pigeons and spear-wielding nomads are as irretrievable as elephants and antelopes on this broken ground. From forever ago until just a moment ago, there was, where wheat now waves, a world. How much of the world is enough for us? Humans and elephants might answer that question differently. The elephants' answer can suffice for mine.

Gilbert finally calls back. There's a problem. Wendy's collar's scheduled nine A.M. report never came. The other collars all reported.

Several tourist vans appear from nearby lodges, jostling for clear views of Wendy's family. *Snap snap snap* go the cameras. The vapid snapping is the only thing competing economically with killing the elephants. Bless the tourists.

David Daballen and Lucy King arrive. Soft-spoken and sharp-minded, David, a tall, taut polyglot who is ethnically Samburu, is field manager for Save the Elephants. Lucy works to reduce villager-elephant conflict and has rather brilliantly investigated how elephant aversion to bees can help farmers reduce conflicts with elephants while creating new income from honey. Lucy places a call to troubleshoot the failure of the nine A.M. report. Everyone's tense. Suddenly Lucy says, "Dear God," and I brace for whatever fresh horror this way comes. Turns out, it's just that her Internet provider's customer service has *again* placed her on hold. In frustration, she hangs up. No one says anything. "It's a bit worrying," says Lucy finally, with exemplary British understatement.

Now on his cell phone, David is being informed that two gunmen were at the Attan marshes firing shots in an attempt to herd a group of elephants out of the water to a spot where they could slaughter them. The elephants panicked, and village women in their farm plots, seeing the stampeding elephants, began screaming. What I am gathering in the commotion of David trying simultaneously to listen and convey the situation is that the elephants fled north, toward here.

David and Lucy decide to continue farther along the riverbank while Shifra and I stay put.

A few minutes later, Shifra's phone goes off.

It's Lucy. They've found Wendy where a small stream—the Isiolo River—enters the Ewaso Ng'iro, the main river, inside the Buffalo Springs National Reserve. She's fine.

I can almost hear all our bodies relax with relief. By the time we join David and Lucy, Wendy's collar is again reporting, and Lucy has displayed her travels on a computer. Last night, Wendy's group suddenly came straight back here from about sixteen miles away, with no rest. It's called "streaking." Lucy shows us the map, narrating: "See them moving outside the reserve. This wetland here is very lush, so they like it; that's where they've been. And now look here between midnight and three A.M.; they're skirting the village. This is dangerous territory." There are human dwellings, farms . . .

"The hot zone for poaching," offers David.

"Look at them streaking in the dark, absolutely hoofing it."

Now, on the riverbank, we watch in real time for two hours as Wendy's dozing family scarcely moves a muscle. They must be exhausted after last night's stressful foray for food. Eventually they stroll into the river, drink, cross, and disappear up the opposite bank. The ephemera of elephants. Surprisingly hard to follow, challenging to comprehend, easy to love, easy to kill. Easy to lose.

Today the staff of Save the Elephants and the Disney Worldwide Conservation Fund have sponsored a trip to bring kids from the nearby village of Attan—poacher's haven—into Samburu National Reserve to see elephants. Their schoolroom: termite-eaten wooden walls, dirt floors, and rudimentary tables serving as group "desks." The kids: skinny. Legs like sticks.

In the kids' smiles is a lesson about appreciation not found in textbooks. And a challenge to our humanity. Most will grow up with no marketable skills in a world with no opportunities. Tribal warfare and poaching are among the few opportunities for which young men qualify. For vulnerable women, there is always sex.

Even though they live less than five miles from the Buffalo Springs reserve, and even though the school's village is a poaching base, and even though the surrounding farms constitute a dangerous corridor for elephants commuting from the reserve to the outlying marshes, and even though elephants and farmers get into conflict there, most students and even the teacher have never before seen an elephant. Today, in the reserve, they get treated to seeing elephants giving themselves mud baths.

Asked to write about elephants, most kids express fear of the animals and anger at the damage they have done. Is there *anything* about elephants that they like? Yes; they like that elephants mean money, from tourists and from ivory. How to make them realize: one can't have both for long.

❦

Last night, distant lions transported me from deep sleep to a more original place. The awe-instilling resonance of their roars—*OOOWWHHHwwwph, OOOOOWWWHHHhhwwwph, OOWWwwph, oohwph, ooph, uff*—reignited the river's frogs, who'd gone silent after their vesper croakings; they sang another chorus. Finding myself somehow alive on a planet whose rock and dust and waters managed to bring voice to such emphatic midnight affirmations, I savored their sublime exaltations and raw terrors. It takes words for me to tell it, but the experience required wordlessness. Coaxed to dreamy consciousness as the voices rippled from night-black mountainside to riverbank and through my brain, I listened without the usual distracting torrent of diluting thoughts and appraisals. The sounds mapped directly onto my mind, which made pictures of what I was hearing, and aided by my creative subconscious I experienced a strong emotional response, which is to say: I felt the sounds acutely; I understood directly.

This morning along the river and in trees over the camp, monkeys are busy with urgent things while we enjoy breakfast. Dandy male vervets sport powder-blue testicles, while females clutch young who stare wide-eyed at a wondrous world more dangerous than they yet know, more improbable than we all realize. Fellow primates. A familiar and ever-watchful hornbill patiently assesses the exact moment when we are all studying the monkeys, and in that unguarded instant swoops in. I see a pancake take flight. You know what a hornbill flying away with a pancake looks like? Well, it reminds me of the starship *Enterprise*.

The call on this Sunday morning comes moments later, and David Daballen rises to his feet to answer it, walking from the table as he talks. Quickly he returns, announcing, "Another elephant, right off the road across the river, just discovered killed."

That's shockingly close, just three miles or so. "This is the worst it's ever been," David mutters. "We're going in the wrong direction." In the last forty-five days, poachers have killed twenty-seven elephants within about twenty miles of here. This week, almost one elephant a day. But in all the recent poaching frenzy, no elephant till now has been killed so deep inside the reserve, so near tourist lodges and our research camp.

David and I wade across the river. Never mind the crocodiles. "They don't attack adults here," David reassures me. "Only sometimes kids."

David has a vehicle on the other side, in Buffalo Springs National Reserve. We climb in. Something like one thousand elephants—minus several per week now—use the Samburu and Buffalo Springs reserves. But these reserves, like almost every other in Africa, are too small. As at Amboseli, elephants continually roam between traditional feeding and watering sites, but their ancient and proven survival customs can no longer promise survival. Outside reserves, they run into trouble with expanding villages and poachers. Inside, they run into poachers from the villages. With ivory prices rocketed to an all-time high, each elephant's prospects have dropped to an all-time low.

Driving grimly, David startles me by saying, "The poachers are just uneducated young men. They're as smart as we are; they're being used by evil people because they have nothing to lose except their lives."

Ivory is about poverty, ethnic rivalry, terrorism, and civil war. Orchestrating much of this are vicious people—criminals, corrupt government officials, official governments—who are mining elephant populations to finance savage conflict. And as with "blood diamonds," elephant blood lubricates human blood. Blood ivory has been helping finance Joseph Kony's Lords Resistance Army, Sudan's murderous Janjaweed, and possibly Al Qaeda's Al Shabab wing. Fueling all this is simple consumer craving for carvings that people could—quite literally—live without. So ivory is not just about elephants. It would be far simpler if it were.

Of course, ivory is also about elephants. Elephants that are intelligent and sensitive and social and live with their families and need their mothers. From an estimated ten million elephants in the early 1900s, to 400,000 or so and counting, today Africa's elephant population is about 100 fewer than yesterday's. During the ivory crisis of the 1980s, Cynthia Moss estimated that 80,000 elephants were going into the ivory grinder annually. Tanzania lost a staggering 236,000 elephants. In the mid-1970s, Tanzania's Selous Game Reserve harbored 110,000 elephants; by the late 1980s, half had been killed. During the same span of years, Kenya's elephants fell from about 167,000 to 16,000, down 90 percent. The Central African Republic had an elephant population approaching 100,000 that fell below 15,000. Uganda's Murchison Falls "National Park" had 10,000 elephants and then had 25 elephants (yes, 25) because Uganda's government killed about 85 percent of the country's elephants to finance its reign of terror. Sierra Leone saw its final elephants killed in 2009. The Democratic Republic of the Congo's elephants have plummeted around 90 percent. Gabon: nearly 80 percent of its elephants killed in the last decade. Chad, Cameroon, Sudan, Somalia, Mozambique, Senegal: shot to pieces, with few survivors. All of this robs elephants, of course, but it takes from people, too. In Kenya alone, 300,000 people rely directly on tourism for employment, and every tourist comes wanting to see elephants. Poaching for profit is a poverty maker.

Now David is on the phone with someone who is telling him that rangers had picked up the poachers' movements and laid an ambush, but the poachers made a U-turn . . . one ranger is a known poacher's brother. I worry that David is learning a little too much for his safety.

A hundred years ago, Europeans and Americans were the main ivory buyers. Western culture has moved beyond that, and now Chinese culture has moved in. There are only so many elephants, not enough to give everyone in China the beautiful ivory carvings they'd like. A lovely Chinese lady recently came here to see elephants, and like many sane and humane people she assumed that ivory is just picked up off the ground after an elephant dies of natural causes. "People say very arrogant things about the Chinese," Iain Douglas-Hamilton told me in camp one evening, "that they don't care and are not capable of caring. That they'll never change. Well, our ancestors killed off the American bison and the passenger pigeon. Were they less rapacious than the Chinese today? Hardly. I think the one lesson of human history is: people change. Look at Germany in 1943 compared to 1953, or Italian use of birth control."

Agreed: people can change. But is there enough time?

International trading in ivory and other "wildlife products" is regulated through a treaty called the Convention on International Trade in Endangered Species (CITES, pronounced SY-tees). In the 1980s, CITES enacted a legal ivory quota system. It didn't work. Elephant numbers continued plummeting because continuing to allow the sale of some ivory facilitated easy laundering of any ivory. That was Lesson One.

The *only* thing that has ever worked was a bitterly won worldwide ivory ban, first implemented in 1990. Zero allowed. Ivory prices instantly collapsed. Elephant populations slowly increased. The ivory ban worked. Lesson Two.

But it lasted only until 1999. That year CITES allowed Zimbabwe, Botswana, and Namibia to sell fifty metric tons (about 110,000 pounds) of stockpiled ivory to Japan, calling it a "one-time sale." Then China wanted in. In 2008, CITES administrators let China buy stockpiled ivory from Botswana, Namibia, South Africa, and Zimbabwe—the *second* "one-time" sale.

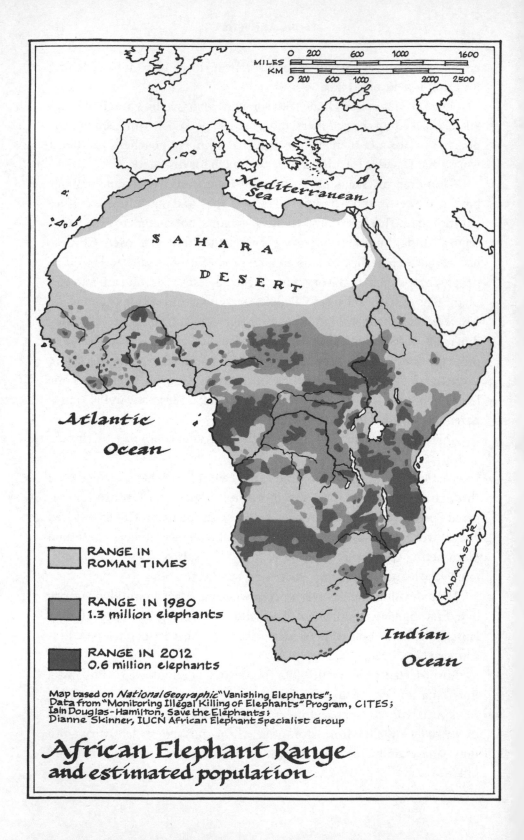

MILES 0 200 600 1000 1600

KM 0 200 600 1000 2000 2500

Mediterranean Sea

S A H A R A

D E S E R T

Atlantic

Ocean

Indian

Ocean

MADAGASCAR

RANGE IN
ROMAN TIMES

RANGE IN 1980
1.3 million elephants

RANGE IN 2012
0.6 million elephants

Map based on *National Geographic* "Vanishing Elephants";
Data from "Monitoring Illegal Killing of Elephants" Program, CITES;
Iain Douglas–Hamilton, Save the Elephants;
Dianne Skinner, IUCN African Elephant Specialist Group

African Elephant Range
and estimated population

No one had learned their lessons. Failure to learn from mistakes is unwise, but failure to learn from success takes true determination.

"Ivory is illegal; don't buy it" is a clear message to consumers, law enforcers, and governments. "Some ivory is illegal, but some is okay" creates confusion that offers perfect cover for killing elephants. Giving China some stockpiled ivory opened the floodgates to laundering illegal tusks. Immediately, poaching surged, condemning tens of thousands of elephants to death while fueling human bloodshed. In Kenya, for instance, the killing ballooned eightfold, from fewer than 50 elephants killed in 2007 to nearly 400 in 2012. Now in Africa an estimated 30,000 to 40,000 elephants are being killed every year—an elephant every fifteen minutes.

Like the one we're headed to.

Vultures flag the huge gray corpse. David and I walk from the dusty road and approach. It's Philo.

Philo was a young male, fifteen years old, only halfway to being a viable contender for breeding. From just below his eyes, Philo's face is entirely mutilated. His miraculous trunk lies a few yards away, like a discarded fathom of hawser in an old boatyard. His tusks, gone.

"They take two teeth and leave four tons rotting. Such a stupid thing." David quietly smolders with a pressurized anger that runs like molten lava beneath his hard-baked crust.

Working backward along Philo's tracks, David determines that he was struck right over there on that rise, ran bleeding two hundred yards to here, then collapsed. After he collapsed, they shot him several times in the back of the head. Like an execution. One of those bullet holes is still bubbling crimson blood.

Four days ago, visiting researcher Ike Leonard captured Philo's last portrait. The photo shows Philo as a promising young bull jauntily showing off a bit of teenage swagger. An elephant keeper with Disney's Animal Kingdom, Leonard had come to see how he might improve the welfare of the captive elephants he cares for in Orlando, Florida—to observe, he'd told me, "how wild elephants live." We are also observing how elephants die.

Acutely, an elephant's problem is ivory. Chronically the problem is room. Rich or poor, humans seem too much of a good thing. The smallest slices of any pie get cut at the most crowded tables.

How with this rage shall beauty hold a plea . . . ?

—Shakespeare, Sonnet 65

The rising tide of humanity has cut these reserves into isolated islands in the stream of time. In just the last forty years here in Kenya, humans quadrupled. Meanwhile, elephants dropped by four-fifths. Since I, myself, first breathed African air in the early 1980s, elephants have lost more than half their African range and more than half their numbers. Not one of them is safe from human rage of one sort or another, something they share with many people in many countries. One wonders where this trend, afflicting humans and elephants alike, is headed. Can we afford to value elephants, and people, more than we do? Can we afford to value them any less? I am very fond of civilization, but what's the plan?

Dear Elephant, Sir:

. . . There are those, of course, who say you are useless, that you destroy crops in a land where starvation is rampant, that mankind has enough problems taking care of itself, without being expected to burden itself with elephants, They are saying, in fact, that you are a luxury, that we can no longer afford you. This is exactly the kind of argument every totalitarian regime from Stalin and Hitler to Mao uses to prove that a truly "progressive" society cannot be expected to afford the luxury of individual freedom. Human rights are elephants, too. The right of dissent, of independent thinking, the right to oppose and to challenge authority can very easily be throttled and repressed in the name of "necessity." . . . In a German prison camp, during the last world war . . . locked behind the barbed wires we would think of the elephant herds thundering across the endless plains of Africa, and the image of such an irresistible liberty helped us to survive. If the world can no longer afford the luxury of natural beauty, then it will soon be overcome and destroyed by its own ugliness. I myself feel deeply that the fate of Man, and his dignity, are at stake. . . .

There is no doubt that in the name of total rationalism you should be destroyed, leaving all the room to us on this overpopulated planet. Neither can there be any doubt that your disappearance will mean the beginning of an entirely man-made world. But let me tell you this, old friend: in an entirely man-made world, there can be no room for man either. . . .

We are not and could never be our own creation. We are forever condemned to be part of a mystery that neither logic nor imagination can fathom, and your presence among us carries a resonance that cannot be accounted for in terms of science or reason, but only in terms of awe, wonder and reverence. You are our last innocence. . . .

I know only too well that by taking your side—or is it merely my own?—I shall no doubt be labeled a conservative, or even a reactionary, a "monster" belonging to another and, it seems, prehistorical era: that of liberalism. I willingly accept the label. And so, dear Elephant, sir, we are finding ourselves, you and I, in the same boat. . . . In a truly materialistic and realistic society, poets, writers, artists, dreamers and elephants are a mere nuisance. . . .

You are, dear Elephant sir, the last individual.

Your very devoted friend,
Romain Gary

David, Shifra, and I are at the river before sunset. As if miraculously, group after group of elephants caravan out of the trees and cross the river toward us. Mothers, babies, elephants of all ages. The world knows what to do. Do we?

Up and down the river, skeins of elephants are crossing, sloshing easily through the slow-flowing sheet of brick-red water. The numbers build to a count of around 250 elephants drinking and socializing. Elephants doing elephant things is a measure of how much good remains.

Elephants try to carry on with normality amid chaos, because, like people blowing out candles on a birthday cake during wartime, it's what they know, what they prefer. Every step is an act of hope, every sip and mouthful an act of faith. Hope and faith might be all we have, and maybe they're all there is. But that's plenty.

Walking upcountry from the river for the evening, slowly grazing, ripping, eating, shortening their distance mouthful by mouthful, step by step, they rise into the low hills that made them.

The old ones remember routes, now blocked and farmed and hazardous, that in their youth, when they followed their mothers, were all one country. Their country. Do they understand? Probably in their way, yes. I hope not. I fear we don't.

An unexpected overcast evens the light, softening the colors, making me aware of how sweet-scented the grass, how resonant the air that carries so much birdsong. The elephants move like time made of clay. Babylon, aged fifty-seven, matriarch of the family named Biblical Towns, is the oldest remaining female in this population. What she must have seen, I would love to know. It would probably horrify me. Approaching too are: the Flowers; the Storms; the Swahilis; the Mountain Ranges, led by Himalaya; the Turks; the Butterflies.

David switches the ignition off, thinking there'll be no engine noise to bother the oncoming families. But they turn round, bunch up, and periscope. Voices without an engine are frightening to them now. Tourists are safe and have idling engines. Poachers don't have engines. David insightfully restarts the engine, and they relax.

One close-passing female with a baby stomps forward aggressively, ears flared. She backs up and shows annoyance and strength by breaking branches off a bush. I'm a bit unnerved, but David understands that so much demonstration means bluff. And she is a magnificent bluffer. But what has happened to make her so uncomfortable around humans?

Young elephants from assorted familes are also here, sorting out the social tatters of heavy assaults. One family lost five big adult females. "Some survivors might join as new families," David says, "brought together by this war upon them." He points: "Ute, that big female there—she is the only adult female of her family left." Aztec and Inca and all the others in her family got killed by ivory poachers. They were just on the edge of the park. "The Planets, that's a horrible story. They were a huge family. Around twenty elephants. They had some of the oldest females. And so they had the biggest range. And that's why they suffered most. Their last group was, I would say, *massacred*. The shooting happened a year ago, about a hundred kilometers from here. From where they were shot, the ones still alive came running toward the park. But they had so much distance to come. Some wounded ones died on the way. Running youngsters got very dehydrated. A lot of them came in without their mothers. They were traumatized, very nervous of course, so they would appear and disappear. So we couldn't rescue them." Eventually almost all the Planets died. "It was so sad to see that family fall apart. The only ones left are these two girls—Haumea and Europa."

. . .

I have a small collection of ivory figurines, about half a dozen, each three or four inches long. Half of these, I was given by an elderly woman when I was in my early twenties, and I cherish the pieces for her memory. They rest on my writing desk. I can reach out and touch them. One is an exquisite spherical ball of tiny carved elephants playfully squirming over one another. The irony is painful. In Canada, as a special spontaneous gift, I was given a small dolphin carved from walrus ivory. I—who would never buy a shark's tooth, a piece of coral, or, for that matter, a seashell—find myself the holder of these pieces, as if we were all lost and somehow found each other. In a humanized world, beautiful ivory carvings would all originate from the tusks of elephants who'd died of natural causes. They would leave larger, more valuable tusks. Ivory wouldn't be a problem at all. It really would be beautiful. The impossibility of that arises only because of the greed of our kind, stuck like a bone in our throats.

Europa turns to look at us. I don't see an elephant. I see someone painfully beautiful.

David seems awash in memories of elephants he misses from families we're watching. "Really, really sad . . ."

"You work to protect some of the most wonderful creatures in the world," I say to David. He is at the moment beyond my words. "These three little babies—so great," I offer.

"Yeah," says David, emerging from grief by virtue of innocence. "Look at them playing."

We watch while time autographs this scene, folds it, and tucks it into my mind.

David adds, "Outside the park, they stick together tight-tight. Inside here, it's a safer haven. So, see, they spread out, because they have no worry."

Where Baby Elephants Come From

A wind blows the clouds from Kilimanjaro on a new Amboseli morning, leaving the mountain's nineteen-thousand-foot snows floating above its blue shoulders.

Katito and I are with Felicity's family. "Such a nice family," Katito says. "I'm glad you got to meet them."

At ten-thirty in the morning, they pour themselves back into the marsh. Into one pool fifty yards long and ten across, attended by several gray herons and sacred ibises, a mixed group of elephants splashes, thrashes, trumpets, and throws mud. They submerge and roll. A big male named Wayne hoses himself repeatedly with muddy water. Babies are kicking the water just to watch such monster splashes, having so much fun that they seem to be smiling. Lubricated by the thick mud, they're squiggling over one another, rejoicing in so fine a bath, squirming upon the muddy banks and rolling back into the pileup. The wetted dust of the plains glistens black on their bodies.

"I never get bored doing this," Katito says. "Twenty years—imagine."

A gray heron nabs a fish that's been terrified to the edge of the pool. The heron was aware that this could happen; herons know their business.

"Oh," Katito coos, "there's beautiful Ottoline." Katito smiles at me and says, "That's how I recognize her, just—her beauty."

Ottoline, thirty-one, is the matriarch of the OB family. Ozora and Oprah are also here. "Oprah I recognize," Katito tries to explain, "because she has a very rounded body and big ears."

Don't they *all*?

Former matriarchs Odile, Omo, and Omega were killed by spear-throwing Maasai. Odile had endured spear hits on three occasions; the third incident killed her. Since then, the family's eight surviving adults have been nervous and inseparable. They've just spent the night outside the park, on a twenty-first-century moonwalk somewhere between companionship and chaos.

Katito points, saying, "This one, Orabel; she look very beautiful to me. I like how she walk, and how she lead her family. She is just a *very* nice elephant to me. Yes." Agreed. "Ohh," Katito breathes solemnly. "These—." The family comes nearer. "These are the survivors of the great matriarch Qumquat." Katito turns to me. "You've heard of what happened?" She turns back to look at them. "It was very bad. You see that hill?" Katito points. "That hill is called Lomomo. They were killed between here and that hill. Just there. Not very far." She gazes in silence, her mind playing a memory.

One morning just three months ago, the much-photographed, magnificently regal forty-six-year-old Qumquat and her two adult daughters were murdered for their tusks, orphaning Qumquat's nursing infant, Quanza, and her six-year-old son, Qores. Qores disappeared, presumed dead.

But just a few days ago Qores suddenly reappeared, following the WB family. "He looked lost and sad. But to see him alive, I was in tears."

The QBs are now led by Qoral, who was very close to Qumquat. "I feel so sad for this family," laments Katito. Little Quanza—Vicki named her "first" in Swahili because she was the firstborn of the post-drought baby boom—was found standing alongside the corpse of her ten-year-old sister. Too young to survive losing her mother, she was taken in by the Sheldrick Trust elephant orphanage in Nairobi, where I'd visited her.

"This other family makes me sad, too," Katito says as we roll along. "Savita here is only twenty-three, and is the matriarch." Katito shakes her head again. "Most died in the drought. Most of these others are orphans."

Suddenly Katito bubbles, "Oh! *There* is Qores, the son of Qumquat! Oh, gosh. He is moving through all the different families, looking for his family. And his family is not far behind us now. Maybe today, after these months, he will finally meet up with them. Oh, gosh. Yes."

We roll onward. Kaliope, the thirty-three-year-old matriarch of the KBs, has a scoop missing from the outline of one ear. Strikingly skittish and suspicious, she and her sister watch us closely. "Kaliope has had a rough time with the Maasai," Katito says ruefully. "She has been speared three times, and her mother was killed."

But we stop, and let many minutes pass, and she forages closer to us. Within a hundred feet. Yet when we turn the engine on, she turns, gets in front of her baby, flares her ears, and shakes her head.

"I am *sorry,* Kaliope," says Katito. "It is okay now. Bad times for you will be gone."

It's a wish. It cannot be a promise.

Various families begin drifting together, merging, building, until they raft into a herd of about a hundred elephants. We roll slowly along the edge of the vast marsh, taking attendance. I absorb the sight and the light of them; I listen to them; I breathe them in.

A tuskless elephant passes. About one in a hundred are tuskless throughout life. I wonder aloud if tuskless elephants look around at their magnificently endowed companions and wish they had a big, beautiful pair of tusks.

"They lucky they don't," Katito declares flatly.

A massive phalanx—250 elephants—comes in a second wave across the plains, toward the water. At the front are the PCs, led by twenty-six-year-old Petula, whose family of seven are all survivors of the drought and the bullets that claimed other members.

This litany of loss and attrition is the profile of a species going extinct. In a generation or two, the memory of wild Africa will be lost as utterly as an American prairie of head-high wildflowers swirled by bison, darkened by wild pigeons, bordered by towering forests of chestnuts, as it all was, mere moments ago.

In the last hour, a breathtaking four hundred elephants have flowed past us in two great waves. We maneuver alongside and then ahead of this vast herd, coming from the dusty plain toward the emerald oasis. We climb a knoll. For long minutes we watch, enveloped in a parading panorama of hundreds of elephants living their lives. Eating, nursing, growing. The babes climbing playfully over one another. Males testing status. Females keeping a watchful eye—and ear, and trunk. The water channels mirror the open sky above the cloudless, snowy peaks of Kilimanjaro.

The accumulated wisdom of this deeply time-rooted place resides in these elephants. But what would the mountain say, if it could, of how it was, and is. Perhaps only the mountain is old enough to know how it should be. That would be a valuable opinion to pry from the rocks of its lofty heights. Even with that shrinking ice and snow up there, the mountain has long kept a cooler head. As the untold bones buried deep in these timeless plains attest, times move in varied meter. Earth's memory beats many rhythms. Those who dance slowly observe much. Often a slow meter and spare melody make a song that says the most.

Perhaps the mountain's answer is this breeze flowing down its slopes and the whirling dust devils blowing up its flanks. If that is the land talking, I can better understand what the elephants are telling me with their sounds and silences, the slow beat of their kick-drum feet and their rhythmic riff of ripping grass. In so many ways they are saying, "Simply to live. Is not too much to ask. We shouldn't have to."

Driving across dried pans and bleached bones, we soon leave the park. It's not far.

The wildlife does not end at the park border. That's reassuring. We see fair numbers of zebras and giraffes outside the park, but everything feels vulnerable.

A word about the giraffes: they are so large and remarkable that—like elephants, who carry riding egrets and lend gravity to orbiting swallows—the giraffes' very bodies are the foraging scapes of insect-plucking birds. The ones riding the run of their necks now are called red-billed oxpeckers.

We climb a slope whose name in Maa means Red-Rock Hill—simple enough—and gaze into Tanzania and the surrounding Maasai land and the red bed that in the wet seasons becomes a large sheet of water called Lake Amboseli but is right now a runway for whirling demons of ruddy dust. The sun beats through a clear sky, somehow moving the air a little. The only sounds are arid-throated birds and buzzing bugs.

For a long time, it must really have been just like this.

Just.
Like.
This.

Katito's gentle voice suddenly breaks into the heat, almost whispering: "I was there when Echo died." Her voice comes so soft on the dry breeze it actually seems to deepen the silence. "I was the one holding her head. May fifth, 2009, two-thirty P.M.

"One morning I saw Echo with two daughters, one nine years old, one four. Echo was dragging herself like an old grandmother. And I just shook my head. The drought was very bad. And Echo was no longer young. She was sixty-four, you know. I stayed with her two hours, watching her lift one leg, then the other, walking with so much difficulty. Next morning, six-thirty, I got called: 'The elephant with the crossed tusks . . .' And I just thought, '*Shit.*' I rushed there. Echo had collapsed, near where we live. I'll show you the spot. She was lying on the ground, kicking, opening her eyes, trying to raise herself. People came with a truck and a rope. They said, 'We'll put the rope under her and try to pull her up.' I said, 'No.' I knew she was dying. Natural death. Caused by drought. I said, 'We will just stay, and watch her.' Two of Echo's daughters were there. They didn't even chase us.

"The rangers wanted to shoot her. I said, 'No!' I asked them, 'If your grandmother is dying, are you going to make her die?' They say, 'No.' 'So why do you want to shoot her? Let her die peacefully.' I say, 'So let us stay the night with her, so hyenas do not attack her.' We stayed all night, all the next morning, into the afternoon. People brought food. I was holding Echo's head. Just soothing her, cooling her. Her daughter Enid didn't even move. She was there until her death, like mourning all the time.

"I had my arms around Echo's head and then, she just stretched her leg out very slowly. And she blinked her eye and looked at me. It was so sad to me when I saw that. And then her eye closed. And she died.

"Enid was really hit by her death. Oh, yes. Her sad face; I cannot describe it. Like a human being who has lost a family member and has been crying. That is how her face looked, for a month. Quite a long time. She lost weight.

"Echo's sister Ella had gone to Tanzania for a few weeks. Ella and Echo had never gotten along very well. Ella is very independent-minded. I can say, Ella is mean. Some elephants, you can say they have a good heart, a cool head, they're nice. Ella is mean.

"When Ella returned, she realized Echo was dead.

"Ella is the oldest now, forty-one. She is acting as though she is the matriarch, but she is not behaving like a matriarch should. Eudora is forty years old now, but she doesn't know—. She cannot be a leader. You know, there's people; they are mature in age, but they cannot lead their family. Eudora is also like that. She doesn't know how. Eudora is flaky. No one follows her.

"The one who is behaving like a matriarch is Echo's daughter Enid. You know, if a human is dying, they can say to a child, 'I am going to leave you; you have to take care of the rest of the family.' Echo had been training Enid to take over. Enid is leading the family, even though she is only thirty. Enid is not timid, so if something happens and they are scared, they all bunch to Enid. They feel she will be able to protect them."

Echo's family did exceptionally well under her leadership, growing from just seven members in 1974 to more than forty at the time of her death. Echo never lost anyone except Erin. By any measure hers was a stand-out reign, because of her exquisite abilities to manage her family, return their faith and loyalty, and wisely navigate life's life-or-death challenges in a way that strongly favored safety.

Now Enid makes the decisions. Enid has taken the family away, something Echo—famously a homebody—never did. And at times the family seems to be splitting into three groups, with Enid leading one, Ella another, and Edwina the third. They're not around right now; in fact, they've been gone nearly three months. "We're worried that Enid might have taken them to Tanzania," Katito says. "When she comes back, we'll see whether they've lost anybody."

Late afternoon. We'd gone back to camp to get Vicki, and now we're out again.

The park is full of dust devils, caused by fronts containing rain that we can see but that never quite reaches the park. The fronts drop only dust, onto the dusty plains.

The astonishing gathering of four hundred elephants is beginning to march in waves from the downtown marsh to the bedroom hills. I feel sure

I will never again see so many elephants in one place. They are right here, and we are elephant-wealthy beyond measure. I miss them already.

I've started calling them eles or ellies, terms of endearment, because now that I have met them, I cannot imagine living without them. They will exist in my mind like long-distance family. They will inhabit my sense of who I am. They already know who they are, in their own communities with their own families. They don't need me. They don't need humans in order to be elephants. For millions of years, they and their families and friends carried on meaningful lives, and lived far better prior to us.

This smaller subgroup right here—a few dozen eles—is trailed by about fifteen males. Someone here, probably, is in estrus.

Vicki's caveat: "Females sometimes fake estrus."

I let that sink in a bit.

"Even when they will not adopt a receptive stance or allow mounting, they like the attention of males. They make these alluring poses."

It takes a lot of thinking to fake one's sexual state because you like the attention.

Rumor has it that an extraordinary male named Tim has returned after an extended absence of three months, so we've been scanning the crowd for a glimpse of him.

And, as if it could really be this easy—there he is. We move a little closer.

Now I understand; he's a knockout. Tim, age forty-three, owns two absolutely gigantic tusks, a little uneven in height and length, the larger nearly scraping the ground as he walks. Each weighs easily over one hundred pounds.

He looks like a creature who is no longer possible, like a mammoth that has walked off a cave wall. I had not thought that any male elephants of his size and with so much ivory survived.

In a changed, quieter voice, Vicki says, "Every time I see him—. We're all so relieved each time he reappears. The potential for heartbreak—"

I see tears in her eyes.

"It scares me how much you can love them. It's almost paralyzing."

I look at Tim. He is loitering, waiting for time to ripen.

Vicki appraises him: "Look at how gorgeous this guy is. He makes me fall in love with this work all over again. People say I'm so lucky, and it's true. But the kind of custodianship you accept—. And I'm sure many other researchers working on other kinds of threatened animals—. The caring. It's a really worrying time. When the ivory poachers are done in central Africa, they'll all come here. I'd love to stay here for thirty years, but at this rate they won't be here in thirty years. I just *don't want* a world without elephants. The more you see, the more you understand: how deep their bonds are, their individuality, how they reinforce their relationships every day."

Tim is in musth, dribbling urine, not eating, just maintaining a vigilant presence. Males in musth tuck their chins in and hold their heads up and swagger. Females in estrus come on with a wiggly, rolling, very coy walk, and they'll look over their shoulders at males and you almost expect them to bat their eyelashes; it's funny when you see it for the first time. They act almost flirtatious and we perceive it as amusing; we get it. That's how close.

Tim crosses our path, and I get a whiff of him.

"Musth smells a little like bhang," Vicki says.

Like what? Oh—I was thinking patchouli.

At only forty-three, Tim's got at least another ten years of breeding ahead of him if he doesn't get killed. And because he comes into musth just after the rains, when most cycling females come into estrus, he can father a very high proportion of the babies here, giving them genes for monster tusks.

In few places in Africa do males over forty years old still survive. Despite many imperfections and rising danger, he's here. It's a world still capable of maintaining elephants, the elephant way of life. They don't need to be "conserved." They just need to be left alone. They *know* how to be elephants. Our children's children have to be able to know that we came to some understanding.

Sudden trumpeting and great commotion; dozens of elephants stream in from all directions, running toward a male who is chasing a young, smallish female. Females are lighter and can outrun males; a male catches a female only at her choice and pleasure.

He catches up to her, laying his trunk along her back. She stops, and he mounts. It's all over in about a minute.

I look over at Tim. He has his massive trunk crossed over one of his gigantic tusks. I can't understand why he hasn't rushed in to break up the tryst.

Vicki says, "He doesn't care; that means she's not in peak estrus."

Tim doesn't mind the presence of smaller males, Vicki says. "He knows he can get rid of them if he wants. He's much more concerned about any males closer to his size."

There aren't many males close to his size surviving. Tim's mere arrival was enough to cause another male who had been in musth to drop out of it. Social perception affects hormone levels. And it's better to withdraw from the competition than to risk a fight with a freight train that leads with jousting poles.

After the mating, the others fill the air with roaring and trumpeting. They've had a lot of excitement. Fascinating scents drift on the thin breeze. Young males all want to sniff the holy ground trod by the king and queen of the prom, and check out the female. The female does not wish to be checked out, however. She wants to be back with her family. Her excited sisters also move in to touch and sniff the mated one.

This is a massive greeting; all the females' facial glands are streaming. Their rumbling is intensely resonant in my chest. The mood feels contagiously, festively affirming. "As if they're singing 'I Feel Pretty,'" I say with a laugh. A celebration of joining.

Elephants probably feel only sexual attraction and no romantic love. After all, much human sexual attraction involves no romantic love. Some anthropologists believed, and perhaps some still believe, that people in other cultures lacked romantic love. And some cultures arrange marriages—love entirely beside the point—solely to serve families' utilitarian interests. Surely the freedom other animals have to choose or deny suitors is superior to such human customs. But what feelings attend the tender attentions of these elephants for their just-consumed daughter? What emotions come with the groomings of primates and parrots? These behaviors serve to forge close emotional bonds. And close emotional bonds are just that.

"You hear that rumble?" Katito suddenly comes to attention. "Calling the family."

I hear it, but also the air vibrates and I feel it, too. I see that many of the eles are rallying their families together. Within the vast herd, the family groupings are now becoming much more apparent as the individuals gather with whom they need to, preparing to move upland in bond groups. So *interesting* to watch happening.

We trail Tim as he follows a bond group from the plain into an open woodland of thorn trees that looks so much like the Africa that has inhabited our minds.

I watch two little ones chasing each other, one trying to bite the other's tail and jumping up to put its forelegs briefly on its playmate's back as they walk along. The mood is fun.

There will be more orphans, torment, and terror. Some of these elephants will kill people. Some will be killed by people. That is our time now. What their lifetime holds in the coming days and decades, no one can say.

Samburu Reserve had fabulous guys like Tim, Vicki is suddenly saying. "They're all dead."

But there *are* signs of constructive change: new legislation steeply upping the penalties for tusk trafficking, sharply increased arrests, protest marches by Kenyans against poaching, and new concern across the world. "Here at this moment," Vicki reminds us, "all is as it should be. Free elephants making the most of the good times. I feel that there are positive times ahead."

Katito says, "Bye, guys," and we roll away.

PART TWO

Howls of Wolves

They often lived, right out in front of us, what seemed like epic lives.

—Doug Smith, *Decade of the Wolf*

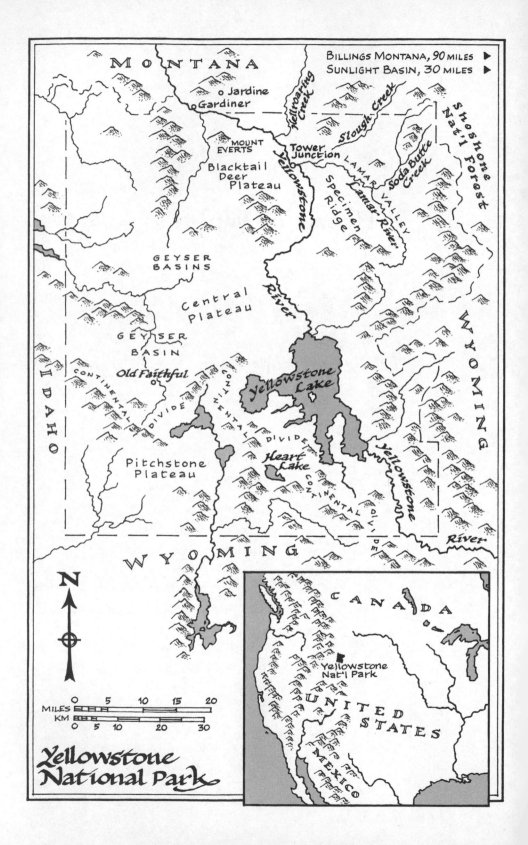

Into the Pleistocene

───•───

From a deep grove of pines on a Pleistocene morning in the original world, a coyote yips an alarm. And when I scope that slope, my view sweeps across snow, sage, the pines—. Wolves. Nearly a mile away but clear enough in the telescope, half a dozen big, long-legged archetypal dogs—primal yet so familiar-looking—are trotting into the valley. Floating down with an easy unhurried motion, they eat distance at unexpected speed. In no hurry myself, I watch as, minute by minute, they grow closer. The wolf in front is gray; two black wolves follow closely, one limping slightly; another gray, two more dark ones, and two more grays. Eight wolves. My first ever.

The wolves of Yellowstone National Park's Lamar Valley attract human attention as nowhere else. The alpha wolf watcher, Rick McIntyre, follows wolves here every day. I don't mean five days a week or weather permitting; I mean that every day for fifteen years so far, every single time the sun's said peekaboo, Rick McIntyre has been in the Lamar Valley. No misses. No matter the blizzards of winter, nor crowds of summer; no matter anything else in the world. A man in his mid-sixties, of angular features, Rick has had his eyes on wild wolves for more hours than any human ever has, quite possibly more than any living creature that isn't a wolf. Rick's typed notes run ten thousand single-spaced pages so far. "You get to know individuals, and you see their descendants, and you want to keep with it," he sums up, as if it's that simple. "It's a never-ending story."

Rick can glance through a telescope at a wolf on a ridge a mile away and instantly tell you who it is by name, and recite its life. As a career ranger who's worked from Death Valley to Denali, he's seen the best of the parks. And when offered the opportunity to observe wolf reintroduction into Yellowstone seven decades after they were exterminated here, Rick recognized a once-in-a-lifetime opportunity, "as if you were a historian in 1860 and got the chance to spend every day in the Lincoln White House, witnessing history."

As Rick sees it, wolves and humans must deal with similar life problems, "such as figuring out when to face the risks of leaving home, finding your place in the world—. There are endless similarities," he says. He notes, though, one difference between wolves and himself: "Certain wolves I've known—they were better at being a wolf than I've been at being a person."

Two more wolves who've been lying on the snow on a sunlit slope have just roused. "Okay, the two gray females that were bedded are coming down, too, now." Rick points to a pair of wolves gliding across the snow at an intercepting angle. "The one with the raised tail is Eight-twenty—that's her."

Some of these wolves wear electronic collars to help researchers understand their movements, and they're usually named for their collar number. If you have a receiver—Rick has one—you can sometimes find and identify particular wolves by the collar's beeping signal.

The elephants have names; the wolves, numbers. Are names or numbers more objective? Jane Goodall's first scientific paper on chimpanzees was returned by the *Annals of the New York Academy of Sciences* because she'd named, rather than numbered, them. The editor also insisted that she refer to a chimpanzee as "it" rather than "he" or "she." Goodall refused. Her study got published anyway. Do names or numbers bias us, or do they help us see? Even if a rosebush were named Dorothy, no botanist would argue that it showed love or insight. Juliet's plea to Romeo "O, be some other name!" may reveal more of men than of mice. Bringing the animals too close and keeping them too distant are equally bias-inducing, if what you need to do is see them in clear focus. Designate a wolf "25," and wolf watchers will begin to think of Twenty-five as the animal's name, because wolves reveal themselves as individuals, with relationships and personalities. A wolf is a "who."

Precocious at age two, Eight-twenty stands out—even compared to her two sisters who are a year older. Die-hard wolf-watching regular Doug

McLaughlin, in his early seventies, comes most mornings. He explains, "Eight-twenty is *so* much like her mother. Even at two years old, she's independent-minded, self-confident. She's got the natural-born-leader personality. And she's already an able hunter—which her mother, Oh-six, was *famous* for."

The ten wolves are converging on the valley flats. Deep-chested adults and lanky, hackle-backed yearlings.

"Okay," Rick dictates into his recorder. "Big rally."

The wolves greet energetically, tails raised and wagging, lots of body pressing and face licking. They're greeting one another the way our dogs greet us when we come home.

It's my first glimpse of the deepest impression I'll take away about the comparison of dogs and wolves. Wolves orient and defer to their elders the way dogs do to their human keepers. Maturing wolves, though, become captains of their own lives. Dogs remain perpetually dependent on and submissive to humans. It's been a simple substitution, with arrested development. Dogs are wolf pups who never get to grow up to take charge of their own lives and decisions. Wolves take charge. They must.

Rick disentangles what has become a blur of furry action. "That black one and the gray one on the left are both females and are nearly yearlings. The gray was the one bedded alongside Eight-twenty. She's Eight-twenty's younger sister, and she has no collar." She's very social and has been nick-named Butterfly. "See her pushing with her paw; that's a puppy thing meaning 'I want to play.'" Just to Butterfly's right, "those two blacks and that gray—they're a year older and helped raise her." Butterfly has to show them respect by submissive postures such as lowering her body and ears, similar to human ritualized lowering as in bowing, genuflecting, curtsying, and lowering the gaze. The message is: "I am not in a posture to attack or challenge; I make myself vulnerable to you." "That's no issue for her," Rick explains. "She's very social, everybody's friend." Of course, the explicit submission helps protect the lower-ranking individual from aggression. Usually.

There's an acute show of submission by one wolf in particular, head low and ears down and tail tucked. A sudden further escalation of aggression puts her on her back as three wolves tower over her. The one on her back is the proud and precocious Eight-twenty.

When their mother, Oh-six, was alive, she was the clear alpha, period. But that was a few months ago. Now the females in this pack are in competition. Of the three sisters towering over Eight-twenty, one, a year older, is very take-charge. She's also probably pregnant. Eight-twenty might also be pregnant. She's been accepting attention from two new males; that's a bit out of line. Two litters in one pack would be in direct competition with each other for any food the pack members can deliver. All of this makes Eight-twenty a threat to her older sister's status. That sister, backed now by Eight-twenty's two black female littermates, intends to nip this situation in the bud.

Pinned on her back, Eight-twenty is not fighting, just trying to hold her sisters off with outstretched legs. There's a tense pause.

Suddenly, a fierce escalation of violence. The others begin vigorously biting Eight-twenty. This isn't just a ritual display; this is more than simply putting one wolf in her place. Eight-twenty is whimpering and yelping in pain. One sister is biting her in the belly, another on her hip. And now her older sister is at her throat—this is how wolves kill wolves.

When Eight-twenty gets a chance to move, she runs away. But only a short distance.

She circles back, crouching in intense submission, wanting at least to be allowed to stay in her family. Her sisters aren't open to any compromise; they want her out. Snarling and threatening, they make it clear: coming closer—bad idea.

Eight-twenty vanishes into snowy undulations of sagebrush. This very moment—banishment by her own sisters—is the final turning point in Eight-twenty's life.

The main turning point was four months ago, when someone killed their famous mother, Oh-six. The end of Oh-six's life launched a raft of turmoil in the lives of her family's survivors.

To understand why Oh-six was such an exceptional individual and why her death matters so much, one must go one generation back to the royal pedigree of her lineage. Her grandfather was Yellowstone's most famous wolf: Twenty-one.

A Perfect Wolf

———

"If ever there was a perfect wolf," Rick says, "It was Twenty-one. He was like a fictional character. But he was real."

Even from a distance, Twenty-one's big-shouldered profile was recognizable. Utterly fearless in defense of his family, Twenty-one had the size, strength, and agility to win against overwhelming odds. "On two occasions, I saw Twenty-one take on six attacking wolves—and rout them all," Rick says. "Watching him felt like seeing something that looked supernatural. Like watching Bruce Lee fighting, but in real life. I'd be thinking, 'A wolf can't do what I am watching this wolf do.'" Watching Twenty-one, Rick elaborates, "was like watching Muhammad Ali or Michael Jordan— a one-of-a-kind talent at the top of his game, the extreme high end of the skill set, talent outside of 'normal.'" And normal for a wolf isn't like average for a human, because *every* wolf is a professional athlete.

Twenty-one distinguished himself doubly. He never lost a fight. And he never killed any defeated opponent. Twenty-one was a superwolf.

Twenty-one came into the world in the first litter of pups born in Yellowstone in nearly seventy years. His parents had both been trapped alive in Canada and shipped to Yellowstone specifically to reintroduce wolves into a system that had gotten out of balance, with too many elk for the land to bear. After almost seventy years without wolves, the elk had built to such numbers that winter for them meant scarcity and hunger. For the introduced wolves, though, the imbalance meant plenty of food.

But even though wolves had been absent longer than most people could remember, just before Twenty-one was born, someone shot his father.

A wolf does not do well as a single mother. Researchers reluctantly decided to capture her and her pups and feed them for a few months in a one-acre pen.

When humans brought food to the pen, all the other wolves fled to the opposite fence, but one pup would pace a little rise in the enclosure, putting himself between the humans and the rest of his family. This pup would later be given tracking collar number 21.

At age two and a half, Twenty-one left his mother—and an adoptive father—and his birth pack. Twenty-one waltzed into the family known as the Druid Peak pack less than two days after the Druids' alpha male had also illegally been shot. The Druid females welcomed this prime male wolf; their pups loved the big new guy. He adopted the pups and helped feed them. With no hassle at all, Twenty-one had left home and immediately become the alpha male of an established pack. It was his big break in life.

Twenty-one was "remarkably gentle" with the members of his pack, says Rick. Immediately after making a kill, he would often walk away to urinate or lie down and nap, allowing family members who'd had nothing to do with the hunt to eat their fill.

One of Twenty-one's favorite things was to wrestle with little pups. "And what he really loved to do," Rick adds, "was to pretend to lose. He just got a *huge* kick out of it." Here was this great big male wolf. And he'd let some little wolf jump on him and bite his fur. "He'd just fall on his back with his paws in the air," Rick half-mimes. "And the triumphant-looking little one would be standing over him with his tail wagging.

"The ability to pretend," Rick adds, "shows that you understand how your actions are perceived by others. It indicates high intelligence. I'm sure the pups knew what was going on, but it was a way for them to learn how it feels to conquer something much bigger than you. And that kind of confidence is what wolves need every day of their hunting lives."

Early in Twenty-one's run as an alpha, three females in his pack gave birth. That was extraordinary. Usually, only the alpha female, or "matriarch," breeds. The three litters reflected the unnaturally abundant food supply. An astounding twenty pups survived, swelling an already large pack to a hard-to-believe thirty-seven wolves, the largest ever docu-mented. Because the pack's size resulted from a food base so artificially swollen after seven decades devoid of wolves, the three-dozen-member pack might have been the world's all-time largest.

"Only Twenty-one had what it took to run an outfit that large," Rick McIntyre comments. It wasn't all peaceful. The high density of wolves likely produced unnaturally high wolf-on-wolf conflict. In territorial defense and in pursuit of expanded territory, Twenty-one participated in plenty of fights.

Wolf territorial fights resemble human tribal warfare. When packs fight, numbers count, but experience matters an awful lot. As adults of both packs beeline to or away from rivals or battle for their lives, juveniles can seem lost in the confusion. Wolf pups under a year old often seem dis-mayed by an attack (it seems even wolves must learn violence), and a juvenile who gets pinned by attackers may simply give up. Wolves often target the alphas of the rival pack, as if they fully understand that if they can rout or kill the experienced leaders, victory will be theirs.

Fatal conflict between tribal groups isn't just a human or chimpanzee thing. The second-most-common cause of wolf death in the Rockies is get-ting killed by other wolves. (Getting killed by humans is first.) But as mentioned, Twenty-one distinguished himself in two ways: he never lost a fight; he never killed a vanquished wolf.

Twenty-one's restraint in letting vanquished rivals go free seems incred-ible. What could it be? Mercy? Another term for a person who does not press their advantage against a threatening opponent is: magnanimous. Can a wolf be magnanimous? And if so, why?

When a human releases a vanquished opponent rather than killing them, in the eyes of onlookers the vanquished still loses status but the vic-tor seems all the more impressive. You can't be magnanimous unless you've won, so you have proved yourself by winning. And if you show mercy, your lack of fear shows tremendous confidence. Onlookers might feel it would be desirable to follow such a person, so strong yet inclined toward forbearance.

History's most esteemed, highest-status leaders are not ruthless strong-men like Hitler, Stalin, and Mao, though they ruled hundreds of mil-lions. They are Gandhi and King and Mandela. Peaceful warriors earn higher global status than violent ones. The person who has been called the most famous man in the world, Muhammad Ali, was a practitioner of ritualized combat who spoke of peace and refused to go to war. Though his decision cost him millions of dollars and his heavyweight title, his status rose to unprecedented height with his rejection of killing.

For humans and many other animals, status is a huge deal, preoccupying one's mind, occupying one's time, and costing energy. And for it, much treasure and blood is risked. Wolves do not understand *why* status and dominance are so important to them, any more than do humans. Without consulting our opinion—or even bothering to inform us of the underlying strategy—our brains produce hormones that make us feel strongly compelled to strive for status and assert dominance. Dominance feels like an end in itself. We don't need to know why. Here's why: high status aids survival. Status is a daily proxy for competition for mates and food. Then, whenever mates or food are in short supply, the high-status individual has the advantage. The thing at stake is survival, and ultimately in survival the thing at stake is reproduction—the chance to breed, to count. Dominance lets you outcompete others for food, mates, and preferred territory—which boosts reproduction. Like dogs who love car rides simply because they go to exciting places, we don't need to understand why or how it all works. We just need to know we want it. One could hardly expect that wolves would understand, any better than we do, what drives us all.

So back to the question: Can a wolf be magnanimous? In humans, as we've noted, letting a vanquished rival go free is a show of both extra strength and extraordinary self-confidence. We value both. In free-living animals, the public display of excess is sometimes called the "handicap principle." The message is: "Notice that I have enough to spare. I have so much, in fact, that I can afford to handicap myself." Almost any kind of excess will impress, as long as it's something that's valued—like bravery, beauty, or wealth. In humans, elevating one's status by displaying excess wealth is called "conspicuous consumption." But the message in a collection of antique automobiles is little different from a shrike making a highly public display by amassing a bunch of dead mice it's not bothering to eat and hanging them on thorns for all to see.

Many animals bid for status by flaunting excess accumulation (mice and mansions), excess beauty (peacock tails and long, luxurious hair), or excess risk (in sports, war, and business). The iconoclastic Israeli researcher Amotz Zahavi, who first perceived and coined the handicap principle, studied birds called Arabian babblers, who live in groups. He noticed that the birds actually compete with one another for the opportunity to fight rivals. He considered such birds altruistic because the fighters vie for the honor, one might say, of being seen putting themselves at risk on behalf of their group. If they were soldiers, they'd come back to the nest wearing medals. Zahavi writes, "The altruistic act can be considered to be an investment (handicap) in the claim for social prestige, demonstrating the reliability of the claim." You're not just claiming that you have more of what it takes; you're demonstrating that you actually do. Onlookers are impressed—and they should be.

Releasing a beaten but potentially lethal rival greatly ups the ante. An individual who shows such exceptional confidence boosts their own status. Some of those confident animals might be wolves. Some might be superheroes.

"Why doesn't Batman just kill the Joker?" asks Rick rhetorically before volunteering his answer. "In admiring the hero who restrains his strength, we are impressed with the hero's power," he says. "A story in which the good person kills the bad guy isn't nearly as interesting as a story where the good guy has a moral dilemma. In what's been called the greatest movie of all time, Humphrey Bogart has won the love he has sought. But he arranges things so that the other man does not lose his wife and is not hurt. We admire him for that. When we see strength combined with restraint, we want to follow that individual. It greatly enhances their status." Obviously Rick has thought about this quite a bit.

The character in the movie feels bound by his ethics. But do wolves have morals, ethics?

Rick chuckles at the thought. "It would be scientific heresy to say they do. But—"

In Twenty-one's life, there was a particular male, a sort of roving Casanova, a continual annoyance. He was strikingly good-looking, had a big personality, and was always doing something interesting. "The best single word is 'charisma,'" says Rick. "Female wolves were happy to mate with him. People absolutely *loved* him. Especially women. Women would take one look at him—they didn't want you to say anything bad about him. His irresponsibility and infidelity; it didn't matter."

One day, Twenty-one discovered this Casanova among his daughters. Twenty-one ran in, caught him, and began biting and pinning him to the ground. Various pack members piled in, beating Casanova up. "Casanova was also big," Rick says, "but he was a bad fighter. Now he was totally overwhelmed and the pack was finally killing him.

"Suddenly Twenty-one steps back. Everything stops. The pack members are looking at Twenty-one as if saying, 'Why has Dad stopped?'" The Casanova wolf jumped up and—as always in such situations—ran away.

But Casanova kept causing problems for Twenty-one. Well, why *doesn't* Batman just kill the Joker so he won't have to deal with him anymore? With Casanova and Twenty-one, it didn't make sense—until years later.

Fast-forward. After Twenty-one's death, Casanova briefly became the Druid pack's alpha male. But he wasn't effective, Rick recalled: "He doesn't know what to do, just not a leader personality." And although it's *very* rare for a younger brother to depose an older one, that's what happened to him. "His year-younger brother had a much more natural alpha personality." Casanova didn't mind; it meant he was free to wander and meet other females.

Eventually Casanova, along with several young Druid males, met some females and they all formed the Blacktail pack. "With them," Rick remembers, "he finally became the model of a responsible alpha male and a great father." Meanwhile, the mighty Druids were ravaged and weakened by mange and diminished by interpack fighting; the last Druid was shot near Butte, Montana, in 2010. Casanova, though he'd been averse to fighting, died in a fight with a rival pack. But everyone in his Blacktail pack remained uninjured—including grandchildren and great-grandchildren of Twenty-one.

Wolves can't foresee such plot twists any more than people can. But evolution does. Its calculus integrates long averages. By sparing the Casanova wolf, Twenty-one actually helped assure himself more surviving descendants. And in evolution, surviving descendants are the only currency that matters. Anything that's helped descendants survive will remain in the genetic heirloom, an evolved proclivity in the behavioral tool kit.

So in strictly survivalist terms, "should" a wolf let his rival go free? Is restraint an effective strategy for accumulating benefits? I think the answer is: yes, if you can afford it, because sometimes your enemy today becomes, tomorrow, a vehicle for your legacy. What Rick saw play out over those years might be just the kinds of events that are the basis for magnanimity in wolves, and at the heart of mercy in men.

Early on, when Twenty-one was young and still living with his mother and adoptive father, one of their new pups was not acting normal. The other pups were a bit afraid of him and wouldn't play with him. One day, Twenty-one brought back some food for the small pups, and after feeding them, he just stood there, looking around for something. Soon he started wagging his tail. "He'd been looking for the sickly little pup," Rick says, "and finding him, he just went over to hang out with him for a while."

Rick suddenly seems to be searching inside himself for something deeper he wants to express. Then he looks at me, saying simply, "Of all the stories I have about Twenty-one, that's my favorite." Strength impresses us. But what we remember is kindness.

The majority of wolves die violently. Despite a violent, eventful life even by wolf standards, Twenty-one distinguished himself to the very end: he was a black wolf who grayed with the years and became one of the few Yellowstone wolves who died of old age.

One June day when Twenty-one was nine years old, his family was lying bedded down when an elk came by. Everyone jumped up to give chase. He jumped up, too, but just stood watching the action and then lay down again. Later, when the pack headed up toward the den site, Twenty-one crossed the valley in the opposite direction, traveling purposefully somewhere, alone.

Sometime later, a visitor who'd been way up high in the backcountry reported having seen something very unusual: a dead wolf. Rick got a horse and rode up to investigate.

That last day, it seems, Twenty-one knew his time had come. He used the last of his energy to go up to the very top of a high mountain. In a favorite family rendezvous site, where he'd been with his pups year after year, amid high summer grass and mountain wildflowers, Twenty-one curled up in the shade of a big tree. And on his own terms, he went to sleep for the last time.

Rick had seen Twenty-one essentially every day of his long life and watched his career from pup to powerhouse to his last walk across the valley. Before he rode up to investigate that day, he told Doug McLaughlin that when he got back, he'd tell him what he'd found. Later, when Doug saw Rick returning from the meadow, he headed over, anticipating Rick's promised report.

But Rick went straight to his vehicle. He opened the door, and before he got in, he broke down in sobs. And as Doug McLaughlin recalled this story for me, he choked up, and I looked down at the ground.

Packing and Unpacking

———•———

A wolf pack is just a family. What we call a pack is, at its most basic, a breeding pair plus their pups. We often call the breeders the "alpha female" and "alpha male." Wolf experts, though, consider the word "alpha" outdated and often refer to the breeding female as the pack's matriarch, because she initiates many of the decisions.

The classic idea about pack formation is: boy meets girl, they have offspring—pack. Yes, that happens. But with wolves, everything happens. A lot depends on individual personalities and chance encounters. Sometimes two or three brothers form a new pack with two or three sisters from a different pack. In a year or two, some of them might split off to form yet another new pack. This is the "fission-fusion" aspect of wolves and humans (shared with elephants).

The wolves in an alpha pair show deep loyalty to each other in matters of defense and assistance. (Loyalty in the dogs we love—their "best friend" character—is the wolf in them.) And alphas depend heavily on their children in crucial matters such as hunting, feeding and guarding pups, holding territory, and defending against attacking rivals.

Like humans, wolves both follow and break rules, playing many variations on the family theme. Like many "monogamous" humans, wolves sometimes color outside the lines. Males might slip across pack borders looking for hookups. Females generally tolerate wandering males. For a male, however, being inside another pack's territory is very dangerous. Yet males sometimes risk a nighttime tryst.

Extended child care is a major part of wolf society and family life. Pups stay with their parents for several years. Older children help care for the younger ones while maturing into young adulthood, creating multigenerational groups. Eventually they leave their parents to start their own families. From dens and rendezvous sites—secluded spots for stashing very young pups—adults take turns hunting, bringing back food, playing with the pups, and enduring mock ambushes and having their tails yanked by some of the world's most playful, insistent youngsters.

"Wolves are about three things," says Doug Smith, Yellowstone's wolf research leader, as he counts off on his fingers. "They travel, they kill, and they are social—very *social*. A lot of their life hinges on their socialness—if that's a word. And after studying wolves for over thirty years," he sums up, "I can tell you this: You can't just say, 'wolves do this,' 'males do this,' 'females do that.' No. Wolves have fantastic individuality."

"If you've seen wolves in captivity," Doug says, "they're constantly pacing; they just want to *go*." Wolves travel between five and forty miles in a day. "Not just to hunt. Also to maintain territory. They're very competitive about protecting their turf.

"A fourth thing about wolves?" Smith is telling more than asking. "They're tough."

During the reintroduction operations, researchers worried that the wild-caught Canadian wolves might try dashing straight home to Canada. So for several weeks they kept them in large "acclimation pens." Most of them accepted this arrangement. But three defiant wolves never tolerated confinement. One jumped high enough to latch onto an overhanging section of ten-foot-high fence, then actually managed to curl his body around the overhanging mesh and escape. And *then* he dug back in from the outside—releasing his comrades. The three defiant wolves' relentless chewing on the chain-link fence caused extreme damage to their canine teeth, basically wearing them flat.

"I thought, 'Wow, these guys are kind of doomed,'" Smith recalled. "But after release, you could not tell there was anything at all wrong. I thought, 'How in the world is this wolf without canines killing elk?'" Wolf jaws exert twelve hundred pounds per square inch, twice that of a German shepherd. "That's crushing power."

Four or five times, Doug Smith has caught a wolf to replace a collar and discovered that the animal had a healed-up broken leg. "Since I put their first collar on, I'd been tracking them the whole time; there was *never* an indication that, meanwhile, they'd broken a leg!" Once Smith was in a helicopter over a running pack. "They were doing the porpoising thing in deep snow. I darted the one at the back to put a collar on. When we reached it on the ground, I was shocked to see that it had only three legs. From the air I couldn't see anything wrong with how that wolf was running." In that same group with the three-legged wolf, another wolf got a broken shoulder in late winter, probably from a kick by an elk or bison. "She was *ten* years old"—exceptional longevity for a free-living wolf—"and she lasted all the next spring and summer. I think the others were helping her." In autumn, she faded out.

"When you examine their bones, you see that these guys have a very rough life *and* they're *incredibly* tough." Smith once spotted an alpha female whose leg was dangling; she was attentively watching her pack hunt. Instead of hiding and nursing her break, "she was right there, alert to what was going on." She healed and survived.

"No," declares Doug. "Wolves never feel sorry for themselves. It's never 'Poor me.' They're always *'Forward!'* Their question is always: 'Next?'"

Wolf packs develop distinctive characters. The Druids traveled without regard to borders. In contrast, Mollie's pack established a territory high in elevation, lovely in summer, that in winter turned exceptionally bleak—deep snow and temperatures dropping to forty degrees below zero Fahrenheit—and devoid of elk. Only a few big bison lingered, "tough, supersized behemoths," Smith calls them. Over several seasons, the Mollie's wolves actually became effective hunters of those thousand-pound winter bison. In one attempt, fourteen wolves repeatedly drove a male bison into deep snow, "a move meant to compromise his footing, his kicking power." Though the bison "literally shook the wolves from his back" repeatedly, the wolves persisted and—after a nine-hour siege—succeeded in killing the bison. Bison are at the extreme high end of wolf-pack hunting abilities, and the bison-killing wolves of Mollie's pack were among the very largest in Yellowstone. It's quite likely that this was natural selection in action, with only the hugest wolves able to survive year-round in that cold, going against those giant bison.

. . .

Almost all predators hunt prey that's smaller than themselves. Wolves, though, hunt animals much larger than themselves. Their prey is often *five to ten times* a wolf's weight. That takes cooperation. That's why wolves live in groups. Being a wolf is a team effort. That makes wolves highly social, and that, in turn, makes wolves special.

Predators who hunt animals larger than themselves tend to hunt in organized groups with social structures and division of labor. Only a few species are in this elite category, such as African painted dogs (sometimes called wild dogs or painted wolves, *Lycaon pictus*), lions, spotted hyenas, and several dolphins, including mammal-hunting types of killer whales. And humans. We're special, too.

Lions move into "wing" and "center" positions, and the wingers stampede prey toward the centers, who lie in ambush. Individual lions specialize in playing the center or wing, and wing lions specialize in the right or left wing. Bottlenose dolphins sometimes go to work with a division of labor, with some swimming back and forth to block the escape of trapped fish, while other dolphins actively catch them. From time to time, blockers move in and eaters take their turn blocking, so the dolphins must have some way of signaling a switch to one another. Sometimes they divide their roles into "driver dolphins," who specialize in herding fish toward "barrier dolphins." In those groups, individuals tend to maintain these specialized roles. Humpback whales dive beneath fish schools, then wrap them in a cylinder of rising bubbles. Through this "bubble net," with its packed and panicked fishes, the whales rise and lunge, surfacing with their mouths wide open, gulping fish. Researchers have been surprised to discover that humpback whales sometimes form stable bubble-netting crews, with the same individuals seen working together from one year to the next, and taking the same positions over time. When researchers watched eight humpbacks make 130 feeding lunges over three days, each whale always stayed in the same position relative to its comrades. As with wolves, these creatures seem to know exactly what is going on, what they're doing, and who's doing it, giving themselves their best chance to tip the odds of survival in their favor.

Wolf hunts can initially seem disorganized. Ten wolves might come upon a hundred elk, and what you see, says Rick, is that "everybody's chasing different elk. But in the chaos, they're all looking for a sign that one particular elk might be vulnerable. And they all watch each other. It's an efficient way to sort through a lot of potential prey pretty quickly."

Wolves divide the labor. Big males run slower than females and lighter, younger males. (Females range from about 90 to 110 pounds. A big male—males approach full weight around age four—is 120 to 130 pounds. The very biggest reach about 150 pounds, rarely more than that.) In fast chases after singled-out prey, you usually see yearlings and females out front. Younger wolves are frequently the first to catch up to a running elk. They bite at its hind legs and haunches, slowing it. But young wolves don't know the best way to kill an elk. (And the longer it takes, the more dangerous for the wolves. Wolves have gotten wrecked by mortal stabs from antlers, or a desperate, determined kick that breaks a bone or punches out teeth, creating fatal abscesses.) Now a big wolf rushes in, plunges past his children and past the elk, and, turning, lunges up for a throat bite.

Elders often initiate hunts. Sometimes the younger pack members don't comprehend the strategy. One day Rick watched the Junction Butte pack's alpha male, Puff, try to get his pack to a higher elevation. Nobody wanted to follow. Rick, though, could see some elk up there. Puff went up high, alone, and disappeared into the trees. And suddenly the elk alarmed and bolted, and Puff came running out of the trees behind the last elk, an adult female. "She was making a lot of bad decisions in her route, and he was gaining on her," Rick says. By now the whole pack realized what was going on. Puff's mate sped in diagonally, grabbing the elk's hindquarters. The elk kicked her off, but the slowdown allowed Puff to catch up and grab her by the throat. With a third pack member plowing in, they pulled the elk down. "It's crucially instructive for youngsters to observe how older, experienced wolves manage life and death," Rick notes.

"Alpha male" connotes the guy who is most aggressively assertive, most dominating—the abusive manager who belittles and yells at everyone, who at every moment demonstrates that he's in total control. The snarling boss has become the caricature of the alpha male. Wolves are *not* like that.

Wolves are like this: the alpha male might be a major player in the kill, then go and sleep until everyone is full. "The main characteristic of an alpha male wolf," Rick says, "is a quiet confidence, quiet self-assurance. You know what you want to do; you know what's best for the pack. You're very comfortable with that. You have a calming effect. Point is, alpha males are surprisingly nonaggressive, because they don't need to be.

"Twenty-one was the classic alpha male," Rick explains. "He was the toughest guy in the neighborhood. But one of his main behavioral characteristics was restraint. Think of a very emotionally secure man or a great heavyweight champion; whatever he needed to prove is already proven. Think of it *this* way," Rick offers. "Imagine two groups of the same kind— two wolf packs, two human tribes, whatever. Which group is more likely to better survive and reproduce: one whose members are more cooperative, more sharing, less violent with one another, or a group in which members are beating each other up and competing with one another?"

So an alpha male, in Rick's experience here, almost never does anything overtly aggressive to the other males, who are usually his sons or adopted sons or maybe a brother. He just has a certain type of personality the other males recognize. "The only time you'd be likely to see him assert dominance would be during the mating season, when the number two guy approaches the breeding female and the alpha might snarl and bare his teeth. Or even just look at him. That would be enough." If the alpha moves aggressively toward the other male, usually by the time he gets to him, the other male is on his back; the alpha might then give a brief holding bite on the muzzle or neck that communicates rank but isn't intended to cause harm. The other male never resists. He usually just goes down into a submissive posture or slinks away. "You know how a dog sometimes looks guilty when you reprimand it? That's how the wolf looks." Rick concludes, "Minimal violence promotes group cohesion and cooperation. That's what a pack needs. The alphas set the *example*."

Rick describes Doug Smith as a wolflike alpha male: "Doug is the best supervisor I've worked with, by far. Very easygoing, supportive; he never yells at anyone; he's very understanding of other people's situations. He has a naturally gentle management style. He has a natural confidence in the best sense. Without him even trying, he totally motivates people. People would be willing to work ninety hours a week for him with no complaints. He'd probably be very embarrassed if he heard me saying this."

I decide to get a second opinion on alphas from the alpha himself. "In the old days," Smith begins, "people talked about the alpha male as the *boss*." He grins, adding, "Mainly, male biologists talked that way." In reality, he explains, there are two hierarchies in the pack, "one for males and one for females." So who's in charge? "It's subtle, but it seems that females do most of the decision making." That includes where to travel, when to rest, what route you'll take, when you're going hunting, and the pack's most important decision: where to den.

Some females seem to have more importance to their packs than do others. "Nez Perce pack: alpha female gets killed"—Smith snaps his fingers—"pack dissolves. Gone. Leopold pack: alpha female dies, you couldn't tell; her daughter assumes the breeding role. Seamless."

Everyone who knows wolves tells you, as Smith is telling me, "Personality matters for wolves." Individual personality influences how playful a wolf is, how they'll hunt, how long a young wolf stays with their parents before leaving to seek a farther fortune, and how—and whether—they will lead.

"Couple of examples," offers Smith. "Wolf Seven was the dominant wolf in her pack. But you could watch Seven for days and say, 'I *think* she's in charge.' Watching over years, I saw she *was* in charge. She led by example. So when I use the word 'matriarch,' I mean a wolf whose personality kind of shapes the whole pack."

Contrasts: Seven led by example. Wolf Forty led with an iron fist. Doug emphasizes this, slowly: "Very . . . *different* . . . personalities." Seven you could study for weeks, her leadership was so subtle. "You could watch Forty for just one hour and see: in charge and—*bitch*!" An exceptionally aggressive wolf, Forty had actually deposed her own mother from top status. (After being deposed by her daughter, the mother wandered out of the park. And one December night, a barking dog resulted in a door opened, a light shined, a gun fired, and the mother dead.)

For three years, Forty ruled the Druid pack tyrannically. A pack member who stared for a moment too long would, said Doug Smith, find herself slammed to the ground, a bared set of canines poised above her neck. He recalls, "Throughout her life she was fiercely committed to always having the upper hand, far more so than any other wolf we've observed."

Forty heaped her worst abuse on her own same-age sister. Because this sister lived under Forty's brutal oppression, she earned the name Cinderella.

One year Cinderella split from the main pack and dug a den, something wolves do only to give birth. Shortly after she finished the den, her sister arrived and delivered one of her infamous beatings. Cinderella did nothing to fight back; she just took it, as always. It's not clear whether she gave birth that year. If she did, Forty likely killed the pups; no one ever saw any.

The next year, though, Cinderella and her bullying sister (now age five) and a low-ranking sister all gave birth, in dens dug several miles apart. (As I've mentioned, this is highly unusual; it reflected the unnaturally high density of elk in the early years just after reintroduction.)

New wolf mothers nurse and guard constantly; they rely on pack members for food.

That year, few pack members visited the bad-tempered alpha at her den. Forty's mate—the famous superwolf Twenty-one—delivered almost all her food. Cinderella, though, found herself well assisted by several pack members, including her adult sisters.

Six weeks after giving birth, Cinderella and several attending pack members headed out, away from her den. Near Forty's den they stumbled into the queen herself. With what, "even for her, was tremendous ferocity," Forty immediately attacked Cinderella. She then turned her fury onto one of her younger sisters who'd been accompanying Cinderella, giving her a beating, too. Soon Forty headed toward Cinderella's den. They were all trotting toward Cinderella's den as dusk settled in.

Only the wolves saw what happened next. But here's what seems to have gone down. Unlike the previous year, this time Cinderella wasn't about to remain passive and let her sister reach her den and her six-week-old pups. Close to the den, a fight erupted. When a fight breaks out between two wolves, others quickly join and take sides. In just a one-on-one fight, Cinderella probably would have lost to her sister. But this time there were at least four wolves, and Forty had earned no allies among them. It was payback time.

At dawn, Forty was down by the road, hiding, barely alive. She was covered in blood, and her wounds—including a neck bite so bad that her spine was visible—indicated an attack of horrific vehemence. One hole in her neck was so deep, said Smith, "I could bury my index finger all the way with room to spare." Shortly afterward, she died. Her jugular vein had been ruptured; her long-suffering sisters had, in effect, cut her throat.

It was the only time researchers have ever known a pack to kill its own alpha. Forty was an extraordinarily abusive individual. Credit the sisters' decision to act outside the box of wolf norms, to mutiny.

Remarkable enough. But Cinderella was just getting started. She adopted her dead sister's entire brood. And she also welcomed her low-ranking sister and *her* pups. And so that was the summer that the Druid Peak pack raised an unheard-of twenty-one wolf pups together in a single den.

The low-ranking sister, out from under Forty's brutal reign, developed into the pack's finest hunter. She later went on to become the benevolent matriarch of the Geode Creek pack. Goes to show: a wolf, as many a human, may have talents and abilities that wither or flower, depending on which way their luck breaks.

"Cinderella was the finest kind of alpha female," Rick McIntyre says. "Cooperative, returning favors by sharing with the other adult females, inviting her sister to bring her pups together with her own while also raising her vanquished sister's pups—. She set a policy of acceptance and cohesion that allowed the Druids to swell into the largest wolf pack ever recorded." She was, Rick says, "perfect for helping everyone get along really well."

The Wolf Named Six

———

In the glancing light of a new morning, fresh powder has turned the ice kingdom into something like a dream. No wind. Utter stillness. Humbly witnessed.

It's pretty, but we've got no wolves in view. So we talk about—wolves.

"She had an unbelievable ability to sense when things weren't right in the pack," says Laurie Lyman, die-hard watcher and wolf-news compiler for *Yellowstone Reports*. She is, of course, talking about the wolf whose birth year became her name, the famous Oh-six: most regal granddaughter of the great Twenty-one; alpha founder of the Lamar pack, which we're not seeing at the moment; mentor and mate to Seven Fifty-five and his big-bodied brother; mother of the precocious, now-banished Eight-twenty; and unwitting, unwilling martyr.

"She was the alpha female who most made her own rules in life," chimes in Doug McLaughlin, who never misses an opportunity to extoll Oh-six. "She did things her way," he says, "and did them spectacularly well. The more you watched her, the more you admired her."

"So, big loss, really sad," reflects Laurie. It's only been a few months, and the pain still shows on their faces, and in self-recrimination. Laurie confesses, "In a way, we loved her to death; in the park she'd so often seen so many people. So outside the park, she wasn't particularly worried."

Oh-six's grandfather was the superwolf, and Oh-six earned her own reputation as both a superlative hunter and a master tactician.

One day, Rick saw sixteen members of Mollie's pack—this bison-killing pack had already killed other wolves—heading toward the Lamars' den. Wolves who discover a rival pack's den sometimes proceed to kill all the pups, as well as any adults in their way. This day, that's just what was unfolding.

On their way up, they disappeared into deep timber. All of a sudden, seventeen wolves came running out of the trees, away from the den site. Oh-six was in front and well ahead at first, but all sixteen enemy wolves were chasing her, and they were closing fast. She was racing across an open slope that terminates in a high cliff. She was heading straight for the cliff.

"I could see that in her panic she'd made a major mistake," Rick remembers. "I could see that when she got there she'd realize her mistake and her only choice would be to turn and fight." But at sixteen against one, that was hopeless. "We'd watched her whole life," he says, "and now we were about to watch her death.

"But what she knew—that I didn't know—was that there was a tiny gully that ran across that cliff face, and that she could run it all the way down to the valley floor. So she plunged down along that gully. And when the other wolves got to the top of the cliff, they couldn't figure out how she'd gotten down.

"A fundamental problem remained: all they had to do was follow her scent trail back and they'd discover the den, where the pups were helpless.

"At that point, one of her adult daughters appeared and did something that I thought was stupid. She just stood, in plain sight. The attacking wolves saw her and charged. She ran east. She was a very fast wolf and easily outdistanced all of them. But in the process she pulled them far away from the den and pups." By the end of all that chasing, the Mollies looked confused, tired, and disorganized. They went into the valley, swam across the river, and didn't return.

And those pups that survived that day, because their adults decoyed the attackers, are some of the yearlings we're now waiting for.

Oh-six earned a reputation as the best hunter in Yellowstone. People had seen only four instances where the wolves managed to kill two elk in a single hunt. And as you'd expect, killing two elk in one hunt had always required a pack. "That was before Oh-six got started," Doug McLaughlin says with something like pride. On three separate occasions, Oh-six killed two elk in the same hunt, solo.

One day a five-hundred-pound elk and her half-grown youngster emerged from the trees. A hundred yards behind them, walking casually, came Oh-six. The elk picked up her pace. Her objective: get to the river and stand in water deep enough that a wolf would float before it reached them. The elk knew what she needed to do, and she accomplished that goal.

Oh-six decided she'd take a number and wait. She had once kept an elk in the water for three days, then eventually killed it. She lay down on the bank.

The two elk split up: mother downstream, young one upstream. As the increasingly vulnerable young one reached a shallower stretch, the tension mounted.

"And in seconds," Doug says, "Oh-six was suddenly all over the *mother* elk."

While the humans had focused on the more vulnerable youngster, Oh-six had figured the situation differently: if she attacked the smaller one, she'd be trying to kill the youngster with a holding bite while the horse-sized mother came on in full fury with sharp hooves flying.

What happened: Oh-six couldn't grab the mother elk in the water, so from the land she goaded the elk into charging. Sure enough, the elk rushed the bank, kicking furiously with her forelegs. Oh-six watched for her opening, then leapt up through the flailing legs and seized the elk by the throat.

They both tumbled down the bank, falling into the water. Oh-six's head was underwater. So she immediately let go of her bite and used her whole body to hold the elk's head underwater. "We saw her demonstrate total knowledge of her prey in a way I've seen no other wolf do," Doug tells me. "And it was the *quickest* killing of an elk that I have ever seen." It can take about ten minutes for wolves to kill an animal with a neck bite, but "this elk drowned in just a couple of minutes."

But now Oh-six had a dead elk in deep water. She tried dragging it out and couldn't. So she planned another strategy. She pulled the elk into *deeper* water, floated it downstream to a bit of beach, and pulled it up there.

She ate some, then lay down to rest on the bank.

The calf, meanwhile, seemed to be doing some thinking of its own. "It had come out of the water and walked clear over by where we were standing," Doug says.

Oh-six seemed to expect that the young elk would return to the river at some point. And when it did, it entered not deep water, where it would have an advantage, but a stretch too deep for it to run fast yet shallow enough for a wolf to reach. As soon as it did that, Oh-six was up and running.

"There was a tremendous amount of chasing, splashing, and thrashing back and forth, back and forth. The young elk already weighed about two hundred and fifty pounds, and it took Oh-six a long time, maybe ten minutes, to get it. And when she did get the elk by the neck, it screamed and screamed and screamed. This was not quite the perfect choke hold. People who were watching with young children started leaving," Doug recalls grimly. "It took another ten or fifteen minutes for the poor elk to die."

Rick has a story involving Oh-six and coyotes. One springtime in this valley, there was a pack of coyotes organized like a wolf pack—pretty unusual—with half a dozen coyotes based around a den site. Coyotes usually fear wolves, and with good reason. But these sharp-witted coyotes had developed a strategy of aggressively harassing single wolves, especially yearlings, who were headed up to the wolf den where Oh-six had pups. Any wolf traveling toward the pups was always full of food intended for delivery. (A wolf can can carry twenty pounds of meat in their stomach.) The coyotes would surround and threaten the wolf. Coyote extortion. The wolf would avoid getting badly bitten by regurgitating its meat to the coyote bandits, then run away safely. And the next time the coyotes spotted that wolf, it would again be full of meat and . . . You get the picture.

One can almost hear the coyotes laughing and telling stories. In Native American lore, Coyote is often a trickster. In real life . . . a coyote is often a trickster. One day, four of the coyotes were at the half-eaten carcass of an elk the wolves had killed when a single female wolf sauntered in. This is usually the cue for any coyotes to make way for the wolf. Instead, one of the coyotes went to the wolf with a wagging tail, as if inviting play—then gave the wolf a sharp bite, as if to say, "Four of us, and we're not budging!"

Oh-six wasn't laughing. "One day," Rick says, she left her den, bringing her whole pack with her, and headed toward the coyote den, "as though she'd had enough." When they got within sight of the den, "she seemed to somehow signal her pack to sit and watch. Anyway, they did." Oh-six approached the den and, sure enough, the coyotes started orbiting and harrying her, snarling, teeth bared, heads down, hackles up, closing in.

Oh-six ignored them.

She dug into their den. One by one, she pulled out each of their pups. One by one, she shook it dead. And in front of the coyotes, she ate all their pups. "She turned and trotted back toward her waiting family as if to say, 'And *that's* how it's done.' That's the only time we've *ever* seen a wolf eat coyotes."

These creatures—in their ancestral homelands or a reasonable facsimile—know what they're doing. At times they let us glimpse their capacity for insight, for planning, for understanding their lives. They remain in context, in a way that we do not. They know what their lives are about. And while I would not trade places (theirs is not my context), I do admire them. Greatly. They belong.

Oh-six, it seems, really did live on her own terms. Her inexplicable approach to romance and her odd sexual proclivities, for instance, led her to become the founding matriarch of the Lamar pack. As a young venturer, she took up with a highly competent male who later became the alpha in the Silver pack. But she stayed for only a week or so and then struck out on her own. She had many suitors, including some whose status and skill made them worthy of her. One breeding season she was observed mating with five different males, a record. She failed to bond with any of them. Rick says, half-joking, "Because she had high standards, she dumped every one of them." He knows that can't be the real explanation, because high standards could never explain her choice of a certain two brothers.

The brothers Seven Fifty-four and Seven Fifty-five, only recently dispersed from their birth pack, had taken up with the four females remaining in the Druid pack. By then the Druid females were suffering from mange. When Oh-six showed up, Seven Fifty-four and Seven Fifty-five took one look at her—this healthy young female—and left those four females for just her. At her choosing—not theirs—she did something else quite unusual among wolves: mated with both brothers.

Why she chose so hapless a pair of males as Seven Fifty-four and Seven Fifty-five is anyone's guess. Maybe she just really liked being clearly in charge. She was four years old, a highly experienced hunter who had ably managed on her own. They were half her age, and their hunting skills were nowhere near her level. She paid for their undeveloped skills the first year by having to do more than her share of hunting for their pups. And once, something funny happened after the brothers had fed on an elk she'd killed. Their job was to return to the den and regurgitate meat for their pups, but when Seven Fifty-four met Oh-six on the trail to the den, he regurgitated the meat to *her*. Doug McLaughlin recalls, "She looked at him like, 'You clueless wolf; you're supposed to do this up *there*.'" But later, they shaped up.

After a while, Seven Fifty-five earned a nickname: the Deerslayer. He learned that though he wasn't as fast as a deer, he had much more stamina. "You can still see that Seven Fifty-five has the slim physique of a marathon runner," Rick remarks. "We saw him start chasing a deer way over by Soda Butte Cone; he chased it deep into the Lamar Valley. The deer crossed the river and went south again, and he went up along the hill behind the Confluence (where the channels of Soda Butte Creek conflue—one might say—into the Lamar River) and kept pacing the deer, with his eye on it the whole time; and when it finally stopped at one of the gravel bars, he came running downhill and out into the open. The deer saw him coming and—did nothing. Was completely spent. Offered no resistance.

"You'd probably guess," Rick predicts, "that for every wolf, hunting and killing is the biggest thing on their minds, that they'd like to go hunting every day of their life. But that's not the case." Usually only two or three wolves do most of the pack's killing, most of the time. All share in the eating. "For some individual wolves, hunting just isn't that big a deal."

For instance, Rick elaborates, Seven Fifty-four was much bigger than his brother Seven Fifty-five, but he preferred to hang out with the pups. He would follow them around like a shepherd, trudging along no matter where the pups went, and if one pup bedded down away from the rest, he'd go over and keep an eye on it, providing the needed protection. That freed up Oh-six and Seven Fifty-five. They were faster, anyway. But when they were having a hard time bringing down a very big elk, Seven Fifty-four's size came in handy; he'd plow in for the tackle and takedown. That's one reason elder wolves matter.

So, that's how Oh-six, Seven Fifty-five, and his brother Seven Fifty-four became the Lamar pack. She'd been an independent career girl and was four years old the first time she gave birth, pretty old for a wolf to start raising youngsters. She gave birth in each of three years.

One of Oh-six's daughters, from her second litter, is the precocious Eight-twenty, the one Rick pointed out during my first morning in the Lamar Valley, the one we've watched getting run out of the pack by her own sisters.

Rick and Doug and Laurie's stories explaining who Oh-six was are helping me understand the history behind these particular wolves I've been seeing, why they are together. I'm about to learn why the pack is now coming apart.

A Shattering of Promises

———•———

Cold weather began to lock the park down in November, four months before I arrived. It was a tougher than average winter in Yellowstone. Most elk and deer migrated directly down to lower elevations, seeking better food outside the park.

Oh-six and the other Lamar wolves ventured to their territorial borders. But they no longer found the resistance of other packs. They did find better hunting.

During the second week of November, the Lamar wolves ventured unopposed into lower elevations, traveling as far as fifteen miles or so outside the park's borders. They were in more lucrative territory—with a lot more elk. It was all new terrain; they had never before in their lives been there.

The Lamars could not have known the reason they found no resistance from other wolves at the eastern borders of their usual territory. They could not have understood that they had just gone from being protected by a national park and the Endangered Species Act to becoming targets in a newly opened hunting season. The Lamars hadn't changed. But human promises had.

Because they'd lived in Yellowstone, they were used to seeing people and weren't particularly cautious about remaining unseen.

Enter the proud arch marking Yellowstone's gated community, and the park impresses as a big piece of country. But a map shows that it's just a postage stamp, a remnant of a once-vast West that was won and lost in the same grab.

Until a moment ago, there were no safe-tucked "parks" huddled in the protection of postcard peaks. There was only the world. In 1806, when Lewis and Clark reached the Yellowstone River near what is now Billings, Montana—well outside the present-day park borders—Clark used some of his precious ink to tell us, "For me to mention or give an estimate of the different species of wild animals on this river particularly Buffalow, Elk, Antelopes and Wolves would be increditable. I shall therefore be silent on the subject further."

Yellowstone looms large; actually, it's too small. The park's straight-edge boundaries were delineated for the tourist appeal of Yellowstone's geysers and hot springs and scenery. How poorly the park works for wildlife was beside the point in 1872. If animals had to leave the park each winter to find food, who cared? One might as well worry about geese flying south. For deer, elk, and bison, the park is mainly high-summer pasture, not year-round range. Winter at seven thousand feet is just too brutal. Come autumn, the whole high interior plateau empties. Of Yellowstone's seven elk populations, six migrate out. Most deer and many bison leave. The territory needed by the park's larger animals, the "Greater Yellowstone Ecosystem," is eight times as large as the park. Can a wolf live a life entirely inside the park? It's been done. Could a viable population of wolves exist entirely within the park? No; it's far too small. Wolves, too, must come and go. When the animals go, many never come back. So each autumn the park's larger creatures still drain into the lower valleys and skirting plains, availing themselves of the food that might sustain them through the winter. But when they get there, they have walked into a place of bullets.

On November 13, thirteen miles outside the park in Shoshone National Forest, hunters shot a wolf weighing perhaps 130 pounds. He was the pack's largest male. The hunters were interested only in his skin. That skin housed a crucial component of the pack's adult skill and experience. That wolf was Seven Fifty-four.

The pack retreated to the park. But only briefly. The brothers Seven Fifty-four and Seven Fifty-five had probably been together every day of their lives and had gotten along very well. Seven Fifty-four's absence was obvious to the whole pack. But because the hunters had removed his corpse, the surviving Lamars never saw his body. They had no certain way of knowing why he wasn't there. Sometimes wolves simply travel away from their packs for a few days, then return. It's hard to say how much the Lamars did or didn't see of the shooting or could understand about a missing member.

After their brief stay inside the park, the Lamars ventured out again. They might have decided to go look for Seven Fifty-four. Or they might simply have gone for the same reason they were there in the first place: good hunting. Whether they went to grieve, search for him, patrol new territory, hunt where there was more food, or some combination of those motivations, the point is that they went back. They went, interestingly, right near the place where Seven Fifty four was last alive.

On December 6, someone killed Oh-six.

Her death was a seismic shift for the surviving members of her family. It was seismic for wolf watchers, too; they had never experienced such a time as this, when wolves they knew so intimately could so easily get shot.

The Endangered Species Act allows for listing a species as endangered if it faces extinction "in all or a significant portion of its range." Wolves clearly qualify. Wolves have been exterminated from nearly all of their former range. Researchers estimate that before Europeans arrived, likely over a million wolves once ran the lower forty-eight U.S. states, with 380,000 wolves ranging across the western United States and Mexico alone. By 1930, humans had wiped wolves off 95 percent of their holdings in the lower forty-eight states. That is why, for decades, they'd been designated as endangered.

Before men from Europe stepped onto North America, wolves laid tracks over essentially the whole continent. In fact, for something like three-quarters of a million years, wolves held the entire northern world, from Atlantic Europe east across the continental immensities of the Asian landmass to the Pacific and Indian Oceans, and in North America from the western Arctic to Greenland, south throughout the great eastern forests, west across the Great Plains to the spine of the Rockies, sloping to the West Coast, south into Mexico. That is one exceptionally well-adapted, flexible creature, a supremely successful social being.

Their recent reappearances in parts of the U.S. West are limited in area and sparse in number. Nonetheless, over several recent years the federal government weakened wolf protections. Among these moves, they declared that 30 breeding pairs and 300 wolves in the entire northern Rocky Mountain region constituted a "recovered" population. (Comparisons: 300 is about one-half of 1 percent of their former numbers there; it's fewer than eight-tenths of one one-thousandth of the 380,000 that once ran the U.S. West; in what is now Yellowstone National Park, in 1871–72 pelt dealers sold more than 500 wolf skins.) On September 30, 2012, the United States Fish and Wildlife Service deleted the words "gray wolf," specifically in Wyoming, from the federal list of endangered species. Open season on wolf killing in the state began instantaneously, on October 1. Every raven knows that the land is one country; the rectangles "Yellowstone Park" and "Wyoming" bear false witness to the topography of time and the contours of memory. But Wyoming officials designated their rectangle open to wolf killing year-round. No license required. No limit on the kill. The only good wolf . . .

In just over two months, Seven Fifty-four and Oh-six were dead.

———✦———

To consider "the wolf" in literature and culture is to study not a living thing but the projected fears of people insecure about civilization. Wolves are—among other things—group hunters. Wolves do sometimes kill domestic animals, and wolves have attacked humans, especially in the Old World. Humans, of course, kill domestic animals and sometimes attack other humans. But wolves' metaphorical power is so strong, people seldom view them simply as the social hunters they are. "Sometimes a cigar is just a cigar," psychoanalysts acknowledge. But a wolf is seldom thought of as just a wolf.

When they get inside the human mind, wolves become a metaphor for the feral and precivilized, the gang, for people living outside the bounds of convention and conformity. Maybe humans also hate wolves because in their dedication to their families, in their interest in eating the same kinds of animals we are interested in killing and eating, we recognize so much of ourselves that we respond to wolves as if they were a competing tribe, or thieves. People cast a wolf as the villain, then confuse the actor with the character they play.

But through the centuries—whether the devil du jour is Lucifer or the federal government—"the wolf" has become a reflecting pool and amplifier for whatever humans dread.

In Europe's Middle Ages, the church considered wolves "the devil's dog," literal proof that Satan was out for a stroll, right around here somewhere. Wolves weren't just exterminated; they were persecuted—burned at the stake like witches and heretics, and publicly hanged. They were dangerous not just physically but also as tempters to evil deeds. Humans were occasionally put on trial under suspicion of being wolf charmers or werewolves. Centuries later, in America, trapped wolves were sometimes set on fire, or had their lower jaws cut off or wired shut before being released to slowly starve. Doug Smith describes this as "a vengeance applied to no other animal."

Anything a wolf did provided a pretext for hating wolves. Early in the twentieth century, people started poisoning carcasses. So, Doug Smith notes, wolves very quickly learned not to return to a kill for a second meal. Wolves who thus avoided poison were then accused of "wasting meat" and, by extension, "killing for fun." "Killing for fun" became moralized to a kind of capital crime, perfect justification to kill wolves for—well, for fun. It's still so. When writer Christopher Ketcham entered a wolf derby in Idaho during the year I was writing this book, a "nice old man" in a bar shared a pointer: "Gut-shoot every goddamn last one of them wolves." Don't just kill wolves; make them suffer.

Contempt for animals who hunt is mainly Western civilization's thing. And nothing is more western than the American West. "The West is politically reactionary and exploitive . . . guilty of inexplicable crimes against the land . . . culturally half-baked." That was Wallace Stegner's opinion, and he lived there. His hope was for a time when westerners would fashion "a society to match the scenery." Maybe he'd been reading Hemingway, whose travels far and near had led him to opine, "The country was always better than the people."

Some people detest wolves with a hatred so deep it feels racial. They have weaponized wolves in the West's peculiar culture wars. When two women in their sixties went hiking and had not returned by the expected time, a Western political website's headline screamed, "Liberal's [*sic*]

Wolves Murder 2 Women Hikers." The article began thus: "Let's cut the politically correct crap. But for the mentally defective wolf-loving liberals, these 2 women would still be alive." Another website asserted, "Wolves Kill Female Hikers, Liberals Cover It Up." A few weeks later, the first website (the second remained silent) printed this retraction: "They were wearing only t-shirts and jeans and were exposed to sub-freezing temperatures. There is no evidence of any wildlife encounters. . . . The two women died of exposure."

When the Congress established Yellowstone National Park, in 1872, there was no federal agency to protect it. Poaching for commercial markets was so rampant that in 1886 the U.S. military was sent in to fight it. After hunters on the Great Plains killed tens of millions of bison, the twenty-three bison found standing in Yellowstone were recognized as crucial to the species' salvation.

Predators were treated differently. After the Congress established the National Park Service, in 1916, rangers were instructed to pursue the extermination of mountain lions, lynx, bobcats, coyotes, and other carnivores. A key park administrator happened to like Yellowstone's bears; that saved them from eradication. Rangers looked for wolf tracks, listened for howls, found dens and pups. In 1926, a park ranger killed the last Yellowstone wolf. Now there were no wolves across America, where there had been hundreds of thousands.

For sixty-nine years, no wolf howled in Yellowstone. You'd think it was elk heaven.

"There is no peace for prey in a land without predators," Doug Smith tells me. "There are only alternate sufferings." Either predation makes them die or starvation makes them die. Predation is dramatic and awful, but starvation causes more widespread suffering, is more prolonged.

As the Yellowstone elk populations irrupted in the absence of wolves, wildlife managers started killing elk or shipping them to places as far-flung as Arizona and Alberta, whose elk had been completely shot out. From about 1930 to 1970, Yellowstone National Park shipped and killed thousands of elk. When that stopped, the elk again surged.

Famished elk and deer so thoroughly scrounged Yellowstone's willows and aspen seedlings that everything from fish to birds had their lives reordered. No wolves meant too many elk; too many elk meant almost no food for beavers, which meant almost no beaver ponds for fish, which meant . . .

As elk fear wolves, one might say that trees and rivers fear elk. In his classic essay "Thinking Like a Mountain," Aldo Leopold observed, "I have lived to see state after state extirpate its wolves. I have watched the face of many a newly wolfless mountain, and seen . . . every edible bush and seedling browsed . . . to death . . . every edible tree defoliated to the height of a saddlehorn. . . . Too much safety seems to yield only danger in the long run. . . . Perhaps this is the hidden meaning in the howl of the wolf, long known among mountains, but seldom perceived among men." He offered, with memorable resonance, "Only the mountain has lived long enough to listen objectively to the howl of a wolf."

It's January 12, 1995, at this exact spot. A pickup truck pulling a trailer has just stopped. In that trailer: wolves trapped in Alberta, Canada. Six of them—the alpha pair and four male pups—are headed for an acclimation pen a mile south of here. The wolves will be held for two months, then released.

After release, that pack decided that the Lamar Valley suited them fine. Tens of thousands of people saw them, an experience wolves and people had never shared. A total of thirty-one wolves released in 1995 and 1996 capped a two-decade fight that drew in the entire U.S. Congress and provoked a splattering of lawsuits. All to merely return, to one abused quadrangle of land, its main natural hunter.

With the return of wolves, Yellowstone finished regaining its full roster of native mammals. Mountain lions had snuck back into Yellowstone on their own in the late 1980s. (Wolves likely would have, too, eventually. In the 1990s wolves from Canada were accomplishing their own self-reintroduction into the U.S. Rockies.) Yellowstone now has essentially everything that used to live here, everything that belongs. So wolves gave Yellowstone its groove back. Not that predation is pretty. Yet predation is the author of much beauty.

What but the wolf's tooth whittled so fine
The fleet limbs of the antelope?

—Robinson Jeffers

Wolf numbers flourished; elk overcrowding declined. Wolves helped liberate aspens, cottonwood saplings, and other vegetation from the tyrannical appetites of too many elk. With the vegetation recovering, beavers were able to return to stream banks, where the wind again whispered in the willows. Into the quieted pools behind newly beaver-built dams swam muskrats, frogs and salamanders, fishes, ducks. Even stream-bank songbirds reappeared. If the animals and plants in Yellowstone could have voted, a majority would likely have elected wolves. Since their peak in the mid-2000s, wolves have declined, too, as the system rebalanced and other factors came into play. Of course, the story is more complex, but in broad strokes that's it.

"Yellowstone is the best it's ever been," says Doug Smith, who has been in charge of wolf studies in Yellowstone since before wolves returned. That's the bottom line.

Sweet success? Some elk hunters certainly don't think so. "In the time it takes to drink a cup of coffee," claimed one elk-hunting advocate, "a wolf will run through and kill a dozen elk calves. It's a slaughterfest." Nonsense like that is less about protecting elk, more about who gets to kill them easily. Some people love having Yellowstone function as an elk farm that grows animals who will migrate from the park into their gunsights.

After reintroduction, it was again possible to find wolf tracks in northern parts of the U.S. Rockies. But despite the wolves' tenuous toehold—and because of it—pressure from western congressional representatives intensified. The politics caused the U.S. Fish and Wildlife Service to declare wolves "recovered." In 2012, Congress—with a precedent-setting intervention—acted to remove wolves from the endangered species list by including the measure in a rider in a budget bill. In the first six months after wolves lost their Endangered Species Act protection, hunters and trappers in Montana, Idaho, and Wyoming killed more than 550 wolves—out of a population estimated at 1,700. In the U.S. West, most wolves die because people kill them. Inside Yellowstone National Park, wolf-on-wolf violence has accounted for about half of all wolf deaths. (This might be unusually high for wolves. In the early years after reintroduction, unnaturally high prey density facilitated unusual wolf density, and packs frequently encountered one another.) Outside of Yellowstone, in the U.S. Rocky Mountains, people account for about 80 percent of wolf deaths. The irony is, killing wolves can cause the surviving wolves to kill more livestock, as shattered packs lose their most experienced hunters, destabilize, and hungry individual wolves move around more.

Oh-six's collar showed that she'd spent 95 percent of her time inside Yellowstone National Park. Hunters that season shot a total of seven wolves wearing expensive research collars that had been fitted inside the park. Wolf lovers suspected hunters of using receivers to pick up the beeps from wolves' collars. They weren't paranoid. The website HuntWolves.com offered this: "If you have the capability to scan collars—search from 281.000–291.000 Mhz step at .003 Mhz."

"Does it hurt our research? Yes, very much so," Doug Smith told the *New York Times*. "It's a huge blow."

Oh-six was Yellowstone's most famous, most watched wolf. A few days after her death, the *New York Times* published what was essentially her obituary, titled "Mourning an Alpha Female." Unlike most human obituaries, hers included testimonials from humans who hated both the deceased and the mourners. One person decried wolf-loving "pagans." The president of the Montana Shooting Sports Association likened Oh-six to "a psychotic predator stalking Central Park and slitting the throats of unwary visitors." But Nathan Varley of Yellowstone Wolf Tracker Tours in Gardiner, Montana, who earned most of his money guiding wolf-seeking touists, complained that hunters were killing "million-dollar wolves."

Million-dollar wolves? A study in *Yellowstone Science* concluded that in one year, "approximately 94,000 visitors from outside the region came to the park specifically to see or hear wolves." They spent "a total of $35.5 million in the three states." The market value of cattle and sheep killed by wolves (the value ranchers would have gotten when they sold them for slaughter) was "about $65,000 per year." Seventy cents from each of the

94,000 extra visitors who spent an average of $375 per person could have easily covered that cost. "Weighing the economic impacts of increased tourism against reductions in livestock production and big game hunting," the study found, "the net impact of wolf recovery is positive and on the order of $34 million in direct expenditures."

All of that is why the Lamars could travel east without running into resistance from other wolves. That's why they crossed an imaginary straight-edge park border, toward where most of the prey had gone for the winter. That's why their biggest male and their matriarch were shot to death.

The battle rages. Two years after Wyoming declared war on wolves, as I was putting this book to bed, a federal judge made her own declaration. She voided Wyoming's wolf-management plan and restored Endangered Species Act protections to wolves in Wyoming. But no one expected this to be the last word.

Newborn getting lifted to his feet for the first time by his twenty-five-year-old mother, Petula (at back, foot raised), and her cousins.

Babies often rest in shade while adults stand guard.

Carl Safina

Carl Safina

After a severe drought, a baby boom. For several years, youngsters remain close enough to touch their mothers.

Carl Safina

Carl Safina

Carl Safina

Water—and mud—makes elephants happy.

Carl Safina

Elephants often greet by touching trunk to mouth, a kind of combined handshake, hug, and kiss.

Carl Safina

Facial gland streaming from high emotion just after mating, this female (front) returns to her family, who excitedly sniff and reassure her.

Carl Safina

Dr. Vicki Fishlock identifies an unfamiliar male under Mt. Kilimanjaro in Kenya's Amboseli National Park.

Carl Safina

Katito Sayialel can identify nine hundred individual elephants on sight.

Iain Douglas-Hamilton, father of elephant research and founder of Save the Elephants, with Carl Safina in Samburu National Reserve, Kenya.

Last photo of Philo. Four days later, poachers killed him.

David Daballen of Save the Elephants.

Carl Safina

Placida, at left, age thirty, consorting with Tee-Jay, twenty-four, an enormous male with a mellow personality. Placida gave birth as this book was being finished.

Carl Safina

Tim at age forty-three. His magnificent tusks are a liability in a time of ivory poaching.

Carl Safina

Rick McIntyre has watched Yellowstone wolves every single day for more than fifteen years.

Mark Miller

The superwolf named Twenty-one, who never lost a fight yet never killed a rival, and died of old age on his own terms.

Seven Fifty-four (top right) and Oh-six were shot dead after wandering beyond Yellowstone National Park's border, despite their prominent research collars.

Beaten and banished, the once proud and precocious Eight-twenty being escorted from her birth pack by her own littermates at the turning point of her life.

Seven Fifty-five, whose life turned upside down when his brother and mate were killed.

Two Lamar wolves seen through a scope eating an elk, attended by magpies and "the wolf birds"—ravens.

Chris Bahn with hand-raised wolves at Howlers Inn.

Jude, bottom left, with Carl and Chula.

Ken Balcomb has studied killer whales for four decades.

Tall-finned thirty-six-year-old male L-41, with forty-two-year-old L-22 at his left side and two other L pod members traveling Haro Strait.

The transient T-20, approximately fifty years old, who with his companions has just eaten a harbor seal.

Dan Mahon appears entertained by the startling proximity of a Ross Sea killer whale, who apparently shares the sentiment.

Catherine Forbes

Luna, the lost young killer whale whom any mother could love—and trust.

Ken Balcomb

L-86 with her daughter Victoria, whose death at age three appeared to be caused by U. S. Navy bombing practice, though the navy denied it.

Carl Safina

The night after this mortally ailing young humpback whale drifted ashore, the lighthouse keeper fifteen miles away at Montauk heard "incredibly mournful whale sounds," as if a distressed mother was searching for or mourning her lost child.

Carl Safina

A humpback whale off Montauk a few years later.

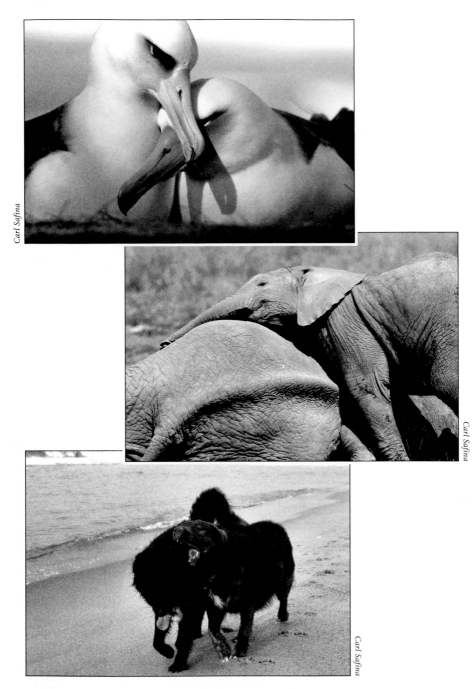

Humans are not the only animals who love one another. Laysan albatrosses; a young elephant giving a snoozing relative a trunk-hug; and best friends forever Jude (left) and Chula.

In a Time of Truce

———

Native hunters have sometimes had a more sensible, more spiritual, closer-to-truth view of wolves (and other predators, including lions and tigers). Recently, Native American groups have tried to block the opening of wolf hunts. When Wisconsin opened hunting for wolves in 2012, Mike Wiggins, chairman of the Bad River Ojibwe Tribe, responded, "Is nothing sacred anymore?" *Ma'iingan*, the wolf, is sacred to the Ojibwe. "Killing a wolf is like killing a brother," said tribal member Essie Leoso. *Ma'iingan* walked with the first man. (And actually, wolves orbited dwellings of the earliest humans, scavenging scraps.)

Ojibwe belief teaches that whatever happens to one will happen to the other. Indeed, it has; white settlers considered the Ojibwe, like *ma'iingan*, a competing tribe to be contained. The Western view often reflects goals of domination or extermination. The native view of other animals is often compatible with a long-term accommodation. It's not that the native view is more scientific, but in sensing deep relationships, their belief web is a truth catcher.

For a long time, the power in other creatures instilled in humans deep respect and a working détente; during this long, dream-filled period of truce and magic entreaties, we asked the stronger, craftier creatures to hold nothing against us, and merely hold their peace. As human craftiness increased, our respect eroded. Our weapons became stronger. Their strength no longer compelled our respect. We kill wolves and whales and elephants and others not because they are inferior but because we can. Because we can, we tell ourselves they are inferior. As with people's treatment of other peoples, intellectual and moral superiority is beside the point. Usually it comes down to deadly force and what the strong can get away with. The seventeenth-century Dutch philosopher Benedict de Spinoza wrote, "I do not deny that beasts feel; what I deny is that we may not consult our own advantage and use them as we please." "Might makes right" is appealing, simplifying as it does our decision making in the treatment of everything from meat to men.

Other animals cannot negotiate, but that's not the deciding factor. People *can* negotiate. But only from strength. The oppressed, the enslaved and exploited—. Being able to speak up for yourself using complex language with syntax gets you only so far. Money talks, guns speak, and neither needs syntax to get their point across. We permit ourselves the excuse that animals can't talk. Truth is, they can't fight back. Weaker people, too, often find themselves overpowered, devalued, dehumanized. "The Oriental does not put the same high price on life as the Westerner," said U.S. general William Westmoreland, who was running an industrial war in Vietnam. "Life is cheap in the Orient . . . life is not important." That delusion let him do his job.

One of the things that "makes us human" is: the strong obliterate the weak. Humans do both magnificent and horrific things. In our treatment of other animals, of lands and waters, there is little malice aforethought because there is little forethought. But into the fabric of the future we are burning gaping holes, living as though we are smoking in bed.

It is deeply unexpected that even when other animals retain the advantage, they sometimes seem more able to consider us than we are of considering them. For instance, people have come "face-to-face" with wolves in the backcountry while out alone, as Doug Smith has. Yet it appears that no human has ever been attacked by a wolf in the lower forty-eight U.S. states. North American wolves virtually always flee humans immediately and don't view people as potential prey. (In the 1940s, two Alaskans were bitten by rabid wolves.) Free-living wolves are known to have killed only two people in North America, one in Saskatchewan in 2005, the other in Alaska in 2010. Essentially, wolves kill fewer people than any other cause of human death. Surely wolf packs often do detect vulnerable hikers. And yet, the calculated shyness or forbearance of so well endowed a pack of predators is a bit puzzling. One wonders what they are thinking.

• • •

Modernity's self-imposed exile from the world seems to have degraded an older human ability to recognize the minds in other animals. Yet it can seem that other animals recognize human minds. In *The Tiger,* John Vaillant describes how Amur (Siberian) tigers had a kind of ancient understanding with local peoples. People long accustomed to living with Amur tigers, such as Udeghe and Nanai hunters, knew enough to stay out of a tiger's way, but also left a cut of their hunted meat. It was ebb and flow; human hunters sometimes scavenged from tiger kills. The balance of powers and considerations in the deep northern taiga forests yielded a kind of mutual courtesy, an understanding of mutual nonviolence. It was a peace all the more impressive because tigers live by meat-making minds inside meat-driven bodies weighing up to five hundred pounds.

But when Russian colonists began arriving, in the 1600s, writes Vaillant, "these carefully managed agreements began to break down." The tide of fur-, gold-, and timber-seeking colonists and their missionaries accelerated, doing unraveling violence both to the local animists' delicate culture of balances and to the non-human members of the forest community.

Violations of that pact carried consequences, suggesting that it had been a true two-way understanding. Commenting on what he calls "the Amur tiger's capacity for sustained vengeance," Vaillant relates a story told by a modern hunter about what happened after they scared a tiger off its kill and took some of the meat. "The tiger destroyed our traps, and he scared off the animals that came to our bait. If any animal got close, he would roar and everyone would run away. We learned the hard way. That tiger wouldn't let us hunt for an entire year. . . . Very smart, and very vengeful." It's as if the tiger was not just a hunter but the manager of its hunting territory.

During a lean time, a hunter decided to eliminate a tiger that he perceived as a competitor. He set up a trap whereby disturbing a trip wire would cause a gun to fire. The tiger tripped the wire, but the bullet merely grazed its fur. On a second pass through, the tiger again touched the trip wire. Its tracks in the snow showed that it stepped slowly backward, and—seemingly understanding who was trying to kill him—did not even follow the hunter's tracks but went straight to the hunter's cabin. The hunter saw the tiger in time to scramble inside. The tiger waited outside for several days, then left the area. A former chief inspector of tiger attacks told Vaillant, "If a hunter fired a shot at a tiger, that tiger would track him down, even if it took him two or three months. . . . Tigers will sit and wait specifically for the hunter who has fired shots at them."

Consider the abstract thinking or precise intuition enabling the tiger to comprehend that the bang from a gun represents intent of harm, or that a painful wound actually originated from the midsized upright creature who had been standing many paces distant. Perhaps most strangely, biologists who catch, sedate, collar, and release tigers in that region have no experience of being stalked, no attacks. If all the foregoing is indeed true, a tiger can understand intent to harm. One particular tiger certainly did. After a poacher named Vladimir Markov wounded him, the tiger anticipated Markov's return from an extended hunting trip, waiting outside his cabin for several days. As Markov approached his home, the tiger attacked not out of hunger but in revenge, not simply eating the poacher but leaving his remains scattered over a wide area behind his cabin, "like a heap of laundry . . . thoroughly and gruesomely annihilated."

In the unciphered span of time that the San people (formerly called "Bushmen") lived as hunters somewhere in the coordinates of the vast space and deep antiquity of the Kalahari Desert, they did not hunt lions. Their courtesy was repaid. Lions and the San had somehow forged a solid truce. Even when commandeering prey from lions—even when outnumbered by lions—the San spoke to the lions firmly but respectfully. It was a respect not paid to leopards or hyenas, whom the San merely ignored when taking a kill. No one had ever heard of a lion killing a human. Leopards, yes, sometimes at night. But lions, never.

White people, of course, knew no such truce. As a teenager in the 1950s, Elizabeth Marshall Thomas lived among the Juwa and Gikwe San; there she saw the old way, and watched it crumble. (Her mother was the path-finding ethnographer Lorna Marshall, and Elizabeth chronicled her own experience in the books *The Harmless People* and *The Old Way*.) Once, when Thomas was camped with her family and an Afrikaner, five lions approached, their presence revealed solely by their eyeshine beyond the campfire. To the horror of Thomas and her family, the Afrikaner immediately fired into the darkness, hitting two of the lions. Having just created the dangerous situation of two wounded lions around the camp, the

Afrikaner refused to follow them into the night. So a horrified Marshall, her brother, and another man set off on foot into the starlight. "At last we heard a soft moan,"she wrote. Their flashlight discovered a young full-grown male, badly wounded, unable to get up. "He was evidently in pain, for he had been biting the grass." Finishing him required several more shots. Thomas recalled, "The lion turned his head aside, to look away from us as we stood over him and shot him. I wonder now if by averting his gaze he was trying to limit our aggression." He cried each time a bullet hit him.

They couldn't find the other lion until, at dawn, they spotted the tracks of a lion who'd taken two great leaps. Her body was lying dead at the end of the second leap. Her fur and the surrounding grass were cold and wet with dew except for one warm, dry spot beside her where the grass was still rebounding from being depressed—another lion had just left her side. From the size of the tracks, the just-departing lion was enormous. "This huge lion . . . had stayed beside the dead lioness, within sight of our camp, listening to all our comings and goings, listening to the shots and cries . . . [yet] had groomed the body of the dead lioness, turning her fur the wrong way."

The San never hunted lions, and lions never hunted the San. Perhaps each side knew that the other was potentially dangerous. Each could have tested the other's limits. Yet they did not. Thomas writes, "No one can explain the truce, because no one understands it." But they chose not to tamper with one another, lived well without doing so, and passed the custom to their children. Maybe that is the explanation. Maybe it was that simple. It no longer is. They no longer are.

"In the 1950s," wrote Thomas, "the lions of Gautscha belonged to one continuous population, a single lion nation occupying a more or less undivided country." Then came Europeans, bringing into a land of fleet-footed herds their plodding cattle, taking the land from all its inhabitants for more ranches and farms. And true to script, "what had once been the uninterrupted lion nation . . . became more precarious." The lions around the new cattle posts had held prospering territories. In the old days, lions sometimes spread out in a line a mile or more long, keeping in touch with one another by roaring. But as the farms expanded, "the lions who lived there became the unfortunates . . . the poor." Farmers took the lions' lands, shot out their antelopes and other animals, shattered the lion economy and culture and the lions themselves. And European settlers did the same to the Juwa and Gikwe "Bushmen." After describing how a lion she was watching yawned immediately after she yawned, and did so several times, Thomas wrote, "Lions are excellent observers, and observation is important to them—hence their empathy."

Magnificent Outcasts

———•———

Oh-six's death instantaneously threw the Lamars' alpha male, Seven Fifty-five, into a very bad position. His brother *and* now his mate and hunting partner were both dead. Even if he found a suitable female to invite into the pack, his adult daughters might not allow it. The nine other surviving Lamars included eight daughters and a male pup born that spring. Two of the daughters were almost three years old. They would now be interested in mates for themselves, and higher status. Seven Fifty-five's problems were acute.

With two ranking adults dead and their father wandering the territory trying to pick up the pieces, the daughters encountered two prime males who had left the Hoodoo pack, based outside Yellowstone in Sunlight Basin, Wyoming. One was a tall, gray, in-control wolf; the other was huge, whitish, and mellow-tempered. Breeding season was upon the wolves, and they all felt it.

In the Lamar females the Hoodoo males found a welcoming reception and a plum opportunity. But the daughters' gain came at the direct expense of their father, Seven Fifty-five. With those new Hoodoo males in the pack, Seven Fifty-five no longer had a place in his own family.

Hour by hour, colder. Five degrees Fahrenheit. That this is a "dry cold" accomplishes nothing toward making it feel less frigid. My brand-new boots are rated to sixty below. My feet are not. My feet are cold. I never stop feeling the cold—except when wolves are in view. For the span of any wolf-filled while, I forget that I am, nonetheless, not warm. I've got snow pants on, three shirts, a vest, parka, earmuffs, my scarf, my fisherman's hat with ear and neck flaps down, and my hood up. We've got no wolves in view.

Temperatures low; spirits high. We get it from the wolves, who seem not to notice what for us is fatal cold.

For a brief while, it looked like things would sort themselves out. Seven Fifty-five lured off a Mollie's pack female whom he'd previously met. They mated and she became pregnant and he brought her back with him to the Lamar Valley. Den sites are special places that exert a strong pull on wolves. Seven Fifty-five showed her the den that had been in his family's use for fifteen years.

It looked as though Seven Fifty-five would continue as the valley's alpha male, in his territory. His daughters and their Hoodoo males were outside the park. Everyone had what they needed.

That the Mollie would be the next wolf to give birth in the Lamar den was ironic. The Lamar pack and Mollie's pack had been tribal enemies. She had probably been among the Mollie's wolves who had come to invade the Lamar den when Oh-six had given them the slip down the gully at the cliff.

After three tumultuous months, the Lamar daughters and their Hoodoo males returned to Yellowstone a changed pack. When they detected the new female with their father, they might—or might not—have borne some recollection of her scent from the day the Mollies came to attack. More likely, they simply viewed her as an intruder at their den, or perhaps as competition for the hunting territory. The destabilizing effects of Oh-six's death kept rippling through the surviving wolves, a bit like how the power vacuum following the killing of a chief or a prince can lead to bloodshed among human groups.

Before dark, the Lamar females attacked and badly injured her. But people watching could also see that the black Lamar near-yearling male pup "wanted to see Dad," as they put it. "Seven Fifty-five had been howling behind us," Doug McLaughlin recalls, "and a lot of the pack had answered him, but they were keeping their distances. Yet it was as if that young guy decided, 'I'm a pup; I want to see my Dad,' and so he came up away from the rest and scent-trailed his father for almost two miles."

When he reached him and realized a new female was there, "he became confused." He didn't recognize her scent. "He would get on her trail and then backtrack to find his dad's trail. He also wanted to find out who the strange new one was, but he acted like he wasn't sure whether he was walking into some sort of an ambush." So he proceeded hesitantly, "and when he finally made visual contact, it was like, 'Dad!—but who's *she?*'" The pup crawled over to his father on his belly in intense submission, communicating to both elders that he posed no threat. Though high-ranking wolves can be a little rough when reasserting dominance on family members they haven't seen in a while, Seven Fifty-five just wagged his tail. Perhaps he was relieved. Maybe, in his way, he simply missed them all.

When the youngster went over to the new Mollie, she'd already been seriously injured by his sisters. She snapped at him to make him keep his distance. But she also seemed to understand that he had not come to hurt her, that he was young and low-ranking, and that he was known and liked by her trusted new companion.

And that's where things stood when sundown closed the curtain.

Before dawn, the Mollie female's signal was coming from a different hill. Soon part of the Lamar pack descended from that same hill. Not a good sign.

Seven Fifty-five showed up on the road in the darkness just before first light. Four of his offspring were by the road visiting with him.

But the two Hoodoo suitors weren't about to tolerate their new father-in-law. Yet the Hoodoos hesitated. They were up the hill across the road, and having grown up outside the park, they didn't like roads. The social goings-on they were watching might have perplexed them. They might not have understood his relationship to their new girls. Or maybe they did, by his scent. Or from the way the others were acting with him, familiar and deferential.

The Hoodoos didn't come down at first. And when they did, Seven Fifty-five moved off just a little. He seemed unsure about what to do. This was his family. *His valley.* But bottom line, it was two prime males against just him.

Seven Fifty-five didn't move off any farther. His family stayed put. The Hoodoos didn't advance.

"So then," Doug McLaughlin recalls, "Seven Fifty-five *crosses* the road, to *their* side. They're just looking at each other."

And then Seven Fifty-five turned, and just trotted away.

"If they wanted to get him?" says Laurie Lyman. "They would have been on him in a *second*. Seven Fifty-five isn't a wolf afraid for his life. But he has reason to be cautious—these males are huge."

Apparently Seven Fifty-five *was* feeling cautious. He continued westward as a lone wolf who never slowed, never circled back to look for his new mate. He'd probably understood by dawn that she was dead.

Predators must understand death in some operative way. They know they are trying to end the struggles of prey, and they shift gears from killing to feeding when the prey relaxes.

As unlikely as it might be for wolves to share a human concept of death, it would seem more unlikely that they have no concept of death, since death is a wolf's living. A wolf requires a working knowledge of "alive" and "dead." Perhaps the wolf simply understands the difference as "No longer moving; I can now stop killing it." When you watch a hunting creature, you sense a skilled professional, experienced and knowledgeable.

I'm not saying that wolves have insight into death, or know the inevitability of their own mortality. After all, why would we expect them to understand more than we do? Most people cannot conceive of an end to themselves. Most people believe they will exist forever, in a place called heaven or in a wheel of karma and reincarnations. That's both the breadth and the limit of human imagination. We exist. We cannot imagine that someday we will not exist. The conceptual limits of the human mind, for most of us in an everyday way, lie remarkably confined by what we've already experienced.

How does a wolf *feel* when its mate dies? "This has always stuck with me," Doug Smith recalls. The alpha male of a Yellowstone pack near Heart Lake was quite old. He'd aged from black to bluish-gray, "so we called him Old Blue." Old Blue had reached the almost supernaturally ancient age of 11.9 years (eight years is considered quite old). He'd been spotted struggling to keep up with his pack, and then one day, Old Blue died. The next day, his mate, Fourteen, did something no wolf scientist had ever seen. She left. She left her territory, left the children who were her pack— left her nine-month-old *pups*. Unheard of. "She wandered westward through the snow," Smith relates, "crossing terrain so inhospitable it contained not a single track of another animal." Miles and miles later, she paused alone on a windblown slope of the Pitchstone Plateau. Then—she simply continued westward for another fifteen miles. A week later, she returned, reuniting with her family. "Though none of us wanted to say she was mourning," says Smith, "I wonder."

Rick tells of an alpha female getting killed by another pack. For days afterward, her mate howled and howled. So: one loses her mate and goes walkabout; one loses his mate and howls—for *days*. The first time my wife, Patricia, and I went on a trip together and left our dogs in the company of a friend in our own home, the ever-happy, ever-ravenous Chula did not eat for two days. What was she feeling?

Missing a loved one is why we grieve when a person or special pet dies. Other animals, too, clearly miss a close companion who's died. While they are alive, they call to each other, look for each other, and return to the same nest or den. Their behavior clearly shows that they envision their mates and their dens and homesites. They anticipate their mate's return. When the mate vanishes, the survivor continues to look for them. They know who they are looking for. In other words, they miss them. Then, as with us, they adjust and life goes on. Sometimes it goes on in a very changed way.

Seven Fifty-five didn't stop putting distance between himself and his estranged family until he was well past Hellroaring Creek, approaching the Blacktail Deer Plateau, something like twenty miles as the raven rows. In all his life, he'd never before been there.

Just weeks earlier he'd been the proud alpha male of the whole Lamar Valley, mated to Yellowstone's best hunter and backed by his enormous, gentle brother and three generations of offspring. Imagine his situation. In the last four months he lost his brother and mate to humans, and because of that he lost his new mate to his own daughters, and his daughters have attracted hostile males he cannot handle. He is no longer safe in his own home among his own family; at the bitter end of winter he has no help hunting, and no hunting territory. Going into pupping season he has no mate. Basically, his life is over.

And we've seen the jealous sisters collude to eject their precocious sister Eight-twenty.

"Hunters like to say that if you take out an alpha, it doesn't matter," notes Laurie Lyman, who used to be a schoolteacher. "It matters. The pack becomes a classroom with no teacher."

Ironically, the Lamars' two most competent survivors are now the outcasts. The alpha male Seven Fifty-five and his precocious daughter Eight-twenty are now the ones most radically upended, each out alone, their prospects tenuous.

I had known that a wolf pack is a family, a breeding pair plus their offspring, who help raise the next generations of youngsters. I had known that as offspring matured, they left to make their own lives, start their own packs. What I had not imagined was the politics involved, the personalities, the vendettas and coalitions, the family turmoil following tragedy, the loyalties and disloyalties. It seems . . . all too human.

And partly it is. Humans triggered these events. As anthropologist Serge Bouchard observed, "Man is a wolf to Man, which, you will agree, is not very kind to the wolf."

❧

A light all-night snow has re-wintered the slopes and valleys. First light makes pink the fresh powder. Sixteen degrees Fahrenheit.

Thousands of miles east, back home on my sea-level coast, spring peepers calling from vernal wetlands are livening the mid-March evenings, and returning ospreys are reaffirming their immense nests. But here at seven thousand feet, winter holds a grudge. The only meager sign of spring is a half dozen geese motoring overhead. Yet the fresh snow is just a lie against the lengthening days, and the down-jacketed geese know that the sun tells the truer story.

After concerted searching we find wolves on a high slope, bedded down. The Hoodoo males are looking very much at home among the hereditary Lamar wolves. Tall Gray is sleeping at the edge of a snowdrift with his chin on the new powder, his paws hanging over the ridge. He is acting alpha. When the yearling male pays his respects, both new Hoodoos greet him, friendly, licking faces and wagging tails. This pack is settling down, the relationships nearly sorted out.

A radio crackles. Two wolves have appeared a couple of miles up-valley, and their beeps confirm their identities: Seven Fifty-five and his banished daughter Eight-twenty. We go.

High on a ridge above an open snowy slope, near the end of vision even in our telescopes—there they are, traveling. Seven Fifty-five already has covered an astounding amount of ground since yesterday. All the way to Hellroaring Creek and back, maybe forty miles round-trip. He knows this valley as his home, and he knows Eight-twenty as his daughter. So in this immensity of miles and snowy mountains and timber and sage, they've found each other.

At about six miles per hour, they're covering significant landscape. Eight-twenty is trotting along holding her tail straight out behind her—an alpha posture. She's feeling good. At age two, she is a prime-of-life wolf, with a classic gray coat pattern and a darker grizzled cape, light cheeks. He is a born-black wolf silvered toward seniorhood with a fifth birthday coming up in two weeks. They are running now, across snowy slopes, in and out of timber.

How very wolflike of them to have found each other; how very human of us to share their relief at their reunion. But I predict that the happy time will be short. A new beginning isn't so simple. With Eight-twenty's alpha personality, she'll likely not tolerate her father acquiring a new mate. Likewise, if Eight-twenty herself got a new mate, the situation would be intolerable for her father. And there is the detail of territory: Where can they hunt? Eight-twenty and Seven Fifty-five are now, in fact, only about a mile, line of sight, from the rest of their family—the wolves who have given them such trouble.

Meanwhile, the main Lamar group is back to slumbering. We hang around in the cold, watching wolves sleep. One yearling wakes, trots to a hidden cleft, reappears with part of an elk's lower leg, and lies down, happily chewing like a pooch with a bone.

Around three in the afternoon, the Lamars rouse and rally. Then the pack begins howling. The humans fall silent.

Their voices surprise me, higher than the deep, chesty bawls I'd expected. And unexpectedly varied: some yowling and others yipping, some wavering their tones, others singing long, spare notes that they hold and let taper, the singing so different among the vocalists. And the impression—when I close my eyes—is of many more voices than there are wolves.

The howling fills the valley, seeming to my human brain as solemn and yearning as a sacred chant in a cathedral. It reaches right in. I hear affirmation and mournfulness, but how do they mean it and what do they hear? Rallying cry? Emotional release? A warning? Whatever they are saying and however wolves hear it, the impression on me is of some ancient story, wordless as a dream at dawn.

If Eight-twenty and Seven Fifty-five howl back, it could provoke a violent confrontation among wolves who, now, all hold a deep claim to this valley. All players understand the dynamic. Eight-twenty and Seven Fifty-five shrewdly maintain their silence. But they can't hide in this valley any more than they can avoid leaving scent as they travel through. Sooner or eventually, push will come. Wolves and people want their once-and-for-alls. Eight-twenty and Seven Fifty-five are in a bind.

She melts into deep timber. He follows. The howling trails off until the air is again filled only with sunlight and cold.

At around six P.M., Eight-twenty starts howling.

Tactical mistake. Immediately the Lamars rouse, answer—then mobilize.

The Hoodoo brothers have no quarrel with Eight-twenty. Nonetheless, with the females leading, the Lamars are heading directly to where they've heard their banished sister's wails.

They disappear into some low timber and reappear high up on a flat bench of land above a snowy swath on a wide mountainside.

Eight-twenty next appears a considerable distance away. Her late-day calling was likely intended for Seven Fifty-five. But he has vanished utterly. No beeps. Howling was her calculated risk, miscalculated. She has failed to draw her only remaining friend in the world. She has drawn all her new enemies.

Eight-twenty is a superior wolf among average sisters of similar ambitions but lesser abilities. Wolf politics are tricky. Even a wolf can be too good for her own good, and made to pay. We're seeing it playing out in the politics of this pack, before our eyes. As the light fades, Eight-twenty is traveling; with her tail tucked this time, she looks dispirited and unhappy. I can see the pack, and I can see her. I can't tell if they have each other in sight, but clearly they all know who's where.

Where the Wolf Birds Lead Us

Eight-twenty and her father spent less than one day together. Now Seven Fifty-five's collar signal cannot be located by handheld antennas waved in the winter air. He has left this valley. Eight-twenty, companionless but detectable, stays out of view. If she *is* pregnant—a probable reason her older sister, also likely pregnant, turned on her—and she experiences a sharp drop in food intake because she's on her own, her body will likely abort and absorb her fetal pups.

The deaths of Seven Fifty-four and Oh-six completely unraveled the calculus of life in the politics of the pack. Death takes not just the lives of wolves killed; it changes the game and the prospects of survivors, even descendants. Individuals matter. A wolf is not an "it." A wolf is a "who."

Laurie searches the valley as a raven might, carefully scrutinizing all details for signs of tracks, a bit of movement, the ground beneath an eagle in a tree—anything.

I see—nothing.

When Laurie says, "I have them," she might as well have pulled rabbits out of her hat. My question: Where? I am looking where she's looking. I still see—nothing.

She steps aside with an inviting gesture, and when I put my eye to her telescope I see—and this is incredible—eight wolves at a kill *two miles away*. Looking in that direction with my binoculars, I spot an oblong dark smudge. Black pepper on snow. The ravens. Of course.

By the time wolves kill an animal they've been chasing, ravens are already arriving. This has been going on so long that ravens have been called "wolf birds." Wolf kills often attract ravens by the dozen. Yet if humans put out elk carcasses, ravens generally ignore them. Ravens trust wolves. Ravens don't trust humans. The memory of the poisoned carcasses must still be a lesson in the raven educational curriculum.

It wasn't always like that. The Norse god Odin, though father of all gods, had certain shortcomings of sight and memory and knowledge. Odin drank only wine and spoke only in poetry. He needed help getting by. Compensating for his godly shortfalls were the two ravens Hugin and Munin (mind and memory), who perched upon his shoulders to bring news of the wide world, and the two wolves at his side, who provided meat and nourishment. All were one god-man-raven-wolf superpack. The power resided in the synergy of that coalition. Biologist and author Bernd Heinrich has wondered whether the Odin myth captured "a powerful hunting alliance, a past we have long forgotten as we abandoned our hunting cultures to become herders and agriculturists." And ranchers.

Researcher Derek Craighead was astonished when he discovered that the flying young of one pair of ravens sometimes spent a night in the active nest of other ravens on the opposite side of a mountain. "We always believed ravens were territorial," he noted, "but they seem to have a vast networked society, not as simple a thing as we thought."

Wolves, apes, elephants, whales—obviously bright. But birds have a lot going on despite their much smaller brains. Especially wolf birds and their crow-family relatives the jays, magpies, jackdaws, and rooks. They're *smart*. They're keenly observant, and some share with dolphins, elephants, and certain carnivores a tool kit of reasoning, planning, flexibility, insight, and imagination—at an ape's level of intelligence.

In Yellowstone, where ravens have dotted their black exclamation points onto the white pages of the snows of many thousands of winters, they've taught themselves something new: how to unzip hikers' packs. The relative size of the forebrain—the "thinking" part—in ravens and their relatives is significantly larger than in other birds, with the exception of some parrots. A raven's brain is the same size relative to its body weight as a chimpanzee's. Some scientists credit this forebrain enlargement as the thing that gives members of the crow family "primate-like intelligence."

In one experiment, ravens encountered something they'd never seen before: meat hanging on a string. The only way to get the food is to pull the string up a little with your bill, clamp a foot on the string after each pull, and repeat this till the morsel is within reach. Some ravens nail this solution on their first encounter. That means that just by looking at the setup, they understand cause and effect and can *imagine* the solution. They don't fumble around with trial and error. In another experiment, ravens rapidly solved a puzzle that left a human toddler and two poodles (who'd been previously familiarized with the components) acting like they "don't even realize there's a puzzle to solve."

Now let's get personal. Betty is a New Caledonian crow who uses pre-vious experience to reason through problems. Having learned what a hook is, she bends straight wire into hooks to reach food deep inside tubes. Pre-sented with an array of wires, Betty chooses the correct length and diam-eter for the task before her. There's no reason to suspect that Betty is exceptional among New Caledonian crows. She just happened to find her way into an experimental situation with a bunch of humans. New Cale-donian crows can use tools to solve an eight-step puzzle to get at food (you can watch it on the Web).

Crowlike rooks have no difficulty figuring out a clear plastic appara-tus that requires the birds to drop a stone down a tube to release a tasty grub. Plus, they choose the largest of several available stones. When exper-imenters narrowed the tube, three out of four birds immediately chose *smaller* stones that would fit the narrower tube; they didn't even try the larger stones they'd previously used. When they could not get a stone but were given a stick, all the tested rooks immediately inserted the stick into the tube, then pushed down to release the treat. When experimenters gave them either a stone that was too large plus a stick that would work *or* a stone that would work plus a stick that was too short, each bird—on the first try—chose the tool that would deliver the treat. When given a stick with side branches that needed to be snapped off before it would fit down the tube, each rook handily snapped the branches off, often before the first try. When the grub was in a little bucket in a tube and the rooks were given a straight piece of wire, they all made a hook to snag the bucket handle and retrieve the snack. They knew what they wanted and they understood what they were doing to get it. This is true insight. Cockatoos, which are parrots, also use insight in solving never-before-encountered puzzles involving locks, screws, and latches.

Crows remember—for years—the faces of researchers who have caught and handled them for purposes like marking and measuring. When they see those people walk across campus, they loudly scold them. From those scolding crows, other crows learn who these seemingly bad and dangerous individuals are and give warning alarms at the sight of them. Researchers have resorted to wearing masks or costumes when catching crows so that they won't be yelled at for years afterward.

These birds and we apes have differently structured brains (we have the mammal neocortex with ape enlargement, and they have the bird nidopallium with corvid enlargement). But great minds think alike, and we have converged on some of the same mental abilities. Two researchers wrote, "New Caledonian crows and now rooks have been shown to rival, and in some cases outperform, chimpanzees in physical tasks, leading us to question our understanding of the evolution of intelligence." Scientists have concluded that, overall, ravens, crows, and their kin "display similar intelligent behavior as the great apes." Who knew? And what else don't we?

We've been talking a bit about tool-using birds. And that's a good enough excuse for a quick look at tool using in general. As with other major concepts about behavior, there isn't one agreed-upon definition of "tool." Mine is: a thing that isn't part of your body that you use to accomplish a goal.

In 1960, Jane Goodall rocked the world with "news" that chimps were using twigs—in other words, *tools*—to extract termites. Up to that moment, scientists had believed that only humans made any tools, and that tools "made us human." But—wait a minute! In 1844, a missionary to Liberia named Thomas Savage wrote that wild chimpanzees crack nuts "with stones precisely in the manner of human beings." Science did not rediscover the missionary's position for more than a century. And in 1887 another observer reported seeing macaque monkeys routinely using rocks to break open oysters at low tide. How could such a thing, reported in writing, be severed from memory? Perhaps tool use didn't seem so surprising until, by the Space Age, our estrangement from nature had grown so thorough. Somehow the world forgot—and *then* Goodall's rediscovery prompted the preeminent anthropologist Louis Leakey to famously respond, "Now we must redefine tool, redefine Man, or accept chimpanzees as humans." It forced reevaluation of the human monopoly on reasoning and culture. It made us seem a bit less special. But the only thing "new" about it was our awareness of it; chimpanzees had been making tools for hundreds of thousands of years. And now we know of simple tool use in primates, elephants, sea otters, dolphins, various birds, octopuses— even insects.

While Jane Goodall's Tanzanian chimps use tools, they do not use *stone* tools. In certain other regions, such as Guinea and Ivory Coast, chimpanzees skillfully wield rocks or wood hammers to smash nuts. Cracking nuts occupies 10 to 15 percent of their feeding time, and during three or four peak months a chimpanzee can crack into thirty-five hundred fat-rich food calories daily. Nut smashing allows chimpanzees access to at least six species of nuts that would be inaccessible without their tools. These fat-city chimps enjoy a higher reproductive rate and more gregarious grouping habits. And yet many chimpanzee populations across Africa with access to the same rocks, logs, and nuts make no use of the rich nuts or the potential tools sitting right there in front of them. In one place they puncture the ground using a stick, then use a flexible tool to dip in for termites. In some places chimpanzees make tools in advance; sometimes they use two tools to accomplish one task. From dipping for ants and pounding palm nuts to sponging up water with leaves to using spears for hunting bushbabies in tree holes, some populations do, some don't. The techniques are learned; they're cultural.

Though very much like chimps and so smart, free-living bonobos haven't been seen using tools. Most people think gorillas don't, either, but Vicki Fishlock and her colleagues discovered gorillas testing the depth of marsh water with sticks, and using staves to lean out over water, and moving logs to make bridges over swampy places. One gorilla in captivity spontaneously invented and became proficient at cracking nuts using a club-and-anvil technique. Capuchin monkeys transport heavy stones to nut-cracking sites, choosing those of appropriate size as anvils and, as hammers, stones of weights appropriate for splitting open different kinds of nuts.

Faced with food out of reach inside a tube, orangutans spit water into the tube to float the food within reach. Rooks and Eurasian jays in similar experiments got the same result by adding stones to raise the water level until they could reach the floating food. At our house, the parrots use water as a softening tool. When we give our parrots a dry bread crust, Kane immediately goes to the water and drops it in. After a few moments, he picks up the soggy bread and carries it to the opposite side of the cage, drops it into his food bowl, and begins eating the now nicely water-softened treat. Rosebud often does the same thing. (We were not in the market for parrots, but when I noticed Kane in the pet shop intentionally softening food with water I was so intrigued that they both came home with us. One of them must have invented it and the other imitated it. They're different species—he is a quaker and she is a green-cheeked conure—so their food dunking counts as interspecies cultural transmission, a phenomenon apparently unknown to science. You read it here first!)

Elephants make at least six types of tools, mostly for scratching and removing ticks. They might make a back scratcher one day, and the next use rocks or logs to flatten an electric fence. Sea otters smash shellfish with stones while floating on their backs. New Caledonian crows and wood-pecker (carpenter) finches use thorns to probe tree holes for bugs. Some other crows press automobiles into service as nutcrackers, dropping nuts on active roads. Gulls drop hard-shelled prey such as clams, scallops, and whelks onto hard surfaces. If they didn't, they would not be able to get at the food within those fortresses. Seizing rock-hard prey below sea level, they fly upward with obvious intent, fly over a surface that will accomplish the job they need done, then release the prey, using gravity as an acceleration tool. If at first they don't succeed, they fly again.

I've countless times watched gulls crack shellfish by dropping them on stony shorelines, roads, or flat roofs. (But *only* flat ones. My neighbors can tell when it's going to be a good year for scallops by how much their home gets bombarded. Luckily for me, I have a pitched roof.) White scavenger vultures crack eggs with rocks. Green herons fish using insects as bait or a loose feather dropped onto the water as a lure, or even bread. An amazing online video shows a heron using a piece of bread to bait fish into range; the heron is quite persistent and repositions the bait several times before nailing a big fish. (Search for: green heron catching fish.)

Humpback whales blow rising circles of bubbles to "net" schools of prey fish, in a kind of "corral and confuse" strategy. When they lunge upward through the net for a massive gulp, they blow the roof off the sea in great explosions of water, one of the world's most spectacular sights.

And here's something no one would ever have guessed: in the Bahamas, bottlenose dolphins hit the sand with their flukes or flippers to create a swirling, moving vortex of water that looks like a sand tornado. The tornado moves along the bottom and then stops and hovers. Where it hovers, the dolphin digs its snout into the sand. What is going on? Turns out, a vortex is drawn to a low-pressure spot such as is created when it encounters a hole. The dolphins are making visual vortices as a tool to find fish holes! "It was one of the most amazing things I had ever seen," wrote Denise Herzing, "but it looked pretty routine for the dolphins."

Many tool-using animals begin their technological careers by playing with sticks and stones, a little like human children learning to talk by babbling, or experiencing the physical world by playing with blocks, able to explore their capabilities with no pressure.

A scientific article has an excellent video of a cockatoo named Figaro making and modifying sticklike tools from a section of bamboo, to rake food into his cage. (Two other cockatoos offered bamboo did not make raking tools, indicating that birds, like us, vary in insight.) I thought it was astonishing when I saw an orangutan using straw to sweep within reach food that had been placed just beyond her grasp, but blue jays will do something similar: they'll tear paper into strips to rake in food pellets.

Among the fishes, surprisingly, some wrasse species use rocks and coral as anvils to break open urchins and shellfish. Wrasses also have a relatively large brain-weight-to-body-weight ratio, like tool-using birds and primates. Some cichlids and catfish glue their eggs to leaves and small rocks, then carry them away if their nest is threatened. Archerfish knock insects from overhanging leaves and branches by spitting jets of water.

Insect tool use is astonishing, because it's so unexpected and looks so conscious. Various ants, upon encountering liquefied food such as rotting fruit, go away and return a minute later with leaves, sand grains, or soft wood to sop up the substance; then each ant can carry its weight in liquid food to the nest. Other ants harass competitors by tossing sand grains into their nest entrances, essentially throwing sand into the gears of their economy, costing them time and trouble. Still other ants lure ground-nesting bees from the safety of their burrow. John D. Pierce describes how they manage it: "Upon discovering the bee, the ant normally paused several seconds at the rim of the nest, then wandered over the surrounding area, picked up a small piece of soil . . . headed straight back to the nest entrance, held the soil over the entrance . . . hesitated for about 1 second, and then dropped the soil." A few seconds later, the ant goes for more. Meanwhile, other ants arrive. The bee is now at the surface, lunging with its mandibles. This is dragon combat in miniature. When the bee attempts to bolt from its now-spoiled protection, the ants attack, killing the bee.

Certain wasps use pebbles and earth to lock their prey into a hole along with the wasps' eggs (which will hatch and feed on the prey). Pierce again: "The major pellet is placed deep in the burrow and additional, smaller objects are placed above it. . . . On some occasions the female uses a pebble in the manner of a hammer to pound the fill into a compact plug." Assassin bugs hunt termites by first dressing in camouflage, sticking pieces of the termites' nest to their body so they smell like the nest. After catching a termite and sucking its body hollow, the bug holds the carcass in front of its head, "jiggling it slightly in a movement that may be described as 'tantalizing.'" When a termite grabs the carcass, the bug, pulling steadily backward, draws the clinging worker termite slowly from the nest. As soon as the worker's head is in an accessible position, "the bug grasps it quickly," dropping its carcass-lure, and injects its poison.

These are just a few examples of insect tool use. Never mind the astounding construction, ventilation, food production, and heat-trapping functions of termite mounds, beehives, spiderwebs, and the like. Does this mean that tool-using insects are very smart? Or does it mean that tool-making doesn't imply intelligence? Or is toolmaking less impressive if tiny-brained insects do it? And how *about* those tiny brains: Are they aware? How aware? How are they making decisions, judging their progress? Does our own brain—as the science seems to show—come to a decision and then inform our conscious mind, making us merely believe that we thought of it?

Ironically, as the best toolmakers, we are the most helpless of beasts. We do not sleep, eat, or even defecate without resorting to tools and devices to aid our efforts and accomplish our goals. If we managed to survive a night in a wilderness lying naked and toolless on the ground, our most urgent imperative would be to start making enough implements to keep us alive. Yet rather than make tools, most of us just use tools made by others. From items in nature, most people cannot create the most basic human tools: a fire, a piece of cord, a knife, any article of clothing. Virtually none of us has ever invented anything. I am using a computer at this moment. I have no idea how it works or how it was made. As a species, we are pretty impressive. But as individuals, most of us, given bolts of cloth wrapped in a bow, couldn't sew a decent shirt.

Yet we enjoy congratulating ourselves for collective human achievements in which we individually deserve no credit, achievements most of us don't comprehend. Humanity's collective horrors, we generously don't like to claim credit for. (In the twentieth century, civilized people killed over one hundred million other civilized people, and this century hasn't gotten off to a great start.) We'd rather focus on our ability to make planes and computers, a soothing delusion to those of us who don't actually know how to make planes and computers, which may be just as well. Dogs don't know that people make cars. About what it actually takes to put together a car—the mining, the metallurgy, the chemistry, the design and assembly, the factory origin and distribution—dogs know slightly less than most of us, who just hop in and go for the ride.

Wolf Music

We hop in and convoy east. From directly across the valley, it's now easy to see black ravens on white snow surrounding a reddened patch. Into focus in my scope come several rouge-faced Lamar wolves yanking mightily at the newly exposed rib cage of a freshly erstwhile elk they're rapidly reducing to a bony rack. Its crown of sharp antlers now entirely beside the point, the elk's severed head lies faceup in the snow like a set-aside trophy. Little seems left for the ravens and magpies, but their presence and patience assure them that it will be enough. Working such kills is their profession. In all, nine wolves attend. Seven, bellies already full, are sprawled contentedly on nearby snowy ground.

Pause to ponder the metaphysics: an elk running for its life is converted to wolf flesh and wolf bone and wolf nerve whose dedication becomes chasing elk who run for their lives to avoid the fate that is pursuing them, a fate built entirely from creatures just like themselves. Predator presages Borg. Overhead the sky livens with playful croaks also made of elk. Later, predator falls, freeing all former elk made wolf, made raven, made bear, to resume a brief stint as grass. Grass's predator, elk, grazes. Grass again becomes elk, and one of Forever's many pinwheels clicks one full turn. Humanity, of course, becomes Forever's disruptor, Borg-eating super-Borg.

I stamp my feet to see whether they're still there. As we stand around waiting for the wolves to sleep off their food coma, we watchers watch, chat, snack, compare boots and gloves again, and generally do everything except warm up. Rick starts telling me about a sickly yearling named for the white triangle on his chest. It was bad times. The pack was rife with mange, which was sapping its members' strength, and rival wolves had killed their matriarch.

One morning, Triangle the yearling and his three-and-a-half-year-old sister were confronted by three hostile wolves. Triangle and his sister ran and—perhaps as a strategy or just in sudden panic—split up. The intruders pursued the sister. She was the pack's fastest runner, but one of the attackers caught her and pulled her down. She instantly jumped up, wheeled, and ran for the river. He caught her twice more; she jumped up each time, running with all she had.

When she was tackled for the fourth time, all three brothers piled in. Now she was on her back, fighting desperately, with two wolves violently shaking their heads as they bit her belly and hindquarters while the biggest wolf moved in and clamped his jaws on her throat for the kill.

As she continued fighting, the big wolf stepped back. He had bitten into her radio collar housing. But he seemed to figure it out and repositioned for a bite that would avoid the collar. Rick was watching through his telescope, and in that instant a small black blur turned the scene to chaos. It was Triangle, the little, sick yearling, in effect trying to snatch his big sister from the jaws of death.

His arrival distracted the attackers, two of whom broke off their assault to chase him. His sister leapt to her feet, streaking toward the river. Triangle only briefly distracted all three attackers. They caught his sister just as she reached the riverbank, and all four tumbled into the water. She had no chance against all of them. But Triangle again rocketed in. In the confusion, his sister splashed across the river and, emerging with a seriously bleeding gash across her chest, ran across the valley and upslope to the north, toward her family's den.

Meanwhile, the three males were all chasing Triangle. And in a race that might have set a record in odds beating, the sick, small wolf outran his tormentors. They gave up and went off across the valley at a slow trot, headed south.

A week and a half passed before Triangle's big sister reappeared. She survived her wounds and got well. Triangle continued to hunt and be seen with the pack for months, but over time his mange infection and his injuries from the fight must have weakened and eventually overcome him.

Rick considers Triangle "a hero."

Hmm. Humans can be heroes, but what could Triangle have been thinking?

Rick says, "We judge heroism not by what is thought but what is done." What are firefighters thinking when they rush into a burning room to rescue a stranger's child and there is no time to think? If a hero is someone who risks their life for the life of another, then as for Triangle, the sickly little-brother wolf who saved his big sister—you tell me.

After a couple of hours of snoozing, the Lamars rouse, enjoy an enthusiastic greeting rally, then fan out just a few paces and begin howling. The human chatter quickly attenuates to silence, and we listen. The deep fascination. Felt. Yet inexplicable. The wolves' voices waver, change pitch. Both gleeful and mournful. Haunting.

We pay rapt attention to their singing. It seems to matter to us, somehow. Our reaction stands in contrast to how much other animals seem to ignore our music. So, does music—and how moved we are by music—"make us human"? Or is howling the music of wolves, by wolves and for wolves?

Our own music is—obviously—in the range of human hearing, usually at tempos corresponding to human heartbeats or footbeats, and with patterns and intonations comparable to qualities of human speech. These qualities of sound, tempo, and tone are technically called "paralinguistic features," and they all come under the umbrella term "prosody." Prosody refers to the sound qualities of human speech. Prosody is why, for instance, listeners can distinguish lullabies from yelling in any language. It's why a piano, violin, saxophone, or guitar solo can sound mysteriously like a person telling a story, though it is devoid of words.

Sound sometimes carries emotion across species. Dogs understand when people are arguing. And we understand a growl as a warning. Some of the emotional freight carried by animal sounds has ancient roots. Our shared capacity to perceive it is part of our deep inheritance. Whether the receiving ears belong to a human, a dog, or a horse, several short upward calls cause increased excitement, long descending calls are calming, and a single short abrupt sound can pause a misbehaving dog or a child with a hand in the cookie jar.

Psychologists who study these roots and shared perceptions speak of the "prehuman origin of prosody." For humans and likely others, the template is prepared in utero. A human just prior to coming into the world has been hearing the beat of its mother's heart, the tonalities of her voice, the pace and pattern of her steps. The capacity to perceive meaning in a mother's tone of voice is present at birth. (Many birds begin vocalizing to their chicks as soon as the chick has chiseled a tiny hole in its eggshell.) In many cultures, most musical instruments produce sounds between about 200 and 900 hertz, the frequency range of the adult human female voice. Not a coincidence.

If there's a need to get more explicit, lyrics can do that. But who hasn't swooned to a Brazilian bossa nova singer even without being able to understand Portuguese, or been moved by religious chants or world music with unintelligible singing, or by an opera with unintelligible singing, or rock music—with unintelligible singing? Singing in another language presents some of the purest prosody; we don't understand the words, so we respond entirely to vocal sounds and rhythmic patterns. Sometimes leaving the lyrics' verbal meaning on the other side of a language barrier purifies, one might say, the music that a voice sends. If the lyrics were the most important thing, we'd just listen to poetry. Or simply read the libretto. But no; the *sound* is the thing.

Music, in a sense, abstracts the tone and rhythm of our lives and hands it back to us as an aural package of pure emotion-triggering stimulation. Hearing music changes our brain chemistry, leading to, for instance, increased norepinephrine levels and the associated sense of well-being. The word "musicality" seems to refer subconsciously to how successful the music's sounds are in capturing, conveying, and triggering emotions. But how much of the emotional content of music comes across to the listener depends a bit on how culturally familiar the listener is with the music's *prosody,* its tonal and rhythmic qualities. In humans, some of this is universal, but some of it is cultural. In a given culture, instruments often reflect the tonal qualities of the language. Think of the twang of Oriental instruments or the drawl of American country and western music's pedal steel guitars.

Why aren't other animals into human music? It's not for lack of trying by humans. Researchers report, for instance, that "pigeons trained to discriminate between Bach's Toccata and Fugue in D Minor for organ versus Stravinsky's *Rite of Spring* for orchestra could eventually discriminate between the pieces, but learned slowly and did not reach high levels of performance."

Some animals *are* into music. My friend Darrel says that his tortoise "loves Mexican music" and starts running around when he hears it. Our green-cheeked conure, Rosebud, struts a lively dance to music having a strong beat, especially if we bring out the percussion toys. The Internet is replete with dancing parrots, such as Snowball, a sulphur-crested cockatoo.

But the fact is, many other animals find much of our music somewhere between uninteresting and annoying. Given a choice of human music, two species of monkeys preferred slow tempos to fast, Mozart to rock; but given a choice among various types of human music and none—they preferred silence.

It looks, however, like that was because they were subjected to *human* music. Human music presents sounds and rhythms corresponding to *human* characteristics. When tamarin monkeys were played calming human music and agitating human music, they calmed in response to both. The "fast" music that agitates humans had a beat merely matching the resting heart rate of the monkeys. Humans feel it as invigorating, but to the tamarins it was nothing to get excited about.

How about translating the things that make human music appealing to humans—and creating *monkey* music? Well, researchers did that.

They looked at the frequency range, tempos, and pitch changes of the vocalizations of cotton-top tamarin monkeys and their heart rates. (For instance, while almost all human music is pitched between 200 and 900 hertz, tamarin threat calls come in frequencies of 1,600 to 2,000 hertz.) The researchers then created music within those parameters. They avoided imitating tamarin calls; used human musical techniques such as counterpoint lines, ending phrases with resolution to a chord; and applied a structure such as A-B-A. They wrote music intended to be calming and music intended to get the monkeys agitated. The music was played on a cello. It was the world's first tamarin music. The monkeys responded to the monkey music as the composers had intended. After hearing the calming monkey music, the monkeys moved less and ate more. After hearing the agitating music, they tended to sit up and take notice.

Music composed for monkeys appeared to evoke the intended kind of emotional responses. (The researchers noted, "We and others who have listened to the tamarin music do not find it particularly pleasant and one might suspect that the tamarins might react to human music in a similar way.") Sound can convey emotional *qualities* such as anger, fear, joy, affection, sadness, and excitement, plus varying *intensities* of those emotions. Music can capture and convey these emotions. Researchers have noted that "music is one of the best forms of emotional communication known." The emotion in music affects your own emotions; exciting music gets you excited. This is another example of "emotional contagion." Music, indeed, *relies* on emotional contagion, which derives from the human brain's ability to trigger an emotional match. In a word, the ability to form an emotional match is: empathy. Feel the music.

After the haunting howling vanished into the thin air, the wolves ate a little more, then enjoyed some romping play. Then, another food coma. When two coyotes come to the carcass, the wolves, lying on the snow less than twenty yards from the rack of bones, are so gorged they don't care. They will eat and sleep all through the following day and night. I leave them to their wolf dreams. Voices come and voices go. The song remains. But songs, too, can be silenced.

At dawn, minus three Fahrenheit. Another wintry springtime day. Another fairy dusting coats the Lamar Valley. Stillness, silence.

I'm alone, determined in this ironclad cold to discover wolves on my own. I scope along the valley's far slopes, searching for wolves by not looking for wolves. I'm looking for a pack's tracks somewhere in the fresh snow, maybe ravens gathering.

Doug McLaughlin arrives.

Intent on finding something good before he does, I am glassing down one particular snowfield when he says, "Got one."

The bastard.

On the far skyline of a snowy ridge above timber walks a wolf. A gliding bald eagle leads me down, down the snowy slope. And just at the toe of that slope, where it meets the expanse of the valley floor, I discover a riddling of tracks, and a broad patch of hair and blood and ravens. Down behind a very slight rise, I see just the head of that now-landed eagle, pulling energetically on something. So the main carcass is there, just out of view.

Almost directly upslope—Doug points this out, too—that eagle's mate is already on eggs, sitting on a huge stick nest in a cottonwood canopy.

I've never been in a place where spring and winter collide so forcefully. A coyote trots in and begins tugging jerkily on the piece of the carcass that the eagle had been working.

Now a total of nine Lamar wolves, four blacks, five grays, just coming out of the timber, are descending the long slope, breaking a new trail in the snow, past the patch of scattered hair and blood, ambling toward the carcass as casually as if returning to the salad bar for seconds. The domineering sister is on the left, acting every bit the alpha. Her low-ranking littermate sister, Middle Gray, walks next to her. They seem peaceable with each other right now.

The scrambling coyotes sense the wolves' supreme assurance. Fully convened in core territory, luxuriantly fed, warm in their furs, they're in charge and, essentially, untouchable.

From behind the little declivity, one wolf pulls up into view the red rib cage and spinal column of an elk. No head. Another wolf draws over a big piece of hide. Others tear off individual ribs or find leg bones and plop down, chewing contentedly. These wolves need about three elk per week. Less than a mile away from the belly-full wolves, I see three elk browsing peacefully on the river's re-willowed banks.

After the wolves have fed, and fed again, the nearly yearlings chase and play bitey-face, just like our dogs at home. You'd think wolves wouldn't need to play snap-dragon after actual big-game hunting and a massive gorge. But all work and no play . . . Apparently, wolves need balance in their lives, too.

After the frolic, they drift a few yards away and scatter themselves like furry throw rugs, sprawling like they're at the beach, making no attempt, while lying on the snow, to curl up or conserve heat. Profligate and fat. They are neither cold nor hungry. That's one difference between them and me.

Middle Gray wakes. She's a sweet-tempered pup-loving three-year-old. Her domineering sister—the same sister who won't tolerate Eight-twenty—is the source of her low status. Middle Gray disappears uphill.

"Is she looking for Eight-twenty?" Laurie wonders aloud.

· · ·

A couple of hours later, the rest of the pack members wake, stretch, pee. They rally, tails wagging, licking faces. A little bit of bounding play. Then for several minutes, all howl. Then all rest.

An hour later, Rick gets a strong signal from Eight-twenty. She's in line with the wolves sleeping on that slope. Approaching them? She must be conflicted.

Her nemesis sister remains asleep.

A while later, it's clear that Eight-twenty is some distance away from the rest—and staying there.

"And where's 'Fifty-five?" Laurie would like to know. Seven Fifty-five isn't beeping in. All day yesterday, he wasn't heard from.

"He has good reason to be afraid," Doug comments. They talk without taking their eyes from their scopes, searching for a glimpse of Eight-twenty.

"Yes," Laurie agrees provisionally, "but if those males really wanted to kill him? They would have done it the last time."

Midmorning, snowing heavily. Nobody moving much.

Earlier, somebody had seen a grizzly ambling into the willows at the Confluence. Because we don't have anything better to do than drive in a snowstorm, we travel a couple of miles to there, where the willowed braiding channels of Soda Butte Creek finger their way into the Lamar River.

In the waters of March, an otter is swimming upstream in a blizzard.

The bear had been at an old elk skeleton that's poking through the snow. Rousing from hibernation into the wintry side of spring, the bear likely spent a nighttime cracking marrowbones, perhaps pop-suckling from the frozen, brainful skull. Winter carcasses maintain their value here for weeks, feeding many. Wolves, coyotes, foxes . . . Ravens, eagles, magpies . . . Life depends on death. As Wolf reaps, so Wolf sows.

A black Lamar wolf who had been sleeping where we just came from— is here! What? And now we see that the pack has somehow drifted through the snow ahead of us. We thought we'd left them to drive here. Yet here they are. Like magic.

In heavy-slanting snow, they almost float. This is the closest we've been, only about a hundred yards between us. I've got a binocular-eyeful of the Hoodoo male Tall Gray trotting along a willow thicket, his amber eyes shoot me a straight glance. But he shows no interest, and his gaze doesn't hold.

After sniffing the frozen bones, they all sprawl in blizzard contentment, as snugly at home as Chula and Jude on our rugs. If anything about the wolves frightens me, it's simply their comfort, which so highlights my frailty.

Fog and a heavier horizontal snow squall descend briefly, like a white stage curtain, and when the curtain rises, all the wolves have somehow ghosted from view.

At three-thirty in the afternoon I am no longer in Lamar Valley. Two distant, unseen wolves are howling back and forth across some span of air, of time. The howls grow a little fainter and a little stronger. These wolves are moving. Who are they? Like smoke signals of sound, howls continue rising into the air at intervals. The message, we can't yet deciper.

We get just a glimpse of a black wolf traveling across a small clearing on a heavily timbered slope. Nape hackles, lanky-looking; this individual is younger than two years. But that's all we can tell. This wolf is going *away* from the other caller, who seems to be trailing.

Taking my eye from the scope, I watch the moving black grain that is the wolf disappear over a ridge. We drive two miles to get a view of the mountain's opposite slope and stand outside, waiting, as the temperature drops, hoping for the black grain to reappear.

Two hours later we're still waiting, now occasionally hearing the same wolves' intermittent, muffled howls. They're coming.

Four hours since our glimpse. Occasional howls traded. No further glimpses. We can hear that the black one we've seen is still traveling and howling.

There is the black wolf again!

And from a hill at least a mile from that black traveler, but now suddenly clear in open air, a strange cry rises. Part howl, part wail. A long, pained, yearning smudge of sound. The word is: anguished. Is this as its author feels it?

Up there—. A lone gray wolf steps onto the skyline above us, looking down on the valley, looking to where the black one had—just a moment ago—appeared and vanished.

The black wolf, continually howling though again unseen, continues moving away from the gray.

I glance back up to the gray, who shows the indecisiveness of a lost dog, turning this way, then that. The gray wolf finally decides to turn *away*, trotting up and over the back of the ridge on which it had suddenly appeared, toward where it had come from.

"The black one *has* to be Jet Black," Laurie says. A young female, of the Junction Butte pack.

"The gray has to be Seven Fifty-five." That's McLaughlin's opinion.

A long silence seems to settle. And yet—am I still hearing him or are my ears playing tricks? His yearnful howling seems lodged in my head, and I almost think I hear it continually haunting the thin breeze.

My companions shake their heads; they're not hearing what I'm hearing.

Rick calls. Seven Fifty-five's signal is coming in. Not far from the Junction pack. And Eight-twenty's signal is coming in, too, from Slough, not too far from her father.

Is that why he just turned around?

Dusk leaves those questions in the air.

The Hunter Is a Lonely Heart

———•———

Rick's radio informs him that Seven Fifty-five has been detected way down, west of Lamar Valley, about seven miles from here. We go. Walking to a low rise, we find Seven Fifty-five's fresh tracks in the snow right around us. Some of us think we hear one deep, resonant howl, from a heavily timbered hill east of us. I'm not sure.

Then another wolf—one of the Junction Butte pack—howls as if replying from a partly fog-shrouded mountainside.

Now in our scopes we can see several Junction Butte wolves traveling along in the snows of a high timber-fringed ridge about a mile away. The Junctions' two alphas, the male Puff and his noticeably limping mate, Ragged Tail, lead two gray and three black wolves through fresh powder in bright sunlight, breaking trail while descending a series of cascading tiers of land called benches. "He's a good leader," Rick says, his eye still pressed to his scope. "He likes to stay ahead of the pack."

High on the precipice of one bench, overlooking expansive sage flats and the winding bison-dotted banks of Crystal Creek, the Junction wolves pause as if admiring their holdings.

Heads thrown back, they raise into the wide sky a minutes-long chorus that sounds like morning in the original world. Masters of their lives. Keepers of the place that keeps them. Truly first nations. For more than an hour, they continue alternately traveling and howling—sometimes both—slowly descending, in and out of timber. Through the broad landscape they continue down, down, stopping to howl, down across open snow, howling again, into a maze of tall sage and—. Gone.

We, of course, pack up and travel, too. We'll wait for them about a mile away, where they should reappear. Partly because I am so cold, partly because they are out of sight, I wonder at our dogged determination to keep seeing, seeing, seeing them. Why not just feel glad that we saw and heard wolves, and call it a day? Why this so interests us is almost as mysterious as where they'll be next. But day by day it grows more special. Something true is here, something real. Something deeply proven, saner, and lasting. They live with a kind of faith in themselves. They have endured. So I'm into waiting out the next sighting. Laurie says we keep at it because wolves *do* things. When wolves are doing nothing, we want to know what they will do next. She adds, "When someone says to me, 'There's a grizzly bear just down the road!,' all I want to know is 'Is there a wolf with it?'"

One *sees* bison and bighorns, but one *watches* wolves. Even the bison and bighorns watch wolves. When we are not actually watching wolves, we wait until there are wolves to watch. "When I was a classroom teacher," Laurie relates, "I loved watching the kids. How they all fit in. In elementary school, some liked the sandbox, some liked chasing each other; and I watched them develop over years. That's how I look at the wolves. It's kinda the same thing. It's not just *wolves* we're following. It's wolves' *stories*."

The howling continues, off and on, wolves telling their own stories.

Suddenly, through the crystal air from the east—behind us—comes a reply more resonant and mournful than the Junction pack's chorus. Seven Fifty-five. We don't see him. How individual and unique he sounds!

Wolves may not have words. What they have is: recognition, motivation, emotion, mental images, a mind map of their landscape, a roster of their community, a bank of memories and learned skills, and a catalog of scents with meanings attached as definitions. As we see in dogs, that's easily more than enough to understand who's who and what's where in a lifetime.

For over an hour, back and forth they keep the conversation going, taking turns or overlapping. Humans play music, sometimes for long jams.

I've done it. It's a very social experience. The tribe convenes. Listeners gather. We must get a lot out of it, because the experience is worth the time of the players, who send sounds to one another and to those who stay to listen. There is a kind of story there, wordless but full of life.

Seven Fifty-five is the baritone I'd imagined a big, howling wolf would be. So distinctive, I would recognize him easily tomorrow and the next day. I hear his recent tragedy in his song. But do the other wolves hear his pathos? Am I projecting? Or is he?

Seven Fifty-five remains unseen, howling from a heavily timbered, heavily bouldered slope caged in slanted tree shadows. With our scopes we are performing a minute inspection of those shadows. I'm searching in vain when Laurie says, "Got him."

Laurie's near-supernatural powers of sight exceed her explanatory prowess. "By the big tree to the left of that boulder" is not helping me narrow my scrutiny of an entire mountainside sprouting big trees and prickled with boulders. It's easier to just look through her scope. So I step up and look in.

I see a rock in a patch of sunlight under the bough of a pine. And a silvered ruff of fur. And from that, Seven Fifty-five suddenly materializes, as if my eyes needed a moment to paint him there, curled on a boulder with his chin resting on his front paws like a pup on a porch. Waiting for—a thought? A decision? A little company?

"How the hell did you ever see him?"

"I don't know—I just saw fur."

Seven Fifty-five sits up on that big boulder. He's just perched there in a patch of sunlight like a fluffy dog, looking across the valley toward the howling Junctions.

He'd been born black, but in his late middle years he is graying, making him two-toned from any angle, with a distinctive two-toned face. Dark forehead, dark ears, dark snout; abruptly contrasting light gray from his lower jaw out to the deep fur of his wide facial ruff; he has a dark cape and dark tail but creamy-looking sides. A very distinctive wolf. He throws his head back. It takes a second or two for his howl to reach me. So he's about a third of a mile away.

He looks directly into my scope. People have told me that a wolf looks *right through* you. But you know what I realize? That's because a wolf isn't interested in you. It's always hard for humans to accept that we're not the most important thing anyone's ever seen. To him I am not significant enough to look right through. He looks right *past* me. His yellow eyes merely note me momentarily: "human." Like something useless that a fisherman throws back: "Can't eat these things."

The Junction female Jet Black, howling as she goes, moves down onto the sage flats, across the steep-cut creek bank, and into willows. This is the wolf Seven Fifty-five was trailing yesterday, who was moving away from him.

Now the Junctions have all moved down to the valley floor, strung out with their alpha couple, Ragged Tail and Puff, leading, going in and out of view in the willows, howling occasionally.

Seven Fifty-five remains alert to the Junctions' intermittent callings, turning his head a bit, triangulating, maintaining his fix on their precise movements in the valley.

He angles his head again, seeming to look straight into my telescope. I keep my gaze on him long enough—*those eyes, that face*—that the wind makes my eyes water up. I look away to wipe them, and when I look back into the scope I see an empty rock. Seven Fifty-five has vanished.

Suddenly, incredibly, he's sauntering across the same low ridge we are standing on, just two hundred yards to our left. I turn and get him square in the middle of my telephoto lens and trigger off a series of images of him nicely side-lit, his focus attentively ahead, two-toned like no other wolf I've seen. Riding his long legs at a brisk lope through the sagebrush, he's heading straight toward the willows that screen Jet Black. From our hill, we can see both him and her and the Junctions. But from *his* angle on the valley floor, they are over the creek bank, out of sight.

Puff stiffens, then goes into a stalk. Puff has a silly name, but he is a survivor and, says Laurie, "He's a gutsy wolf for his size." Abruptly Puff charges into the sagebrush, running fast and hard. Seven Fifty-five bursts from the sage into the wide open. But Puff seems to be chasing his own daughter, Jet Black, as if reprimanding her. Now he breaks off the chase.

The Junction yearlings are rallying together, tail flags flying, noses and bodies rubbing. Is all the adult maneuvering making them anxious?

It's making me anxious.

Seven Fifty-five runs straight back in their direction. He seems determined to make contact. He submerges deep into the sagebrush. The Junctions are looking around as if they don't know where he is.

Ragged Tail's bushy tail suddenly snaps straight out behind her. She has seen him.

Seven Fifty-five abruptly banks. He is taking a big risk. Or maybe he understands his odds. Quite likely, he is acquainted with the Junctions. Puff has earned a reputation as a wolf who avoids fighting (that might be why he's still alive). Still, Seven Fifty-five has cause for caution. But he seems determined to woo. He needs a partner and has come here to get one. He knows whom he wants. He appears conflicted between attraction and fear. And logically so. Even if Puff isn't very aggressive, Seven Fifty-five has no guarantees. He's outnumbered, vulnerable.

Rick comments, "If you're a male with a high degree of social intelligence, you might be able to gain a pack's acceptance through displays of submission. Or you might be able to lure an adult daughter away. These things happen." He adds, "So there are a lot of similarities between wolves and what you already know about human behavior."

Years ago, when the Druids and the Slough wolves were bitter enemies, a Druid male made friends with all the Slough pups. Then he made friends with all the adult females. Rick says, "This took him some time. But he kept away from the big guy. When the big guy came toward him, he would kind of tuck his tail and walk away, showing he was no threat at all and withdrawing." Later, when the alpha male approached, "he stayed put but rolled on his back, then licked the big guy's face." And that worked. "If he had played it differently, he might have been killed."

We would not guess that a wolf could have a long-term social strategy, Rick acknowledges. "But when you actually watch them day after day, year after year, the best-fitting explanations are that they can have a strategy, that they sometimes do, and that outcomes depend on how individual personalities play their hand, in a sense. You never really know what to expect."

Seven Fifty-five is suddenly face-to-face with the matriarch Ragged Tail, atop the creek-bank bluff. Their meeting could be described as cordial but cool. No aggression. But why doesn't Puff attack? He has to realize that Seven Fifty-five is meeting his mate.

It's hard to suppress the impression that Seven Fifty-five is greeting the lady of the house like a nervous suitor before a date with her daughter. Seven Fifty-five and Jet Black seem mutually interested in each other but keep a distance. I think they've previously met. Laurie calls her Miss Personality, but at just under two years old she is on the lowest rung of the Junctions' female ladder.

So Jet Black's decision is high-stakes: she'll either leave her parents and siblings and try to breed—with a single male who has no pack and no territory—or stay, remain low-status, and basically live to help her parents. The key word is "live."

To my amazement, Seven Fifty-five and Jet Black mingle momentarily. It's very brief; the two alphas show themselves immediately, and their mere appearance is like pointing Seven Fifty-five toward the door. Puff and Ragged Tail seem interested in keeping their pack under some semblance of control. It doesn't serve them to lose a pack member.

Seven Fifty-five returns into the maze of snowy sage. I wonder how he's feeling. I know this isn't the end of the story.

A Will to Live

In late March, the wolf mosaic remains in full flux. One morning during the third week of March, while springtime has decided to sleep in at *minus* seventeen Fahrenheit, Doug McLaughlin sees an explosion of wolves chasing Eight-twenty. The biggest Hoodoo male and Eight-twenty's domineering big sister are in it. Butterfly is there. But it isn't brutal like before. Most crucially, though, reconciliation isn't in the cards. Eight-twenty tries to follow, but they reject her again.

The next day we see Eight-twenty way west, over at Tower Junction, eating from a carcass killed by the Junction wolves. Risky. Eight-twenty has never been there before. She appears to be scent-tracking her father. He's gone to Hellroaring Creek.

The Lamars head in the opposite direction, east, out of the park to where the Hoodoos had come from, into that strange and imaginary place of real dangers called Wyoming.

During March's final week, Eight-twenty is still occasionally beeping in from the western part of the park. Seven Fifty-five is still investing a lot of time wooing Jet Black from the outskirts of the Junction pack, and dodging Puff. Meanwhile, Puff seems content to just chase. Everyone says he isn't one to fight, and he isn't.

In early April, hundreds of elk begin returning to the park. A bit perplexingly, Seven Fifty-five has been hanging with a new, unfamiliar female, who seems to return to him some youthful vigor. They play on a snow slope and slide all the way down. Then *she* mounts *him*—and this isn't even the breeding season anymore. "Whoever she is," comments Laurie, "she's a frisky one."

Meanwhile, Eight-twenty has fallen in with her older sister Middle Gray and a huge new gray male. Middle Gray, formerly living a reduced-status life under her domineering littermate, has never shown any aggression toward Eight-twenty. She's got one of her black sisters with her, but when that sister starts to bully Eight-twenty, Middle Gray slams her to the ground and stands over her. Is Middle Gray seeing herself as a new alpha? Is the Lamar pack fissioning further?

This could work out for Eight-twenty. Yet reason doesn't entirely rule the decisions of wolves or people. And maybe that black sister just won't cut it out. At any rate, it isn't long before Eight-twenty is again gone.

She travels back westward alone, for miles and miles. And over near Hellroaring she finds her father, with his new female. The new female probably treats Eight-twenty as a rival. The next day, Eight-twenty is missing.

Why can't this family get along? They did—before hunters shot up the pack.

At Slough, a group of elk are pointed like weather vanes at seven wolves coming through a gap. The Lamar wolves are back. The bigger of the Hoodoos, known as Tall, quickens his pace. One of the black two-year-old sisters starts running in the opposite direction. Next, one elk, separated, is running hard across the flats toward the water. Behind the elk, a black streak is steadily gaining. It's a long chase. The black wolf grabs the elk by its hock and hangs on while being whipped up and down like a fluttering leaf. The elk makes it to the creek just as the other wolves converge. Some very wet wolves accomplish their task.

In a surprise appearance, Middle Gray suddenly emerges, looking pregnant—and gets a very warm greeting from all the Lamar wolves. Where is her huge new male? What's going on? Six months ago, the Lamars were a cohesive group. Now the tribe is in continual flux.

April 18 delivers a steely minus five degrees Fahrenheit with a spiteful wind. Winter seems to have its jaws locked on Yellowstone's throat. Yet

heeding internal alarm clocks, grizzly moms with new cubs are emerging from hibernation, showing themselves here and there. Pronghorn
"antelope" are back up in Lamar Valley.

The Lamars slow their trot to look at a newborn bison. It would seem
easy, but bison have their own sense of life and death, and like most people,
they prefer life. The small band of bison adults charges the wolves, easily
routing them. Doug tells me that sometimes bison even have "funerals,"
involving a solemn group inspection of a fallen comrade, reminiscent of
elephants' habits. I never knew.

Meanwhile, Laurie wants to rename Puff and has chosen "Hunter." Inso-
far as hunting is what wolves do, I don't think Hunter is a very distinguishing name for a wolf. So I'll let Laurie tell you what she just saw him do:

"Puff split an elk herd that had started to run and picked out a healthy
yearling. The elk was already probably twice Puff's weight and was running
like a rocket. But Puff was pouring on extra speed, closing the gap. He
briefly got a throat hold, then a leg hold, but two adult female elk came to
its defense; one seemed to trample Puff. This let the yearling bolt. It put a
lot of distance between itself and him. At that point, the elk should have
escaped. But incredibly, Puff ran a wide circle around those other elk, and
followed the one he'd attacked. Again he poured on extra speed and was
soon beside the galloping yearling elk. Puff lunged and latched onto the
elk's throat, but the yearling elk was strong and had no intention of going
down. Puff then body-checked the elk while applying a violent twist, and
the elk stumbled and fell. Puff's pack caught up and all ate heavily. Puff is
not a large wolf. But having survived a ravaging mange that gave him his
name, he has turned into a relentless and seriously effective hunter."

In May, Seven Fifty-five and Eight-twenty are taking turns sending beeps
from Mount Everts, near the park's northwest border. Father and daughter seem to have reunited. But they don't appear to be spending their time
together. Likely Eight-twenty can't get along comfortably with her father's
new mate. Eight-twenty drifts north, out of the park.

Meanwhile, the Lamars' Middle Gray has pups, in the old Druid pack
den. No one has seen the pups, but she's obviously nursing, and her mate
and her black sister have been hauling plenty of food up toward the den

site. The rest of what had been the Lamars are out east of the park again in Wyoming, where the Hoodoo males are from.

Someone has the courtesy to share this on Facebook: "Middle Gray would make a nice rug." The taunts show that shooting wolves isn't just hunting. It's a way of acting out some people's desire to inflict pain not just on wolves but on people who aren't like themselves.

By July, Eight-twenty is fairly stationary, outside the park near Jardine, Montana. To a wolf like Eight-twenty, who has been in the vicinity of people and has crossed roads all her life, Jardine offers plenty of opportunities for misunderstandings.

> *THE BILLINGS GAZETTE,* August 26.
> 1 HOUR AGO—A young collared female gray wolf was shot by a Jardine-area resident on Saturday after the wolf had recently come in close proximity to a number of homes. . . . It was shot while eating a chicken.

Having dined on a few chickens myself, I pause to ponder getting shot for doing so. The article notes, without quite tying the earlier deaths to the cascading turmoil among the wolves all winter and summer, leading to this latest shooting loss:

> Two other members of the Lamar Pack were shot last fall during Wyoming's hunting season, one of which was the pack's alpha female. All together, hunters in surrounding states shot 12 wolves last year that spent part of their time inside Yellowstone's boundaries. Six of the 12 wolves were collared.

So ends the sad ballad of Eight-twenty, a wolf in her precocious prime who, in a better world, might have matured to lead a worthy wolf enterprise. She'd never quite learned—despite the killings of her uncle and her famous mother—that humans can be murder.

On a happy note—if you like wolves, and I do—Seven Fifty-five is finally keeping steady company with Jet Black. She was the lowest-ranking Junction wolf. As an underdog, she seems worth rooting for. When she and

Seven Fifty-five greet, they are all over each other with wagging tails and happiness. Amid such death and tragedy, there is in their daily ritual of renewal a genuinely redemptive quality. Their affirmations of each other easily come across. We all feel it.

Though the catastrophe that befell him and his pack the previous autumn seemed to suggest that his life was over, Seven Fifty-five would endure. Two years after he lost his mate, his brother, his pack, and his territory, I finished this book. On the day I did, I logged in to Laurie Lyman's Yellowstone Reports. And there he was. Seven Fifty-five, still alive and well, having proved himself a survivor against all odds. It reminded me of a point Doug Smith had made emphatically. "Wolves are tough," he'd told me. "Very—*tough*."

Domestic Servants

In wolves' personalities, abilities, and social dynamics, I've perceived self-governing dogs who get the chance to grow up and take charge of their own lives. They have their own families; their own social order, politics, and ambitions; they make their own decisions and earn their livings. They are full captains of their lives, sometimes cruel and violent with one another, often friendly, loyal, and supportive. They know who to protect and who to attack. They're their own masters, their own best friends. Always unleashed. No food bowls. They have freedom, and with freedom comes hazard. Wolves have plenty of both. They're always playing for keeps.

The similarity with dogs runs deep because all dogs are domesticated wolves. The communicative postures we see in dogs—the crouching invitation to play; the submissive rolling onto the back, tail between legs; and the loyalty—these are wolf behaviors that survive in the domesticated wolves we live among.

One very important thing before we proceed: "domesticated" means genetically changed from wild ancestors by selective breeding. One way to think of it: zoos have wild animals in captivity; farms have domesticated animals. Arboretums have wild plants; farms have domesticated plants. "Domesticated" doesn't mean tame. A wolf that has been captive-born and bottle-raised and is entirely tame is a wolf in captivity; it's not *domesticated*. Pet parrots, even captive-bred, are not domesticated.

Domestication implies intentional human creation of animal and plant varieties or breeds that don't exist in nature. Classically, that's

accomplished by selective breeding, but now technicians use genetic engi-
neering, too. Farmers, fanciers, and researchers select traits they want and
promote them. They breed individuals with those traits together, resulting
in many varieties of domestic chickens, cows, pigs, pigeons, laboratory
rats, terriers, farmed salmon, corn, rice, wheat, and so on, all genetically
changed from their naturally evolved, wild ancestors.

Dogs make domestication *very* interesting. Dogs *may* be the only creatures
ever to have domesticated themselves. And—they *might not* be the only
such creatures.

So, all dogs were domesticated from free-living gray wolves. Their
domestication occurred, at most, just a few times—maybe only once—by
about fifteen thousand years ago. All dogs are a domestic *variety* of wolf. A
highly *variable* variety. Outwardly, many dogs look so different from
wolves that scientists first assumed dogs were a different species. Taxon-
omists had named the domestic dog *Canis familiaris*. Gray wolves are
called *Canis lupus*. And, obviously, dog breeds—greyhounds, mastiffs,
dachsunds—are genetically different from one another. But as scientists
peer into dogs' DNA, they've realized that while the visual differences are
major, the genetic changes are minuscule. One can argue over the definition of "species" (many do). But very little has changed *genetically* between
wolf and domestic dog. So little that scientists have changed dogs' Latin
name back to wolf, back to their maiden name, *Canis lupus,* telling us
who they were before we adopted them, who they really are. Dogs are
now *Canis lupus familiaris*. Wolf. But *familiaris* says they are *our* wolf.

When people first realized that dogs are direct descendants of gray
wolves, they imagined Stone Age people finding wolf pups and bringing
them into caves as the first pets. But as best we know now, the origin of
dogs instead goes like this: wolves hung around human camps and caves,
scrounging cast-off bones and the remains of butchered carcasses. The
less skittish wolves came closer and got more. Wolves with fuller bellies
raised more pups, more of which were born carrying those successful
genes for less skittishness. Those slightly changed pups grew up around
humans, prompting more and friendlier interactions.
   These wolves' tendency to alert at the approach of strangers and

predators would have been valuable. The humans would have encouraged such guards to hang around by providing more scraps. The extra scraps would have boosted the survival of more people-friendly wolf pups.

This went on for centuries. These human-oriented wolves specialized in exploiting humans as a new resource. Human camps were a new habitat. Friendlies got the most food. Eventually they were regulars around camps, started guarding human camps as their territories, and began to tag along when humans went hunting. Those friendly genes proliferated.

Researchers now believe that's how the first dogs happened; by making the first overture, wolves unintentionally *domesticated themselves* to humans.

But that first unintended domestication wasn't entirely one-way. Because dogs received survival advantages, they evolved to be oriented toward humans. And because humans received survival advantages from dogs, we became oriented toward dogs. As our unique emotional response to their wagging tails whispers, they domesticated us a bit, too.

Dogs pick up on human cues such as pointing in a way that even chimpanzees, surprisingly, do not. (Elephants can also follow human pointing.) Wolves, too, can follow human pointing to find hidden food—without being trained to do so. Sometimes, wolves perform better than domestic dogs. After all, free-living wolves must be finely attuned to where one another's attention is directed. Dogs understand fully where humans' attention is focused, so if you throw a ball and turn away, your dog will bring the ball around to where you're facing. Most important, though, the wolf researchers say that "domestication is not a prerequisite for human-like social cognition." Human-like social cognition—remember that.

Humans, meanwhile, became very dog-oriented. But did humans actually *evolve* an orientation toward dogs? I think of it this way: Is there anything a cow, chicken, bunny, goat, or pig does with its body that gives you the same feeling you get from seeing a dog's wagging tail? Of course, some people don't like dogs—some love the purr of a cat or the sight of a pig—but many people feel their dog's bond as part of the family's. Humans' moods match dogs' moods more intimately; most people seem to experience more emotional contagion—in other words, more empathy—with dogs than with any other species.

So I think, yes, to a certain extent, humans and dogs coevolved.

Humans became dog-reliant, perhaps even dog-dependent. Dogs were trackers and hunting partners, dogs were alarm systems and well-armed guards; dogs defended and played with human children. Dogs cleaned up. Dogs were hot-water bottles. Humans provided dogs with food, and dogs served as security personnel and guides. And helped secure food, too.

Once we had them, they had us; we could not do without them. Dogs accompanied people to the far ends of the earth. It's likely that hunting peoples would not have penetrated the high Arctic without them. In the Far North, dogs were transportation and freight haulers, and in the toughest times, dogs became food. Dogs went to Australia, too (where, faced with a new continent and no competitors, some rewilded, becoming dingoes). Dogs came across the Bering Sea to the Americas. In *Empire of the Summer Moon*, S. C. Gwynne writes of an 1860 army attack on a Comanche camp: "In the midst of the struggle, the white soldiers found themselves under attack from fifteen or so dogs from the Indian camp, who tried valiantly to defend their Indian masters. Almost all were shot and killed." The dogs' loyalties and self-identities made them enemy combatants. Dogs seem to be wherever people are. I once visited Papua New Guinea to work on sea turtles. On that wild coast, tiny villages of just twenty to eighty inhabitants were separated from one another by distances requiring hours of walking. Yet each village had several semiferal dogs hanging around, living off scraps—as their ancestors had started doing tens of thousands of years ago.

Thousands of years later, we're still uncovering dogs' hidden abilities. At least one border collie responds to an unfamiliar word by choosing the unfamiliar object. Asked to "Get the dax!," the dog apparently reasons along these lines: "There's a ball here, but she didn't ask for ball. 'Dax' must mean this other thing that I've never seen before." Such skills of inference, scientists write, "have only been demonstrated previously for language learning in human children."

Even dogs have some perceptual gaps, though. Non-human great apes are good at inferring the location of hidden food by, for instance, noticing that one board is lying flat and another is tilted up, indicating that there's something under it. Dogs are terrible at that (that's a visual cue; dogs excel at searching by smell). Ravens—the wolf birds—are able to figure out which of several crossed strings is connected to the treat. Primates do such tasks easily. Dogs are terrible at this, too (again, it's purely visual).

But a raven probably couldn't guide a blind person across the street or warn you of an oncoming seizure. Dogs can do this in stride, with pride.

Wolves are social, and humans are *enormously* social. Dogs can depend on us because we're both social enough to understand each other. Depending on humans, though, comes with costs (as we all know). Dependence requires giving up freedom, self-sufficiency, and a sense of self-reliance. When dogs and wolves are presented with a locked box containing food, the dogs almost immediately stop trying and start looking back and forth from the human to the box, as if saying, "Can you help me?" Wolves keep trying to solve the task until the test times out. Wolves perform as well as or better than dogs on practical problem solving and memory tasks. Dogs' social skills are their wolf heritage, but dogs' *orientation toward humans* resulted from domestication.

We're at a strange place in a unique relationship: Dogs domesticated themselves. Dogs domesticated not *only* themselves—dogs domesticated humans, too. In becoming reliant on us, they made us reliant on them. We became like each other.

During dogs' ancient first domestication, the genes that changed "overlap extensively" with genes that were changing in humans, too. These include genes involved in digestion and metabolism of starches, as humans and their dogs transitioned from hunters to agricultural omnivores. They also involve genes that affect certain neurological processes and cancer, as well as genes having pivotal roles in transporting dietary cholesterol.

Dogs' friendliness results from their genetically altered brain chemistry. Ours does, too. In both dogs and humans, increasingly crowded living conditions put pressure on the serotonin system to reduce aggression. "Humans have had to tame themselves," said Adam Boyko of Cornell University, adding that "similar to dogs—you have to tolerate the presence of others." In both dogs and humans, the same gene controls a protein that transports serotonin, a key neurotransmitter. Variations in this gene cause pathologies of aggression, depression, obsessive-compulsive disorder, and autism. Strikingly, dogs and humans share several compulsive disorders and respond similarly to the same antidepressant drugs, such as serotonin reuptake inhibitors. I've often wondered why free-living animals never seem to suffer psychological problems or mood disorders (with the possible exception of elephants driven mad by interactions with humans). Now it seems that those problems come in a bundle with living in dense proximity to people. Commenting on how much we can learn from dogs about human disorders, the serotonin researchers concluded, "Our best friend in the animal kingdom might provide us with one of the most enchanting systems for illuminating our understandings of human evolution and disease."

It would seem that wolves, as our canine companions, have come to join in the human conversation in some unique and telling ways. And remarkably, we understand each other pretty doggone well.

But why did dogs start looking less like wolves and more like dogs? *That* happened on its own, too. Turns out—and no one could have predicted this, and no one did—that animals with genes for friendliness look different. The same genes that deliver desire for friendly contact with humans bundle a raft of stowaway *physical* traits. In discussing selective breeding in domestic animals, Darwin in the first chapter of *On the Origin of Species* noted, "If a man goes on selecting . . . he will almost certainly modify unintentionally other parts of the structure, owing to the mysterious laws of correlation." Weirdly, in various mammals (not just dogs), genes that create the hormones that reduce fear and aggression and increase friendliness *also* create floppy ears, curly tails, blotchy markings, shorter faces, and rounder heads.

Though he didn't understand why (genes were unknown then), Darwin did observe that "not a single domestic animal can be named which has not in some country drooping ears." Now, floppy ears are *not* found in *any* wild animal adult. But don't we just love floppy ears? Some of the traits that humans find so endearing and huggable in dogs are exactly the ones that come along, by sheer coincidence, with a genetic predisposition for friendliness. Our emotional response to those floppy ears makes it seem as if *our own* friendly feelings toward dogs did indeed coevolve with theirs toward us, so that we experience a positive emotional reaction to animals who *look* most friendly. They *are* most friendly. And as I've mentioned, how about our instant response to that wagging tail? Humans and dogs, it appears, learned to love each other in deep, genetic ways. It sure can feel that way.

But how do we know that friendliness, floppy ears, and a curled tail are tangled genetically? To explain, we need to bring in the famous Russian foxes. In 1959, scientists in Siberia began a decades-long experiment on the genetic basis of behavior. To see whether friendliness has a genetic basis, they set up two populations of captive foxes. One population bred randomly. In the other population, only foxes who acted less aggressive, less fearful, and friendlier to humans were allowed to breed. The researchers were interested *only* in aggression—not looks. They got more than they'd bargained for.

Over several generations—faster than expected, in fact—the experimental foxes got friendlier. (It wasn't because of mere captivity; decades later, the randomly breeding foxes continued to both look and act like wild foxes.) But what really surprised the scientists—and everyone else—was that from generation to generation, the line of friendlier foxes started to *look* different. Researchers were getting foxes with droopy ears; splotchy coats of differing textures; curling, wagging tails; shorter legs; smaller heads with smaller brains; and shorter faces with smaller teeth. And in addition to having kinky hair, some had kinky ideas, showing out-of-season and nonreproductive sexual behaviors (hold that thought). As adults, the friendly foxes continued to behave like juveniles, by acting submissive, whining, and giving higher-pitched barks. Foxes, in other words, more like dogs.

In the bred-for-friendliness foxes, scientists found reductions in blood levels of various hormones affecting fear and fight (including glucocorticoids, adrenocorticotropic hormone, and the adrenal response to stress). They also found changed chemical activities in brain regions that regulate emotional and defensive responses. (These changes affected the serotonin, noradrenaline, and dopamine transmitter systems.) It's not surprising that foxes born friendlier have different brain chemical activity than foxes fearful and aggressive with people. They would have to, because brain chemicals create behavioral tendencies.

So: genes resulting in invisible brain changes for friendly behavior also result in highly visible changes in how foxes look. The scientists did not care how the foxes looked; they selected *only* for friendly behavior. The changed looks came along for the ride, tangled into the friendliness genes.

Some researchers call the whole set of traits that hitchhike on friendliness genes "domestication syndrome." Among the controlled chaos of DNA are multitasking efficiencies such that the *same* hormone—dopamine, say—that affects mood might *also* affect coat color.

Researchers and farmers might have *thought* that they were selecting for mellow personalities, but they were really selecting for juvenile-style adults, perpetual pups. Cows and pigs, goats, rabbits—similar physical changes came along with tractability. The human breeder says, "Don't bite," but the genome hears, "Never grow up." So maybe a better name than "domestication syndrome" would be "Peter Pan syndrome."

Some wolves seem to have self-domesticated into dogs. In the process, they domesticated us to them. And none of this was planned; it just happened. That means: simply preventing aggressive individuals from breeding can eventually get you a population of more juvenile-like adults—regardless of species.

Two Ends of the Same Leash

Let's raise the stakes. We're going to move from dogs to apes.

With no training, chimpanzees can cooperate to pull ropes together to retrieve a heavy box of food. But they seldom do. They have a problem. The problem is: they can be their own worst enemies. Chimpanzees will not cooperate on rope pulling unless: (1) the food can be shared, (2) the partners cannot reach each other, and (3) the partners previously shared food. If those criteria aren't met, chimpanzees will not cooperate. The reasons: subordinate chimpanzees won't risk attack by dominants, and dominants can't seem to control their aggressive impulses toward subordinates who are getting some food—even if by not cooperating, the dominant one doesn't get any food, either. They can't cooperate even when cooperation is actually quite selfish. "Be nice, and everybody eats" is too much to ask of a chimpanzee.

Chimpanzees lack dogs' human-like skills because chimpanzees lack dogs' human-like cooperative tendencies. We know dogs got it as wolves. But where on Earth did the human-like temperament of *humans* come from?

Some researchers believe that early humans had to evolve a conciliatory, friendly, human-like temperament *before* communicative and cooperative behaviors could offer such enormous advantages.

Well, if the advantages are so great, why haven't chimpanzees evolved a conciliatory, friendly, human-like temperament? Some, it seems, did. And this is constructive for considering humans. Ever wonder why, when chimps are often so nasty, bonobos are so friendly and sexy with one another? Self-domestication seems to be the answer. Bonobos, like wolves, seem to have self-domesticated. More remarkably in the bonobo case, their self-domestication had nothing at all to do with humans. Bonobos evolved after the Congo River formed, about a million years ago, isolating a population of chimpanzees south of the river. Somehow, for the bonobos, a lot changed.

As chimpanzees reach adulthood, they become less playful and largely intolerant of sharing. Bonobos are like chimps who never quite grow up. Adult bonobos play with each other the way juvenile chimpanzees play with each other. Bonobos famously indulge in copious sex play and non-reproductive sexual behavior. This sexiness with one another greatly dissipates tensions, boosting food sharing and cooperation and friendly meetings between groups. In the same setup where chimpanzees could not overcome their aggression to cooperate in pulling ropes to access a treat-filled box, bonobos played, foreplayed, and happily shared the food like youngsters. "Adult bonobos," researchers commented, "performed at the level of juvenile chimpanzees." If, compared to their warmongering, covetous, political chimp cousins, bonobos sound like kids playing and being cooperative—that's the point.

Chimpanzee between-group encounters are always tense and can at times be warlike. For males caught without their group's support, such encounters sometimes turn lethal. And males sometimes kill babies of other groups. In contrast, bonobos meeting strange groups of bonobos often just backtrack into their own territories. But sometimes bonobo groups mingle, flirt, and frolic, using the opportunity for a social call of grooming and horsing around. And if the mood is right, they may indulge in a polite—though, by chimpanzee standards, wildly promiscuous—orgy.

Chimps are jealous, ambitious, frequently aggressive within their own group. Chimpanzee groups are male-dominated. Male chimps form coalitions against other males, and dominance is mainly about monopolizing fertile females (result: dominant males achieve disproportionate fatherhood; this is the main advantage of their aggressive, status-seeking side). A bonobo group's dominant individual is never a male, always a female. Female coalitions dominate, preserve the peace, and keep males socially submissive. Female authority dampens male aggression.

A male bonobo's closest lifelong bond is to his mother (as in killer whales). Fights are rare, and various sexual combinations often settle disputes. Females choose whom they wish to mate with and when—and they're not very choosy. Females prefer belly-to-belly copulation and often initiate sex—things that self-respecting chimp females would never think of doing. Bonobos, it might be said, are trisexual; they'll try anything with anybody. Sharing is caring. Many males in the group sire similar numbers of young.

Were the chimpanzee ancestors of bonobos who found themselves newly cut off on the south side of the Congo River a small group with mostly females? Even so, how would female dominance and leadership become institutionalized? Mysteries.

As in all of us, bonobo personality parameters are brain-related. Compared to chimpanzees, bonobo brains have more gray matter in regions involved in perceiving distress in others. Bonobos have a larger nerve pathway for controlling aggressive impulses, inhibiting harm toward others. This limits stress, dissipates tension, and reduces anxiety to levels that open up room for sex and play.

Even as adults, bonobos have brain hormones and blood chemistries typical of juveniles, including higher levels of serotonin, which suppresses aggression, and lower stress hormones. Brain chemistry typical of juveniles prompts juvenile behaviors such as playfulness, friendliness, and trust. The underlying genetic changes result in a suite of behavioral, internal, and physical features. For instance, compared to chimpanzees, bonobos mature more slowly physically, psychologically, and socially, and they learn skills more slowly. The *same* genes that lower aggressiveness by creating a more juvenile-like brain chemistry also create more juvenile physical features. An adult bonobo's skull looks like an adolescent chimp's. More to the point, an adult bonobo's skull looks like a juvenile *bonobo's* skull. Their heads are more like juveniles' heads in shape and size, and bonobos have smaller canine teeth (20 percent smaller than male chimpanzees'). Compared to chimps, bonobos have smaller jaws in flatter faces. Female chimpanzees lose the labia majora as they mature; bonobos, like humans, retain them into adulthood. Female bonobos' clitoris and genitalia are situated more toward the front than are chimpanzees', helping explain their preference for the missionary position. Bonobos have lost their lip pigmentation; they have fetching pinkish lips.

Why and how bonobos self-domesticated is still not clear, though there's an intriguing possibility that relates to bonobos having wandered into a sort of food-filled Garden of Eden. That's a bit of an exaggeration, but food abundance might be the difference. Adult chimpanzees can remember many more places where they've seen food hidden than can bonobos, suggesting that food for chimps is scarcer and requires more searching, more skills, and more work. And in fact, bonobos forage for shorter periods of time, over smaller areas. No gorillas live where bonobos live. So to the limited extent that gorilla and chimpanzee foods overlap, there's more food for bonobos in their gorilla-less domain. Fights between chimps can result in serious injury or death. Chimps often forage at some distance from one another, and females spend significant time alone. Bonobos' more concentrated food supply facilitates larger foraging groups. So it seems that bonobos had to deal with the tensions and friction caused by closer, more frequent contacts. This necessitated a capacity for more peaceful interpersonal relationships. Somehow, bonobos achieved this, almost completely liberating themselves from violence.

Primate expert Richard Wrangham describes bonobos as "chimpanzees with a threefold path to peace. They have reduced the level of violence in relations between the sexes, in relations among males, and in relations between communities." Japanese primatologist Takeshi Furuichi, the only person who has studied both free-living chimps and bonobos, observed succinctly, "With bonobos everything is peaceful. When I see bonobos, they seem to be enjoying their lives."

"Following this line of reasoning," say Brian Hare and Michael Tomasello, sounding very cautious as they tiptoe into a suggestion, "one might seriously entertain the hypothesis that an important first step in the evolution of modern human societies was a kind of self-domestication."

How's that? Hare and Tomasello, recalling those Russian foxes in which only the friendly ones survived to breed, speculated that humans "either killed or ostracized those who were over-aggressive or despotic. Thus, like domestic dogs, this selection for tamer emotional reactivity put our hominid ancestors in a new adaptive space," preparing the ground for evolution of "modern human-like forms of social interaction and communication."

Well, killing the overly aggressive doesn't sound too friendly. But isn't that the whole history of democracy and the struggle for human freedom and dignity? And today don't we give governments the job of killing, and isolating the overly aggressive among us by putting them behind bars?

Aren't we, by fits and starts, even through the darkness of unspeakable human horrors, always searching for peace, always seeking more perfect ways of taming ourselves? Self-domestication does indeed seem part of the human program. The process of becoming more civil is called civilization.

I've long thought that humanity seems to be in a juvenile phase, and have assumed that we were somehow on a trajectory of maturation. If the self-domestication idea is correct, it means that we *are* in a juvenile phase, but that we're going in an increasingly infantilizing direction.

The juvenile traits of adult humans are so apparent that as early as 1926 one scientist summed us up this way: "If I wished to express the basic principle of my ideas in a somewhat strongly worded sentence, I would say that man, in his bodily development, is a primate fetus that has become sexually mature."

Experimental foxes, our family dogs, and free-living bonobos all show that along for the ride with a genetic predisposition for friendliness come other incidental, unselected changes programmed into the same stretches of DNA. Turns out that in all domesticated animals a bundle of things accompany a tamer, human-caused life. Over many generations of domestication, most mammals (cows, pigs, sheep, goats, even guinea pigs) actually got smaller, with slenderized skeletons compared to those of their more robust free-living ancestral relatives. Typically the skull's brain case becomes smaller, as does the brain itself. The muzzle shortens, causing relative flattening of the face. This creates tooth-crowding problems, and teeth themselves become smaller. Size differences between males and females narrow. Hair colors and textures diversify. Fat-storage capacity increases under the skin and in muscle. Activity decreases, and docility increases. Breeding seasons lengthen, along with increases in courtship behavior, sexual stimulation, nonconceptive sexual behaviors, multiple births, and milk production. Juvenile behaviors, including play and low levels of male aggression, extend into adulthood.

During domestication, dogs lost as much as 30 percent of their brain size relative to body weight compared with wolves. Pigs, ferrets, about the same; minks, about 20 percent; horses, about 15 percent. Domestic animals gone feral don't regain brain size, showing that the loss is indeed genetic. Compared to their wild progenitors, domestic guinea pigs are

less interested in aggression, more interested in sex, and pay less attention to the environment around them. Genetic changes that alter the
endocrine system drive domestic animals toward such differences.

In the Late Pleistocene, numerous similar physical changes also appeared
in some human populations. Let's consult the human fossil record. Though
we tend to assume that civilization made humans larger, earlier humans
actually shrank. By about 18,000 years ago, the shrinkage totaled a considerable four inches (ten centimeters) of height in Europe. This trend
toward diminishment continued during the transition into agriculture.
Climate warming can probably be ruled out as a reason for shrinking.
Humans tend—with notable exceptions—to respond to warm climates
over evolutionary time by getting taller, because in us, longer limbs increase
cooling capacity. This suggests that some other transformation was
causing human shortening. (Improvements in health and nutrition over
the last 200 years have again made Europeans as tall as their Paleolithic
ancestors.)

Other changes came as humans attained our modern looks. Compared
to Neanderthals, the first modern humans, at 130,000 years ago, "had much
smaller faces," according to American anthropologist Osbjorn Pearson.
At the end of the Pleistocene, certain human groups *and* their associated
animals begin progressively to show *parallel* reductions in size and stat-
ure, shortening of the face and jaws, tooth crowding, and reduced tooth
size. Pearson says that size reduction of our face and teeth began during
the long process toward settled living.

Experts debate whether human brain size *relative* to body weight
has declined. But regardless, we have smaller brains than did Neanderthals. Australian males in both sedentary and nomadic populations, for
example, underwent a 9 percent decline in skull volume from the Pleistocene to our present epoch, the Holocene. By roughly 12,000 years ago,
such changes characterized nearly all humans. Our modern brains, with
a volume of about 1,350 cubic centimeters, are 10 percent smaller than the
1,500-cubic-centimeter brain formerly possessed by Neanderthals. With
agriculture, those physical changes generally accelerated.

Animals under early domestication received shelter, a diet altered by agriculture, and protection from predators through relative confinement.

This reduced their sensory needs, facilitating further domestication. As our domesticated animals settled in for a life of reduced activity and stimulation, so did humans. As people provided safer, more sedentary conditions for their livestock, they did the same for themselves. The confinement was mutual. By moving out of nature and settling onto farms, we became in a real sense just another farm animal. Caltech brain researcher John Allman says that through agriculture and other ways of reducing daily hazards of existence, humans domesticated themselves. We now depend on others to provide food and our shelter. We're a lot like poodles in that regard.

Domestic creatures don't need to live by their wits. It behooves them to be accepting of their lot, not uppity. Cows and goats don't seem very alert to their surroundings; they don't have to be. And neither do the people who keep them. Archaeologist Colin Groves writes, "Humans have undergone a reduction in environmental awareness in parallel to domestic species and for exactly the same reason." He explains that domestication is a kind of partnership in which "each partner is, to a degree, sheltered by its association with the other." Groves says security has cost us a certain dulling of senses, explaining that brain changes have caused in humans "the decline of environmental appreciation."

I find that statement arresting. He uses the word "environmental" to mean our total surrounding environment. But I think, too, about our awareness of the natural world. "To speak truly," observed Emerson long ago, "few adult persons can see nature. Most persons do not see the sun."

I always thought humanity's alienation from nature was just a habit. Clearly, there have recently been tribal hunter-gatherers living in close resonance with the living world. Yet what if the problem of alienation from nature—the idea of the banishment from the Garden—is embedded into real human nature? Is ours a human nature altered by self-domestication? Have we been domesticated by our own domestic animals? What if "domestication syndrome" is human nature?

Robinson Jeffers:

> . . . the race of man was made
> By shock and agony . . .
> . . . they learned to butcher beasts and to slaughter men,
> And hate the world.

． ． ．

So: Did the changes we imposed on ourselves in the process of settling into our civilizing "domesticity" really bring to humans changes in fat storage, sexuality, frequency of multiple births, declining sensory abilities, flatter faces with crowded teeth, and docility similar to those we see in other domestic animals?

What is certain: our view of ourselves as postevolutionary, purely cultural creatures, standing outside of selective pressures and in control of our fate is wrong. We tend to think that humans evolved, then stopped evolving and started culture. Far from it. The onset of agriculture and the flowering cultures of civilization were themselves enormous changes in the human environment, massively altering selective pressures. Pressures to maintain a hunter's size and strength and senses relaxed, while pressure to behave cooperatively, expand social skills, and suppress violent urges intensified. Small, slender, thin-boned people might not have excelled at the rigors of mammoth hunting. But people requiring fewer calories might have survived better during crop failures. Darwin coined the term "natural selection" because he was comparing the mechanics of what happens in nature with the artificial selection applied in raising livestock. But nature doesn't really select; it filters. The environment works as a filter, and as the environment changes, it filters differently. The point is: as the pressures change, we remain a work in progress.

Look at the evolving creature in the mirror. Realize that we've got a ways to go before we're universally as good to one another, or as much fun with one another, as are bonobos.

───

It's been said that no two species are more alike than wolves and humans. If you watch wolves not just in all their beauty and adaptability but in all their brutality, it's hard to escape that conclusion.

Living as we do in family packs, fending off the human wolves among us, managing the wolves within us, we can easily recognize in real wolves their social dilemmas and their status quests. No wonder Native Americans saw wolves as a sibling spirit.

Consider the similarities between male wolves and men. They're quite striking. Males of very few species *directly* enhance the survival of females or young year-round. For example, most male birds provide food to females and young only during the breeding season. In a few fishes and a few monkey species, males actively care for young, but only while the young are small. Owl monkey males carry and protect babies, but they don't feed them. Male lemurs challenge predators, allowing females to escape, but they don't provide any food.

Helping procure food year-round, bringing food to babies, helping raise young to full maturity over several years, *and* defending females and offspring against individuals who threaten their safety is a very rare package to find in a male. Human males and wolf males—that's about it. And of the two, the more dependably faithful isn't us. Male wolves more reliably stick with the program, helping raise young *and* actually helping females survive.

Chimpanzees seem much closer to humans, but male chimps don't help feed babies or bring food back to a home site. Wolves and humans can understand each other better. That's one reason why we invited wolves, instead of chimpanzees, into our lives. Wolves and dogs and us; it's not surprising that we found one another. We deserve one another. We were made for one another.

In our kitchens, on our floors and sofas, in our laps and in our beds, hidden in plain sight among humans who've forgotten the ancient origins of our eager pets, wolves in dogs' clothing riddle our homes and transform our families and our hearts, wagging their sweet tails, being our working partners and best friends. It's not as ironic as it might seem that a creature as violent as a wolf could domesticate itself into humanity's most beloved companion. They could say something similar about us. In the form of their dog avatar, wolves mesh with humans through their astute, innate grasp of in-group, out-group living. A wolf knows who to protect and who to attack and how to defend to the death. That obsession for distinguishing friend from foe is one we share. It's why we understand one another, on the one hand, and fear one another, on the other hand. It's why since deep antiquity we have viewed wolves as everything from guards to gods.

To watch wild wolves is to recognize a kindred creature by turns riveting, horrifying, and admirable. It's also to see how many of our dogs' tendencies and talents were fully formed in the wild, and remain intact in our homes.

Dogs have been diversified into an enormous range; think of Great Danes and Chihuahuas. Yet even at a distance, a dog seems to recognize the difference between another dog—no matter what the breed—and a cat. And so do children.

Rick McIntyre likes to tell people that because many households have dogs, we already "know about both."

"You mean both wolves and dogs? Or both wolves and humans?" I ask.

"Right," he says.

"Does my dog love me, or does he just want a treat?" A professor who is an expert in climate change—not dogs—recently asked me that question. I've often asked it myself. Short answer: your dog really does love you. Part of the reason is: because you are kind. If you were abusive, your dog would fear you. And they might *still* love you, out of duty or need—not so different from many people trapped in abusive relationships. But to answer the question directly: what we know about dogs' brains, their brain chemistry, and the changes to their brains caused by domestication tells us that yes, your dog loves you. A dog's ability to feel love for humans comes partly from the love wolves have for wolves, partly from the genetic changes of their domesticated ancestry. In dogs, we've bred the people we wish we could be: loyal, hardworking, watchful, fiercely protective, intuitive, sensitive, affectionate, helpful to those in need. No matter how they originated, their feelings are real to them. Your dog genuinely loves you, as you, in your domesticated state, activating the deep, old parts of your brain, love your dog.

Just outside Bozeman, Montana, Chris Bahn and his wife, Mary-Martha, run a bed-and-breakfast called Howlers Inn. On four fenced acres right next to their home, they provide for several captive-born wolves who needed a haven. Chris and Mary-Martha had raised these wolves by hand, bottle-feeding them from the age of three weeks. They are real wolves, not wolf-dog hybrids. When I drove up, they came to the fence like dogs, curious.

Having read about the Russian friendly foxes with the curly tails and theories that friendly wolves domesticated themselves—which all made perfect sense—I was nonetheless unprepared for the first time I saw a man interact with tame, undomesticated wolves.

When Chris entered the enclosure, he was wearing a canvas jumpsuit to protect himself from the enthusiasm of their surprisingly long and sharp claws. What surprised me most, though, was their doglike friendliness. They were wagging their tails, happily rallying round him. (I had to remain outside.)

"Wolves are extremely expressive," Chris said, looking up at me while kneeling in a sea of swarming wolves. "Probably even more so than dogs. You always know what a wolf is thinking, whether they're happy or relaxed or uncomfortable."

The alpha male, aged six, came for vigorous rubs and then rolled belly-up. Chris crouched down and obliged, while others gave him licks to the face, just as Jude likes to do while I'm rubbing Chula's belly at home. I asked Chris where he is in the pack order. He says he's not; he has no dominance role. His role is caretaker.

Seeing these wolves, I found it perfectly plausible that wolves who'd acquired a habit of hanging around human habitations began to hold dual citizenship and then, as centuries came and went, started to integrate into the human social lattice, departing from their origins. It would have been a good career move.

PART THREE

Whines and Pet Peeves

*Our present subject is very obscure,
but, from its importance, must be
discussed at some little length; and it is
always advisable to perceive clearly our
ignorance.*

—Charles Darwin, *The Expression of the
Emotions in Man and Animals*

*The problem is that rules are simple,
and animals are not.*

—Bernd Heinrich,
The Geese of Beaver Bog

Never Mind Theory

———•———

Experiments showed at first that wolves could not follow human hand pointing to find hidden food. Dogs often can. But the wolves had been tested with a fence separating them from the human who was pointing. Dog tests were of course barrier-free, and dogs usually had their most familiar human companions with them. When experimenters finally leveled the playing field, wolves did as well as dogs—with no training.

Experiments can be powerful for learning about behavior. But sometimes, experimental situations are so pinched and artificial—as with wolves behind fences—that they hide capabilities they're trying to investigate. Real-life behaviors and decisions can't always be stuffed into an experiment.

Any ecologist who watches free-living animals feels humbled by the depth and nuance of how they negotiate the world and how easily they slip the noose of human observation as they go about their business of working to keep themselves and their babies alive.

On the other hand, laboratory studies seem preoccupied with "testing" academically generated concepts such as "self-awareness" and—my pet peeve—"theory of mind." It's not that these *ideas* aren't helpful. They are. It's that animals don't care about academic classifications and testing setups. They have no interest in arguments over wafer-thin slices of categories, such as whether an otter smashing a clam with a stone is using a tool but a gull dropping a clam on a stone is not using a tool. They care about survival. Some academic researchers, meanwhile, chop concepts into so many pieces, you'd think behavior was shish kebab. So in this section I want to have a little fun with some muddles that behavioral scientists have created. We'll be blowing away some smoke and breaking some mirrors. And as for the kebab, the first skewer goes to "theory of mind."

"Theory of mind"—such an awkward phrase—is an idea. Exactly what the idea is depends on whom you ask. Naomi Angoff Chedd, who works with autistic children, tells me it is "knowing that another can have thoughts that differ from yours." I like that definition; it's helpful. Dolphin researcher Diana Reiss says it's the ability to feel that "I have an idea of what's on your mind." That's different. Still others assert—oddly, I think—that it's the ability "to read the minds of others." The "mind-reading" camp gets the most press, and its adherents get the most carried away with themselves. Italian neuroscientist and philosopher Vittorio Gallese writes of "our sophisticated mind-reading abilities."

I don't know about you (I guess that's my point), but I cannot read anyone's mind. Informed guessing based on experience and body language is just about all we can really do. If a sketchy-looking stranger crosses the street to come toward us, our first problem is that we *can't* know what they're thinking. If "theory of mind" is defined as understanding that another can hold thoughts different from yours, then fine, there's that. But claims about humans' "sophisticated mind-reading abilities" are nonsense. That's why we say, "How are you?"

"Theory of mind" was coined in 1978 by researchers who tested chimpanzees. With an impressive lack of human insight into what could be an appropriate context or meaningful to a chimp, they showed chimpanzees videotapes of human actors trying to access out-of-reach bananas, or trying to play music while the record player was unplugged, or shivering because a heater wasn't working, and so on. A chimpanzee was supposed to prove that it understood the human's problem by choosing a photo of the solution to the problem. It was supposed to choose, for instance, "a lit wick for the malfunctioning heater." No, the researchers *weren't* kidding. If the chimps didn't select the correct photo, the researchers declared that chimpanzees didn't understand the videotaped human actor's problem and, thus, had no "theory of mind." (Now, imagine you're a chimp, led into a room, shown a video of a man shivering next to a heater, and without anyone being able to explain the problem, the experiment, or the uses of fire, you're supposed to choose a lit wick. Imagine, for that matter, that you're Thomas Jefferson being shown a video of a man trying to play a phonograph that is unplugged. You'd have no idea what you were looking at.) In the decades since, and many studies later, scientists in the field have finally suggested that those results might have been affected by the test's setup. Science marches on. Well, hello.

So far, some scientists grant theory-of-mind ability—basically, understanding that another can have thoughts and motives that differ from yours—to apes and dolphins. A few allow elephants and crows. Occasional researchers have admitted dogs. But many continue to insist that theory of mind is "uniquely human." Even while I was writing this, science journalist Katherine Harmon wrote, "In most animal species, scientists have failed to see even a glimmer of evidence."

Not a glimmer? It's *blinding*. People who don't see the evidence aren't paying attention. Frans de Waal pays attention. The shenanigans of chimps who like to spray water on unsuspecting zoo visitors, he says, reflects, "a complex, and familiar, inner life."

Whether researchers do or don't think that chimpanzees, dogs, and other animals "have theory of mind" hardly matters. What matters: What do they have, and how do they have it? What do dogs do? And what motivates them? Rather than asking whether a dog or chimp follows a human gaze, let's ask how dogs and chimps direct one another's attention.

Humans are better at reading humans than we are at reading dogs. Dolphins are better at reading dolphins. Chimps at chimp reading. We judge the sketchy stranger's friendly or evil intent by their body language. But so do our dogs. Other animals are highly skilled body-language readers. The stakes can be life or death, and they can't ask questions. Our orphaned raccoon, Maddox (whom we bottle-raised but never caged; she lived free-range), could sometimes read my intent almost as fast as the thought occurred to me, though I couldn't understand what cue I was giving. She'd suddenly bristle and put her back up, for instance, if I'd just decided that it was time to stop playing in the kitchen and usher her outdoors. I used to joke that I had a mind-reading raccoon. (It must have been something in the way I looked at her, but, wow, was she sharp. And so were her teeth.)

Watching free-living animals negotiate the world on their terms shows you their rich mental abilities. And you can start by looking at who's scampering around your house, gazing up at you imploringly, awaiting your response.

～

In the morning I'm making coffee, and because it's chilly I raise the screens and lower the storm windows; the phone rings, and I answer it. Chula follows all my movements, looking me in the eyes for any clues that I might wish to interact—or perhaps move toward the jar of treats. She does not understand coffee, screens, or phones. A human from most of our history or a Native American from an intact tribe in 1880 or a hunter-gatherer today would also not understand anything I am doing. The difference between my crazy dog and Crazy Horse is that Crazy Horse could have learned everything I am doing (and perhaps vice versa). But, again, the point is not whether dogs are just like us. The point is that they are like themselves. The interesting question is: What are they like?

Our daughter, Alexandra, aged twenty, sees our other dog, Jude, appear at the screen door and indicate his desire to come in. Usually the doggies are both either in or out together, but Chula happens to be inside when Jude comes to the screen. Alex sees the whole thing and describes it like this: "Jude whined to be let in. Chula went to the screen and stared at Jude like, 'Ha,' as if teasing him like she does before they start playing; then she put her paw to the door, but just lightly, just like a person would open the door, and just opened the door and turned and went back to the bone she'd been chewing. She knew what she was doing. She had already turned around by the time Jude entered. She just got up to open the door, like, 'Okay, fine, come in.' The specific thing that was so interesting," Alex wants to emphasize, "was how she opened the door for him and then turned away and went back to what she'd been doing, just as I myself would have let Jude in."

We grab our jackets, and Chula and Jude get excited. They hope—it's safe to say—that we're taking them for a run. I open the door and say, "Car," and they run for the car's back hatch.

At the river, we let them out. They love this, of course. A swan sees them running along the shore. He steps gingerly into the water, paddling just out of easy reach. The dogs go into the water up to their bellies and bark at the swan a few times. The swan is actually stemming the current in place, not paddling away, not even drifting away. Either he doesn't want to move from this point along the shore, or he's taunting them, or he feels some conflict between challenging them and fleeing. But it's not nesting season, and the swans are not being territorial with one another. It seems he's taunting the dogs, but why would he? I don't know why he's holding right there—but he must know. Is this his idea of fun?

Chula weighs her option of swimming to the swan. You can see her trying to figure out what to do next. She wades deep enough to almost float but seems to understand that this won't work for her. The swan clearly understands that this won't work for Chula, because he is staring directly at her from just a few strokes away, but not moving one feather farther. In a minute the dogs realize that this is not going to get any more fun for them, and they splash to shore and gambol off.

The swan just showed that he understood that he needed to avoid the dogs *and* that he understood the limitations of their movement in water. He understands how to use the water to stay completely safe while holding himself so close that, were he on land, the dogs could cover the distance in two bounds, requiring perhaps half a second. The swan demonstrated theory of mind and mastery of medium.

Farther down the shore, Chula bounds into the water near where some mallard ducks are floating. They, too, paddle to deeper water but do not fly. A few hundred yards farther along the shore, the river enters Long Island Sound. The river's mouth is perhaps a hundred yards across. Out in mid-river, several hundred scaup—another kind of duck—are diving for mussels. They ignore the dogs. But when four humans appear on the far shore, all the ducks fly up in alarm, leaving the vicinity of the river and flying out into the Sound. As they pass over other sitting groups of scaup and long-tailed ducks, those ducks also take flight and head out over the Sound, in a wide-spreading panic.

Why would the ducks merely paddle away from their age-old enemy the wolf (in domesticated form) yet become panicked by the mere appearance of humans on a farther shore? Because the ducks understand a dog's limits and have learned that humans can kill at great distance—that's why. They know that causing harm can be on a human's mind, and they have some concept either of death or attack or great danger. And because for millions of years of evolution they had no experience of guns, their accurate judgment about what constitutes differing safe distances from dogs and humans is learned and recent. Do they "have" a theory of mind? The question gets less interesting as the richness of behaviors and perceptions become more apparent. What the birds do and why; that's what's so interesting.

When we get home, I towel off Chula, whose fur is full of sand and damp with brackish water. She endures it but doesn't love it. Yet as soon as I unfurl the towel, Jude dives headlong into it, tail wagging widely as he snaps his jaws randomly while prancing like a terry-cloth ghost. Jude loves playing blindman's buff. The game is to grab and release his muzzle while he's blindly snapping. Take the towel off, he stops snapping and tries to get into the towel again. Chula has no interest in this game, or in Jude when he's being so silly.

Later, in the yard surrounding our house, the dogs chase each other in totally unnecessary play. They fake each other out when racing around the shed or cottage. Chula will try to double back to intercept Jude, but Jude will stop to see from which way Chula is coming. They know what is going on, and they seem to understand that the other is trying to fool them. That's "theory of mind," too. One is evaluating what the other is thinking, each showing clear understanding that the other might be faked into a false belief about which direction they'll be charging from. Because they're playing, there's both cleverness and humor in this. (Unless they're just two unconscious machines interacting without sensation or perception. Some people still insist that "we can't be sure." That's what I mean by denial.)

A dog who has never before seen a ball would not bring it to a person and lay it at their feet. But a dog experienced with balls comes to invite play. They envision the game, plan a way to start it, and execute the plan with a human partner who they understand is knowing. Theory of mind.

Any dog who goes into a play bow is inviting you, understanding that you might engage. (The play bow isn't strictly canine; Maddox the raccoon frequently invited play this way.) Dogs and others don't play-bow to trees, chairs, or other inanimate objects. Our puppy Emi play-bowed to the first ball she ever saw when I rolled it her way. She assumed anything moving so purposefully along the floor had to be alive—but she did that only once. In moments she realized that this was a wonderful new thing but that it was inanimate, not capable of an aware response or voluntary play. It therefore needed no further invitation, nor consideration, nor restraint in being chewed, flung, and pounced on.

Chula once barked at a life-sized concrete dog, but only once—a sniff told her that its shape had lied. A dog—or an elephant, say—often validates the authenticity of things by scent. A dog that loves chasing rabbits will give one perfunctory sniff to a porcelain rabbit. It obviously recognizes rabbits on sight but is too clever to be fooled by a fake. To a dog, if it looks like a duck and quacks like a duck, it's not a duck unless it *smells* like a duck.

These little stories reveal dogs' shrewd ability to discern what has a mind—and what doesn't. Theory thereof. You can't bring swimming swans and flocks of diving ducks into a lab. Sometimes, rather than "testing" animals in contraptions and contrived setups where they can't be who they are, we might simply define the concept we're interested in, then watch the animals in free-living situations appropriate to their lives. Do they show an understanding that others hold different thoughts and agendas and can even be fooled? Yes. It's happening all around us, twenty-four/seven, blindingly obvious. But you have to have your eyes open. Lab psychologists and philosophers of behavior often don't seem to know about how perceptions function in the real world. I wish they'd go outside, watch, and have some fun.

Sex, Lies, and Humiliated Seabirds

———•———

Our two young dogs came from the shelter in springtime. They grew up during the summer, and all during the warm weather they could come and go from the house at will through a propped-open door. They almost never had to ask to be let out. On very rare occasions when the door was closed and they were inside, wanting out, they'd stand by the door; they never barked to get someone to open it. They'd go out for the last time at about ten P.M., then come up to the bedroom, where they'd bed down for the night on their floor pillows. They would rest well until first light, when they'd get active and wake us up. During October of their first year, we were out one evening later than we'd expected, and we fed them unusually late. Disrupted from their usual schedule, at four A.M. they got the urge to go and went downstairs to the door. I became aware of their need because one of them barked several times. They'd *never* barked to be let out before; they'd never had to. Why would they bark now? They apparently understood that we were upstairs, asleep, and that, having found the door closed downstairs, they needed to get our attention. So they sent a message that we received and understood; that's the definition of communication.

The first time Patricia drove separately with the dogs to our cottage at Lazy Point, I had been there for several days. When she arrived, Chula did a double take at the sight of my car and immediately went to it, looking for me. I'd gone for a walk, but Chula ran excitedly into each room of the house, hoping—it seemed to Patricia—to find and greet me.

You can't know what your dog is thinking—except when you can. You both know if you're about to go for a walk or get into the car; you both understand when you're preparing to give them some leftovers. True, most of the time I *don't* know what they're thinking. But most of the time I don't know whether my wife is thinking about how much she loves me or what she'd like for dinner. She can tell me or show me. Love and dinner occur to our dogs, too, but a dog's ability to tell is limited. Their ability to show is a bit better. But they have whatever thoughts they have, regardless. And we find sufficient currency, in our few words and gestures, our deep affection and trust, for a shared life.

Jude is one of the sweetest dogs I've known but not the sharpest. We call him "the poet" because he always seems to be daydreaming, seldom paying attention. At least that's what I thought. Once day I took him and Chula for a beach run. Halfway down the beach they caught a deer scent and disappeared into the woods atop a bluff. Usually they return in about five minutes. This time their absence stretched to twenty, twenty-five minutes, with me calling the whole time. I finally climbed the bluff. Calling, calling. Nothing. Then I saw Jude back down on the beach, galloping full speed in the direction we'd been headed when they'd bolted.

This was odd. Chula is *always* ahead of Jude, and Chula is *always* the first one who comes looking for me. I called Jude, and he immediately stopped and came scrambling up as I scrambled down the vine-tangled slope. On the beach, I leashed him. Now I was worried; where was Chula? Bad possibilities included: an injury, getting taken by someone who thought she was lost (she does wear a tag), a run-in with a car. Minutes peeled off the clock. No Chula. Maybe she'd gone *back* to the car. Jude has done that twice during lesser separations. I decided I'd walk back to the car, about half a mile, and if I didn't find Chula, I'd put Jude in the car and come back.

Jude would have none of it. He resisted the change of direction. Very clearly, he wanted to keep going in the direction we'd all been headed. Was this because he was having too much fun? Unlikely. Usually when he's had this much activity, he's ready to stay close and go home. His insistence on pressing forward was odd. Then far, far down the beach—farther than we'd ever walked—I saw Chula running very hard, zigzagging. What a relief. But she was running *away* from us. I called as loud as I could and waved my arms, hoping the wind might help my voice reach her.

She heard and, in an instant, turned, saw me waving, and began running hard toward us. She must have thought that the whole time they were in the woods I'd continued walking in the same direction—as, in fact, I usually do when they run off briefly. Apparently, she'd returned to the beach about where she'd expected to intercept me. By how fast she was running when I saw her, it seemed that she was trying to catch up and find me. Did Jude know she was down there? Did he fear that I was going to abandon Chula? No way to know, but that's certainly how he acted. *Yes, you sweet boy, I'm talking about you* (he's lying next to my desk as I write this). In retrospect, I think the dogs knew what they were doing the whole time; I was the one who'd gotten confused.

We interrupt our days with doggies to bring you a news bulletin from *Science* magazine titled "Dogs Are No Mind Readers." Well, who is? This is news? As if an experiment might have shown that dogs are clairvoyant? Purportedly, the article highlights an experiment "which shows that dogs continue to trust unreliable people and therefore lack a so-called theory of mind." We're going to forgo the temptation to ask whether clients of Bernie Madoff or victims of any petty scammer lack a so-called theory of mind. Does the writer mean to imply that humans never trust unreliable people? Sometimes people apply a weird double standard: we start with the premise that other animals are not as intelligent as humans, then we hold them to a higher standard of performance. And by the way, it's going to turn out that what the news item says the experiment showed is *not* what the experiment showed.

The researchers tested two dozen dogs. They used two buckets that smelled equally like food. Only one bucket actually had food in it. Beside each pair of buckets stood a human the dog had never before met. Half of the humans always pointed to the bucket with the treat. Half always pointed to the empty bucket. Over five test sessions, each dog got a total of 100 trials with each kind of human. The truth tellers and liars were mixed among the trials. The dogs followed the pointing of the truth teller more than 90 percent of the time. On the *first* trial with a liar, they followed the liar's suggestion only 80 percent of the time, *and* they took more than twice as long to even approach the person who was lying (14 seconds versus 6 seconds for the truth-telling stranger). Seems pretty doggone intuitive. Over time, the dogs went to the bucket the liar pointed to less and less, as the dogs learned to lose faith in the misinforming people. By the last test session, the dogs were essentially ignoring the deceptive humans and choosing based on chance, about 50-50. The researchers concluded— as would most sane people—that "the dogs were learning to treat the cooperator and deceiver differently."

But then the researchers spun their result, suggesting that "the dogs stopped trusting humans not because they could intuit what the humans were thinking but merely because they had learned to associate certain humans with a lack of food reward." Wait a minute! No human in this setup would "intuit" what the person was *thinking*. The person was *showing* whether they were reliable or not. And the dogs learned who was and who wasn't. (After all, the dogs had never before encountered a lying human.) But the researchers were saying that the dogs would have to literally read humans' thoughts in order to "prove" that they have theory of mind. And that's just absurd. For goodness' sake.

The researchers somehow failed to see that the dogs actually *did* prove that they had so-called theory of mind. The dogs understood that a human could know the whereabouts of a treat when the dogs themselves did not know; that *is* theory of mind. Understanding that some humans' indications are not reliable: that *is* theory of mind. It's not that dogs don't have a theory of mind; it's that humans often miss the point. Faced with a lying human, dogs refused to choose *either* bucket one-fifth of the time. They understood at some level that, in nontechnical terms, something was up, that the humans were messing with them. The researchers somehow concluded that their experiments "offer no support for the idea that dogs understand human intentionality." So let's try another experiment: accidentally trip over your dog, then intentionally kick him. See how surely dogs understand intent.

Some experiments say more about the researchers. When researchers can't intuit the animals' thoughts or viewpoint, it shows that many *humans* lack a theory of mind *for non-humans*. Many animals, though (mammals and birds, for starters), realize that if another animal is looking at them, it sees them. And they realize that their interests don't always harmonize. (Unless, like Shackleton's dogs, they've learned absolute trust and know only loyalty.)

SHACKLETON'S DECISION

At a certain point he decided they could not afford
the dogs. It was someone's job to take them one by one
behind a pile of ice and shoot them. I try to imagine
the arctic night which descended and would not lift,

a darkness that clung to their clothes. Some men objected
because the dogs were warmth and love,
reminders of their previous life where they slept in soft beds,
their bellies warm with supper. Dog tails were made

of joy, their bodies were wrapped in a fur of hope.
I had to put the book down when I read about the dogs
walking willingly into death, following orders,
one clutching an old toy between his teeth. They trusted

the men who led them into this white danger,
this barren cold. My God, they pulled the sleds
full of provisions and barked away the Sea Leopards.
Someone was told to kill the dogs because supplies

were running low and the dogs, gathered around
the fire, their tongues wet with kindness, knew
nothing of betrayal; they knew how to sit and come,
how to please, how to bow their heads, how to stay.

—Faith Shearin

No one has ever suggested that tigers have theory of mind. If a tiger had theory of mind, it would know that you can discover that it is stalking you, and that you could act on that realization. Well—they do. In the Sundarbans delta in India, villagers working in the forest defeated a serious problem of tiger attacks by wearing Halloween-type face masks situated backward, so that the eyes and face were on the backs of their heads. Tigers would not attack if they thought they were being watched. Tigers had been killing about one person per week. But after the mask ruse was implemented, no one wearing a mask was attacked, though tigers were seen following mask-wearing humans, and in the same span of time they killed twenty-nine more people not wearing masks. (Talk about old habits dying hard; why didn't everyone just get a mask?) Like mothers who want the kids to think they have "eyes in the back of their heads," numerous butterflies, beetles, caterpillars, fishes, and even some birds have prominent "eye spots," usually in the rear. The spots are an attempt to fool predators into thinking that potential prey is staring back, that they've lost the element of surprise. In sum, various predators operate with widespread understanding that prey can sometimes see you trying to sneak up, and that prey can act independently on that knowledge. That *is* "theory of mind." It's precisely why predators are stealthy, why they hide, approach from behind, and so on.

In Tanzania's Ngorongoro Crater one morning, I watched a particular lion family wake and rouse, its members greeting one another. Then they walked single file to the ridge of a low, grassy hill. Beyond the hill, about half a mile off, grazed a small group of zebras. With no apparent signal, one lion sat. The others kept walking. Another lion sat. The rest kept walking along the ridge. Another sat. This continued until the hill was lined by an evenly spaced picket fence of lions sitting upright in tall golden grass facing the distant zebras. One lion had not sat; she went toward the zebras. I'd just watched them set up a well-planned ambush. The walking lion's job was to frighten the zebras toward the hill. The waiting lions had a commanding field of view from the hiding cover of the tall grass, and a downhill sprint at any zebras that might be forced to run uphill. It seemed tactically exquisite. But the zebras, no fools, detected the stalking lion early—and moved farther away from the hill.

Watch, and you easily see that many creatures' lives depend on deciding—quickly and correctly—whether a predator is hunting or just traveling, whether a rival feels apprehensive or plans to attack, and that animals make other crucial judgments about the intentions of others.

Richard Wagner's work involves watching birds living their real lives. We've known each other since we were both ten years old. In our twenties, together we studied seabirds and shared great adventures across Kenya. Now we're sitting in my backyard on a summer day in the shade of maples and he's telling me about seabirds called razorbills. He's studied them at their breeding colonies for a long time, watching hour after hour, day upon month upon years. "When you watch razorbills," he says, "you get to see who the good fighters are, who the good mates are, and who the hussies are. One female found her mate mating with another female. She pushed her mate off. The following day, she encountered that same female. She knew who she was. She lunged at her and pushed her off the rock she was standing on."

Why would she care—might the male be sneaking a little food to the other female, or to her chicks? "That doesn't happen," says Wagner. "I've watched them for thousands of hours, and I've watched for exactly that. They don't do it." The reason for the aggressive behavior, Wagner found, is that the *next year* the male might run off with the other female. "Copulations this year lead to pair bonds next year. The female mate guards her pair bond. Meanwhile, the male guards his mate to protect his paternity." Is that how the birds actually think of it? Likely not. But I'll bet they feel something we'd recognize as jealousy. After all, jealousy—not a probabilistic understanding of evolutionary genetics—motivates humans to guard our own mates.

"The razorbills know each other like kids on the school bus know each other," Wagner explains. "They don't make mistakes. Razorbills are *social*. They see each other every day. They come to the same rock. They can live *twenty* years! They know who's flying in before they land. Say a female arrives. Male A mounts her; Male B pushes Male A off and mounts her himself. Male C mounts Male B. He's just seen Male B demonstrate that he's a male. The mounting isn't a mistake made in a frenzy. It's a fighting tactic. The one that got mounted has very publicly been dominated. Turns out, mounting other males helps eliminate competition. The more a male gets mounted by a male, the less he continues to show up on the mating rock. It's possible that they feel something like what we'd call humiliated. They lose status." We strive for status, too, but we don't really *understand* our drives any more than they do theirs. Status boosts reproduction, but we don't feel the calculation about lifetime reproductive averages that evolution has made and given to us on a crib sheet called urges. We *feel* the motivations of jealousy, of status seeking. And we often perform the behaviors we are driven to perform.

While we tend to lack a theory of *their* minds, other animals seem to have a theory about ours. They know that we can know. One day my good friends John and Nancy noticed a pair of free-living mallard ducks on their lawn. They gave them some bread. The ducks came back the next day. They fed them cracked corn. The ducks became regular lawn visitors. No surprise there. But one day John heard a knock at the door. He opened his front door and looked through the screen door, but apparently whoever was knocking had left. The screen door had a metal lower half, and he heard the knock again and looked down. Now, could a duck that was "not conscious" or "not self-aware" or had "no theory of mind" waddle to the front door and *knock*?

When a capuchin monkey in Trinidad came away from its group into a tree over our heads and started breaking branches and throwing them at us, it was clear that the monkey saw us, perceived us as potentially dangerous (people hunt them there), and was trying to discourage us from pursuing by intimidating us with hurled branches. It was not clear whether he was intentionally trying to protect his companions, but that was my impression. He was clearly communicating, "Go away." My doctoral professor Joanna Burger used to watch capuchin monkey interactions at a tiny, nearly dry water hole. The monkeys didn't like her hiding in an observation blind; they were less disturbed if she remained leaning against a tree, where they could see her. Each day, an hour before dawn when no monkeys were nearby, Joanna filled a plastic tub adjacent to the hole with water she brought in a bucket. When the monkeys came, they could drink from the tub instead of descending so far into the water hole that they couldn't be seen. While she observed them, the pail was tucked behind a nearby tree. On Joanna's last day she went for a final brief look but didn't bother filling the plastic tub because she had no time for observations. Seeing that she had not filled the tub, one monkey went behind the tree, got the bucket, and brought it to her. A clear communication, understanding one another's understanding.

Conceit and Deceit

———

The door-knocking duck and the free-living monkey bringing the bucket to the professor seem to be *envisioning* an outcome they desired, a state of affairs different from the immediate reality they were simply observing. Sometimes animals can even communicate their desires to us. When our dogs come looking for us in different rooms, they are *imagining* finding us. They're seeking something more suited to their interests than what they have at the moment, and they know what they're seeking. Their mental pictures, imagined scenarios of cause and effect and desired outcomes, are their thinking. Imagining a route to something desired—first this, then that—might even be a glimmer of storytelling. What else are these "folks" saying?

Jude and Chula *sound* and *look* like they're battling as they growl and bite. Guests to our home have asked in alarm, "Are they fighting?" But the pupsters know they're playing, and so do we. We easily hear it because we understand their tone of growl; we're in on their joke. We all understand the intent. We humans also appreciate our own verbal play. As humans, we understand metaphor and detect the difference between the humor of a well-meaning joke and the offense of a sarcastic one. But we don't hold a monopoly on judging subtle cues.

You might already have taken in stride the idea that dogs and apes indicate and understand intent. But what about, say, a fish? A tasty fish, at that. The more we learn—well, it can rock our boat.

We think of apes as smart because apes *are* smart—*and* because they look like us. But the science of cognition is becoming peppered with reports of "apelike performance" in some other animals. Newest among them: certain fishes. Our rarefied list of beings who use gestures to direct the attention of companions—humans, bonobos, dolphins, ravens, African hunting dogs, wolves, domestic dogs—must now include groupers. Yes, the same fish that's in countless fried fillet sandwiches; they're among the smartest.

When its intended prey escapes into a coral crevice, the grouper rotates and points down in the direction of the hiding prey. If no help is forthcoming, the grouper might go to where it knows a giant moray eel is resting in its day lair and rapidly shake to say, "Follow me." The eel, who can get into the squeezes, often follows the grouper to the hiding prey. To make sure the moray is following, the grouper turns to check. If the moray isn't quite getting the message, the grouper will sometimes "try and push it in the direction of the previously indicated crevice." When they get to the hiding prey, the grouper faces the spot and shakes its head. The grouper and the eel don't share the catch, but they split the proceeds: sometimes the moray gets the hiding fish, sometimes the hiding fish bolts and the grouper nabs it.

If no moray is nearby, the grouper might recruit a Napoleon wrasse, who can break the coral, or an emperor fish. The groupers signal until they get help, then immediately stop signaling. These gestures are intentional and directed to another fish, whose response is voluntary. At least two species of groupers do this. Researchers say that the groupers "regularly hunt collaboratively with other fish species" in the Red Sea and also "collaborate with octopuses" on Australia's imperiled Great Barrier Reef. Furthermore, the groupers' patience, waiting above hidden prey for up to twenty-five minutes for a passing potential partner, suggests "an ape-like level in a memory task." In new experiments, researchers found that groupers so quickly learned which moray was a good or poor collaborator that groupers' abilities in choosing the more effective partner are "nearly identical to that of chimpanzees." Groupers' hunting collaborations come as news—surprising news, at that. But the groupers have probably been guiding their hunting partners for a few million years.

Flexible interspecies cooperation of the sort shown by groupers and their partners is so rare, even humans engage in it with only two or three species. Honeyguides are birds who lead badgers and humans to beehives so they can share the feast of a broken-into hive. Humans hunt with dogs or birds of prey but humans control and contrive it. Dolphins, however, have controlled and contrived their own situations, using humans—and, in a couple of cases, seemingly training humans—to help them catch food.

In both Brazil and Mauritania, dolphins drive mullet schools toward a line of fishermen. On the coast of Brazil, the dolphins seem to have trained the fishermen; along Mauritania's shore, the fishermen seem to have trained the dolphins. Brazilian bottlenose dolphins use head and tail slaps *to direct the humans* about when and where the fishermen should cast their nets. The dolphins nab fish that become confused or injured by the nets. Only a small proportion of the lagoon's dolphins do this—they learn from their mothers to be fishers of men—and the fishermen know them well enough to give them names, such as Caroba and Scooby. Mauritanian fishermen who spot mullet beat the water with sticks to call bottlenose and humpback dolphins, who then herd the mullet against their nets and share the profits. They've been in business together since 1847.

Most extraordinarily, for about a hundred years, starting in the mid-1800s, the world's largest dolphins—killer whales—had humans trained to be their hunting partners in Australia's Twofold Bay, near a town called Eden. The killer whales apparently herded large whales into the bay, then actually went and alerted human whalers, who'd come in for the attack. The killer whales understood that they'd get a share of the whalemen's kills. The killer whales reportedly even grabbed the ropes attached to harpooned whales to further slow the stricken giants, helping to subdue them.

Conventional wisdom holds that only humans can consciously plan. But when jays store perishable and nonperishable foods, they use up the perishable food stashes first. This means that they evaluate and then act on their categorization of different foods' time-sensitiveness. At Sweden's Furuvik Zoo, one particular chimp would gather stones together, planning to use them later on to bombard unsuspecting human zoo-goers (fortunately, chimpanzees have terrible aim). Over the span of a decade, he made hundreds of piles of ammo. Each morning before the zoo opened, keepers had to search the chimpanzee exhibit to remove his collections of stones. At another zoo, an orangutan figured out that by wrapping a piece of wire around the latch of a locked furnace room door and pulling, he could let himself and his orang friends out for a frolic in the zoo's trees. He did this several times before baffled zookeepers figured out how he was getting out. Meanwhile, he'd kept his wire hidden, fully intending to continue using this tool he'd so insightfully crafted.

The orangutan was being crafty, sneaky, and a bit deceptive. Deception involves conscious attempts to instill a false belief in another mind. That's why deceit shows that humans have a "theory of mind." Humans excel at dishonesty, so we deal with deception—lying politicians, tricky sales-people, our children—every day. Nature is full of deception, from camouflage to clever lies. Even in intentional deception, humans aren't unique.

When a bird called the fork-tailed drongo sees mammals such as meer-kats or birds such as babblers with food, the drongo mimics their specific alarm calls, sending them fleeing to cover so the drongo can swoop in and steal their morsels. Plovers are shorebirds who use a "broken-wing act" to draw predators away from their nests in the sand and their chicks. Their main goal, in acting disabled, is to foil the predator by creating a false impression. They vary the intensity and direction of their act according to how well the predator is falling for the deception. I've seen it many times; I've often been the plovers' target. They know their business.

Living in social groups gives you motives to lie and someone to lie to. Vervet monkeys sometimes cry "Leopard" when their troop is losing a fight with another troop. The shrewdly strategic false alarm sends every-one scrambling into the trees, ending the fight. One vervet monkey was known to sometimes scream "Eagle!" in order to clear the competition out of a fruit tree. The other monkeys would scatter—and he'd quickly stuff his face. Similarly, monkeys knowing of treats hidden in a box "ignored" the box when other monkeys were around, so others would not see how to open it.

Among chimpanzees in the famed Gombe Stream National Park, researchers used a remote control to open a locked food box. One chim-panzee happened to be next to the box when they opened it. But, seeing that a more dominant male was coming, he closed the box and moved away. Once the dominant male had passed, the first chimp reopened the box and loaded up with bananas. But the dominant male had hidden himself just out of sight; he swooped in and scooped up the fruit.

In experiments where rhesus monkeys can steal a grape from either of two humans, they steal from the person who is situated such that they cannot see what the monkey is doing. This shows that the monkeys believe that the human would object to their theft and that they need to be sneaky about it. Similarly, monkeys prefer to take food from containers that don't make noise. Stealthy stealing shows that they understand that it's best not to alert anyone to their larceny. Similarly, dogs are less likely to snatch forbidden food when a human is watching than when the human is looking away or is absent. They understand that we understand, and that our goals can differ.

You don't have to be a mammal to fool your friends. When western scrub jays notice that another jay has watched them hiding food, they will move the food after the watcher leaves—but only if they themselves have robbed another bird's food. They must form a concept of stealing based on their own experience and basically realize, "That bird might steal my food." Sometimes they only *pretend to* move the food. Jays who've been watched *but* have never stolen another jay's hidden food don't move their own food. This requires projecting their own larcenous motivations onto another bird's possible decisions. The jay has to imagine another jay's viewpoint. Scientists call this "mental attribution" or "perspective taking," and they make a big deal of it. To the jay, it's not a big deal; it's just what you have to do in a world where "people," including jaybirds like themselves, can't be trusted. They know that the other bird can know. And they know that what goes around can come around, and perhaps that life can be unfair.

A sense of fairness puts some animals into another exclusive club. A researcher offers a capuchin monkey a slice of cucumber. Mmm; the monkey likes cucumber. The researcher gives an adjacent monkey a grape. Monkey One watches Monkey Two enjoy the grape. When offered another cucumber slice, Monkey One takes it, then throws it back at the researcher. Unfair! Cucumbers are fine, unless your colleagues are getting something sweeter. Ravens, crows, and dogs are also sensitive to fair payment for the same task. Humans too, of course, can be aware of what's fair—when we want to. Why don't all humans see it as unfair when women are forced to accept less pay for equal work? Maybe another thing that "makes us human" is our ability to create double standards.

Apes are more than just clever; they're often insightful, strategic, and political. Sometimes that's shown during a high-stakes operation between the humans who would fool them fatally and the apes who cheat the cheaters to stay alive. A baby gorilla trips a poacher's snare and dies. Days later, conservation workers watch a four-year-old male named Rwema break a bent tree branch that is the trigger stick of a snare, while a female of about the same age named Dukore disables the snare's noose. The pair then see another snare nearby. Rwema and Dukore, joined by teenager Tetero, disable that trap, with a speed and "confidence" that cause a watching researcher to think this isn't the first time they've saved themselves some grief. (Who is the better person, the human who set the snare or the gorillas humanely protecting themselves and their family?)

Spotted hyenas live in societies far more complicated than those of wolves or any other carnivore. Spotted hyena clans have up to ninety members, all of whom recognize one another individually. They understand and use kin and rank relationships when making decisions. Spotted hyenas also lie. Researchers studying free-living hyenas have observed scenes like these: While higher-ranking hyenas are feasting, a low-ranking hyena falsely calls out an alarm that scatters them, then races directly to the carcass to snatch a few fast bites before its clanmates realize there's no danger. To disrupt hyenas who are fighting with her offspring, a mother sometimes utters a false alarm call. A subordinate hyena who knows where food's hidden sometimes leads other accompanying hyenas astray, later returning alone to claim the prize. Researchers were watching a group that was traveling when a low-ranking male saw a leopard crouching motionless in a creek bed beside the carcass of a young wildebeest it had killed. None of the other hyenas noticed. The low-ranking male hyena looked directly at the leopard and its kill as he continued past. When all the hyenas were well beyond the creek, the low-ranking male turned and loped straight back, commandeering the carcass from the leopard without having to contend with competition from higher-ranking companions.

Yet—*incredibly*—the researchers describing *all* this conclude: "However . . . spotted hyenas appear to show no understanding of the thoughts or beliefs of others."

What? They've just described hyenas' skills of *deception*. Inexplicably, the researchers state, "We have no evidence that hyenas know anything at all about [other hyenas'] current mental state or future intentions . . . unless they directly perceive sensory cues that provide them with such information."

Well, where does one start? Perceiving sensory cues—seeing you, watching you interacting—is the *only* way I can "know anything at all about" your current mental state or your intentions. Isn't that—*obvious*? My question: Why do researchers judge the mental performance of other animals against a standard that humans could not possibly reach? Lying proves that the liar understands that another can have competing interests—and that you can keep them ignorant so you can benefit. That *is* "theory of mind."

In Tanzania, each of two rival higher-ranking male chimpanzees need the support of one particular subordinate male to maintain their dominance. Each courts the subordinate's favor by allowing him access to fertile females. By shifting his allegiance whenever the male he's been backing gets a little stingy, the lower-ranking male keeps the sex coming his way. In another instance, researcher Craig Stanford watches a lower-ranking chimpanzee seem to stage a dominance challenge. This gets the real dominant male so carried away displaying his dominance to the whole group that he doesn't realize the lower-ranking chimpanzee has used the confusion to sneak a little sex with a willing lass. Reviewing dozens of studies over three decades on the question of what chimpanzees know about others, one team concluded what the chimps themselves already know: "Chimpanzees understand both the goals and intentions of others as well as the perception and knowledge of others." Chimpanzees pursue power, and they keep track of favors given and received "as relentlessly as some people in Washington," says Frans de Waal. He observes, "Their feelings range from gratitude for political support to outrage if one of them violates a social rule," adding that "the emotional life of these animals is much closer to ours than once held possible."

Does that closeness reflect well on the chimps—or poorly? Chimpanzees hold a mirror up to us, challenging us to see the ape reflected. Often, we don't recognize ourselves. Chimpanzees can be as darkly, murderously ambitious as Roman senators, as if there is a human pent up inside them, brachiating toward Eden and our birth, a genie waiting to be released from its bottle and let loose upon the world. But we humans are already out of the bottle. In who we are, in how we are, we have much reason to feel pride and shame. If cruelty and destructiveness are bad, humans are by a wide margin the worst species ever to infest this planet. If compassion and creativity are good, humans are by a wide margin the finest. But we are neither simply good nor bad; we are all these things together, and imperfectly so. The question for all is: Which way is our balance trending?

Chuckles and Wacky Ideas

I'd never deny that formal scientific research in controlled conditions has been exceptionally helpful. I'll also never lose sight of the fact that the real lives of animals are too expansive for laboratories to adequately reflect. Yet many behaviorists work only in labs (or, far worse, philosophy departments). Now we'll see how, by slicing reality salami-thin and marinating it in jargon, researchers who confuse sometimes amuse.

The search for intelligent life on Earth produces a few chuckles along the way. One dog-loving researcher videotaped dogs in a neighborhood park during two years before arriving at the following conclusions: If a dog wanted to play with another dog it was facing, it would usually perform the "play invitation" (that familiar bow: front end crouched low, rear end high). But if the dog the play seeker wanted to romp with was facing away, the play seeker would first get the other dog's attention—with a paw, for instance, or by barking. In one of those science-marches-on moments, the researcher tells us, "They seem to be reacting to distinct cognitive states." In everyday terms: from two years of video analysis she discovered that a dog can distinguish another dog's face from its butt. May I please say this: a dog's behind is not a "distinct cognitive state." Why not just say that dogs get other dogs' attention before inviting play? Too obvious to seem like science?

Just minutes after I started searching the formal academic literature for "theory of mind," a typical recent study popped up. Titled "On the Lack of Evidence That Non-Human Animals Possess Anything Remotely

Resembling a 'Theory of Mind,' " it was published in the *Philosophical Transactions of the Royal Society*. The authors begin, "Theory of mind entails the capacity to make lawful inferences about the behaviour of other agents on the basis of abstract, theory-like representations of the causal relation between unobservable mental states and observable states of affairs." (Translation: by watching another's behavior, we can guess at what they may be thinking.) They continue: "We are entirely agnostic (for our present purposes anyway) about whether an organism's states are modal or amodal, discrete or distributed, symbolic or connectionist or even about how they come to have their representational or informational qualities to begin with. . . . Of course, there are innumerable other factors that also contribute to shaping a biological organism's behaviour."

I can probably understand that study—I just don't want to.

Two guys from Rutgers University (where I got my own PhD, so I am favorably inclined) have published a review called "Reading One's Own Mind: A Cognitive Theory of Self-Awareness." Here we go: "We'll start by examining what is probably the most widely held account of self-awareness, the 'Theory Theory' (TT). The basic idea of the TT of self-awareness is that one's access to one's own mind depends on the same cognitive mechanism that plays a central role in attributing mental states to others. . . . Theory Theorists argue that the TT is supported by evidence about psychological development and psychopathologies. . . . After making our case against the TT and in favor of our theory, we will consider two other theories of self-awareness to be found in the recent literature."

No, thanks! Theorizing about theorizing seems a very poor substitute for actually watching living beings do their thing.

"Theory of mind" is probably the most oversold concept in human psychology, as well as the most underappreciated, oft-denied aspect of non-human minds. We've all been in relationships where we thought, "I don't know where I stand with her" or "I don't know what to expect of him."

As John Locke said in the 1600s, "one man's mind could not pass into another man's body." The painter Paul Gauguin wrote of his thirteen-year-old Tahitian wife, "I strive to see and think through this child." Joni Mitchell sang, "There's no comprehending, / Just how close to the bone and the skin and the eyes / And the lips you can get / And still feel so alone." The Roman poet Lucretius—in what W. B. Yeats called "the finest description of sexual intercourse ever written" (not to mention a good translation)—observed bleakly,

> *They grip, they squeeze, their humid tongues they dart,*
> *As each would force their way to t'others heart:*
> *In vain: they only cruise about the coast,*
> *For bodies cannot pierce, nor be in bodies lost. . . .*
> *All ways they try, successless all they prove,*
> *To cure the secret sore of ling'ring love.*

"The tragedy of sexual intercourse," Yeats howled, "is the perpetual virginity of the soul." Paul Valéry, another poet, noted that "the interchange of human things between men requires that brains be impenetrable." Praise the poets for being good scientists. The scientist Nicholas Humphrey says, "There are no doors between one consciousness and another. Everyone knows directly only of his or her own consciousness and not anyone else's!"

If I want to sneak up on you, or fantasize while flirting, or steal from you, it is crucial that my mind remain unreadable. The more we *could* open into each other's minds, the more our brains would need a way to get up and lock the door. So yes, we observe, we resonate, but ultimately we guess. That's the most we can do. We can choose to reveal ourselves or hide our cards. But the choice is ours.

⌁

Chimps have mainly a theory of chimp mind, if we might put it that way; dolphins, mainly of dolphin mind. Humans often experience difficulty understanding even human needs and predicting other people's actions. And humans who assume that other animals are not even conscious—or who ignore their capacity for conscious experience—show how faulty our theory-of-mind talents are.

People in Japan and the Faeroe Islands kill dolphins and pilot whales by running steel rods into their spinal columns while they squeal in pain and terror and thrash in agony. (In Japan, it's illegal to kill cows and pigs as painfully and inhumanely as they kill dolphins.) The lack of compassion for dolphins and whales indicates that humans' "theory of mind" is incomplete. We have an empathy shortfall, a compassion deficit. And human-on-human violence, abuse, and ethnic and religious genocide are all too pervasive in our world. No elephant will ever pilot a jetliner. And no elephant will ever pilot a jetliner into the World Trade Center. We have the capacity for wider compassion, but we don't fully live up to ourselves. Why do human egos seem so threatened by the thought that other animals think and feel? Is it because acknowledging the mind of another makes it harder to abuse them? We seem so unfinished and so defensive. Maybe incompleteness is one of the things that "makes us human."

While some people seem unable to sense the minds of non-human animals, other people see human-like minds in everything. Our minds automatically discern human-like faces in things like clouds, the moon, even in food. Many believe that rocks, trees, streams, volcanoes, fire, and other things have thoughts, that *everything* has a mind and is inhabited by spirits that might act for or against us. That's called *panpsychism*. The religion that follows from this primal human assumption is *pantheism*. It is common among tribal hunter-gatherer peoples, and it's also alive and well in modern life. On the summit of Mount Kilauea, in Hawaii, I've seen offerings of money and liquor, put there by people who think that volcanoes have a god within who watches, tallies favors, and sometimes acts vindictively. Don't get the volcano mad by ignoring it. A little more booze and a few more bills, some flowers and some food and a roast pig occasionally, and the volcano's fiery goddess, Pele, will perhaps be mollified. And this is in the United States, where anyone can just stroll into the visitors' center and learn some volcano geology. (Park rangers have asked visitors to stop leaving offerings of food, money, flowers, incense, and liquor on Kilauea because in sum the offerings are more clearly appreciated by rats, flies, and roaches than by the goddess.) It appears that deep belief in the supernatural comes naturally to us.

"Nonhuman animals may arrive at beliefs based on evidence," writes philosopher Christine M. Korsgaard, "but it is a further step to be the sort of animal that can ask oneself whether the evidence really justifies the belief, and can adjust one's conclusions accordingly." Yet it is many *humans* who are demonstrably incapable of asking whether evidence justifies their beliefs, then adjusting their conclusions. Other animals are great and consummate realists. Only humans cling unshakably to dogmas and ideologies that enjoy complete freedom from evidence, despite all evidence to the contrary. The great divide between rationality and faith depends on some people choosing faith over rationality, and vice versa.

Other animals' actions and beliefs are evidence-based; they don't believe anything *unless* the evidence justifies it. Other animals attribute awareness only to things that are actually aware. While a dog might bark to rouse someone sleeping on the living room couch, they never seek assistance from the sofa itself. Or from volcanoes. They easily discriminate living things from inanimate objects and even from impostors. True, skilled duck hunters' decoys and calls fool passing ducks enough to get them to swerve into gun range, but the ruse must be elaborate or it won't work. Fish can be hard to fool even with artificial lures painstakingly designed to look and act like the real thing.

Years ago, while doing research that involved tagging migrating falcons, I lured the falcons to my net with tethered live starlings. The frightened starlings did not enjoy this; nor did I. So I put a stuffed starling on a string, wings in flight position, behind the net. Of course, in nature absolutely everything that looks like a bird and is covered with feathers and has a gleaming eye and moves up and down *is* a bird. Yet the stuffed bird never fooled one single falcon. They all sized it up, at a glance, as somehow "not real," and ignored it. *That* is impressive. Other animals are exceptionally good at identifying and reacting to predators, rivals, and friends. They never act as if they believe that rivers or trees are inhabited by spirits who are watching. In all these ways other animals continually demonstrate their working knowledge that they live in a world brimming with other minds, as well as their knowledge of those minds' boundaries. Their understanding seems more acute, pragmatic, and, frankly, better than ours at distinguishing real from fake.

So I wonder: Do humans really have a better-developed theory of mind than other animals? People watching a cartoon of nothing more than a circle and a triangle moving around and interacting almost always infer a story, involving motives and personalities and genders. Children talk to dolls for years, half-believing—or firmly believing—that the doll hears and feels and is a worthwhile confidant. Many adults pray to statues, fervently believing that they're listening. When I was a teenager, our next-door neighbors (Americans who'd been born and raised in New York) kept religious statues in every room except their bedroom, lest the Virgin witness human lust. All of this indicates a common human inability to distinguish conscious minds from inanimate objects, and evidence from nonsense.

Children often talk to a fully *imaginary* friend who they believe listens and has thoughts. Monotheism might be the adult version. We populate our world with imaginary conscious forces and beings—good and evil. Most present-day people believe they're helped or hindered by deceased relatives, angels, saints, spirit guides, demons, and gods. In the world's most technologically advanced, most informed societies, a majority of people take it for granted that disembodied spirits are watching, judging, and acting on them. Most leaders of modern nations trust that a sky god can be asked to protect their nation during disasters and conflicts with other nations.

All of this is "theory of mind" gone wild, like an unguided fire hose, spraying the whole universe with presumed consciousness. Humans' "superior" theory of mind is in part pathology. The oft-repeated line "Humans are rational beings" is probably our most half-true assertion about ourselves. There is in nature an overriding sanity and often, in humankind, an undermining insanity. We, among all animals, are most frequently irrational, distortional, delusional, worried.

Yet I also wonder: Is our pathological ability to generate false beliefs, to elaborate upon what does not exist, also the very root of human creativity? Is our tendency to imagine and even cling to what is false the foundation of all our inventive genius?

Perhaps believing false things comes bundled with our peculiar, oddly brilliant ability to envision what is not yet, and to imagine a better world. No one has explained where creativity arises, but some human minds lurch along sparking new ideas like a train with a stuck wheel. It's not rationality that's uniquely human; it's irrationality. It's the crucial ability to envision what is not, and to pursue unreasonable ideas.

Perhaps other animals don't need to manipulate logic because their actions are logical. They don't need tools because they are self-sufficient in their special abilities. Perhaps humans need logic and tools because without them we cannot survive, in a sense unable to succeed just as we are. Perhaps this is intuited in the story of the Fall, the trade-off in going from self-contained creatures like all the others to creatures needing a new way to access new knowledge so that, with much craft and effort, our distinctly human abilities might compensate for our distinctly human frailties.

Insight, shared to various degrees by other apes, wolves and dogs, dolphins, ravens, and a few other creatures, relies on an ability to see what is not there. As does turning homeward, or waiting for the mate who happens to be gone at the moment. Perhaps the depth of human insight comes with genes that give us a capacity not just to imagine what isn't there but to insist on it, to fervently hold and pursue unmoored beliefs. What is more irrational than a nonexistent melody, or the dream of human flight, or holding fixed the light of an image, or capturing a musical performance so that it may be heard again and again, or diving deep into the sea and breathing underwater? Who could have imagined such things? Who else.

Along for the ride on that singular ability to imagine comes sheer brilliance and utter madness. And maybe more than anything, what "makes us human" is our ability to generate wacky ideas.

Mirror, Mirror

Another pet peeve worthy of roasting on a skewer is the "mirror mark test." Devotees say it detects whether a creature has "self-awareness." The test goes like this: A person or other creature is marked—a smudge of makeup is surreptitiously placed on a toddler's forehead, for instance. If the creature later notices the smudge in a mirror and tries to remove it from its body, it clearly understands that the mirror shows an image of itself. True enough. Apes and dolphins do this, some birds, occasional elephants. But if an animal does not wipe at the smudge, they are deemed to lack self-awareness and the capacity for self-recognition. Well, that's *quite* a leap. The mirror test doesn't actually show whether the creature has self-awareness. Actually, the mirror test is often interpreted exactly backward, as I'll explain.

First, there's a definition problem. Psychology professor Gordon Gallup—who invented the mirror mark test in the 1970s—has said, "Self-awareness provides the ability to contemplate the past, to project into the future, and to speculate on what others are thinking." That's quite a definition. Try finding that in a mirror. The other end of the confusion spectrum is the "introspection" school, typified by Wikipedia's entry: "Self-awareness is the capacity for introspection and the ability to recognize oneself as an individual separate from the environment." Introspection doesn't reflect light. And recognizing yourself in a mirror doesn't show whether you understand that you are separate from the environment. So in just two definitions, the innocent phrase "self-recognition" supposedly refers to: the ability to understand time, to guess what someone is thinking, to examine one's own mind, and to understand that you are distinct from the rest of the world. None of which can be seen by recognizing one's image in a mirror.

For our purposes, "self-awareness" will mean what it sounds like: understanding that you are an individual, distinguishable from others and the rest of the world. Self-recognition means simply that you recognize your *self* from everything else. That was easy. Let's proceed.

On the beach near my home one autumn morning, two dozen sandpipers are scurrying along between the wipe of waves. Suddenly one gives an alarm call, and the flock rises rapidly, bunches up tightly, and flies out over the ocean. I turn and see a peregrine falcon powering in after a single sanderling that has not reached its massed comrades.

The sanderling is in a very bad spot—alone over open water, no cover anywhere—with a very determined falcon rapidly closing. The sanderling is flying as fast as it can, flat out, at around sixty miles an hour. The peregrine's advantage: it's the fastest living thing. The sanderling's situation is hopeless.

In the precise instant that the overtaking falcon extends a snatching foot, the sanderling shifts sharply right, and the much faster falcon, unable to alter course at this speed, streaks by. The sanderling has abruptly changed direction.

The falcon shoots skyward, using the momentum of its failed approach, effortlessly adding all the potential energy of gravity and the advantage of height. The sanderling's directional change widened the gap, but this bird has no place to go. Having rested its wings for a few seconds during the upshot, the falcon launches a refreshed attack. The sanderling suffers the added disadvantage of continuous exertion at the extreme of its ability. The falcon could afford the miss. The sanderling can afford nothing. And eventually the sanderling has to tire.

The falcon easily powers into another overtaking dive, coming in right behind the sanderling. Which shifts again. The falcon streaks past, again shooting itself skyward without a wingbeat.

The sanderling pivots, speeding away in the opposite direction. It has already gotten a hundred yards farther when the falcon half-rolls and planes into its next attack. The sanderling cannot maintain this level of exertion. That is not possible.

Yet, again, the sanderling shifts and the falcon shoots past. This is a life-stakes bullfight with the bull charging from behind at a hundred miles per hour. The sanderling, coordinating flight, sight, and perfect timing, is proving itself less a hopeless victim than a consummate opponent.

Maybe the falcon and I were misjudging the situation. I was certain that the sanderling's energy would be failing by now, but I detect no change in its flight speed. And maybe speed isn't the whole game here. You'd think the peregrine's superior speed—displayed on every attack—would absolutely make the difference in a chase. But at the moment when it matters most, the sanderling is using the falcon's speed against it. By precise and finely timed shifts, the sanderling is repeatedly turning the falcon's speed advantage into a disadvantage.

The sanderling's speed is critical. The faster the sanderling flies, the slower the falcon's relative speed. This gives the sanderling the added fractions of a moment to judge the progress of the coming rocket and to shift at just the right instant. But the *absolute* speed of the falcon prevents it from shifting abruptly with the sanderling. So while the sanderling needs to be going fast enough to avoid the falcon, it also needs to be going slow enough to make the shifting maneuvers that the falcon cannot match. And while speed keeps working for the sanderling, speed is simply not working for the falcon.

Again the falcon closes. Misses.

They are covering a *lot* of airspace. I watch six or eight attacks over maybe three minutes. Each attack spans about a quarter mile. Only the sanderling's very abrupt changes in direction—and my binoculars—keep the drama in view.

Another miss. The sanderling continues flying flat out. But the falcon—gives up!

Astonishing!

Each animal is a professional at what it does. Whether the falcon succeeds or the pursued bird escapes depends utterly on each creature being precisely aware of itself, of its distinction from the other, and of its masterful use of space, speed, and other aspects of its environment. Falcons and humans have been hunting partners since antiquity because we have a compatible understanding of the world. When you are out with a falcon you've trained, you share anticipation and feel their excitement, as you both examine the world for something you have in mind.

. . .

Somehow the mirror test became the standard for determining whether an animal "has self-awareness." That's silly. The test cannot make that distinction. A creature *lacking* self-concept would be unable to differentiate itself from anything, so it would *assume* that the reflected image is itself. But a mobile creature unable to differentiate itself from anything could hardly exist. It could not navigate the real world, escape, mate, or survive. Obviously, many, many animals know the difference between themselves and the rest of the world. But very few recognize themselves in mirrors. Even humans seeing a mirror for the first time don't fully comprehend their reflection. When first shown a mirror, New Guinea tribesmen reacted with "terror." So recognizing one's self in a mirror must mean something else.

It does. When an individual "fails" to recognize their reflection, all it proves is that they don't understand reflection. Because only a few species recognize themselves in a reflection, and because that's been confused with lack of self-awareness, science writers give the impression that self-awareness is rare. In reality, it could hardly be more commonplace. All day and everywhere, life and death continually depend on high-performance self-awareness and razor-sharp distinctions between self, environment, and others. And all without a mirror.

Most animals simply don't understand reflection. Others simply might not care. One morning soon after we'd adopted our dog Jude, I woke and saw him facing the tall dressing mirror in our bedroom. When I sat up, I could see his face in the mirror. Without turning, he began wagging his tail. It seemed that he saw and recognized my reflection. He did not turn around to look at me (though he knew where I was and had just heard me sit up). It was as if he just enjoyed the moment of seeing me reflected in the mirror.

Everyone "knows" that dogs "lack" mirror self-recognition. But now I wonder. Puppies recognize animals in videos but soon lose interest, probably because the images are not interactive and don't have scent. Maybe dogs know that the reflection in mirrors is themselves and don't much care. Dogs don't *mistake* mirror images for other dogs; they don't try to greet or attack them, as many birds do. Maybe dogs simply aren't interested in examining themselves visually, because they're so smell-oriented.

That's why I was intrigued when Jude wagged his tail as my reflection appeared in the mirror he was facing. Creatures who use mainly scent to ground-truth the world may smell a rat in the mirror's lack of confirming odors. Interestingly, dogs *can* recognize images. They recognize computer-displayed photographs of dogs and of humans they know. Even more impressive to me, dogs recognize photographs of dogs, regardless of breed, as all being in the category "dogs," distinct from other species. Deciding whether a dog has self-awareness by whether it examines its mirror image is like a dog deciding that we lack a concept of self because we don't linger to sniff our own, uh, shirt.

Apes do figure out that the image in the mirror is themselves. Zookeepers had been watching apes recognize themselves in mirrors for over a century, doing things like examining the insides of their mouths, which they love to do. But not until 1970 did four chimpanzees undergo the first formalized test. Researchers surreptitiously placed a dye mark on the chimpanzees' foreheads. Later, encountering their reflection in a familiar mirror, the chimpanzees touched the marked spot on their own skin. The researcher concluded that this was the "first experimental demonstration of a self-concept in a subhuman." It was nothing of the sort. But the assertion has been dogma ever since. We put a mirror in a cage to see if the creature goes, "That's me!" If they do, we say they have a "concept of self." Otherwise, they "fail," as most researchers put it: no self-awareness.

Um, no. When a bird, say, *attacks* the mirror, it does so precisely because it believes the reflection is *another* individual—*not itself.* This proves that it understands that it is distinct from others. It demonstrates self-concept. It doesn't "fail" the mirror test. An animal that *attacks* its reflection clearly knows the difference between self and not-self. It is attempting to attack what it thinks is not-self. If the subject shows fear of the reflection or solicits play—as monkeys and some birds do—it has likewise proved that it has a self-concept. It just doesn't understand reflection.

All the mirror test shows is whether an animal understands reflection of itself *and* cares about its reflection. Mirrors are extremely primitive tools for understanding the complexities of minds. It's preposterous to say that animals who don't understand their reflection don't distinguish "self" from "not-self." Self-recognition is why a wolf eating an elk's leg doesn't bite into its own leg. A concept of "self" is absolutely basic.

One morning years ago, I walked a short distance from my home to cut a branch that had grown across a path I frequented. I went home and shortly came back out for my usual walk with our dog, who always trotted a few yards ahead. When she got to the cut branch, she sniffed it over and over, seeming surprised to find my fresh scent, doing an olfactory double take, because, clearly, I was behind her. Sight is not dogs' main mode, and smell is not ours. But, mirror or not, they know themselves, and their friends, well.

Even creatures who eventually recognize their mirror reflections assume at first that they are looking at another individual. They try social responses and perhaps threats, then often try to see behind the mirror. But the select group of reflection solvers—including apes, dolphins, elephants, and a few others—eventually realize that the individual in the mirror is doing everything they're doing. They start testing their hypothesis with exaggerated, obvious movements such as rocking, circling, cocking their heads, opening their mouths, wiggling their tongues. "Is that one—*me*?" And soon they realize it is. And then they do what we all do: look at places that are hard to see without a mirror, especially the insides of their mouths, their genitals, and for dolphins, their blowholes (human children like to look into their own nostrils). One dolphin Diana Reiss worked with liked to spin while keeping his eyes fixed on the mirror for much of each rotation, like a ballet dancer practicing pirouettes. If a dolphin likes looking at their body in a big mirror and you replace the big mirror with a small one that lets them see only a part of themselves, they'll back up until they can again see their whole body. Dolphins know exactly what they're doing.

Ironically, mirror-test enthusiasts overlook what's perhaps the most interesting thing: understanding reflection means that you understand that the reflection is not *you;* you understand that it *represents* you. Fathoming "representation" means that the mirror gazer's mind has *symbolic* abilities.

That's a bigger deal. If you see a member of your own species, then realize that, because the image is doing everything you are doing, the image must represent you (even though you've never quite seen yourself before), that demonstrates rare abductive reasoning. So apes, dolphins, and elephants recognize their mirror images as representing "me." These are all smart classmates. Magpies do, too, which makes us wonder who else is hiding in the mirror.

One species that is very good with mirrors sees itself not *only* in the mirror. It also sees itself in the moon, in clouds; it assumes that the whole universe revolves around it. Maybe a mirror is mainly a test for which species is the greatest narcissist.

And Speaking of Neurons

Any active player in the world must have ways of sensing the "me" from the "not-me." Animals must build a fortress (body, immune system), surrounded by a moat (the mind's self/not-self boundary), but we need a drawbridge when the self has to mingle with the not-self—for instance, in judging the mood of another who is a potential ally, rival, or mate. The drawbridge is composed of nerve cells in the brain that have been given the name "mirror neurons."

The problem with talking about "mirror neurons" is that they've been crazily hyped and need to be dialed back quite a ways. Still, they're helpful to know about.

Before we get to "mirror neurons" and their hype, though, just think of them this way and don't worry about what to call them, and you'll be scientifically up-to-date: certain nerve networks in the brain help put us in emotional sync with others. Is this a strictly human ability? Hint: "mirror neurons" were discovered in a monkey. Hint: when I hug our dog Chula, Jude wags his tail. If Patricia and I argue, both dogs slink under the furniture. Is it uniquely mammalian? Hint: parrots sometimes get crazy jealous. The coordinated flocking of so many birds, the schooling and coordinated hunting of many fishes, the preference of certain tortoises for certain humans, and the presence in worms of the same mood-making brain chemicals that cause humans to feel love—all of these phenomena show that the roots of tuning in to others go deep, blurring across species and into the fade of time. We aren't exactly alike, but we're not simply different. Being related means there are bridges and connections. Look around; you'll see them.

Though discovered in macaque monkeys, mirror neurons were instantly hailed by some researchers and many popular accounts as the "great evolutionary leap forward that made us human." Turns out, V. S. Ramachandran (his friends call him Rama), at the University of California at San Diego, has *a lot* to say about mirror neurons. Maybe too much. He says they: create empathy, allow us to imitate others, accelerated evolution of the human brain, and catapulted our ancestors into a cultural burst-out, starting seventy-five thousand years ago. Quite a list—anything else? You betcha! Also: tool use, fire, shelter, language, and the ability to interpret another person's behavior—all triggered by "the sudden emergence of a sophisticated mirror neuron system. . . . This is the basis of civilization." Anything else these cells make possible? "I call them Gandhi neurons," Ramachandran says. Ohhh-kaaaay—why? "Because they dissolve the barrier between human beings." Really? "Not in some abstract metaphorical sense." Really. "And this, of course, is the basis for much of Eastern philosophy." *Philosophy!* "There is no real distinctiveness between your consciousness and someone else's consciousness. And this is not mumbo jumbo." Who ever said it was? But are the triumphs of mirror neurons a teeny-tiny bit exaggerated? "I don't think they're being exaggerated," he answers. "I think they're being played down, actually."

It's odd that some researchers and the media appropriated nerve cells discovered in the brain of *monkeys* as "the thing that makes us human" and seized this to explain our "extraordinary human capacity for empathy."

We're obsessed with filling in the blank for a Mad Libs line that goes: "_____ makes us human." Why? Scratch and sniff the "what makes us human" obsession and you get a strong whiff of something that could fit into that blank: our insecurity. What we're really saying is "Please tell us a story that distances us from all other life." Why? Because we desperately need to believe we are not just unique—as all species are—but that we are so very special, that we are resplendent, transcendent, translucent, divinely inspired, weightlessly imbued with eternal souls. Anything less induces dread and existential panic.

Everybody, please, calm down. Be human, strive, act with kindness and compassion, serve, dance every now and then, appreciate life while you can—that's about the best there is. It's our chance to be magnificent. But I digress.

One thing about mirror neurons is: actually, no one understands what they really do. A review of two decades of studies, published as I was working to understand why people were hailing mirror neurons as the driving force behind the humanness of humankind, concluded, "The functional role(s) of mirror neurons . . . remain to be solved."

The other thing about "mirror neurons" is: as a distinct cell type, they might not really exist. A variety of types of neurons, in several parts of the monkey brain, light up when the monkey performs a goal-directed action (such as moving a hand) or watches another monkey or researcher perform such an action. Why do they fire? What does it mean? Do they fire to create the mind's recognition of the other's action? Or does the recognition occur elsewhere in the mind? Fact: no one yet knows. The gap here, between what's actually known and what some researchers have claimed they know, is a large crevasse.

Why did popular magazine writers run so hard toward mirror-neuron hyperbole? "I myself am partly responsible," Dr. Rama admitted, "because I made this playful remark, not entirely serious, that mirror neurons will do for psychology what DNA did for biology." Perhaps he was still feeling playful when he added, "Turned out I was right, but . . . a lot of people, anything they can't understand, they say it's due to mirror neurons." That couldn't include you, Rama, could it? And then, as if belatedly remembering where it all started, he said, "If mirror neurons are involved in things like empathy and language and all of that, then monkeys should be very good at these things." Um—right. This shows, he noted, that mirror neurons aren't solely responsible for what he said they were responsible for. So he's probably sorry about any confusion, right? "Those kinds of errors are quite common, but that's okay. It's how science progresses. People make overstatements, and then correct them." Sometimes people do.

But if you sort carefully, there's value in the discovery (if not the discussion) of such cells. Think of it this way: *somehow* our brains create understanding of what we and others are doing and why. Calling the different kinds of neurons involved in this "mirror neurons" reminds us that the art of understanding what's going on around us doesn't "just happen" to us. Specialized nerve-cell networks are required to make understanding possible. Mental disorders help show that different neurons do different things. People with certain kinds of autism can't sense other people's goals or desires, or social norms. Yet such people often function well in other areas. Brains are very diverse, hugely complex internetworked multisystem syndicates.

In a real sense, there isn't such a thing as "the" brain; it is not "an" organ. Any sliver of a liver is pretty much the same. Not so brains. Brains are layered and compartmentally specialized; you can see their evolution in their structures and functions. Brains lie quartered in the head, but in those corporeal suites, different departments represent varied companies functioning within the parent conglomerate. We result from acquisitions and mergers and novel additions from the distant depths of living time to the relatively recent era. The same is true of the brains of every other species, in their ways. Many species share an inheritance from common ancestors. On top of that common core, evolution has added to each species some signature flourishes that "make us human," *or* make us chimpanzee, *or* a white-throated sparrow singing, *Oh Canada, Canada, Canada.*

When we look for "intelligence" in other species, we often commit Protagoras's error of believing that "man is the measure of all things." Because we're human, we tend to study non-humans' human-like intelligence. Are they intelligent *like we are*? No, and therefore—we win! Are we intelligent *like they are*? We don't care. We insist that they play our game; we won't play theirs.

What other animals must learn, the problems they must solve, and how they must solve them differs greatly. A human must make a spear; an albatross must travel four thousand miles from her nest to find a meal and then return across open ocean to an island half a mile wide and pick out her own chick from among thousands. A dolphin or sperm whale or bat might pity us for staring dumbly into the night while their brains virtually "image" a high-definition sonic world at great speed, allowing them to hunt, identify others, and catch fast-moving food in darkness. We might seem to them as utterly bereft of crucial abilities as they seem to us disabled by lack of language—though actually they are extremely enabled, in some ways we cannot match. Many creatures blow us away at sight, hearing, smell, response time, diving and flying capacities, sonar abilities, and migratory and homing abilities (even under the sea). Many are super-hunters. Extreme athletes. (Humans are the best at running on two legs—if you exclude ostriches.) Different brains emphasize different abilities, enabling different living beings to excel at exploiting different circumstances. There is room and reason here for respectful appreciation, for a sharing of the world.

The supposed unknowability of other animals' experience was raised in a famous essay by Thomas Nagel called "What Is It Like to Be a Bat?" The idea is that a bat's life is *soo* different, we can't begin to answer that question; we can only know what it's like to be a human. But do we really know what it's like to be human? Do we know what it *means* to be human? To some extent yes, to some extent no. When I've visited Arctic natives or sailed with Polynesians, I've found that we share the basics, yet we differ in detail. The differences are a lot, but the similarities are enough. I don't *entirely* know what it's like to be them.

In the post office and supermarket, I see the same rows and shelves as do those neighbors who clean my other neighbors' homes; we see and inhabit the same world, but I don't know what it's like to be them; they don't know what it's like to be me. What is it like to have grown up as a New York girl whose immigrant father committed suicide in the Great Depression? My mother, who gave me my life, has lived that different life. What is it like to play the harp in the New York Philharmonic? What is it like to be a child soldier? I probably better know what it's like to be a hungry poodle in a suburban home than what it's like to be a hungry, hopeless person in a Nairobi slum, though I've seen that place in person. When our dogs are happy or tired, it's obvious; I know what it's like to be happy or tired myself. But I don't really know—it pains me to guess—what it's like to be hungry and hopeless.

So while there is a lot about being a bat that is different, there's a lot about being a person that is different, too. Bats feel comfort, rest, arousal, exertion, maternal urges; they're mammals, so there are shared basics. And are we referring to sonar-using insect-catching bats, or to pollinating bats, or to fruit bats? About 20 percent of all mammal species are bats, so to be cheeky about it, I guess we must specify, What *kind* of bat? There are more than twelve hundred species.

Ludwig Wittgenstein, the philosopher, famously said, "If a lion could talk, we wouldn't be able to understand it." Like most philosophers, he had no data. Worse, he seems not to have known any lions. Such impediments never give philosophers cause for pause. But okay. He implies that humans, at least, understand one another. Yet do we? Our words often fail. When Arabs and Israelis talk, do they understand each other? Can Sunnis and Shiites talk to each other? Many of us can't communicate effectively with our own parents or children. So, Wittgenstein, come off it. We all seek food, water, safety, and mates. We seek status so that we can have preferential access to food, water, safety, and mates. If a lion could talk, he'd likely bore us with the mundane: the water hole, the zebras, the warthogs, wildebeest ad nauseam. Sex. Cubs. More sex. Anxiety about those two new threatening brothers with their gorgeous thick manes. What's so hard to understand? Their concerns—food, mates, children, safety—are our concerns. After all, with lions on the same plains, with both of us following the same prey and stealing each others' kills, we became human. We have a lot in common. It's not the lions' fault if some humans later became philosophers.

People of an Ancient Nation

———

Early winter. I've just stepped outside my writing studio. The pooches Chula and Jude are lying in a nice patch of sunlight in a pile of recently fallen leaves. They're not in shade, as they'd be in summer. They're doing exactly what we'd do. Soaking up the remaining sun, feeling comfy. (Comfy is also why they lie on their pillows at night rather than the hard floor—except in summer, when the hard floor is cooler.) I crunch a few leaves walking over; they glance up at me. Chula looks me in the eyes, wondering if I've come with a request or an offer. I stand still and her gaze drifts toward the street; the sound of the school bus is familiar to us both. She knows it and has no need to go investigate. In familiar territory, listening to familiar sounds at frequencies we both hear, enjoying the warmth of this winter sun, we share much the same moment. We're using the same senses: sight, smell, touch, temperature, hearing. I see many colors. They smell many scents, and their hearing is more acute. Our experience isn't the same. But it's comparably vivid.

This morning, when I accidently cracked an egg while removing it from our chicken coop, the pupsters were immediately there, lapping it up. We share taste, too. Shared senses. Why else would they have eyes, ears, noses, sensitive skin, and those adorably sloppy tongues, all connected to a brain? Hmm? *Right? You good girl.* I know more than approximately what it's like for Chula to be feeling *soo sleeepy* that she can hardly keep her eyes open beside the woodstove on a winter night. Later, when it's time to turn out the light and they're getting into their beds, I know what that is like because I am doing the same in our shared home, in the same bedroom, in our shared routine. It's not much of a stretch.

But other aspects of Chula's experiences, of what she senses when we go for walks and she is sniffing, sniffing, and what thoughts and feelings those scents excite—I can't know exactly. But Jude can. Yet I know enthusiasm when I see it, joy when I feel it, love when I share it. There's plenty there. They might not contemplate their own death or imagine next summer's vacation. Neither do I, most of the time. In the moment they're highly perceptive and alert. Except, of course, when they're just snoozing in a sunny pile of leaves. My dogs are my friends and part of my family. I know them better, actually, than I know the man living across the street. I do what I can to care for them and to keep us safe and well. They share more of my life than do my human friends. Like most of my human friends, my dogs and I are together by accident, and I just enjoy their company. Being around them makes me feel good. Why, exactly? Dog only knows. When Jude, say, chooses between the rug and the sofa, his every action—including his reaction to our coming home and finding him on the couch, where he's usually not allowed—shows his consciousness of choice and the logic of his brain's sensations.

When I am out at dawn looking for a swirl of fin, my eye is drawn to ospreys and terns, who are also looking for the same fish, with the benefit of a birds'-eye view. I've spent many hours studying terns, and I feel that we have a lot in common. What is it like to be a tern? I don't quite know, except that in some ways, I kind of do. I've been among them in their nesting neighborhoods on hundreds of days, watched them courting and raising their chicks, year after year; I've seen how hard they work, followed in my boat the ones who knew where the fish were on many a given morning. They are experts, athletes, professionals. I've learned a lot from them, about their world as they know it, and the world we share.

Acting hungry, happy, or scared in contexts that make sense to us, so many creatures behave as if they feel human-like emotions. If you play with a ferret or young raccoon, for instance (or almost any mammal and some birds and reptiles), you see how much fun they're capable of, and you sense that their play includes elements of humor. On most mornings or evenings, our hand-reared orphaned squirrel, Velcro, descends from the trees for treats and play sessions. She can easily spend an hour hopping around on our laps and shoulders, wrestling our hands and flipping herself upside down for vigorous belly tickles. We interpret Velcro's vocalizations as a form of squirrelous laughter (she makes us laugh, that's certain). Rats playing with one another or being tickled by human researchers produce sounds very much like the laughter of human infants. (Rats' laughing sounds originate above the range of human hearing, but researchers can downshift the sounds into the human-hearing range.) Rodent mirth arouses the same brain area aroused by joy in humans.

So do squirrel joy, rat joy, and human joy feel similar? Rodents who seem to be having fun apparently are. "Young animals we have tickled become remarkably friendly toward us," writes leading researcher Jaak Panksepp. Our squirrel friend Velcro can't get enough. We often have to put her back on her big old maple tree and leave her, because we have things like jobs to go to and can't spend a whole morning just playing. At those moments, she seems to have her priorities in better order. She certainly knows how to have a good time. I had no idea squirrels had such interactive playfulness in them, but because we hand-reared her, she revealed a lot.

For full-blown humor, though, apes are the practical jokers. Frans de Waal relates that when the senior male bonobo at the San Diego Zoo descended into the enclosure's dry moat, a junior male sometimes quickly pulled up the chain that allowed access back up. De Waal writes, "He would look down with an open-mouthed play face while slapping the side of the moat. This expression is the equivalent of human laughter; Kalind was making fun of the boss. On several occasions, the only other adult, Loretta, rushed to the scene to rescue her mate by dropping the chain back down, and standing guard until he had gotten out."

You have to deeply deny the evidence to conclude that humans *alone* are conscious, feeling beings who can enjoy living and desire to continue doing so. In other words, life, liberty, and the pursuit of happiness. People who play with a dog—or a squirrel or a rat—and then believe that the animal lacks consciousness, themselves lack a certain consciousness. Such people certainly lack, in a peculiarly human way, the wider empathy that our dogs and others so generously, so naturally grant to us.

Thing is, though, a lion or a squirrel—even Chula—cannot talk. Communicate, yes. But talk, no. Especially not to humans. Some notable birds (such as crows, mynahs, and parrots) and a few mammals (including dolphins, elephants, and some bats) can learn and utter new and different sounds. Most monkeys and apes, however, seem to have instinctive calls that they can't change very much. Humans have universal instinctive calls—distress scream, laughing, crying—plus, we acquire languages.

Humans have a universal brain *template* for acquiring language. Onto this template we *learn* to speak in Italian, Malagasy, and so on. Humans speak using the same physical structures that dogs use to bark and cats use to meow. Humans' unusually fine and facile capacity for control of sound production appears to be just a matter of unusual brain wiring. In an arrangement unlike those of other primates, human brains have a direct connection between the part of the brain cortex involved in voluntary movements (the lateral motor cortex areas) and the brain area called the "nucleus ambiguus," which facilitates motor control of the larynx, or "voice box." Other apes and even mice have the gene called FOXP2, which helps enable human speech, but our version contains a minute mutation—two amino acid changes—that makes a shattering difference in vocal control, facilitating language capacity. This innovation in the human lineage appears to have been a prerequisite for speaking and singing. In a sense, the primate vocal tract—jaw, lips, tongue, with their muscles and nerves from the brain—was sitting there waiting for the larynx to come under fine voluntary control. As it did, speech became possible.

Most other animals do indeed lack the physical ability for speech. Apes like Kanzi the bonobo can understand hundreds of spoken human words and use keyboard symbols but cannot utter human speech. Though humans' differences from other animals are small, and just a matter of degree, small degrees eventually make a big difference. Complex speech enables our brains to network our minds and form multigenerational memories more complicated than the learned traditions at work in some other animals. Complex language allows complex storytelling. Not simply a monkey or bird's present-tense "Hey, I see a snake" but one human's ability to convey to another, "I saw a viper there yesterday, so be careful."

Because apes generally cannot make human-like sounds, in the 1960s researchers Allen and Beatrix Gardner, their student Roger Fouts, and his research-partner wife, Debbi, raised a chimpanzee in a family setting, teaching her sign language. She became the world-famous Washoe. Later Washoe taught other chimpanzees to sign things like "Give me apple." Chimpanzees can combine signs, so "fruit" plus "candy" means "watermelon." Some signing chimpanzees' sentences stretch to half a dozen words.

"Give me apple" may be explicit, but its complexity pales compared to the mental processes and group coordination among free-living chimpanzees cooperating to cut off the escape routes of colobus monkeys who themselves are freaking out with fear and knowledge as the chimps prepare to attack. Chimpanzees would not be able to live in our communities with us, and we would not be able to live in theirs with them. But they know what they need to know and do, in great detail. Chimpanzees remember the locations of *a thousand* or so fruit trees, keeping track of their ripening progress over weeks while the band patrols its large territory.

When you think about human work with captive apes, remember that they are highly social creatures whose laboratory and zoo populations were founded by kidnapped infants plucked from their social context and cultural history. People captured at different locations and thrown together as slaves communicate in what's been called "the crudest shadow of human language, virtually without any grammar." By analogy, these apes taken as infants from murdered mothers were likely denied the chance to develop the richness and nuance in communication skills seen in natural, deep-rooted ape communities.

Free-living chimpanzees don't use words with specific definitions. They use dozens of calls and as many gestures whose meanings rely partly on context but convey much information. A breakthrough in translation was recently announced by ape researchers (who not only study apes but who actually—formally—*are* apes). Turns out, all apes use gestures to communicate. These gestures are understood by all individuals in the group. They're directed at specific individuals, who understand them, and they're used intentionally and flexibly. Researchers in Uganda have produced a first "lexicon" of 66 gestures used by chimpanzees to deliver 19 meaningful messages, such as "Come here," "Go away," "Lets' play," "Give me that," and "I'd like a hug." Gorillas use more than 100 meaning-bearing gestures. And bonobos use a human-like wave to beckon another to come over and then, with a debonair twist of the palm, indicate a direction in which the waver is inviting the wavee to go for a discreetly private sexual tryst.

The bonobo Kanzi was born in captivity and grew up with his mother at a research facility in Georgia. Under intensive contact with researchers, he's used special touch screens to wield a 300-word vocabulary, making comments and requests and combining words. He understands more than 1,000 English words, including sentences with syntax. Videos show Sue Savage-Rumbaugh with him on a picnic. She asks him to prepare a hamburger and light the fire. He does. Primate expert Craig Stanford wrote, "If there is a difference between what Kanzi comprehends and what a human toddler comprehends, scientists have not yet discovered it." But I have: you wouldn't trust the toddler with the lighter. (YouTube has fascinating videos of Kanzi using syntax and flaking and using a stone knife; see "Kanzi and Novel Sentences" and "Kanzi the Toolmaker.")

Anthropologist Dawn Prince-Hughes, who as an autistic child had difficulty acquiring language, found a kind of identity with a group of gorillas in Seattle's Woodland Park Zoo, eventually getting a job as their caregiver. She calls the gorillas "the first and best friends I ever had . . . people of an ancient nation." Meanwhile, back in the Georgia lab, Kanzi had been watching videos of the gorilla Koko and, unbeknownst to his humans, had picked up some of Koko's American Sign Language. (Kanzi, remember, had been taught to communicate using symbols on a keyboard.) When Kanzi met Prince-Hughes, he watched her mannerisms for a brief while, then signed, "You gorilla, question?"

By 1982, Washoe had given birth to two babies but lost both, one to a heart defect and one to an infection. When research assistant Kat Beach became pregnant, Washoe expressed great interest in her belly, signing, "Baby." Beach had a miscarriage. Roger Fouts wrote, "Knowing that Washoe had lost two of her own children, Kat decided to tell her the truth. MY BABY DIED, Kat signed to her. Washoe looked down to the ground. Then she looked into Kat's eyes and signed CRY, touching her cheek just below her eye. . . . When Kat had to leave that day, Washoe wouldn't let her go. PLEASE PERSON HUG, she signed."

Though some non-humans can learn to use a few human words, human capacity for extensive language appears unique. (By "language" I mean a system of extensive vocabulary with grammar and syntax.) Human children pick up and master the complexities of speech intuitively. When a child beginning to use the past tense says, "I thinked," instead of "I thought," they are applying a grammatical rule they've never been taught. Harvard psychologist Steven Pinker believes that a child's ability to create verbal structure means that human brains come preprogrammed to acquire grammar. Apparently, humans are born with a human language instinct. If that's close to true, then human language comes as naturally to humans as rumbling and trumpeting comes to elephants, howling and growling to wolves, and sonar clicking to dolphins. Which, come to think of it, should seem obvious.

But the implications are unsettling. Perhaps we are as truly, deeply, and biologically *incapable* of understanding the richness other species perceive in their own communication as they are incapable of understanding our species. What if their communication modalities are lines we can smudge but never truly cross? One of the great dreams of humanity, to "talk with the animals," may be off the table. Talking with the animals may be impossible, not just because they can't talk to us but because we might be as incapable of having a conversation in elephant as an elephant is of commenting on the prospects for rain in English or Farsi.

And yet. There's a little more to it. When humans ask dolphins and sea lions to find an object that isn't in their pool, they either look extra hard—indicating that they know what they're looking for—or they don't bother looking—indicating that they know that what they're being told to look for isn't there. Significantly, because there is nothing round about the word "ball," the human word is an *abstract representation,* a symbol. Yet any animal who understands that "ball" means ball understands the abstract symbol. Chimpanzees can form abstract concepts like "food" and "tools" and can sort objects, as well as *symbols* for objects, into these categories.

"When we ask things of animals, they often understand us," Elizabeth Marshall Thomas wrote. "When they ask things of us, we are often baffled." Orangutans can evaluate how well a human is understanding their gestures. When gestures fail, they sometimes pantomime what they would like from the human. When the human has seemed to partially understand their meaning, researchers wrote, "orangutans narrowed down their range of signals, focusing on gestures already used and repeating them frequently." When misunderstood, however, the orangutans came up with: *new* signals. Orangutans are able to establish shared meaning—if the humans prove capable of understanding what they're trying to express.

Shared meaning. Understanding. That's the quest.

PART FOUR

Killer Wails

*Exception might be taken to the name
bestowed upon this whale . . . for we are
all killers.*

—Herman Melville, *Moby-Dick*

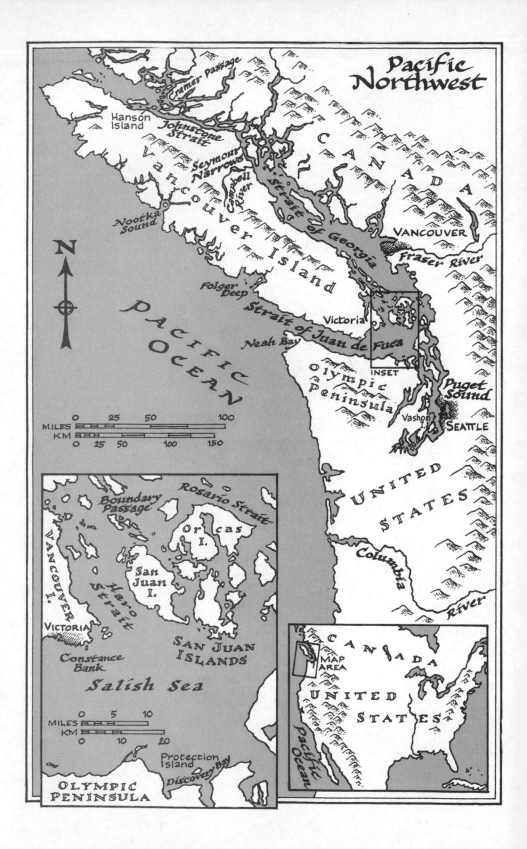

Sea Rex

———•———

Ken Balcomb inhabits an otter's home in a deer's meadow with an eagle's view, his house perched among pines on a slope that toes to the sea, granting an expansive panorama from San Juan Island across Haro Strait.

Today the strait is whitecaps and foam, the wind spitting rain, with gulls shooting by on near-gale gusts. Across the strait, Vancouver Island, Canada, appears as mountains beyond blue mountains between blue sky and blue water. The strait's manifest denizens include the world's largest constellation of sea stars, the planet's most far-reaching octopus, and the world's largest dolphins—killer whales. Shore to shore and surface to sea-floor, the whales know it as one country. Their country.

In no other living room have I ever felt so at sea. And on a low coffee table rests a skull, three and a half feet long, weighing 150 pounds. Its enormousness and those rows of interlocking teeth make it the closest thing to *T. rex*. It's Sea rex. And it lives. Somewhere out there right now swim creatures wielding skulls like this one, taking their living by these massive jaws and those rows of thumb-thick daggers. Feared in our own time by even the sea's greatest whales, killer whales exert power without peer since dinosaurs sighed out, sixty-five million years ago. But the killer's subtle, sensitive side makes a hunter with complex notes that *T. rex* could never have hoped to emulate: intelligent, maternal, long-lived, cooperative, intensely social, devoted to family. They are, like us, warm-blooded milk-makers, mammals whose personalities are really not much different from ours. They're just a lot bigger. And notably less violent. The brains—also a lot bigger—manage the tasks of family, geography, social networking, and the minute analysis of sound.

Ken has just started explaining how the whales create and use sonar when, for some reason, my gaze shifts past the windows, to the moving water.

Just beyond the near-shore kelp bed, my eye catches a sudden puff of vapor. But no fin. So I'm thinking, Dall's porpoise? Then: a steamy blow. I can't imagine that a killer whale could breathe without showing its high-flying dorsal fin, but at that moment the sea slits open and out bursts a starkly black-and-white head.

Holy—! But why haven't they announced themselves? The speakers on Ken's kitchen windowsill continually stream sound from a nearby array of underwater microphones called hydrophones, via OrcaSound.net. So far, the speakers have been conveying only the sea's white-noise hiss.

Hurrying to the big, tripod-mounted binoculars at his kitchen windows, Ken scans. "Could be transients," he says intently. "They're usually silent."

There are a couple of fins now.

"Not going particularly north or south," he says, almost to himself. "A few gulls following. Not traveling fast, just looking around . . ." He scrutinizes the scene, then adds, "Fairly broad-based fin on that male. Long dive time. More and more like transients."

Transients: mammal eaters. The "resident" killer whales are fish eaters who mainly chase salmon; they're usually chatterboxes, very vocal. The transients can be quiet stalkers, cloaked in silence from the seals, dolphins, sea lions, and occasional whales they seek—for whose breaths and bubbles they listen.

We step out onto Ken's kitchen deck. We might as well be on the deck of a boat. The low sun shoots glitter across the sea. Ken spreads the legs of his tripod-mounted camera.

A fishing boat labors by. But minutes pass with no sight of blow or fin. I ask, "How could they just—disappear?"

"Oh, transients can do that. Soft blows, like that first puff you saw. Not putting a fin up, long dives—. Many a careful watcher has gotten the slip from transients."

Fully a quarter of an hour later, there they are again, off the point.

"Oh—" breathes Ken, his eyeballs buried in the binoculars. "That's, I think, T-19." An identification seems impossible in the wind-roughened whitecaps. "See the fin leaning slightly toward the left?"

T, for Transient. No routes or routines. Constantly they move. Abruptly they can disappear. Suddenly here they are.

There's another male with a more erect fin. And another, possibly a young male. Coming on slowly. Close to shore. Farther off, two females.

"Oh yeah, yeah, yeah," Ken says, his eyes glued to his binocular lenses. "Oh boy."

You'd think a guy who studies these whales full-time might be a little less excitable. But if he were, he wouldn't still be here, four decades in.

Well ahead of the males, a harbor seal pops its head up. Looks around. The males are moving with deceptive speed, and the seal is, one might say, dead ahead.

"The seal hasn't—" Ken starts. "Reaction is crucial, but—"

The seal slips from the surface like a raindrop. Visibility underwater here is only about ten feet. The seal is about a hundred yards from the nearest whale. Its problem: timing. Three lurking giants capable of echo-imaging the open water just came around the corner. To sonar-wielding whales, the seal might as well be a black silhouette on a light table. Even if the whales are moving cloaked in radio-blackout silence to avoid detection, they're swimming listening posts of exquisite sensitivity and analytical ability.

And though the seal might be surprised and perhaps inexperienced, the whales know the drill. This kind of seal is more than half their diet.

Suddenly the three nearby males are surging through a spreading patch of slick water.

"Well, that seal should have acted immediately," eulogizes Ken.

Natural selection, in real time. Two gulls dip. One of the whales lunges through the surface, jaws clenching part of the seal. Dismemberment has its privileges; they've shared it.

A neighbor rings the phone. She's seen it all, too. Another neighboring couple suddenly rounds the point just north of Ken's house in a small outboard boat as the high-finned males parade past, dwarfing them. These males are twenty-six to twenty-eight feet long and weigh about seventeen thousand pounds. The seal they've just torn to pieces probably weighed about as much as both people in the boat. Yet mysteriously, no free-living killer whale has ever killed a human.

I'd have thought that they'd get vocal after a successful hunt, but we still haven't heard a squeak from these whales over the hydrophones. "Must be looking for more," Ken says. Harbor seal–hunting killer whales need about a seal a day each, roughly 250 pounds. They'll chase, catch, and consume seals several times a day, sharing them. Food sharing is rare and rarefied among adult animals. The list is short but varied. The few species who hunt in groups—such as lions, hyenas, wolves—share big kills. Vampire bats share regurgitated blood with relatives and friends, who later return the favor. Social insects share food. Some monkeys share. Humans share. Some housecats bring "gifts." Chimpanzees sometimes share meat—though often grudgingly and almost always with political allies or sex partners. Bonobos, on the other hand, will actually release an unrelated bonobo from an adjacent room and eat together instead of eating all the food alone. Then there are the rarely observed instances: an online video shows a horse feeding another in an adjacent stall; an injured crow places choice morsels against its enclosure netting, where familiar free-living crows can reach it.

Killer whales share all the time. A whale who catches a salmon that could be swallowed in a gulp shares it with family members three-quarters of the time. Sometimes killer whales wait at the surface while one of their group goes for a long dive, surfaces with a fish, and gives it to waiting comrades. In Argentina a killer whale named Magga caught ten sea lion pups in two hours, taking each to waiting juveniles, then returning to the shoreline for another.

People uncomfortable with the word "killer" have long since called these whales "orcas" after their Latin name, *Orcinus orca*. But the word "orca" itself refers to a demonic underworld; it's not very flattering. And scientists will probably formally recognize several different species of *Orcinus* whales, but only one will retain the name *orca*. Then calling the non-orcas orcas will get awkward.

Like roses and elephants, they've been given many names. In this region, fishermen call them blackfish (confusing: pilot whales are also called blackfish, killer whales aren't all black, neither one is a fish, and there's a fish called the blackfish). Kwakiutl natives call them *max'inux,* and the

Haida call them *ska-ana*. In the western Pacific, the Aino people of the Kuril Islands refer to the *dukulad*. Over in the eastern Arctic, the Inuit call them *arluq*. Down at the tip of South America's Tierra del Fuego, the Yahgan people call them *shamanaj*. Just as the different elephant species are all called elephants, researchers tend to call the different killer whales simply "killer whales." Because they're the world's largest dolphins and so starkly black and white, were it up to me, I might have called them "domino dolphins." "Sea pandas" has even been tried. But undeniably, they're the baddest whales out there. They're the sea creature that nothing in the sea dares to hunt. So I think of them as "killer." Often enough, they own it. As I'm about to see.

In under five minutes, Ken has downloaded his photos and is confirming IDs of the seal-hunting whales by comparing the photos he just took to his digital database, matching dorsal fin irregularities and the distinctive white "saddle" patches. That's what you can do with a million or two photos taken over decades—if you're exceptionally organized. "That was T-19, T-19b, T-19c, T-20 . . ." T-20 is about fifty years old. Ken clicks through the pages of these whales' photos and genealogies. Births. Deaths. Family relationships.

Mysteries, too. No one had ever seen the T-20 group before 1984; now they show up annually. One whale, T-61, vanished for thirteen years—then returned.

Ken's VHF radio crackles sporadic chatter from whale-watch boat captains thirty miles away in Admiralty Inlet. They're saying that some killer whales are moving toward Puget Sound. Ken hears the captains and the sea itself with the ears of a professional listener. But so far the sea has been issuing merely its continued hiss. For eight years in the U.S. Navy during the Cold War, Ken—a big, amiable man, easygoing to a fault—listened to the ocean for sounds of submarines. Ken could also hear something else: whales. But the project was secret. "I couldn't tell anybody about what I was hearing," he says.

Now Ken's talking. He is explaining how killer whales are masters at the production and analysis of sound. Like all dolphins, they live in an aural soundscape of their own creation. Even in a world of cold, green, often murky water, they generate sound to unveil prey far beyond visibility and to stay in touch with their comrades and children dozens of miles away.

Ken shows me how the killer whale skull's contours are sculpted for the production and reception of sound. Unlike human and other mammalian voices produced in a larynx, whales and dolphins manufacture sound in their skulls. Highly specialized sound. Ken says that he believes these whales can probably focus and shape a beam of sound. Some researchers have suggested that they might disorient or stun fish with focused blasts of sound. When they want to, dolphins can generate something over 220 decibels, loud enough to be painful if you're near them underwater. Ken thinks they might be able to adjust how loudly they hear their own sonar blasts, using their huge trigeminal nerve to control incoming sound intensity. (The skull's trigeminal nerve cavity is so large that I can place two fingers in it.)

Ken explains some differences between the mammal-eating transients and the fish-eating residents. Transients' calls differ from resident whales'. Transient groups don't form stable "pods" but, rather, split and merge. They're more "fission-fusion." Transients hunt in small, quiet groups. Residents sometimes form chatty, playful multipod aggregations. Transients often hold their breath for fifteen minutes. Resident whales seldom stay down more than five. Big differences.

When mammal-eating transients hear the fish-eating residents' cheerful chirps a few miles away, they detour or even turn around. You might guess that the mammal eaters are fiercer—transients do pack more robust jaw muscles—but residents usually move in larger groups.

Once, ten members of a resident pod suddenly started swimming at high speed toward a bay two miles away where several other highly excited pod members were creating a great commotion. Together, they charged farther into the bay. Suddenly the transient T-20—one of the seal eaters I've just seen—surfaced, along with T-21 and T-22. They were clearly fleeing the residents. The whales were so agitated that researcher Graeme Ellis could hear their underwater calling over the noise of his engine. The transients managed to sprint away, with the chasing residents just two hundred yards behind. And the residents weren't fooling around. T-20 and T-22 were marked with fresh tooth wounds. (This instance is apparently the only physical aggression ever documented between free killer whales.)

But when the transients fled the bay, the residents didn't follow. Instead, they milled around for half an hour, until one of their pod members, who had not been present during the attack, suddenly appeared and joined the group. It was the female J-17—and her newborn infant. Had she been hiding? Had her pod's aggression been motivated by anxiety over mammal-eating whales in the vicinity of their family's newborn?

Another time, whale specialist and author Alexandra Morton was watching forty members of the resident A pod splashing around "in high spirits" when they suddenly vanished. They reappeared against the far shoreline, moving swiftly, no longer splashing, bunched tight, babies tucked close. They ducked into the first bay. Morton swung about and caught sight of four transients—again including T-20, who gets around. Did all the whales precisely understand one another's agendas? The whales are under no obligation to tell us. But do you have a better explanation?

We've done a little photo work, talked about killer whales, and from the kitchen we've seen killer whales kill a seal—it's been a typical Sunday at Ken Balcomb's home. From this perch, Ken has spent most of his life on the lookout for killer whales. "He's closer to them, in some ways, than to people," says a friend. "In the night, when the windows are open, he'll wake and say, 'They're here.'"

In the 1960s, when Ken was coming of age, California still had whale-hunting stations. A professor sent Ken to get samples from dead whales. "It was gory," recalls Ken, "but I had the stomach for it." Then, in 1972, Ken watched a fin whale actually getting killed. "I was unprepared to see the whale look at us like, 'Why are you doing this?' I had kind of an emotional breakdown. I was like, 'What have we just *done?*' I felt like I was working at Auschwitz or something, just horrible." When his professor got a grant to count the killer whales in Puget Sound, Ken leapt. "Nearly forty years later," he sums up, "we have more questions than when we started."

A More Complex Killer

Until the 1970s, when pioneering studies began in the Northwest, a far simpler killer whale roamed the human imagination: a worldwide species ferocious enough to kill any whale—and certainly any human—that swam within its furious clench. Aggressive dominant males managed harems whose females bore the commander's young. Wrong. Decades of watching, listening, tagging, cataloging, and genetic sleuthing have pulled the veil off not just a new killer whale but *numerous* new killer whales.

Turns out, several "types" of killer whales swim the North Pacific. We've already met "transients," who travel widely. Individuals seen off Monterey, California, have turned up off Glacier Bay, Alaska, fifteen hundred miles away. "Residents" range about one thousand miles, north to south. They stay closer during summer and fall, swimming this maze of islands, following the fortunes of salmon funneling toward coastal streams for spawning. The rest of the year, they're gone from here. But transients' and residents' *diets*—not their travels—distinguish them. Transients show no interest in fish as they pursue mammals. Their jaws are built for their larger, much more difficult prey. Residents, on the other hand: no interest in eating mammals. And inside that diet difference hide surprises inside surprises. They're like those Russian dolls; you see one but—surprise!—inside it are others, similar-looking but different.

So we have transients and residents—and more dolls. Out in the North Pacific roam little-known "offshores," whose existence wasn't even suspected until 1988, when researchers puzzled over smaller whales, with different calls, hunting sharks. In groups of up to a hundred, they rove far from coasts, between the Bering Sea and South America. One seen off Mexico in 1988 was sighted again three years later off Peru, thirty-three hundred miles distant.

Ranges of the different "types" overlap—but no one's ever seen them mingling. DNA shows that North Pacific fish-catching (resident) and mammal-hunting (transient) killer whales have avoided interbreeding for about half a million years. In fact, North Pacific transients are the most genetically distinct of all the world's killer whales. When free-living animals freely interbreed, they're the same species. When they don't, they're different species. Most killer whale "types" now seem clearly to be previously unrecognized species.

Field guides still show one worldwide killer whale, *Orcinus orca*. It's likely that scientists will eventually amass sufficient data to recognize separate species and bestow new Latin names. Until then, scientists refer to the various "types"—such as Antarctic types A, B, and C, pack-ice killer whales, and the others. At least five types swim just Antarctic waters.

"Pack-ice" killers cruise the Antarctic in small hunting groups, lifting their heads to look for seals resting on ice. A whale finding a seal examines it, "apparently to make sure it is the right species," says killer whale expert Bob Pitman. If it is a Weddell seal, the whale disappears for twenty to thirty seconds, rallying its comrades. A couple of minutes later, the group is gathered, everyone looking at the seal. "After a minute or two of collective appraisal, the group decides either to move on or to move in." If they decide they'll attack, they go as far as 150 feet *away* from the ice floe and the seal. Then, "as if on cue," they turn abruptly toward the floe, tails pumping in unison. A wave approximately three feet high forms above the synchronized flukes. The whales dive under the ice at the last second. The wave breaks over the floe and usually washes the seal into the water.

A different killer whale, half the size of the pack-ice whales, inhabits Antarctica's Gerlache Strait, hunting penguins. "Amazingly," Bob Pitman says, "the whales apparently feed only on the breast muscles and discard the rest of the carcass." The Ross Sea killer whale, the smallest known (males reach only twenty feet, and a third the weight of some larger types), penetrates miles-long cracks in frozen ocean, hunting Antarctic toothfish (sold as Chilean sea bass) that can weigh two hundred pounds. In the North Sea, killer whales herd herring schools into tight balls. There are other types, as well.

So to review: killer whales used to be thought of as one worldwide species. Now it appears that eight or so "types," with differing food specializations, are likely different species. Here's the biggest surprise: spectacularly, some of the largest undiscovered species on Earth have been hiding in plain sight. Amazing.

———

Before dinner, the hydrophone system continues to convey only the sea's deep, vague static, a lonely lifeless hiss, the sound scattered like atoms in interstellar space. When we hear the passing whine of a motorboat, Ken comments offhandedly, "He's radiating about one to four kilohertz in the, oh, hundred-and-sixty-five decibels range." The boat sound builds and softens, returning us to that static hiss.

Humans hear from about 40 or 50 hertz up to about 20,000 (20 kilohertz). Deep bass in music is about 80 to 100 hertz. We speak at about 500 to 3,000 hertz (3 kilohertz). Killer whales' "frequency notch"—the sound they're most capable of hearing—is around 20 kilohertz. "They can hear well at other frequencies, but that's their primo," Ken says. Their sonar is in that range "because you can get pretty fine resolution there." It's generally above most people's ability to hear.

We vocalize with a stream of air, then need another breath. We talk through our mouths. Dolphins, they're different. A dolphin forces air through the nasal passages inside their head, then—this is weird—they process and amplify the vibrations through a special rounded fatty "acoustic lens" in their forehead (this gives dolphins their rounded, "melon-headed" shape). The energy exits the dolphin's head as a beam of sound.

Their hearing is even odder. Incoming vibrations striking their lower jaw get picked up by oil in hollow jawbones and carried to their inner ears. I guess you could say their jawbones perform the sound-collecting function of the outer ears of other mammals, though very differently.

The sonar-using "toothed whales"—the dolphins (including, of course, killer whales), porpoises, and sperm whales—have more than triple the number of nerve fibers in their ears than do land mammals. Their massive hearing nerves are the largest-diameter nerves in any creature of any kind. Why so many and so big? "For transmitting large quantities of acoustic information at very high speeds," scientists say. By comparison, our brain's routing is like a very slow modem. Some dolphins seem able to shift the frequency of their sonar if there happens to be a lot of noise in the frequency range they normally use. It's a bit like switching a two-way radio to a different channel if there's too much chatter on the channel you're using. Meanwhile, they have lost the nerves and brain structure that other mammals use for smell. It's possible that they can't smell at all.

The great "baleen whales" can produce, as do elephants, sounds too low-frequency for human hearing. But an elephant would be astonished to know what a whale can do with sound. The big whales make sounds as loud as a medium-sized ship. You can't hear it; their frequency is too low. Yet whales very, very far apart can hear one another. Whales such as finbacks swimming *hundreds of miles* from one another can migrate "together," their calls letting them stay in touch during their travels. The animal kingdom is symphonic with mental activity, and of its millions of wavelengths, we're born to apprehend the minutest sliver.

After dinner, before bed, laptops closed, we're sitting in Ken's kitchen just chatting, having a glass of wine, when through the little speakers' white-noise static comes a single whistle that stops all conversation.

A soft shimmering starts seeping through like a slow flooding of sound. The quiet nighttime kitchen fills with squeaks, chatters, whoops, buzzes, whistles, whines, and squeals. It's as if, on an empty, dark road, a Dixieland band had just come round a distant bend. Coming nearer, getting louder.

For twenty minutes, from out in the darkness, they parade past us, whistling and chirping like rain-forest birds, sounding confident and energetic. Their crescendo and diminuendo builds and peaks. It's a surprisingly reassuring confirmation that such beings survive here with us in some numbers. And then the sound begins fading. And when the last of the living music reaches us, I sense what we'd lose if we lost them.

When the hiss again envelops us, it seems changed. No longer empty, but pregnant with possibility. It's the way a good fisherman feels, within his untouched line, a vast, anything-can-happen-now potential that floods him with the patience of a hunter. Which is to say, the whales have me; I'm hooked.

Just Very Sexual

———•———

In the morning, Ken comes floating downstairs in his bathrobe, saying buoyantly, "We have coffee. And—we have whales!"

He's tuned in to the hydrophones at Lime Kiln, a few miles south of us. His windowsill speakers weave for us an abstract aural tapestry of whines, whistles, whoops . . .

Who is it?

Ken holds up a finger to pause me. "Oh—there's a K; hear that kind of mewey, meek-sounding call, like little kittens? Uh, there's more than one pod there right now. I'll know better in a moment." Pause. "There's J pod," Ken offers. "J- and L-pod calls are more like honks and horns." Pause. "Okay; I hear Js, Ks, *and* Ls—all three pods!"

We step onto Ken's kitchen deck and look out at the strait. No whales. But then, sure enough, rounding the point a mile to our south, lined up in a broad front, killer whales come bursting energetically through steep whitecaps. Those high black pirate-flag fins, startling each time, slice through the spume as the wind blows their explosive spray into the sunshine. This is a big bunch of whales; from left to right they span my binoculars' entire field of view and then some, even at this distance. "Wow—there might be sixty, seventy-five whales out here!"

"They might *all* be here," Ken says, excited.

Indeed, *all* the killer whales of all three "resident" pods that are ever seen in these waters—J, K, and L pods—are headed our way. It's "a superpod!" Ken exclaims.

My qualifications for judging whale behavior are at the beginner level, but the whales seem to be in a good mood. During superpod aggregations, "the real old and real young ones like hanging out with each other," Ken narrates. "Females who haven't seen each other for months just stay together for days on end, and chat around as if wanting to talk about what they did all winter. The young like rolling and tumbling and chasing."

During their parties, play and love flow freely. They're light on parental guidance, and as in many other dolphins, much killer whale play is a bit X-rated. Young male killer whales start sex play in early childhood. "Even with the little one-year-olds," says Ken, "soon after they stop nursing, there's a lot of rolling around with their little snakes out." Older males aren't exactly inhibited with each other, either. "We see groups of guy whales with their three-foot wangers draped over each other—pink floyd, we call it." Like other dolphins, they frequently indulge in same-sex enjoyment, getting help from a friend's flipper or snout. Many free-living dolphins routinely masturbate against objects, and Ken has even had aroused whales rub against his boat. It's vigorous but not aggressive.

When Diana Reiss put a large mirror in their pool, the seven-year-old juvenile male bottlenose dolphins Pan and Delphi positioned their bodies in front of it—and watched themselves imitate the sex act with each other. (Bottlenose dolphins engage in more same-sexual behavior than any other known creature.) As Denise Herzing concluded, "Dolphins love to have sex and they have sex a lot."

Killer whale females start acting sexual in their teens—and never stop. "It's pretty interesting when postreproductive grandmas start rubbing against males, sliding along them," Ken tells me. In a killer whale version of "cougars," older, menopausal female killer whales seem to entice younger males into sex play. "Any randy young guy," Ken says. "Sometimes, even young males five or six years old. They'll get the males all excited. We haven't seen actual mating, but we've seen a lot of penises draped over whales that are upside down and downside up and sideways. They'll roll over and you can see that their vaginal area is swollen. There's a heck of a lot more sex than there is reproduction. They're just very sexual."

There's no other creature on Earth with a society quite like that of these fish-eating resident killer whales of the Pacific Northwest. As with elephants, the basic social unit is a family led by a senior female matriarch, with her children and her daughters' children. The big difference: although young male elephants leave their family as they mature, male killer whales stay in their birth family for their entire life. (They mate when socializing with other families but are soon back at their mama's side.) Mother-child bonds remain extremely strong, lifelong. And, in fact, in no other known creature do all children—daughters *and* sons—stay with their mother for the duration of her life.

As with elephants, each killer whale family's elder decision-making matriarch has memorized the family's survival manual, maintaining knowledge of the region, the routes and island passes, the rivers where salmon concentrate in their seasons, and so on. She's often out in front. Ken speculates that matriarchs make evaluative decisions, such as "Not many fish here; let's see what it's like at the Columbia River." Such a decision might mean a couple of days' travel; they swim seventy-five miles a day, commanding large areas.

Vocal calls play a strange but important part in the next layers of the residents' social organization. All the whales use certain common calls. But some other calls are used only by particular groups. Several families who share a small number of specific calls that are not used by other families form a stable association called a "pod." (Ken's research assistant Dave Ellifrit assures me, "They sound very different, even to an untrained ear.") Each resident pod uses between seven and seventeen discrete calls. Each whale in a pod has exactly the same call repertoire and uses the entire call repertoire of its pod. Different pods may share some calls, but no pod uses the exact same call repertoire of another pod.

So a killer whale pod is several families who regularly socialize, rather like an elephant bond group. Though killer whale families often travel independently, pods are real, cohesive social units. You see that when, for instance, the families of J pod travel together to the mouth of the Fraser River and K pod goes to Rosario Strait.

Next layer: "clans," composed of several pods whose members use another set of vocal calls not shared by other clans. Clans who socialize at least occasionally are called a "community." Communities *don't* socialize with other communities. Here in the Northwest, the two separate communities are the northern and southern residents. The eighty-some whales of the J, K, and L pods collectively constitute the southern residents. They usually range from the lower end of Vancouver Island, Canada, down to Monterey, California. The northern residents usually travel from

Vancouver Island to southeast Alaska, and their sixteen pods total about 260 whales.

Another thing—and this is also weird—is that these adjacent communities of fish-eating residents avoid mixing, for what appear to be purely *cultural* reasons, learned habits by which they create their own peculiar segregation. Northern and southern residents have been seen feeding less than a thousand yards apart—but never mingling. These whales here have been under a magnifying glass for decades; if they'd mixed, lots of people would have noticed. The DNA shows these non-mingling neighbors as genetically the same species. Yet the usual *behavioral* indication of *different* species is "two populations that do not freely interbreed"—and these whales don't.

We could be seeing killer whales openly in the process of separating into different species. If they continue to thoroughly avoid each other and both communities survive (the southern is now endangered), these different communities could evolve into different species. (Let's check back in a hundred thousand years.) Meanwhile, the only discernible differences between them *are* cultural: their vocal dialects. They seem to share everything else, including their mutual disdain for socializing with each other. This self-segregation of stable cultural groups is so exceptional that, researchers say, it has "no parallel outside humans."

Got all that? Pilot whales in the Canary Islands also seem to have resident (seen often) and transient (seen seldom) pods that don't mix. Sperm whales maintain vast, non-mingling "clans." In the Pacific Ocean, for example, researchers have identified six "acoustic clans" distinguished by patterns of emitted clicks, each clan spanning thousands of miles, each containing perhaps ten thousand sperm whales. Scientists know of no other stable cultural groupings at such transoceanic scale. Bottlenose dolphins have coastal and offshore forms that overlap in range but don't interbreed. That fits the definition of "different species," but they, too, are not yet officially acknowledged as such. Spotted and spinner dolphins also exist in different "forms." They're all here with us, they're big, they're smart—and we hardly know them.

To sum up: killer whales maintain a social structure more complex than chimpanzees'. And more peaceful. For all their heft and dental weaponry, when they find themselves in close proximity they either socialize or leave. Researchers have long been impressed by the absence of aggres-sion among free-living killer whales. Ken's assistant Dave Ellifrit once saw two males "collide with a thump, then go their separate ways." Is that all? Pressed for another example of aggression, Dave tells me, well, he once saw a mom trying to rest while her baby kept bothering her. "The mom smacked the baby with her head, like, 'Leave me alone!'" That's all the aggression he's noticed in over twenty years. After decades of listening to and watch-ing killer whales, Alexandra Morton writes of the synchronized breath-ing among family members, the way all the whales continually touch one another as they swim along, lightly running their flippers along the flanks of their companions or indulging in full-body contact; of the way no killer whale seems subordinate or second-class. She writes of the close interac-tions between mothers and children. She notes killer whales' "acceptance, approval, and peace."

Different physical forms, different languages, different cultures, family values—except for the lack of violent aggression toward their own kind, you might almost think killer whales were people. Some native peoples do believe that they are. Perhaps they intuit that killer whales' stable, tiered, culturally self-defined groups parallel human society. Perhaps they're right.

The superpod of partying whales go off-mike; that means they're headed in our direction. We keep watching—and they bring it. Blasting along in high gear, they stage an impressive show. When they are directly in front of the house, the closest is just half a mile from shore. Spaced fifty to one hundred feet apart, they're in a line formation about a mile across, searching for salmon like a big dragnetting crew, all sending beams of sound. Many more move in loose association out in the strait. Suddenly all the nearby whales seem to dive at once. I envision them rapidly closing a circle around a bunch of salmon, taking turns going in among the fish, eating them, sharing. In under a minute several pop to the surface, their cloud puff of breath heralded by the tall slice of those awesome dorsals. One male turns around with his head out, as if looking to see how many of his companions are up. A few more rise, bunched closely. A few gulls streak to the surface, grabbing floating fish scraps. Success in fishing seems to have the whales in a lighthearted mood, splashing and socializing and looking relaxed.

. . .

When Ken switches to the next set of hydrophones to our north, the northward-traveling whales come on as surely as if we'd stepped into a karaoke bar. A question arises: Do the complex sounds and complex brains of killer whales and other dolphins communicate complex things? Seems the answer is: yes and no. It's, well, complex. Dolphins can understand the syntax of sign-language sentences amounting to "Touch the Frisbee with your tail and then jump over it." Dolphins understand enough to ignore nonsense commands. They can learn several dozen human words and understand short sentences. But the dolphins' real world and society are infinitely more demanding, dimensional, and high-stakes than a pool with a human or two and a few toys.

While dolphins have grasped a bit about human language in the pools where they learned the signs and symbols used by researchers, we've never cracked their code or figured out how to use dolphin sounds to communicate with dolphins about dolphin things. Do they talk to each other and give each other commands and instructions and tell stories? We don't know. What they're thinking: we don't know. What they're saying: we don't know. Can we begin to know?

Like human babies, infant dolphins babble sequences of whistles that become more organized as they grow. At anywhere between one month and two years, bottlenose, Atlantic spotted, and other dolphins develop their own distinctive individual "signature whistles." Signature whistles are a name they create for themselves. The sound is distinctive, and the dolphin doesn't change it, ever. They use it to announce themselves.

Dolphins who hear their own signature whistled by another dolphin call back. They don't respond to a dolphin who whistles a third dolphin's signature call. In other words, they call each other by name, and they answer when they hear their own name called. Dolphins call their close friends' names when they are separated. No other mammal seems to do that (that we know of). Dolphins more than ten miles away can hear each other if water conditions are right. Atlantic spotted dolphins seemingly use names to call together several individuals. When groups meet at sea, they exchange names.

Female bottlenose dolphins stay in their mother's group for life. They develop signature whistles quite different from their mother's, and thus easy to tell apart as they travel together. Male youngsters—who will leave their birth group—develop signatures similar to their moms'.

Researchers have recently realized that various bat species, too, sing songs that include individualized calls. For instance, the European bat known as Nathusius's pipistrelle has a song with several parts; it says, in human terms: "Hear ye, I am a *Pipistrellus nathusii,* specifically male 17, I am of this community, and we share a social identity; please land here." In birds, various parrot species use signature calls to identify neighbors and individuals. Some researchers think that all 350-plus parrot species probably use signature calls. In "an intriguing parallel with human parents naming infants," say researchers, green-rumped parrotlet parents name their young ones, who then use those given names to refer to themselves. And Australian superb fairy wrens teach their unhatched chicks a password, and "the better they learn the password, the more they will be fed." Surely, in the enormous gap between dolphins and fairy wrens, there must be much, much more that we are so far missing, things currently unheard of.

Of course, dogs and others easily recognize their given names. Our smart little Chula knows who to run and find when I say, "Go get Jude" (her adopted brother) or "Go get Mommy" (her lady caregiver—and, admittedly, mine, too). And they can understand terms like "water" or "toy." And, certainly, "treat." When our puppy Emi learned "toy," she didn't just pounce on the nearest thing, like a shoe or sock, but looked for *her* toys, either in a box or on the floor, showing that she understood a concept that included several different items but excluded many others, a *category.*

Dolphins remember and recognize one another's signature whistles for their whole lives. In the experiment that showed this, captive bottlenose dolphins heard recorded signature whistles of dolphins with whom they'd been housed as long as twenty years earlier. They remembered and responded even if they'd known each other only a short while before being separated. The experimenter, Jason Bruck, concluded, "Dolphins have the potential for lifelong memory for each other." That was the first formal study showing social memory lasting twenty years in a non-human. But more informally, apes and elephants and some other species have, after separations of many years, reunited very touchingly with lost companions or human caregivers. Several such heart-rending reunions, caught on video, can be viewed on the Web. When orphaned elephants are brought from the Sheldrick Trust, in Nairobi, to Tsavo National Park, they meet older free-living orphans they may have known back at the nursery years earlier. When I visited, keeper Julius Shivegha explained, "After communicating, the elephants will say, 'Oh—it's you; I could not recognize you; you are grown so big!' Just like people who have not seen each other since one was a child."

Inner Visions

———•———

Something about dolphins—or, actually, about us—impels many to believe that the sea swimmers are better than we are. Perhaps our discomfiture over our own human shortcomings makes us yearn to believe that there is something, someone, more perfected than us, either in the sky or in the sea. We needn't worry. Lots of things qualify, in their qualified ways, as better than we. Including certain people. And, as my dogs are constantly explaining, many of the most important things are said without words. And maybe dolphins *are* better at certain things—but not at talking.

From everything we understand at present, it appears that dolphins' whistles convey information that is simple and repetitive, not complex, not specific, not highly patterned; not a word-based, large-vocabulary, syntax-equipped language. Yet few who love dolphins—myself included—really want to accept that. The calls just sound too complicated and varied. And so, waiting, we listen, hoping someday to hear more.

It must say something about humans or whales—or both—that some people have put a lot of time into listening to whales. In the 1970s, scientists realized that humpback whales sing structured songs. Strangely, even if they're coming from thousands of miles apart, males converging on mating grounds all sing the same song. Humpback song is composed of about ten different consecutive themes, each made of repeated phrases of about ten different notes requiring about fifteen seconds to sing. The song lasts about ten minutes. Then the whale repeats it. For hours in the ocean, in their season of courtship, the whales sing. Each ocean's song is different, and over months and years it changes in the same way for the thousands of whales in each ocean, the song somehow a continual work in progress, fully shared.

Sometimes the change is sudden and radical. In the year 2000, researchers announced that humpbacks' song off Australia's east coast was "replaced rapidly and completely" by the song Indian Ocean humpbacks off Australia's west coast had been singing. It seems that a few "foreigners" made the trek west to east, and their song," became such an instant hit with the easterners that *everybody* had to sing it. The researchers wrote, "Such a revolutionary change is unprecedented in animal cultural vocal traditions." And once a phrase in the song disappears, it has never again been heard, despite over twenty years of eavesdropping. What do the songs mean? Researcher Peter Tyack says, "We may have to thank the evolving aesthetic sensibilities of generations of female humpbacks for the musical features of the males' songs." Songs of humpback whales, by the way, have sold millions of recordings. We share that aesthetic. That might be both the biggest mystery and the best evidence of like-mindedness.

Killer whales in a group can be spread out over 150 square miles—and all be in vocal contact. Through the hydrophones I've been hearing their chirps, whistles, honks, whoops, and whatever you'd call what sounds like wet hands on a latex balloon. Most of the calls have sudden shifts or sweeps in pitch, making them recognizable through background noise. What song are the whales singing? What epic poetry of their origin are they reciting? If there's a code, no one's cracked it. Unless Ken sort of has. "Since the first recording in 1956," he says, "they've been saying the same things over and over and over. I've thought, 'Don't they have anything new to say?' They don't seem to be saying stuff to each other like 'Big fish here,' or whatever. They don't seem to have one call for 'prey' and another for 'hello.'" Each of their calls may be heard whenever the whales are vocalizing; it doesn't matter what they're doing. Ken feels certain, however, that "*they* know— from just a peep—who that was and what it's about. I'm sure that to them, their voices are as different and recognizable as our voices are to us. I'm pretty sure they have names for each other like other dolphins do, and that right now some of what we're hearing repeated are those signature calls."

There may be more communicated in the *emotion* that comes across. "A call might sound like *Ee-rah'i, ee-rah'i*," says Ken. "Does that mean something specific? Or does its *intensity* carry meaning? When the pods congregate, you sense intensity, excitement; it *sounds* like a party. When they're excited, the calls get higher and shorter—in other words, shrill." The calls might not have syntax, but what comes across among the whales is who, where, mood, and, perhaps, food. *Pituuu* is a call that predominates when whales are synchronized in their actions ("We're doing this now; let's keep doing this together"); *Wee-oo-uuo* is a call of tranquillity and relaxed contact ("How we doing—good? Good"). It's enough to maintain coordination, cohesion, group identity, and group integrity—for decades.

So is this calling we're hearing also the sonar they use to find fish?

"No. Sonar sounds like—" Ken rapidly clicks his tongue. "Sometimes they come on the speakers with those clicks; that's them 'looking' for fish."

Clicks return an echo that the brain can use to extract information. Dolphins using sonar can detect a ping-pong ball one hundred yards away, a distance at which many humans would fail to see it. They can track rapidly swimming fish well enough to capture them, meanwhile avoiding obstacles while traveling at high speeds. They click fast: each click lasts just ten millionths of a second, and they make up to four hundred clicks per *second*.

Resident killer whales produce a series lasting about seven to ten seconds, called a click train. Residents produce click trains twenty-seven times more often and lasting twice as long as transients'. Transients are cryptic clickers. Transients sometimes produce just one single, softer click. Seals and porpoises have a hard time hearing one click acoustically camouflaged amid the ocean's constant aural static of little pops and the crackling of calling shrimp and other creatures, which can sometimes sound like something's frying in the ocean. Jacques Cousteau famously called the ocean "the silent world," but sound travels much better in water than in air, and many sea creatures use the ocean's sonic superhighway to great advantage. Or are betrayed by it.

Killer whales don't just make clicks; they're also always listening for a splash or a puff of breath. Consequently, there's an acoustic arms race among the high-acumen killers and their astute dolphin prey. Mammal-hunting killer whales sometimes hunt Dall's porpoises. The porpoises also use sonar, which you'd think would be like ringing a dinner bell on themselves. But their clicks are above the hearing range of killer whales. Such a separation could evolve and be maintained pretty simply: a porpoise whose click voice is low enough for killer whales to hear gets eaten. Higher-pitched callers literally survive at higher frequencies.

Only rather recently have people known about sonar in animals. Researchers didn't grasp dolphins' sonar until 1960. In 1773, the Italian Lazzaro Spallanzani observed that in a totally dark room, owls were helpless but bats flew freely. He was later astonished to find that blinded bats could avoid obstacles just as effectively as bats who could see. But how? In 1798, a Swiss experimenter named Charles Jurine plugged bats' ears; they crashed into things. He was baffled because the bats seemed silent. And when he announced that bats' hearing had something to do with their ability to navigate, his findings were first ridiculed and then, for a century, forgotten. (The history of rejection of new ideas that turn out to be true—including, famously, the idea that microscopic "germs" can cause disease and that physicians and surgeons should wash their hands—should caution us against too quickly dismissing the seemingly absurd. Whales, as you will read in the next few chapters, do some seemingly absurd things, still beyond human understanding.) In 1912, the engineer Sir Hiram Maxim thought bats produced sounds humans couldn't hear; but he suspected that the sound came from their wings.

In 1938, the "Spallanzani bat problem" was solved at Harvard by G. W. Pierce and Donald Griffin, who used a special microphone and receiver and tape-recorded bats emitting sounds above the range of human hearing. When they proved that bats could hear sounds in those ranges, our own bat-sonar blindfold came off. In World War II, humans devised analogous echo-based sonar and radar systems for military purposes. About a decade after Pierce and Griffin, Arthur McBride of Marine Studios (later Marineland), in Florida, noticed that during capture on very dark nights, bottlenose dolphins could avoid fine mesh nets and detect openings. In 1952, two researchers first publicly hypothesized that "the porpoise, like the bat, may orient itself with respect to objects in its environment by echo-location." Then experimenters proved that dolphins can hear sounds too high for humans. And Marineland's curator Forrest Wood suggested that captive dolphins seemed to be "echo-investigating" objects in their tank.

Not until 1956 did researchers report that captive dolphins emitted sound pulses as they approached dead fish, that dolphins could avoid clear glass panels that were moved around their tank, and that they could in darkness avoid suspended obstacles and identify a kind of fish they liked when it was presented alongside a fish they didn't like. (Much more impressively, many free-living dolphins hunt in the dark of night, chasing—and catching—small, agile fish.) When, in 1960, Kenneth Norris placed rubber suction cups over dolphins' eyes, they swam just fine, emitted sound pulses, avoided suspended objects, and navigated mazes. From the 1960s to the 1990s, other experimenters showed that similarly blindfolded dolphins, belugas, porpoises, and certain whales retrieved tossed fish and toys, swam obstacle courses, and basically had no trouble being sightless. Now we know that sperm whales, killer whales, other dolphins, and bats really do navigate by sound. In all the generations before, humans had been blind to the world of living sonar.

So much of a dolphin's head hardware and brain wiring is devoted to production and analysis of underwater sound, it's as if each individual functions as a sophisticated undersea spying station. But we humans, too, in our way, come well equipped for analyzing sound. We listen to recordings of orchestras or rock bands and, from the mere vibration of the speakers, effortlessly reassemble a coherent soundscape of violins, horns, keyboards, and drum fills, instantly identifying our guitar heroes and singing sensations. Whales likely hear their friends and families' social voices quite similarly to the way we hear ours. After all, it's easy for researchers to listen to their calls and know which pod is talking.

But because we're such *visually* navigating animals, sonar navigation is for us almost impossible to imagine. Our analogy is sight. When light bounces off everything, some goes into our eyes, and our brain makes for us an extraordinarily detailed vision of the world around us. We see, in other words, echoes of light.

Imagine being in a dark place with a flashlight, the beam originating from you, bouncing around so you can scan and see what's there. Now imagine that instead of a light beam, your body is producing a beam of sound, and that your brain can still make a detailed assessment of what the beam is bouncing off. Not an image—not visual, perhaps—but enough to tell you with great precision what's there.

When sonar signals are slowed so that humans can hear them, even humans can tell by the sound of the echoes whether the test targets are made of steel, bronze, aluminum, or glass—with 95 to 98 percent accuracy. Turns out, human hearing is very good at making distinctions. Think of how easily we recognize voices on the telephone or follow one conversation in a noisy restaurant.

We can't imagine how animals experience sonar without reference to sight. It's assumed that they hear the echoes and make a kind of auditory sound map so fine that they can use hearing alone to find and catch agile fish. We imagine that whales use sonar to make a sound "picture," as sharply focused as the light picture we assemble into vision. But I wonder: Might they *actually* see their sonar?

Consider: eyes don't see; brains see. Consider, too: there is nothing inherently "visual" about "light."

What we call "visible light" is a narrow range of wavelengths that is a very small part of the electromagnetic spectrum. Above and below the wavelengths that humans *can* see are others, just as real, called gamma waves, X-rays, infrared radiation, ultraviolet light, radio waves, and others. We don't see those because human eyes do not produce and send impulses about them along our optic nerves to our brain. Some other species, though, do see ultraviolet and infrared. Various insects, fishes, amphibians, reptiles, and birds—and mammals including at least some rodents, marsupials, moles, bats, cats, and dogs—see into the ultraviolet. Some snakes use pit organs—not their eyes—like pinhole cameras to *visualize* infrared energy emitted by warm bodies.

Perception of light and experience of vision happen inside the human brain. With our eyes closed, we can still see our desires and dreads in the "mind's eye," and in dreams. You can rummage around in a bin with your hand while visualizing something familiar you're "looking" for. With our eyelids open, our eyes create *impulses* based on the pattern of electromagnetic wavelengths striking our retinas, then send the impulses along optic nerves into vision centers in the brain that decode the impulses; the *brain* creates a picture, then presents the picture to our conscious minds for our viewing pleasure. So our eyes don't really "see the object"; the brain *creates* images from reflected energy. And there is nothing "red" about the wavelengths we see as red; color perception is just how our brain color-codes incoming impulses of certain wavelengths. A video camera sends impulses through wires to a monitor that turns the impulses into pictures.

When you look at the monitor, your eye, nerves, and brain instantly do the same thing.

Like light, sound comes in waves. Like vision, hearing is created in and by the brain. Electromagnetic wavelengths we happen to be able to "see," we call "light," and vibrational wavelengths we happen to hear, we call "sound." Above and below what we can hear and see are other wavelengths that fill the world but lie outside of our senses.

Is it possible that whales' and bats' brains, using sonar-reflection input, create actual vision? I can't see why not. Might a whale's brain take nerve impulses from its sonar echoes, just as it takes nerve impulses from light, and turn them into an *image* that the whale—or a bat—might literally see? Sound and sight aren't as separate as they seem. When some people hear specific musical notes, they actually *see* certain colors. It's called synesthesia. On my boat I have a sonar machine that makes pulses of sound and then collects reflected echoes and turns them into electrical impulses that run through a wire to the machine for processing. The sound collector, wire, and processor act like an ear, a nerve, and a brain. The processed echoes get converted to visual images that appear on a screen. With the help of the machine, I'm using sonar to literally see the bottom contour, boulders, and slopes where fish live, and the position of fish in the water.

Perhaps the most amazing practitioner of echolocation among humans is Daniel Kish, blind since he was one year old, who early in life discovered that making clicking noises helped him get around. Much of his brain must be reassigned to sound, because he uses his own clicks to navigate. He can ride a bicycle in traffic (hard to imagine), and he has founded World Access for the Blind to teach other blind people to use their own sonar—to summon, as it were, their inner dolphin. Sounds from his tongue clicks, he explains, "bounce off surfaces all around and return to my ears as faint echoes. My brain processes the echoes into dynamic images. . . . I construct a three-dimensional image of my surroundings for hundreds of feet in every direction. Up close, I can detect a pole an inch thick. At 15 feet, I recognize cars and bushes. Houses come into focus at 150 feet." This is all so hard to imagine, people have wondered if he is telling the truth. But he's not alone, and his claims appear to check out. He says, "Many students are surprised how quickly results come. I believe echolocation capacity is latent within us. . . . The neural hardware seems to be there; I've developed ways to activate it. Vision isn't in the eyes; it's in the mind."

So, *is* it possible that a dolphin such as a killer whale might actually *see* the echoes?

It's possible; no one knows. The least we can say about our shared, compared sense of the world is that while we are mostly visual and can also hear well, they are mostly acoustical, though they can also see. Same senses, different emphases.

If you imagine the very slow changes over millions of years that turned some mammals into apes and others into whales, we seem to have grown very distant indeed, almost estranged. But is that really a long time, or a big difference? Take the skin off, and the muscles are much the same, the skeletal construction nearly identical. The brain cells, under a microscope, are impossible to distinguish. If you imagine the process very much sped up, you see something real: dolphins and humans, both already having shared a long history as animals, vertebrates, and mammals—same bones and organs doing the same jobs, same placenta and that same warm milk— are basically the same, in merely shape-shifted proportions. It's a little like one person outfitted for hiking and another for scuba diving.

Whales are nearly identical to us in every way except their outer contours. Even their hand bones are identical to ours, just shaped a little differently and hidden in mittens. And dolphins still use those hidden hands for handlike gestures of touch and calming reassurance. (In any group of spinner dolphins, at any given time one-third are usually caressing with flippers or making bodily contact, a bit like primates grooming.) From primates to ponies to penguins to peepers to pupfish, the circulatory, nervous, and endocrine systems work in similar ways. And inside the cells? Pretty much the same structures with the same functions, down to amoebas, sequoias, and portobello mushrooms.

Living diversity is astonishing, but as you peel layers of difference, you encounter *similarities* more stunning. The extreme shrinkage of hind limbs that granted whales their swimming bodies was largely accomplished by the loss of *one* gene. (Geneticists call the gene "sonic hedgehog.") In your body, this *same* gene gave you "normal" limbs. Normal for a human, that is. If you look at side-by-side drawings of human, elephant, and dolphin brains, the similarities overwhelm the differences. We are essentially the same, merely molded by long experience into different outer shapes for coping with different outer surroundings, and wired inside for special talents and abilities. But beneath the skin, kin. There is no other animal like us. But don't forget: there are no other animals like each of them, either.

Diverse Minds

———

The different killer whale types each have very narrow ideas about what constitutes food. (There are parallels among human ethnic, tribal, and religious groups with various food customs and taboos.) Among killer whale types, we have the mammal hunters, shark hunters, penguin hunters, and fish eaters, who often specialize in certain fish—king salmon in the case of these residents, for instance—and seldom eat other fish. Throughout the world's seas, various types of killer whales eat everything from herring to large whales—but probably no killer whales eat all these things. For each prey specialty, the whales show strategic foraging specialties. Off Norway, for example, killer whales often herd a whole school of thousands of herring into a dense ball close to the surface; then, while most of the whales keep the herring balled by swimming around them—scientists call this "the carousel"—certain whales slap the ball's edge with their tails. The whales then dine on the stunned fish.

Transients in the Northwest mostly hunt harbor seals weighing one to two hundred pounds, but sometimes they attack thousand-pound-plus sea lions whose slashing canines resemble a supersized grizzly bear's. A fifth of the transients' diet here is extremely agile porpoises and dolphins. Closely cooperating whales often try to split up the groups of prey, then corner one group against a shoreline. Terrified dolphins have leapt ashore and died. When hunting big sea lions, the mammal hunters' task is akin to attacking a cornered cat with your teeth. I've seen a photo of a killer whale who'd lost an eye. Whales may spend hours beating up a sea lion until it gets sufficiently exhausted that the whales can drown it.

One day, an unusually large troop of transients—eleven—traveled to a place called Kwatsi Bay. Alexandra Morton was following them. The lead whales stopped and waited for nine minutes, until all the whales arrived. For a while, everyone just hung there, breathing. Then, as if cued, all the whales rolled into high-backed dives, indicating that they planned a long submergence.

As I've just seen with Ken, transients sometimes stay under for as long as fifteen minutes. When Morton's stopwatch ticked to fifteen minutes, she glanced up just as "a wall of white water erupted." A thousand-pound sea lion flew end over end through the air. Morton watched spellbound as some of the whales shot skyward while head-ramming three sea lions and other whales whacked them using their heavy tail flukes. Though utterly surprised and vastly outnumbered, the sea lions bunched together, trying hard to slash their attackers. The whales were working to avoid the sea lions' canines. Forty-five minutes into the battering, Morton, listening through her hydrophone, heard the orcas shaking the half-ton sea lions out of their skins, tearing their bodies apart. She wrote, "I had until now never truly realized the power of the killer whale. I sat there feeling amazed and blessed that the orcas never loosed this power on humans."

Killer whales rarely hunt big whales. But when they do, their persistence can be almost relentless. Minke whales (rhymes with "pinky") have superior endurance and can outdistance a killer whale during a prolonged chase. But a team of killer whales may pursue a swift minke for hours if they think they'll have a good shot at getting it. Researchers in British Columbia watched two killer whales in high-speed pursuit of a minke whale who entered a dead-end bay—then vigorously drove himself onto the beach in a desperate effort to avoid them. For more than eight hours, the killer whales remained nearby; as the tide rose, the minke thrust himself farther up on the beach. At nightfall, the killer whales were still milling in the bay. The next morning, the pursuers were gone. But the self-stranded minke had died. One wonders about the minke's panicked grasp of his own plight and failed strategy.

. . .

Whales learn migration routes by following their mothers. For Pacific gray whales, it's a long, sometimes harrowing trek: ten thousand miles from their bath-warm Baja birthing lagoons up through Alaska's Aleutians and—with luck—on to Arctic feeding grounds. They see, know, and deal with about as complex a life as do nomadic human hunter-gatherers. Along the way, and in the narrows of those Aleutian passes, killer whales shadow them.

Before killer whales can drown a young gray whale, they must separate it from its mother. This is difficult and dangerous, because gray whale mothers very aggressively defend their babes by lashing out with their back-breaking flukes. Often grays will lessen their vulnerability en route by clinging to coastlines, because killers cannot drown a whale in very shallow water. To prevent grays from maintaining this refuge, killers sometimes latch onto the front of a gray's pectoral flippers, driving the big whale backward. To counter this, gray whales may spin belly-up to make their pectoral flippers less accessible, or even beach themselves. Power and terror. Minds and counterminds.

One wonders whether the killers' understanding of what it means to protect their own child—coupled with their ability to form concepts—extends to their prey. In other words, do they ever feel bad afterward about killing their food? Likely not; few people do. Evidence is, killer whales don't.

Off California, my friends the whale and seabird experts Bob Pitman, Lisa Balance, and Sarah Mesnick watched thirty-five killer whales (collectively needing about seven thousand pounds of food daily) attacking nine female sperm whales for over four hours. Overwhelmed, the sperm whales formed a huddle at the surface with their heads together, tails out. Adult female killer whales attacked in parties of four or five, using a "wound and withdraw" strategy in which it seemed they were trying to kill through blood loss while avoiding the sperm whales' pounding flukes. Whenever the killer whales pulled a sperm whale from her group, one or two sperm whales "left the formation almost immediately, and despite the vicious attacks this brought upon themselves, they flanked the isolated animal, and led it back into the formation."

While the females attacked, several adult male killers remained distant. But the moment one nearly dead sperm whale rolled over, wrote the observers, "an adult male killer whale charged in and slammed into it, violently shaking the sperm whale from side-to-side. He then spun it around at the surface, throwing huge sprays of water into the air in an immense display of power not shown by any of the females at any time during the attack." At nearly thirty feet long, the male killer whale's mass could have put it at perhaps twenty thousand pounds; the sperm whale, at over thirty feet and much bulkier, might have weighed upward of thirty thousand pounds. Incredibly, another sperm whale came out of the formation, attempting to lead this doomed whale back, subjecting herself to intense attack. In humans, exposing oneself to great harm to aid another would come instinctively, and such behavior would be called heroic.

What followed was chaos and confusion so intense, it wasn't even clear which of the two sperm whales got killed. But the adult male killer whale swam off carrying a large dead sperm whale in his jaws. In the end, the killer whales killed and ate one sperm whale and injured all the rest, leaving some with devastating wounds. Wrote the observers, "We suspect that at least three or four of the survivors eventually died from wounds they received, and it is quite possible that the entire herd died as a result of injuries from the attack." (One cannot—at least, I cannot—imagine such a situation as anything but horrific for *all* the participants, trapped as they are in their own natures and circumstances, even more than are we. But that is precisely their excuse.)

Another time, the same researchers saw five killer whales headed toward a small group of sperm whales about a half mile away. Those sperm whales must have sounded an alarm, because another group of sperm whales immediately came swiftly *toward* the first group. Together they milled, some with heads raised from the water, looking in different directions, others slapping the surface with their tails, as if trying to signal a show of strength. A single adult female killer whale came among the sperm whales and seemed to bite one. Now four other distant groups of sperm whales charged in at full speed to join the main group, one group coming from more than four miles away. Others continued joining for about an hour, until the group built to about fifty sperm whales. Facing such well-communicated, unified enlistment, the killer whales left.

Ingrid Visser describes the strategy of a particular quartet of dolphin-hunting killer whales off New Zealand (she prefers the name "orca"):

The orca are cruising nonchalantly towards a small group of dolphins. The dolphins head away, but not too fast, as they don't want to draw the attention of the orca just in case they aren't really hunting. After following for 30 minutes, one female orca, named Stealth, doesn't surface the next time the others breathe, nor the next, nor for the following 10 minutes. The three remaining orcas take off towards the dolphins at high speed, which is incredibly dramatic as they hurtle through the surface. The dolphins are fleeing for their lives and they know it; they fly out of the water and don't even seem to touch down before they are off again. The three orca are closing fast. But suddenly one of the *front* dolphins goes flying as if it was a tennis ball, tumbling through the air as it turns somersaults. Stealth is also hurtling through the air in the follow-through after hitting the dolphin from below. She grabs the dolphin in mid-air, then falls back into the water with it in her jaws. Together, the four orcas devour the meal.

Visser adds, "I have never seen them miss."

Even stranger, then, that killer whales have overturned no kayak, emptied no rowboat, and slurped no human. It is perhaps the greatest behavioral mystery on our mysterious planet.

❧

Having watched a sizable group of whales pass the house and having eavesdropped on them over the hydrophones as they're moving north, we hop into the truck and sprint to a little marina tucked into a rock cove and backed by evergreen forest and carefully perched homes. It's pretty. I step onto Ken's boat with his assistants Kathy Babiak and Dave Ellifrit. We've barely cleared the harbor when we come startlingly face-to-face with about fifteen or twenty killers. This close, their size is alarming. Five times as long as a human, they weigh more than a hundred times what we weigh. Surging along, their heads push piles and pillows of water, their rising backs so wide that I watch the sea pouring off like water sheeting off an awning. Traveling before a sheer granite cliff under a steep fir-forested slope, they leave their breaths lingering in the air behind them. Their beauty and momentum induce an awe so thorough that I just silently stare.

There are others ahead. The thirty-five fish-eating residents here right now are the entire L pod. This high-finned adult male with the nick halfway up his dorsal's leading edge and the two nicks on its trailing edge is L-41; he's thirty-six years old. The female pushing just to his left, L-22, is now forty-two years old. Many killer whales have lived past their fifties. Whale L-12 was about seventy-nine years old when she died in the 1980s; K-7 was believed to be ninety-eight years old. L-25 is now eighty-five years old. You can feel that these whales are made to stay. You just don't know if they can.

While the topic is longevity, Ken is tapping his fingertip on a photo in his ID guide, saying, "So here's matriarch J-2." Females usually breed until they're about forty, and she's been nonreproductive since the study started, forty years ago. Her last offspring, the study's longest-lived male, died in 2010, and scientists determined that he was sixty at the time. If she was, say, thirty-eight years old when he was born, she'd have been born in about 1912. "That's why we think she's about a hundred years old."

Life after menopause is exceptionally rare in animals. It can evolve only in creatures where grannies help younger family members survive. Only human, killer whale, and short-finned pilot whale females routinely live for substantial periods after they stop breeding. Like humans, killer and pilot whales have roughly twenty-five to thirty childbearing years, then can live another thirty or so. And as Ken's just explained, some live a lot longer. Up to a quarter of the females in a group are postreproductive. These whales are not waiting to die; they are helping their children survive. As human children often benefit from their grandmothers' attention, killer whale grandmothers boost their grandkids' survival.

A rather bizarre twist of killer whale society is that killer whale mothers remain crucial to the survival of their *adult* children. When older killer whale females die, their adult children start dying at high rates, especially males. Male killer whales who are under thirty years old when their mothers die suffer a tripling of the annual mortality rate compared to males in their age group whose mothers are still alive. Male killer whales who are more than thirty years old when their mothers die face death rates more than *eight times* as high as males in their age group whose mothers are still living. Daughters under thirty show no mortality increase after their mothers' death. But daughters older than thirty when their mothers die have more than two and a half times the death rate of same-age females whose mothers are alive.

Males' handicaps of the extra drag of their huge dorsal and pectoral fins and the extra food required for their immense size (at around 20,000 pounds, males can be one-third more massive than females) seem to make them reliant on their working mothers for food. Females don't have the males' impediments, but while raising young, females may rely on food shared by their no-longer-breeding mothers. Adult females share essentially all the fish they catch, and more than half goes to their children. Adult males share their catch only about 15 percent of the time—usually with their mothers. While no one fully understands their strange death pattern following the loss of a mother, extreme parental care is likely at the root. Toothed whales are the world's champion nursers. Short-finned pilot whales continue to produce milk for up to fifteen years after the birth of their last calf, likely nursing other females' young.

In bottlenose and Atlantic spotted dolphins (further study might reveal others), some females *never* give birth. Denise Herzing dubbed them "career females," because their role in society does not include motherhood. They might be infertile. They might be gay. But their contribution is crucial: they do a lot of babysitting. When Herzing entered the ocean with a visiting nine-year-old girl, "White Patches, the eternal babysitter herself, had never seen me babysitting a young human before. Her excitement vocalizations were audible and electric and she continued to swim around us, eyeing the human youngster attached to me." (Researchers sometimes call babysitters "aunts." That's precisely who they often are.) In sperm whales, babysitters are particularly important while mothers are diving deep; their babies must wait near the sea surface, where they would be very vulnerable to killer whales and, perhaps, great white sharks. Sperm whales go one better: a female may nurse the group's various young, and traces of milk have been found in the stomachs of thirteen-year-old sperm whales.

Young killer whales who lose their moms at two to three years of age often survive only with extra attention from other family members. Tweak (a.k.a. L-97) was an infant when his twenty-six-year-old mother, Nootka, died of a prolapsed uterus; giving birth had killed her. Tweak was still completely dependent on milk. His grandmother swam with him but had no milk. Tweak grew thin. "We saw his nine-year-old brother catch a fish and try to give it to little Tweak," Ken says. The older whale tore the salmon into bits, presenting the drifting bits to the baby. But Tweak was way too young to eat. He didn't make it.

Another was more fortunate. When L-85 was three years old, his mother died. His thirty-year-old brother paid particular attention to him after that. "You'd see this little three-year-old just traveling along beside this massive male," Ken recalls, "almost like a mom." L-85 is now twenty-two years old.

Here comes lucky L-87. He's twenty-one years old. After his mother died eight years ago at age fifty, he survived. He is the only killer whale known to have switched pods. He went with K pod for a few years and now usually swims with the Js. Ken says, admiringly, "He's got a lot of personality. He's always spy-hopping to look around at the boats. Sometimes suddenly—*phoosh!*—here he is with his head up right alongside, obviously playing. He likes the reaction of the people. He has a sense of humor. They're not all like that."

The group contains males, females, and babies. As with elephants and humans, babies make families more active. "Best thing," affirms Kathy, "having kids around." Killer whales seem to delight in babies, Dave says, adding, "There have been times when a mom would surface on every side of the boat with her newborn, as if showing off to us." Mother killer whales have even temporarily parked babies at the boat while they swam off a short distance to fish or just socialize. Dave was drifting along with J pod once "when the moms with little kids came and said basically, 'Okay—here. Now y'all play around this boat.' So we had four or five kids, one to six years, playing around the boat while their moms went off foraging." Ken adds, "The kids had a great ol' time romping up to the bow and coming around the stern. They just play with each other like crazy, jumping all over each other."

Right after birth, multiple females often help bring a newborn to the surface for its first breath. "There were so many females," Alexandra Morton said about seeing a birth, "there was no telling who the mother was. They all touched that baby over and over." Mothers with nursing young frequently push them around on their snouts. One researcher saw three killer whales balancing a newborn in the air on their noses. (Quite a feat, since newborn killer whales measure eight feet long and weigh about four hundred pounds.) And tooth marks on a recent J-pod newborn suggest that a family member may have acted as midwife, helping pull the infant from its mother.

All kinds of dolphins nuzzle and nurse their young, with emotional bonds if not arms to hold them, their brains flooded with the same love hormones that bathe ours, their babes seeking and sucking the warm milk, their companions showing similar fussing, excitement, and concern. It's the same. I'm told that adolescent female dolphins, like adolescent elephants and many human teens, are "very, very interested in babysitting or being near babies."

When young dolphins test the limits of adult patience, mothers and babysitters chase and chastise them. Though people have noted dolphins pushing ailing babies to the surface for millennia, not until the age of face masks and behavioral research did anyone see a mother spotted dolphin pinning a misbehaving child to the bottom! But after a brief calming down, once the attending elder lightens up on the discipline, the young ones "resume their out-of-control behavior." After all, they're just kids.

Play and entertainment are part of their repertoire. Ken has seen the whales amuse themselves with a feather, balancing it on their nose, then letting it go and catching it with a fin, then letting it go and catching it with a fluke. "A seventeen-thousand-pound whale—playing with a *feather*," Ken marvels. "Such exquisite tactile control, and at good speed! They just have time for entertaining themselves."

Whatever play is, dolphins are very playful. Play—appropriately, though mysteriously, too—is part of smart. "Play is a hallmark of intelligence and is indispensable for creativity," wrote psychiatrist Sterling Bunnell. "Its marked development in cetaceans makes it likely that they frolic with their minds as much as with their bodies." Young bottlenose dolphins sometimes propel themselves out of the water, onto a dock. When they do, other young dolphins push and nudge them back into the water. It's the dolphin version of kids at a swimming hole.

Then there are bubbles. Bottlenose dolphins don't just blow bubbles. They're master bubble jugglers, skilled practitioners of bubble styling. And bubble juggling does take practice. So they do. Youngsters, mainly. Some first blow a bubble ring by accident, watch with intense attention as it rises, then work on perfecting ring blowing. Then: share and copy, engineer and play. *I'll blow a bubble cap just so and watch it form a ring. I'll spin some water with my tail and blow a bubble into the middle of the vortex. Watch that bubble get pulled into a circle. What would happen if I dropped a fish into a rising ring? Hey—the fish spins and rises! What if I blow the bubble sideways and it rises upright? What if I flick the surrounding water with my snout and set the sparkling ring spinning? What if I snip the ring? Splice the fragments into two little rings? Make a wiggly water-snake string of rising silver?* Inventing, testing, evaluating, modifying—all this, they do. Taking turns trying. How about: *I swim fast in a curve and let a vortex come off my dorsal fin, then turn quick-quick and inject a stream of air into the swirling vortex. Wow—a long silver helix shoots out in* front *of me. Match that!* (No one could; only Tinkerbell could do it.) Just blew a sucky bubble? Flick it; make it go away. Just blew an *excellent* bubble? Try to make a second one join it. Ready to quit? It's important to bite that final ring before it reaches the surface, clear the Etch A Sketch. Game over. On the other side of the glass, an infant, awed by the big kids' bubble mastery, tries a few bubbles. A few more. None form rings. Maybe someday, kid—keep tryin'.

In the Bahamas, free-living Atlantic spotted dolphins often play keep-away with researchers. One day they showed up with a live filefish. "The dolphins carried it ever so gently in their mouths and dropped it, inviting us to grab the terrorized thing," wrote Denise Herzing. "But right before one of us reached the poor fish, the dolphins showed their aquatic superiority and swooped in to grab the fish." It seems extraordinary that these free-living creatures view humans as worthwhile playmates. That they do carries big implications about minds understanding minds. Here they are, and this is *who* they are, coming across that species bridge on their own terms, bringing their own invitation, offering their own game, playing by their own rules. They've done this many times. The terrified fish, meanwhile, show their own understanding of who they need to worry about by trying hard to hide from the dolphins—in the humans' bathing suits, or between a video camera and a human face, as the dolphins buzz and poke to get back their living toy. Herzing said that while she felt sorry for the fish, giving it back to the dolphins "seemed the courteous thing."

· · ·

One day Ken was watching several killer whales who were focused on getting some salmon. All except J-6, a teenage male. "He went from boat to boat and burst his head out right alongside and just looked at everyone, just—showing off." When the whales pass certain land points where people line up, clapping and shouting, Ken claims, "the whales get much more excited and acrobatic and really put on a show." People will be running along the shoreline and the whales will flap their tails and slap their fins and jump. Same if they're near whale-watching boats with people cheering." Why? "Because," he says "I think we're as entertaining to them as they are to us."

Intelligent in What Way?

⎯⎯•⎯⎯

Partway into considering examples of dolphin "cognition," I realized that dolphins are as cognizant as anyone. There are so many examples of them acting aware and clever (because they are aware and clever) that one might as well try to compile examples of humans acting aware and clever. That's just who we are. And it's who dolphins are, too. Dolphins and humans have not shared a common ancestor for tens of millions of years. Yet for all the seeming estrangement of lives lived in liquid, when they see us they often come to play, and we greet them and can recognize in those eyes that someone very special is home. "There is someone in there. It's not a human, but it is a someone," says Diana Reiss.

When we speak of "dolphins," bear in mind that of the more than eighty dolphins and whales, only about half a dozen—bottlenose dolphins, dusky dolphins, spotted dolphins, killer whales, sperm whales, and humpback whales—have been studied in any behavioral detail, and only in parts of their ranges. The seas are home to seventy-plus species of toothed whales (sperm whales, dolphins, and porpoises) and about a dozen large baleen whales (instead of teeth, they strain out tiny bits of food using sievelike brushy plates). Collectively they're called "cetaceans" (from the Greek for, basically, sea monster). They are the swimming mammals with blowholes atop their heads. We've scarcely made their acquaintance.

Academic study of dolphin intelligence got off to a rickety start that cost it about a decade. In some sense it has never recovered from its first publicly noted researcher, who cloaked dolphins with a mystical allure they've never quite shaken. On the other hand, dolphins have earned a bit of mystique.

In the late 1950s and '60s, neurophysiologist and brain researcher John C. Lilly presented us with creatures whose gigantic brains made them our superiors. It was an improvement on the idea that whales felt only an inexplicable urge to swallow humans. But Lilly, too, was wrong. John Lilly pronounced that an animal with a brain the size of a sperm whale's must have a "truly godlike" mind. We'll leave aside the question of what a "godlike" mind would be and what a whale would do with one. Lilly mistakenly assumed that brain size translated directly to thinking ability.

Different species' brains emphasize different abilities. The nerves and brain structure for detecting and analyzing scent is an important part of a dog's brain but essentially nonexistent in a whale's. Meanwhile, a sperm whale's brain devotes enormous resources to creating, detecting, and analyzing sound. Sperm whales' brains are larger than blue whales', though blue whales' bodies are twice as big. What does a sperm whale *do* with its singular brain? It sets courses for long migrations and keeps track of family and friends over decades and across thousands of miles of travel. It prepares for dives deeper than a mile; manages the pumping, distribution, and shunting of blood and oxygen while the whale stops breathing for up to two hours; and controls the tracking and muscle coordination needed while hunting squid the size of your nightmares in total darkness. It does some things that humans cannot do, and it cannot do some things that humans do. It's a brain that's much more interesting and much more useful for the tasks at hand than anything "truly god-like." "Godlike," anyway, was a grandiose Band-Aid for "We don't know." It covered a big intellectual boo-boo in Lilly's own thinking.

Scientists rightly scorned John Lilly. His insistence that we could crack dolphin communication—by teaching them English—proved wrong. But his image of dolphins as superior to humans grabbed the imagination of the public, which remains captivated, waiting for a sign that they're on a higher plane. Perhaps we hope that somehow, someday, someone better will deliver us from our own evils.

It wasn't until the 1970s and the work of Louis Herman's group that inquiry into dolphin cognition got real. Herman showed that a Hawaiian bottlenose dolphin named Akeakamai could respond correctly when shown an arbitrary symbol (not a literal picture) for "ball," followed by a symbol for "question." If there was no ball, she would press a "No" lever. This demonstrated that a dolphin could form a concept of a ball, and that she could call upon that knowledge when presented with a symbol used to represent "ball." It showed that dolphins are, as long suspected, very intelligent. Whatever "intelligent" means.

Dolphins at the Institute for Marine Mammal Studies, in Mississippi, were trained to help keep their pools clean by trading litter for fish. A dolphin named Kelly realized that she got the same size fish for bringing a big sheet of paper as for a small piece. So, under a weight at the bottom of the pool she hid any paper that blew in. When a trainer passed, she tore off a piece of paper to trade for a fish. Then she tore off another piece, got another fish. Into the economy of litter, she'd rigged a kind of trash inflation rate that kept the food coming. Similarly, in California, a dolphin named Spock got busted for tearing pieces off a paper bag he'd stuffed behind one of the pool's underwater pipes, using each shred to buy another fish.

One day, a gull flew into Kelly's pool, and she grabbed it and waited for the trainers. The humans seemed to really like birds; they traded her several fish for it. This gave Kelly a new insight, and a plan. During her next meal, she took the last fish and hid it. When the humans left, she brought the fish up and baited more gulls, to get even more fish. After all, why wait to scrounge an occasional piece of accidental paper when you could become a wealthy commercial bird-fishing dolphin? She taught this to her youngster, who taught other youngsters, and so the dolphins there became professional gull baiters.

A young killer whale at Marineland Canada, in Ontario, somehow figured out that spreading mashed fish at the surface of the pool, then sinking out of view, could bring a little sport into his life. If a gull landed, the whale shot upward, sometimes catching—and eating—the gull. He set the trap many times. Eventually, his younger half brother and three other whales caught on.

Insight, innovation, planning, culture.

In 1979, Dr. Diana Reiss started working with a captive bottlenose dolphin named Circe. When Circe did the behavior that Reiss was looking for, Circe got verbal praise and some fish. When she didn't, she got a "time-out," in which Reiss stepped back or turned away to indicate that Circe had not performed "correctly." (Time-outs are now considered outdated; they can frustrate intelligent creatures.) Circe didn't like tail fins left on her mackerel, and by spitting out the pieces with tails, she essentially trained Reiss to cut them off. One day a few weeks into training, Reiss absentmindedly gave Circe an untrimmed tail section. Circe waved her head from side to side the way we might indicate "No," spat out the fish, swam to the other side of the pool, positioned herself upright, and just looked at Reiss for a short time. Then she came back. Circe the dolphin had given Reiss the human a time-out.

Astonished but skeptical, Reiss planned an experiment. Six times over several weeks, Reiss purposely fed Circe a tail section with the fin on. Circe gave Reiss four more time-outs. Those were the only times Circe behaved that way. Circe had not only learned "reward" and "no reward; time-out" for her *own* behavior; she had conceptualized the time-out as a way of communicating the idea "That's not what I've asked for" and used it to correct her human friend.

Reiss also worked with a young male named Pan. Pan was learning to use abstract symbols on a keypad. (The symbols were never literal; the symbol for "ball" might be a triangle. And the keys were moved around, so that the dolphins had to learn the symbol, not the location, for what they wanted.) Pan didn't care about toys; he *really* wanted fish. When Reiss removed the fish key from the options, Pan found a fish left over from the morning's breakfast, swam to the keyboard, touched the fish to a *blank* key, and expectantly looked Reiss in the eye. Reiss understood exactly what he wanted; Pan was making himself *very* clear.

Not long into the project, the dolphins started copying the different whistle sounds that the computer paired with the various objects. When Pan and his poolmate, Delphi, played with the toys, they copied the computer sounds for "ball," "ring," and other objects. Dr. Reiss explained this to me, then added, "One day, I had given Pan a fetch signal. There was only one toy in the pool, a ball, but Delphi had it in her mouth. Pan swam over to Delphi, and I heard someone do the 'ball' whistle. Delphi passed it to Pan, and they both swam to me with it." They'd learned human symbols and used them for communication with each other.

Another dolphin, also named Delphi, but male, started to play with his food, holding fish in his mouth and then dropping them all over the pool.

Diana Reiss trained Delphi to understand the command "swallow" and would not give him another fish until he had shown that the first was indeed gone. This worked for the next week, while Reiss was away; her students fed Delphi and demanded proof of his "swallow." When Reiss came back, Delphi's swallows looked exaggerated. Sore throat? More exaggerated gulps, more displays of his empty mouth, more fish given. Suddenly, writes Reiss, "Delphi's eyes got really big." He opened his mouth. Seafood; see—food! "I saw all these whole fish in there." He must have been holding them in his throat. "Before I had time to open my mouth in surprise he started to shake his head, left and right, left and right." Fish flew everywhere. "Delphi was obviously having fun, and he had chosen to play this trick on me, not one of the students." Delphi had utterly fooled and manipulated Reiss—and he seemed to relish it. As did Reiss, who says, "I laughed hysterically."

Intelligent creatures, sure. But what *is* intelligence? Something to do with insight, reasoning, flexibility? Curiosity, imagination? Planning, problem solving? Perhaps we have different kinds of intelligences. Perhaps one person is more intelligent at math, another at violin, reading social cues, fishing, tinkering, or storytelling. Could there really be just one intelligence among us or among species?

"I personally do not believe that it is meaningful to attempt to fit different species along a linear scale of intelligence," writes the whale expert Peter Tyack. "There are hundreds of tests for *human* intelligence alone, but we still have trouble even *defining* human intelligence."

Who was more "intelligent," Pablo Picasso or Henry Ford? Each brilliant—differently. Perhaps our word "intelligence" clumsily spans various problem-solving potentials and skill-learning talents.

Talent may be the strangest thing about our brains. In the caves, human minds were already there; their works are on those walls still. Before the agriculture or the technology that now reflect our intelligence, the capacity to invent those things was there. Many, many human hunting-and-gathering cultures remained unchanged generation upon generation for millennia, living with only the same few stone, wood, and bone tools, from antiquity well into modern times. As recently as the 1800s, various native cultures of the Americas, Africa, Australia, and much of Asia still relied entirely on ancient Stone Age technologies; many had no wheels, no tool with moving parts, no iron. Even today, Stone Age cultures persist in a few remote redoubts. All are fully human. And into the verge of the Industrial Revolution, Mozart, Beethoven, and the drafters of the United States Constitution wrote with feathers, working without electricity or engines. Computers, shopping malls, airports, dishwashers, television—in 1900, none of them existed. Smartphones are not what make us human. They're what humans make. And only very recently.

Though human brains shrank with the settled predictability of agriculture and civil life, thousands of years later human brains somehow yielded *Petrushka* and a moon lander. People born in animal-hide huts can learn to create software.

Nobel Prize–winning physicist Max Delbrück wondered about our Stone Age brain's seeming overendowment, commenting, "Much more was delivered than was ordered." And not just ours. Whence comes a dog's capacity for sensing and warning of a human companion's oncoming seizure? Why, when bonobos physically cannot form words, can they understand human verbal language at the level of a young child? Why can flipper-limbed dolphins learn human arm signals; why are they motivated to have sex in front of mirrors and do other things that could never in a million years enter the possibilities of an ocean-living dolphin? Why such *capacity*?

Where *does* intelligence come from? Partly, it's just scaling up; the big bodies have the big brains, the big brains have some extra computing power to play with. The three peaks in brain *size* on planet Earth belong to whales, elephants, and primates. Life has not selected one smartest line with humans as the be-all (though we might yet be the end-all). Sperm whales' eighteen-pound brain is the largest that has ever existed. Bottlenose dolphins weigh several times what humans weigh, so of course their brains are also bigger. Their brain's neocortex—the thinking part—is also larger than ours. Human brains are just a shade larger than a cow's. It gets humbling.

Yet like all good things, size isn't the whole shimmy. Peter Tyack reminds us, "The honeybee, which has a brain weighing milligrams, has a dance language that, to my mind, represents just as high an achievement of animal communication as anything demonstrated in wild marine mammals, no matter how large their brains." Remember the bees' dance that tells companions where food is, how far, how much, and whether there's been any trouble there. So, a cautionary word to the wise: intelligence isn't one thing; it doesn't have one formula.

A big body requires a big brain just to manage the physical mechanics. Being *smart* in a body of any size requires a bigger than average brain for your weight class. Ravens, crows, and parrots—famously clever—have a brain-size-to-body-mass ratio similar to chimpanzees'. Ravens can solve certain puzzles that chimpanzees' much heftier brains cannot, and their insightful problem solving has been dubbed "primate-like intelligence."

To *compare* brain-weight-to-body-size ratios, scientists developed the "Encephalization Quotient" ("encephalization" means "amount of brain"). An EQ of 1 indicates that the species' brain-weight-to-body-size ratio is average for mammals; their brain weighs just what you'd expect for an animal their size. Elephants can trumpet a score of around 2, twice as big as you'd expect. Many dolphins score in the 4 to 5 range; Pacific white-sided dolphins come in handily at 5.3. Chimps brain in at a relatively pale 2.3. Dolphins' disproportional brains are exceeded only by humans'. Humans' EQ is about 7.6. We *do* have the highest brain-weight-to-body-size ratio. (And, judging by your reaction, humans have both the biggest ego and the worst insecurity.)

But mere brain weighing is a bit Frankensteinish, and EQ doesn't quite capture IQ; size isn't intellect. A human's brain is 2 percent of their body mass. A shrew's little brain weighs up to 10 percent of their body mass, yet shrews aren't terribly shrewd. Capuchin monkeys have higher EQs than chimpanzees, but chimps outsmart the monkeys as warring, alliance-building, meat-hunting politicians.

EQ is too coarse because brains have components. We have ancient parts of our brain inherited from fish, and newer parts shared only with mammals. It's not just a matter of gross weight. It's also what the parts are sized to emphasize. Whales have a relatively bigger cerebellum (to manage or automate complex tasks such as swimming, heart rate, and movement) and a major sound-processing allocation but, recall, almost nothing related to smell.

A whale's neocortex—where much of consciousness and thinking happens—has a higher amount of surface area relative to total brain size than a human's does. This is the hardware of awareness, the wiring of thought. What this enables a whale's brain to do, we can see: watch them fill their days with complicated behavior, long-term parenting, athletic performance, and high-level socializing in large group networks. But the human neocortex is twice as thick *and* has much higher cell density.

Don't let this get to your head. We're not done.

Now let's get to the heart of the brain, if you will. Weights and sizes are mere stand-ins for what matters. Nerve cells matter. Neurons. But not just numbers. Their density; how they are organized, networked, and wired with other components; how fast they transmit impulses. That *is* a brain's information-processing capacity. No one weight or measure captures the whole of intellectual capacity. In a way, measuring a brain is like measuring the fuse box in a house. A big fuse box suggests a big house because a big house has more wiring and more stuff. If you remove the fuse box, your lights won't go on. But it's not just the fuse box that lights the place. It's the fuse box *and* all the wiring throughout the house. Where are those wires routed? Where are the outlets, the ground-fault interrupters, the ceiling fixtures and lamps, the cabling for the electric range and the Internet? We see structures in the brain, yes, but how those structures are wired up makes a difference about how we plug into reality, what we can download and transmit, and how our lights shine.

There is one generalization we can make: most important for flexible problem solving and mental dexterity seems to be the sheer *number* and the *density* of neurons in mammals' brain cortex and in non-mammals' equivalent of the cortex. As with any computational system, the number of processing units determines the processing power. German brain scientists Gerhard Roth and Ursula Dicke compared the world's largest brains and concluded, "Humans have more cortical neurons than other mammals, although only marginally more than whales and elephants." Whales, with 6 to 10.5 billion, and elephants, with 11 billion, are breathing close on our cortical heels; humans have about 11.5 to 16 billion neurons in the brain's cortex, depending on whom you consult. Ours are packed densely, so signal transmission is faster.

What about those astonishing crows, ravens, and parrots? No one has counted, but birds generally have much smaller cells than do mammals.

So bird brains densely pack a lot of processing power and speed for their size. As for speed of signal transmission—you can easily see how extremely alert birds are.

A person's individual brain neurons are basically indistinguishable from those of a killer whale, elephant, or mouse—or fly. The synapses, various nerve cell types, connections, even the genes creating those neurons: essentially identical across species. The differences among species' brains are mainly differences of degree. Roth and Dicke conclude, "The outstanding intelligence of humans appears to result from a combination and enhancement of properties found in non-human primates . . . rather than from 'unique' properties."

The Social Brain

If you're going to have a larger, denser brain, you're going to have to pay to run it. And brains are real energy hogs. At just about 2 percent of our body weight, ours costs nearly 20 percent of our body's energy budget (that's why mere thinking can be so tiring). Chronic energy budget overruns can kill; in hard times if you run out of calories, you starve. So why risk having a big brain? Either it's greatly needed or it conveys some incisive advantage.

It's not greatly needed. Plenty of less smart species survive very well, thank you. Killer whales cleverly hunt salmon, but they'd be more abundant if they simply *were* salmon. Abundance is success, so why not just keep the in-head overhead low? Dolphins often share the same waters with tuna, hunting the same prey. Tuna are more energy efficient, and there are more of them. So the question lingers: Why pay the added freight of a bigger than average brain? Spiders and insects succeed in their trillions; their small brains present no disadvantage. In fact, by the numbers it might seem that big brains produce costly drag on reproduction and survival. But dolphins pay to be smarter than tuna; elephants pay to be smarter than antelope. So there must be something about their lives that demands expensive intelligence.

Behavioral ecologists long assumed that the harder it was to secure food, the more intelligent a species had to be. They thought that greater intellect reflected complicated food getting. But those tuna and dolphins school alongside each other, hunting the same fish and squid. Food isn't the cause of their widely different intellects. Tuna are smart in their ways and are marvelous creatures. But tuna don't travel with their young at their sides during their years of learning; they don't aid wounded companions or summon one another. Big differences—*social* differences. If you're a wildebeest, your society is as flat as the plains you graze: no leader, no social ambitions, no family group. So no remarkable brain. Because: no need. Wildebeest eat grass, and elephants eat grass. Grass eating isn't why elephants are more emotionally and intellectually complex.

But what if, in your group, you have to keep track of specific individuals you meet repeatedly, who might want your food or your mate or your rank and who might plot against you, or might plot with you against your rivals, or be there for you when it matters; what if you need to continually balance cooperation and competition among specific individuals? *When individuals matter*—when you're a "who"—you need a social brain capable of reasoning, planning, rewarding, punishing, seducing, protecting, bonding, understanding, sympathizing. Your brain needs to be your Swiss Army knife, packing different strategies for different situations. Dolphins, apes, elephants, wolves, and humans face similar needs: know your territory and its resources, know your friends, monitor your enemies, achieve fertilization, raise babies, defend, and cooperate when it serves you.

In various dolphins, males form alliances in twos or threes to control exclusive access to individual females in breeding condition. Bottlenose dolphin alliances in Florida last up to twenty years. These tight male alliances sometimes merge into coalitions that overwhelm smaller alliances, stealing their females like human tribal raiders. Think of a street gang, with sonar.

Researcher Janet Mann saw an alliance of male bottlenose dolphins surrounding a single female. A *female* coalition swooped in, diverting the males by rubbing up against them and stroking them with their fins. After confusing the males by what looked like playing on their sexual interests, the females—all of them—took off. I wonder if they laughed about it. Alliances can make the difference between who wins and who suffers. When those are the stakes, intelligence matters.

Chimpanzees rise in rank by giving favors and by shrewd judgment about whom to rely on or undermine. Researchers call it "a Machiavellian mind." Primatologist Craig Stanford writes, "Male chimpanzees have political careers, in which the goals stay more or less the same—wield as much power, influence and reproductive success as possible—but the tactics for achieving them vary from day to day, year to year, and life stage to life stage." Why all the effort, expense, and risk for status? Because the highest-ranking male usually fathers the most babies, to whom the highest-ranking female, most frequently, gives birth. Since the behavior reproduces itself, it perpetuates. That's what status seeking is about, whether we status seekers realize it or not. In social settings, intelligence can help you get reproductive access to quality mates.

Species who have the most complex societies develop the most complex brains. Which comes first? They likely evolve together in an arms race where social advantages begin outweighing social costs. Take-home: the most intelligent brain is *the social brain*.

╼

Twenty-five million years before today, dolphins were firmly in possession of our solar system's brightest brain. In many ways it would be nice if they still were. When dolphins were the planet's brain leaders, the world didn't have any political, religious, ethnic, or environmental problems. Creating problems seems to be one of the things that "make us human."

Whales may have "our kind of intelligence," said the researchers who discovered that whales' brains possess another kind of special cells formerly believed to set humans apart from all other creatures. They're called "spindle" neurons for their elongated shape. (They're also called von Economo neurons, after their discoverer.) The brains having these special cells power the great apes (which includes humans, don't forget), elephants, the largest whales, and at least some dolphins. Interestingly, hippos, manatees, and walruses also have them.

Spindle cells are the "express trains of the nervous system." By letting impulses bypass unnecessary stops, they allow very rapid signal transmission. This enables near-instant assessment and reaction. Spindle cells are shaped and positioned to take information from an entire column of brain cells and rapidly output to other brain structures. Scientists think that in fast-changing, complicated social situations, these cells enable fast, intuitive decisions.

Spindle cells seem to help brains track social interactions, perform certain intellectual and emotional functions, and have feelings about the feelings of others. Damage to spindle cells impairs social awareness, the ability to self-monitor in social situations, intuition, and judgment. Some believe spindle cell damage is involved in Alzheimer's disease, dementia, autism, and schizophrenia.

Spindle cells were first discovered in human brains in the early twentieth century and for decades were believed to be a hallmark of human intellectual exceptionalism. Patrick Hof, codiscoverer of whale spindle cells, said, "It's absolutely clear to me that these are extremely intelligent animals, and have evolved social networks similar to those of apes and humans."

—◂—

Like special brain cells once believed exclusively human, like toolmaking, *teaching* was thought to be an exclusive province of the human mind. Killer whales teach. "Teaching" requires this: one individual must take time from its own task to demonstrate and instruct *and* the student must learn a new skill.

When a young chimpanzee watches a skilled adult and then imitates, that's learning, but the adult has not taken time specifically to instruct, so it is not teaching. In the honeybees' amazing waggle dance, the dancer takes time to indicate information about a source of food, but the other foragers learn no new skill. Same with certain ants; same with animals who alarm about the presence of a predator. They do take time to show, but they do not impart new skills to the learners. Killer whales teach skills.

Around the Indian Ocean's subantarctic Crozet Islands, killer whales capture fur seal and elephant seal pups by surging onto beaches. But it's dangerous. The whales risk stranding themselves and must thrash their bodies back into the rescuing surf. So adults teach the young how to do it. They teach in steps, giving lessons.

First, they practice on beaches without seals. Mothers gently push their young onto steeply sloping beaches, from which youngsters can easily wriggle back into the sea. It's the killer whale equivalent of learning to operate an automobile in a parking lot before driving in traffic. This teaching builds skills in a safe environment, eliminating the very real risk of a fatal stranding. Then the young learn hunting by watching their mothers' successful attacks. At five to six years old, young killer whales finally attempt to catch seal pups using the beach-surge technique. An adult female often helps them return to the water, creating a body wave if necessary. The time required for teaching means that mothers catch fewer seals for themselves. This training may well be the absolute height in both teaching and long-range planning among non-humans.

In Alaska, researchers saw two killer whales teaching a one-year-old to hunt by practicing on seabirds. Adults stunned an unsuspecting seabird with their flukes; the yearling whale came and practiced the fluke-slapping technique. Atlantic spotted dolphin mothers sometimes release a prey fish in the presence of their youngsters and let their youngsters chase the fish, recapturing it if it's getting away. Atlantic spotted dolphin youngsters also position themselves alongside mothers who are scanning and prodding sandy bottoms for hidden fish. They can "eavesdrop" on her echoes and imitate her technique, but the mother spends extra time demonstrating. Australian bottlenose dolphin mothers who wear snout sponges to protect against urchin spines and the searing sting of hidden scorpionfish while they're probing the sediment teach their children the sponge-wearing technique.

Teachers are an elite group. Other teachers include: cheetahs and house cats (who bring back live prey and let their young learn to catch it), birds called pied babblers (who teach their young a call that means "I have food"), peregrine falcons (who lure their young away from nesting cliffs before dropping killed prey for them to catch in flight), river otters (who drag their babies into and under water, teaching them how to swim and dive), and meerkats (who first bring to their growing young dead scorpions, then disabled ones, to demonstrate how to dismember the venomous stingers). Humans teach, of course. That's about it; we know of few other teachers, so far. But many more must be hiding in a spread as diverse as that.

Like toolmaking and teaching, *imitation*—considered to reflect high intelligence—is also rare in the animal kingdom. Some researchers believe that only apes and dolphins imitate, but it's a little more common. Our parrots' habit of dunking hard bread crusts in water was probably invented by one and copied by the other. Young dogs imitate older dogs. And dogs imitate people in their way. When I am "doing" firewood by cutting, hauling, and stacking it, Chula "does" wood by finding a suitably sized piece and lying down nearby to chew it. When I am "doing" paper sorting for recycling or burning in the stove, Chula might find an envelope and very inconspicuously lie down with it. Chewing envelopes is usually not allowed, but at these times we both understand that we have paperwork to do.

In South Africa a captive bottlenose dolphin named Daan had watched divers cleaning algae off his pool's windows. He found a gull feather and started cleaning the window, using the same long strokes. He positioned himself vertically, with one flipper touching the glass—like the divers, who'd steadied themselves by holding on to the window frame—and made sounds almost identical to the diver's breathing apparatus, and released a similar-looking stream of bubbles. When a window-cleaning diver left his vacuum-cleaning apparatus in an exhibit, he returned the next morning to discover a dolphin named Haig clasping the hose with her flippers, her snout on the scraper. When the diver took back his equipment, the dolphin found a broken piece of tile and started scraping seaweed off the bottom of the pool. Who *couldn't* use a roommate like Haig?

In a South African aquarium lived a baby Indo-Pacific bottlenose named Dolly. One day while she was just six months old, Dolly was watching a trainer standing at the window smoking a cigarette, blowing puffs of smoke. Dolly swam to her mother, briefly suckled, then returned to the window and released a cloud of milk that engulfed her head. The trainer was "absolutely astonished." Dolly didn't "copy" (she wasn't really smoking) or imitate with intent to achieve the same purpose. Somehow Dolly *came up with the idea* of using milk to *represent* smoke. Using one thing to represent something else isn't just mimicking. It is art.

Woo-Woo

———•———

Many people hope that some day we'll meet an intelligent being from another world. . . . But maybe it won't be like that. Maybe it will be like this.

—Michael Parfit, *The Whale*

"I've sometimes come away," Ken says, "with a real '*Wow!*' feeling. Like I'd just seen something above and beyond. When you lock eyes with them, you get the sense that they're looking at *you*. It's a steady gaze. And you feel it. Much more powerful than a dog looking at you. A dog might want your attention. The whales, it's a different feeling. It's more like they're searching inside you. There's a personal relationship that they set up with eye contact. A lot transmits in a very brief time about the intent of both sides."

Like what?

"In those looks I've felt"—he hesitates to say this—"appreciated. But of course," he quickly adds, "that's subjective."

Appreciated?

Ken started his research in the 1970s, right after the courts ordered Sea-World to stop catching baby whales. "Within a year or so," Ken says, "if someone in another boat started chasing the whales each time they surfaced, or began aggressively circling them, they would often come over and just stay around our boat. The whales understood that we weren't going to be involved in high-speed chases. We weren't going to be shooting any darts and tags. They saw," he says, "that we were cool around them. Which implies, y'know, a consciousness of what's going on."

Could that consciousness encompass a sense of Ken's goodwill? After everything they'd been through with the captures, could they have *appreciated* Ken? Enough to return a favor?

Ken has stories like this one: "For days we'd been following all three pods. They'd come in the Strait of Juan de Fuca, up the west side of San Juan Island, through Boundary Pass to the Fraser River, gone back down to Rosario, into Puget Sound, around Vashon Island, then back up here. One morning they were headed into a dense fog bank. We followed them. This was in the 1970s. No GPS or anything, just a compass. We got lost down near the entrance to Admiralty Inlet, socked-in fog, about twenty-five miles from home. I knew the approximate compass bearing. We put away all the cameras and prepared to run. I started to head along that compass bearing at about fifteen knots. We'd only gone for about five minutes when whales just came porpoising in from all directions until they were right in front of the boat. So I just slowed down and followed wherever they went. I had about half a dozen of them right in front of our bow at all times." Ken followed them for fifteen miles. When the fog opened, he could see his home island. "Well," he says, "I do have the feeling that they knew absolutely that we had zero visibility. They knew exactly where they were. It was the year after the captures ended. They'd seen lots of boats and been subject to a lot of aggressive behavior. But there they were, and as far as I can tell, they were guiding us. It was very touching."

It gets, if anything, more touching. And much stranger. The fact is, killer whales seem capable of random acts of kindness. Acts that defy explanation. Acts that make scientists consider some pretty far-out possibilities. One might conclude that killer whale behavior falls into two categories: amazing behavior and inexplicable behavior.

Fog guidance can seem like an exclusive service that killer whales feel inclined to provide—to people who work to protect them. Once, Alexandra Morton and an assistant were out in the open water of Queen Charlotte Strait in her inflatable boat when she was enveloped by fog so thick she felt like she was "in a glass of milk." No compass. No view of the sun.

Flat calm; no wave pattern to inform a guess. A wrong hunch about the direction home would have brought them out into open ocean. Worse, a giant cruise ship was moving closer in fog so reflective Morton could not tell where its sound was approaching from. She imagined it suddenly splitting the fog before it crushed them.

Then, as if from nowhere, a smooth black fin popped up. Top Notch. Then Saddle. And then Eve, the usually aloof matriarch. Sharky was suddenly peeking at her. Then Stripe. As they clumped close around her tiny boat, Alexandra followed in the fog like a blind person with a hand on their shoulder. "I never worried," she recalled. "I trusted them with our lives." Twenty minutes later, she saw a materializing outline of their island's massive cedars and rocky shoreline. The fog opened up. The whales left them. Earlier in the day, the whales had been unusually difficult to follow and had been traveling west, toward open ocean. The whales had taken Morton south, to her home. When the whales left, they changed direction, aiming back toward where they'd just come from and where they had originally been headed.

Morton felt changed. "For more than twenty years, I have fought to keep the mythology of the orcas out of my work. When others would regale a group with stories of an orca's sense of humor or music appreciation, I'd hold my tongue. . . . Yet there are times when I am confronted with profound evidence of something beyond our ability to scientifically quantify. Call them amazing coincidences if you like; for me they keep adding up. . . . I can't say that whales are telepathic—I can barely say the word—but . . . I have no explanation for that day's events. I have only gratitude and a deep sense of mystery that continues to grow."

My friend Maria Bowling was snorkeling in Hawaii when several killer whales showed up—a freak coincidence. She wrote to me, "After I gently slid off the side of the boat, I heard a very strong clinking sound, like metal on metal, like two scuba tanks hitting one another. It was a very high vibrating sound that did not feel uncomfortable but it did feel incredibly strong! It went right through me. It was the strongest energy that I have ever felt. A wave of energy, like transmitting. It was like a portal opened, or an introduction to another possibility of communication. After the encounter I was so elevated and activated by the power of the event that for days I was a bit dazed. I felt lighter, more integrated, very hopeful, light-hearted and full of joy. This is not very scientific I know, but it's more of a somatic experience than that of the mind or intellect."

If there *is* some kind of yet-unknown energy-wave connection, it has its limitations. When it mattered in a life-or-death moment, the whale named Eve, whose family had guided Alexandra Morton home in the fog, did not transform into a superhero. But maybe it was already too late. And whales are only mortal, after all. As are humans.

One September day in 1986 in British Columbia, Alexandra, her film-maker husband, Robin, and their four-year-old son went to a familiar place, a unique near-shore spot where killer whales came to rub themselves on certain specific boulders they seemed to find somehow special. After a wait, Eve, alone this time, approached. Robin, who'd been trying hard for good underwater footage, suited up, slipped into the water just thirty feet from shore, and ducked under. Morton took the Zodiac a short distance away, out of the shot. "Eve dove toward Robin," Morton wrote. Then Eve "abruptly emerged from the water and charged back toward me. She surfaced beside the Zodiac, paused, then disappeared into the deep." That seemed odd. Morton thought, "She shouldn't have resurfaced so soon." And Eve had seemed in a hurry to leave. While her son was busy with his crayons, Morton watched the water, expecting her husband to surface at any moment. As the wait stretched into excruciating minutes, Alexandra motored over to the spot, looking down at the seaweed and starfish and rocky seafloor. To her ultimate horror, she saw her husband lying face-up on the bottom. His complex rebreathing apparatus had malfunctioned and he had blacked out—and drowned.

Eve had acted alarmed and seemed to have made the connection. But there was no cosmic breakthrough, no retrieval, no pushing the inert human to the surface for air. Wild killer whales' perfect record of never attacking a human defies explanation, but actually raising a dead person might be a bridge too far. Perhaps mouthing a mammal was too creepy a move for a fish-eating resident whale. Or maybe for Eve, coming upon an unconscious Robin was just too alarming, and because she understood, surfacing next to the boat and pausing was her best attempt to alert Alexandra before fleeing in fright. Maybe she was actually trying to communicate in a modality humans lack. Or maybe Eve simply heard her sons calling in the distance and was merely hurrying to join them. Maybe Eve was just a whale.

But there are stories of killer whales seemingly retrieving lost dogs. A small party of scientific people left shore to go whale watching in a small boat. When they returned, their German shepherd, Phoenix, was not on the island. He'd apparently tried to follow them out into the big water and powerful tides of Johnstone Strait. The people searched the strait until eleven P.M. No dog. The dog's owner was sitting on a log, crying, when he heard the blows of killer whales. He thought the worst: that they might have eaten his beloved dog. He could see the whales coming closer because the turbulence of their swimming caused the sea's phosphorescent creatures to glow. Just after the whales passed, he heard splashing. Suddenly, there stood his sodden dog, weakened and vomiting salt water. "I don't care what people say," he declared. "Those whales saved my dog."

It's not an isolated case. At a different research camp, a person went kayaking, and when he returned, *his* dog, named Karma, was missing. Similarly, she'd probably tried to follow him. The researcher was mourning the loss of his faithful companion late in the night when some whales passed. The dog appeared on the beach, soaked and trembling and near collapse. "I was there," said the person who related the story. "There's no doubt in my mind; those whales had pushed Karma ashore."

And then there are other weird stories. In the early 1980s, a marine amusement park wanting whales to train for shows started asking for permission to resume captures of British Columbia killer whales. Captures had been banned in 1976, but talk turned to taking a certain small family: the A-4 group. That family had already suffered. In 1983, someone—they were let off for lack of photographic proof—shot the whale A-10 and her youngster. Whale watchers heard the shots and went right over. One of the witnesses said, "A-10 pushed her wounded calf to my side of the boat. We could see the wound oozing blood. It really seemed that she was showing us: Look what you humans have done." Within a few months, both whales died.

The mere suggestion of someone trapping these whales she'd often seen—years after the capture ban—set Alexandra Morton's blood boiling. At one meeting, even her own friends had to calm her down.

Over the years, there was only one major waterway where Alexandra Morton had *not* seen killer whales: Cramer Passage, where she lived. Two days after the meeting where she'd spoken so passionately against their capture, Morton was following Yakat and Kelsey—who were sisters of the dead whale A-10—and a youngster called Sutlej. In front of the inlet to Cramer Passage the whales started milling around. Morton drifted with them. Then they "trapped" her, with the two sisters on either side and the youngster broadside at the front of the boat, all inches away. Each time she started the engine, they would buzz around, keeping her trapped. They reminded her of transients making a kill, and it unnerved her. But then they turned, leading her into Cramer Passage—and traveling up and down Cramer three times.

"Sometimes I don't know what to believe with whales," Morton said. She allowed herself to wonder: Were the whales trying to communicate something after she'd defended their family? But she'd spoken indoors, at a meeting (not even out in a boat, where the whales—if they were fluent in English—might have overheard her). Their knowing her thoughts while she watched them would require true telepathy. That, she knew, "flew in the face of reason."

Alexandra Morton, as Ken might put it, was deep into "woo-woo" territory.

She knew she was. She wrote, "I know this has no place in science (or even a sound mind perhaps), but could our parameters on reality be set just a little too tight?"

Decades earlier, while watching two captive whales named Orky and Corky swim around their Marineland of the Pacific pool one day, Morton asked a trainer to show her how one teaches a new idea to a whale. (Corky was the captured child of Stripe. Many years later, in the incident I mentioned a few pages ago, Stripe would help lead Morton home in the fog.) Neither Morton nor the trainer had ever seen either captive whale slap its dorsal fin on the water. They decided they'd work on that trick the following week. "Then something happened," Morton later wrote, "that has made me careful of my thoughts around whales ever since." *Corky slapped her dorsal fin on the water's surface.* She did it several more times, then charged around the tank, exuberantly smacking the water with her dorsal fin. "That's whales for you," said the trainer, smiling. "They can read your mind. We trainers see this kind of stuff all the time."

Howard Garrett recalled his and several colleagues' early 1980s experiences with captive killer whales in these words: "We each felt tested and our intentions probed by the orcas, and that the orcas not only learned our limits and abilities, but seemed to have shared their knowledge of us with their tank mates. We felt they became friends we knew well and that we became well known by the orcas. Each of us was deeply moved."

When a very young northern resident killer whale named Springer (A-73) mysteriously showed up near Seattle in Puget Sound, she had just recently been weaned and her mother had been missing. Ken found her playing with a small floating tree branch, pushing it around. "I picked it up and threw it and she'd go after it, very playful. I started slapping the water and she started slapping the water with her pec fin. Then I looked at her, and for some reason I just made a circular motion with my finger, like a 'roll over' signal—*and she rolled over!* I just went, *'Wow!'* To get a dog to do all that, you have to train them. I mean, she knew what I had in mind, like her consciousness was just sort of linked with mine. There are no words for something like *that*." Rolling when he moved his finger in a circle required an understanding that his finger represented a generalized geometric concept of "motion around an axis." Plus, it required an ability to apply to her body the concept she saw in the motion of his finger. It required an innate desire to engage with another life-form, a capacity for play, and, it would seem, a sense of fun. And she couldn't do what he had in mind unless she indeed inferred that he had something *in mind*.

It was astonishing behavior.

In other words, Springer was just being a killer whale. Killer whales simply seem to specialize in acute consciousness. They don't appear to be astonished by us; they take us matter-of-factly. We don't need to continue being astonished at their behavior. Instead, we might simply fully accept them—and be astonished by one thing about ourselves: how long it's taken us.

Luckily for little Springer, the humans hatched the right plan: bring her back to her family. Springer was gently lassoed, then moved into a big net pen in a bay in Canada. The idea: hold her until researchers could locate her family. Her family showed up the next day. So the researchers opened the pen and, Ken says, a "real excited" Springer has been with them ever since. "In fact," Ken points out, "she had her first baby this year. So it's a real feel-good story." Then, however, there's a pregnant, uncomfortable pause. Ken adds, "It was exactly what they should have done with Luna."

Luna was a little male born to L pod's Splash in 1999. From the beginning, his life included bizarre twists. He spent time early on with a K-pod female named Kiska, who'd recently been seen carrying a dead baby on her back. Kiska, missing her own dead child, might have borrowed Luna. Eventually Luna returned to his real mother, but he was never a mama's boy and frequently accompanied other L-pod whales. Then, in the spring of 2001, Luna went missing.

He showed up alone, barely more than a toddler of two years old, in British Columbia's Nootka Sound. "It's only a couple hundred miles from here," Ken points out. Killer whales can travel seventy-five miles a day. "But acoustically, he was in a place where he wouldn't be able to hear his pod's calls."

Luna happened to turn up shortly after the death of a local First Nation chief who'd said, "When I die, I am going to come back as a *kakawin*." The natives called the baby whale Tsux'iit, and to them he wasn't just a whale. He was here, one said, "to wash away hurt, wash away the pain in our lives." Part whale, part messiah.

People had started calling him different names, like Patch or Bruno, before researchers realized that the strangely lost baby whale was the missing L-98, Luna.

Patch, Bruno, Luna, Tsux'iit. He was lost, and people were at a loss over what to do next.

Luna was also at a loss for company. He'd catch a salmon and then hold it in the air. "He was certainly showing us what he had caught," one person opined. "You realize," said another, "this is not a reptile. . . . This is somebody." When he looked at you, someone else said, his gaze "had need in it, and your empathy lit up right away." People saw "an awareness, a presence, a longing." One recreational fisherman related that when he first encountered Luna, he put his hand underwater and waved it, "so he puts his fin above the water and he is waving back at me." Convinced that this must be a coincidence, the fisherman waved again. Luna waved again. Luna left for a few minutes, and when he returned, the fisherman waved once more. Sure enough, Luna waved back. "Here is something," the fisherman realized, "that has got way more intelligence than the domestic animals that we are used to." When a workboat cook encountered Luna and looked into his eyes, she saw something so astonishing and deep that, she said, "I could not breathe."

As he grew, Luna sought to play with boaters and people of all kinds. He had no problem pushing forty-foot logs or turning a thirty-foot sailboat in a circle. But when he went to play with a canoe paddled by two women, or a kayak, he'd nudge very gently. Could Luna have had any idea that the water, his home medium, would kill a person? Like many things about killer whales and everything about Luna, that seems so unlikely. But what else explains it?

Starving for attention, "Luna quickly found," as Ken puts it, "that humans could be a source of pretty interesting interaction." He liked being touched, having humans rub his tongue, getting sprayed with hoses—"all sorts of things you wouldn't think possible with a wild animal," Ken recalls.

But I'm not so surprised. In the early 1980s, while I was studying the seabirds called terns, I was sitting in my boat when I heard a plosive *pfooffh*. I turned and was staggered to see a beluga whale right beside me, about a thousand miles south of its normal range, and alone. For two seasons the beluga frequently sought and often hung out with me (and vice versa) while I was doing my research. I also often saw the beluga visit other boats. That little white whale was a bit shy but got very excited on the occasions when I decided to jump into the water. He or she (I didn't know how to tell) would zoom around me, allowing brief touches that seemed to thrill both of us equally.

Luna showed that he was a social being foremost and deepest, and that being a killer whale was, in a sense, secondary. One Luna observer said that he could "look through your otherness at you." If people didn't have a problem with his being a killer whale, Luna didn't have a problem with them being humans.

But people had a problem. Luna became the center point of a deep divide over whether he was a gift or a dilemma, and whether to ignore him, befriend him, repatriate him to his family—or take him into captivity.

"It would have been *very* easy to train him to follow a recording of his mom's voice—which we have," Ken says. "We could have given him the social contact he kept wanting, and little by little, moving farther out of the sound toward the ocean entrance, just bring him back over to his pod when we knew they were here." Ken looks at me to make sure I understand the simplicity of that plan. "But then the *stupid* Canadian government—" Ken is still seething, all these years later. "I don't know what all their stupid reasons were, but they wouldn't let us do it."

More than anything, Luna's story is that of a lost child needing friendship and guidance home, encountering a species too at odds with itself to extend the essential gesture.

"All he needed was somebody to be with him until he could come back home," says Ken, the man who himself had been guided home by killer whales. "And they *insisted* on keeping all the company he wanted—and needed—away from him. We were dealing with ignorance at high levels." Ken chuckles bitterly, still sounding mournful. "He just needed a few friends."

Luna would hang with a docked boat for hours as the people on it were busy delivering supplies and equipment. But as soon as the people left, he'd leave. Yet if a person remained aboard sleeping, Luna would often stay with the boat all night. One captain frequently heard the sound of Luna's breathing outside his open window. When a passenger's hat blew into the water, Luna went to get it. He came up under it and, with the hat perched perfectly on his head, brought it back within reach. The man got his hat back, thanks to an untrained free-living whale who showed in so many ways that he, at least, was a good friend.

Luna needed his family. In the meantime, he needed company. The government worked hard to prevent all contact. At one point, officials tried to catch Luna. The *stated* idea was: reunite him with his family. *But:* an aquarium wanted to buy him, and the government would not take that possibility off the table.

Luna is the focus of the movie *The Whale* and the book *The Lost Whale*, which vividly document the flaring tempers, showing how people who responded to Luna's invitations to interact got hit by the cops with fines and charged with crimes. Luna's sea filled with lunacy.

Michelle Kehler, who'd been hired with a woman named Erin Hobbs as government Luna monitors, recalled, "When he would come up to the boat, there was a lot of eye contact. It was very soft; it was very genuine." She observed too, that, "his relationship with me was different from his relationship with Erin." Erin is the jokester, and Luna joked with her. "He would spit at her. She would get water in the face. She would get all the gross stuff. She would get all the tail slaps, the pec slaps. . . . He never did that with me. And we are on the same boat, like five feet apart. . . . He was totally different with me. . . . We have different energies. He played to that, for sure. And it was amazing."

But the women were hired to keep Luna away from people—and that soon changed their relationship. "At first he really liked us," said Michelle. But because Michelle and Erin's job was to tell people who were playing with Luna to stop, "we would come, and he would come over and push us away, just say, 'Get out of here! I have not had anyone to play with all day, you know; get out of here!'" Another monitor wrote that Luna "is a sur-vivor, a fighter, a clown; a compassionate, rambunctious, and very loving being."

With friendly people barred from contact, and Luna needing friend-ship, Luna followed a tugboat one day, was struck by its propeller, and died.

The first time Michael Parfit and Suzanne Chisholm encountered Luna, they were going eighteen knots in a light inflatable boat when Luna sud-denly exploded out of the water alongside them. He came up so precisely that his skin slid along the starboard flotation tube. "I could feel his touch in the motion of the boat," Parfit recalled, "but I didn't have to correct for it." Luna "was somehow respecting the two-way care that maintaining this connection required."

One day when Luna was playing a little too energetically with the emer-gency outboard engine on his boat, Parfit said, "Hey, Luna, could you leave that alone for a while?" Luna immediately left it alone, and backed away. Wrote Parfit, "It was hard to accept that level of awareness and intention in something that did not look in any way human." He added, "A sense washed over me that this orca was just as aware of living as I was: that he could perceive all the details that I perceive, the feeling of atmo-sphere and sea, the texture of emotions . . . and what makes us feel safe. This was overwhelming. It was not comfortable."

Luna had taught Parfit that human language is just one way to get at the awareness of living. "It seemed to be our failure that we cannot operate except with these cumbersome symbols," he said, feeling that language was the barrier, and *we* had erected it.

Human awareness is present without words; words are one attempt to capture our consciousness. Nonverbal animals experience pure consciousness. Eventually, Parfit realized that he had finally looked through the otherness. He no longer saw something that didn't look human. He didn't see a killer whale. He saw Luna.

When I myself look at other animals, I almost never see an otherness. I see the overwhelming similarities; they fill me with a sense of deep relation. Nothing makes me feel more at home in the world than the company of wild relatives. Nothing else except the deepest human love feels as right, as connected, or puts me as much at peace.

Dolphins' bodies, with their flippers and flukes, strike many people as alien. But *they* routinely show an understanding of the similarities underneath our outer body contours, and they know which parts of their bodies correspond with ours. The dolphins Lou Herman worked with easily copied human moves. When the human shook a leg, the dolphins shook their *tails*. That's a pretty impressive transfer of the concept of "leg" in the mind of a creature that hasn't had legs in millions of years.

～

When the trainer at Marineland of the Pacific said that killer whales can read your mind, she wasn't joking. But what if she wasn't just serious— what if she was right? What if, like their sonar abilities, which weren't suspected until the 1950s, there's another unknown-to-us modality to their communication and perception? I severely doubt it. But here's a thought: We constantly use radio receivers to listen to music and conversation being broadcast by, one might say, distant minds. That's a sort of technological telepathy. Brains are much more complicated than radios and computers. Considering the enormous survival advantage that would accrue to any truly telepathic mind reader, is it possible that a mind has evolved a kind of two-way radio for thought sharing? Is a dolphin mind an undersea listening-and-analyzing operation that can also detect thought waves of intentions and feelings? Likely not. But maybe you just need a bigger brain than we have. Science fiction used to imagine wise visitors from outer space wielding huge heads housing vastly superior brainpower. The whales certainly have, at least, very big heads.

In the 1960s, Karen Pryor discovered that rough-toothed dolphins could understand the concept "Do something new." If she rewarded them only when they did something they'd never been taught or had never done, then at a specific signal they "thought of things to do spontaneously that we could never have imagined, and that we would have found very difficult to arrive at."

There's even more mystery. When the Hawaiian bottlenose dolphins Phoenix and Akeakamai got the signal to "do something new," they would swim to the center of the pool and circle underwater for a few seconds, then do something entirely unexpected. For instance, they might both shoot straight up through the surface in perfect unison and spin clockwise while squirting water from their mouths. None of that performance was trained. "It looks to us absolutely mysterious," researcher Lou Herman related. "We don't know how they do it." It *seems* as if they confer using some form of language to plan and execute a complex new stunt. If there's another way of doing it, or what that might be, or whether there's some other way to communicate that humans can't quite imagine—dolphin telepathy?—no human knows. Whatever it is, for the dolphins it's apparently as routine and natural as human kids saying, "Hey, let's do this . . ."

During several decades of research on free-living dolphins in the Bahamas, Denise Herzing got familiar with particular individuals. Apparently, the feeling was mutual. After being gone for eight months each year, the researchers would return and all would reunite. " 'Joyous' is probably the word I would use to describe it," wrote Herzing. "And even though I am committed to studying and understanding the dolphins scientifically, I have no problem also feeling like they are friends, of another species, but clearly aware, with feelings and memories, and this was a reunion of friends." At the end of multiweek research trips, she writes, "The dolphins seemed to know we were leaving and gave us a grand sendoff. I have often wondered how they knew."

Seemingly "telepathic" behavior occurred in a more somber incident. At the beginning of one research trip, as Herzing's vessel approached the familiar dolphins she'd been studying, they "greeted us but they acted very unusual," not coming within fifty feet of the boat. They refused invitations to bow-ride, also odd. And when the captain slipped into the water, one came briefly nearer and then suddenly fled.

At that point, someone discovered that one of the people aboard had just died during a nap in his bunk. Spooky enough. But then, as the boat turned to head back to port, "the dolphins came to the side of our boat, not riding the bow as usual but instead flanking us fifty feet away in an aquatic escort. . . . They paralleled us in an organized fashion." After the crew had attended to the sad business at hand, when the boat returned to the dolphin area, "the dolphins greeted us normally, rode the bow, and frolicked like they normally did." After twenty-five years with those dolphins, Herzing never again saw them behave the way they did when the boat had a dead man aboard. Perhaps, in a way we don't understand, dolphin sonar lets them scan inside a boat and somehow realize and communicate among one another that a man in a bunk has a heart that is still. Perhaps they detected that a human had died using another sensory system, one that we humans neither possess nor suspect. And what does it *mean* for dolphins to become solemn in response to a human death?

We don't really have enough to go on; there's not enough to analyze. We have a few stories of free-living killer whales guiding people lost in fog; of whales seemingly returning lost dogs; of free-living killer whales turning in circles as a person makes a circular motion with his finger, or returning a hat worn perfectly for the occasion, or seeing someone wave and waving back, of empathy—of *sympathy*.

In Antarctica, my friend Bob Pitman tossed a snowball near a killer whale and the whale immediately tossed back a piece of ice. These stories could be just coincidences. We don't have other stories in which whales ignored people and did not respond to their thoughts, their dogs, or their snowballs. I am a hard-hearted disbeliever of things unknown. As a scientist, I am persuaded by evidence. And I tend to discount the less material explanations of puzzling phenomena.

More importantly, I don't see evidence that the whales—even if they are more intelligent than us (whatever "intelligence" means)—would be "sending us a message," as one friend of mine believes with all her heart they are trying to do.

Who wouldn't *like* to believe that whales are trying to send us a message? That would make them special. But most important, it would make us *very* special. And how very special we are is our favorite story. If humans have one overriding conceit and one universally shared delusion, it is that the world owes us for being so special.

Me, I am most skeptical of those things I'd most like to believe, precisely because I'd like to believe them. Wanting to believe something can skew one's view.

But the whales leave us with questions so puzzling they are disturbing. Why would these beings declare unilateral peace with humans and not with smaller dolphins and seals, whom they attack and eat? Why would they single us out to give assistance? And why no grudge? Why, after the chronic harassment, capture, and disruption we've visited upon them, do they show no learned and handed-down fears of humans such as wolves and ravens and even some dolphins seem to teach their young? The dolphins of the vast Pacific tuna grounds have such fears. Tuna nets used to kill them by the thousands; they still flee in panic from a ship several miles away if it pivots toward them, or if its engine merely changes pitch. I have seen that myself, in person. The dolphins' hard-learned fear of ships makes sense.

What doesn't make sense is: gigantic mega-brained predators patterned like pirate flags who eat everything from sea otters to blue whales and spend hours batting thousand-pound sea lions into the air specifically to beat them up before drowning and shredding them; who wash seals off ice and crush porpoises and slurp swimming deer and moose—indeed, seemingly any mammal they come across in the water; yet who have never so much as upended a single kayak and who appear—maybe—to bring lost dogs home.

Argentina is one of the places where killer whales sometimes burst through the surf to drag sea lions right off the beaches. You see a video of this and you think it would be insanity to stroll near the shoreline. Yet when park ranger Roberto Bubas stepped into the water and played his harmonica, the same individual killer whales would form a ring around him like puppies. They'd rally playfully around his kayak and come as, by names he gave them, he called to them.

· · ·

Through the squishy anecdotes runs a hard fact: free-living killer whales treat humans with a strange lack of violence. It's especially strange when compared with the rate at which humans continue hurting and killing other humans. How to explain *either* fact? What can explain the whales' striking forbearance? For the sea's *T. rex* to stick its head up alongside a tiny boat uncountable times and *never* hurt a human even in play— that begs for an explanation. More crucially, it demands that we find a way to understand. Is it simply outside our cognition; are their reasons beyond our ability to comprehend? Perhaps one day—.

And not only killer whales. Many anecdotes show other whales being gentle. Photographer Bryant Austin had been photographing humpback whale mothers and babies for several weeks when a five-week-old infant left his mother and swam up to him. Austin wrote, "The newborn maneuvered his five-foot-wide fluke precisely by my mask less than a foot away." While transfixed, Austin suddenly felt a firm tap on his shoulder. "As I turned to look, I was suddenly eye to eye with the calf's mother. She had extended the tip of her two-ton, fifteen-foot-long pectoral fin and positioned it in such a way as to gently touch my shoulder." Realizing that he was now between the mother and her baby, he was frightened by the thought that she could easily break his back. Instead, Austin described her actions as "delicate restraint." Meanwhile, the baby swam over to biologist Libby Eyre. "Time slowed down as I observed the calf roll underneath Libby and then gently lift her out of the water on his belly. She was on her hands and knees looking down at his throat." As Bryant's mind scrambled through a list of things that could go wrong, "the young whale placed his pectoral fin on her back, then gently rolled and put her back in the water."

And not just whales. Remember the elephant Tania, who was chasing a woman who'd annoyed her, yet skidded to a stop to avoid trampling the woman when she fell. Or the elephants who've guarded lost or injured people. What in the world is going on?

Helping in Mind

Stories of killer whales suggest an urge on their part to avert harm, protect, and comfort. Assistance is part of killer whale "persona." In 1973, a ferry's propeller struck a young killer whale. The captain wrote, "The cow and the bull cradled the injured calf between them to prevent it from turning upside-down. Occasionally the bull would lose its position and the calf would roll over on its side. The bull would make a tight circle, submerge, and rise slowly beside the calf, righting it." They cared for the young one with such astonishing faithfulness that fully two weeks later someone else reported "two whales supporting a third one, preventing it from turning over." But researchers never saw that whale again. (Some people call whales and elephants "bull," "cow," and "calf" out of habit. But labels propagate bias. "Male" "female," "baby," "adult," "brother," "mother," and so on are more accurate terms for what and who those whales and elephants are. If we let the terms equalize, our smokescreen begins to clear; the blinders begin to come off. Of course, that's what some people are afraid of.)

But in the case of the young whale injured by the propeller, is the adults' response really indicative—at all—of "astonishing faithfulness," as I just termed it? Is that *my* bias? Maybe the whales perform that kind of helping response by unthinking instinct, something like reflex—a hardwired urge to push a flailing companion upward. Is there any way to judge whether they understand what they are doing? Do they ever assess the situation and flexibly modify their response?

You can be the judge in several quite different scenarios: Pilot whales who were supporting a harpooned comrade near the surface suddenly started pushing their stricken podmate *down* underwater as it was being hauled to the ship. Apparently they first assessed that its main problem was its need to breathe; then they realized that the most urgent thing was to keep it from the ship. They want to live. And when under attack, they try to live. During several well-documented killer whale pursuits of Weddell and crabeater seals and a young gray whale, humpback whales disrupted the attacks. After killer whales washed a Weddell seal off an ice floe, whale experts Bob Pitman and John Durban watched as the seal dashed toward two nearby humpback whales. "Just as the seal got to the closest humpback, the huge animal rolled over on its back—and the 400-pound seal was swept up onto the humpback's chest between its massive flippers. Then, as the killer whales moved in closer, the humpback arched its chest, lifting the seal out of the water." When the seal started sliding back into the sea, "the humpback gave the seal a gentle nudge with its flipper, back to the middle of its chest." Shortly thereafter, the seal scrambled off, swimming to safety on a nearby ice floe. When a young free-living Atlantic spotted dolphin named Zigzag became fearful about escalating rough play from a small group of age-mates, he swam evasively and hung at the surface, making little whimpers. The other juveniles then gently approached and rubbed him, and he rejoined their play. (This seems especially touching, considering the bullying that human children sometimes show to playmates who indicate weakness.)

Not only do they help one another; they also accept help from humans. Sometimes they seek it. Sometimes they provide it. Sometimes they appreciate it.

A humpback whale off San Francisco got tangled in dozens of crab traps connected by about a mile of rope, with weights every sixty feet; the whole apparatus ran to well over a thousand pounds. Rope was wrapped at least four times around the whale's tail, back, mouth, and left front flipper, cutting into the giant's flesh. Though nearly fifty feet long and weighing about fifty tons, the whale was being pulled down and was having trouble breathing when divers got into the water to see whether they could help. The first diver was so aghast at the extent of the entanglement, he didn't think they'd be able to free the whale. Further, he feared that the whale's thrashing could entangle the divers, too. But instead of struggling to break away as soon as possible, the whale remained passive through an entire hour while the divers worked. "When I was cutting the line going through the mouth," James Moskito said, "its eye was there winking at me, watching me. It was an epic moment of my life." When the whale realized it was free, it did not swim away. Instead it swam to the closest diver, nuzzled him, then swam to the next one. "It stopped about a foot away from me, pushed me around a little bit and had some fun," Moskito told a *San Francisco Chronicle* reporter. "It felt to me like it was thanking us, knowing that it was free and that we had helped it. It seemed kind of affectionate, like a dog that's happy to see you."

A riveting amateur video (it's on YouTube) shows a dolphin off Hawaii with a fishhook in its flipper, actively seeking aid from scuba divers. When the divers see what its problem is and they stop, the dolphin instantly accepts the help it had been seeking. How does a dolphin with a fishhook in its flipper decide to seek help from a human diver, a creature so alien in the history of its realm? Would it seek help from a turtle or a fish? Doubtful. Another dolphin? It seemed to understand its problem as well as we might. But can dolphins really understand that we, like them, understand— *and* that we have these *hands*? Apparently, yes. Contrastingly, however, when researchers initiated aid toward a dolphin named Dash who had stainless steel fishing line cutting into his tail, he didn't cooperate. But those stories don't cancel each other out any more than one person seeking help and another not. One dolphin sought and accepted help; one didn't.

During the horror of the *Deepwater Horizon* oil blowout, in the Gulf of Mexico in 2010, fishing guide Jeff Wolkart told me, "A dolphin kept coming around. Its body was covered in that brownish oil, that tannish-colored crude. And he was trying to blow out his blowhole, and he was struggling." Each time Wolkart moved off, the dolphin followed, "coming to us, hanging right alongside," he said, adding that the dolphin "seemed to want help." But Wolkart couldn't think of anything to do, and eventually he had to go, leaving the ailing dolphin let down by humans, yet again, and likely doomed.

One wonders why they might come to us. And one wonders how often other animals have had their hopes of help from humans dashed. Dolphins and other animals who seek our help possess a mind that understands that humans, too, have a mind and can help (if we choose to). To understand that we might understand is more than we often grant to them.

Sometimes dolphins choose to help us. Sometimes people kill dolphins and deny that they suffer. So whose "mind" is more developed?

In *Of Wolves and Men,* author Barry Lopez relates a story told to him by a trapper who approached a large black male wolf caught in his leg-hold trap. The wolf lifted his trapped foot, extended it toward the man, and softly whined. "I would have let him go if I didn't need the money awful bad," the trapper said.

An online video shows a wild raven in Nova Scotia that sat on a fence calling for an hour until a person came and pulled several porcupine quills from its face and neck. There are many such stories of injured creatures seeming purposely to seek out human proximity. In *Out of the Wild,* Mike Tomkies recalls, "It was odd how many sick wild creatures . . . came close to us, as if knowing they would be protected."

We had a sweet dog whose unsolvable bad habit was a penchant for chasing deer. Once, in deep snow, she caught a doe and bit her on the rump. I saw it happen and saw that the deer had a nasty skin wound, but it didn't look too severe. I spotted the same deer over the next couple of days and hoped she would be okay. Then one morning I opened our front door and was horrified to find the deer on our doorstep—dead. Had she come seeking help? Had she come to ask why, or to lay blame, or to beg us to remember? Did she wish to be finished off or to confront our dog? Was it merely a little warmer next to the door for a deer in deep distress? Perhaps all of those things affected her choice. Nothing I can think of seems the likely explanation for the disturbing puzzle of why one deer who had suffered harm by our family had come to die on our very doorstep. The deer knew why; I don't.

Other animals sometimes seem to recognize in us a kind of kindred consciousness that we often fail to recognize in them. Occasionally, at least, we respond well. Gray whales give birth in the lagoons of Pacific Mexico's Baja coastline. During the whaling era, harpooned gray whales sometimes turned on the boats and smashed them to bits. Whalers thought grays unusually aggressive, though they were merely fighting for their lives. After the whales were driven nearly extinct, their fierce reputation survived for decades. Mexican fishermen, in their small skiffs, greatly feared them. "They were known as the Devil's fish," Don Pachico Mayoral told me. "Nobody had anything nice to say about them."

All that changed one magical day in 1972. Pachico was out fishing with a friend when a large gray whale startled them by surfacing mere inches from the boat. "My partner and I were both afraid," Don Pachico recalled. "The surprise was so intense that our legs were shaking." But instead of threatening the boat, the whale cozied up to it, and hung out. And that's when Pachico decided to bridge the gap. "I touched the whale very gently and the whale remained calm." Don Pachico recalled the event for me four decades later, but it was obvious that the life-changing moment remained vivid. "Minutes passed, and I kept petting her, until my fear went away. It was sublime for me," Don Pachico said. "I gave thanks to God."

Eager to share the gift with others, Pachico began taking visitors out to see the whales, and the lagoon's now-famous whale-based tourism business was born. Don Pachico acknowledged, "They forgive all the damage we did. That's why I have a lot of love and respect for them." Shortly before his death, I was lucky enough to accompany Don Pachico into the lagoon. And like many people who've visited, I experienced mother whales swimming up to the boat with newborns, as if proudly presenting them to us, and standing by while we stroked them. Don Pachico and his son Jesus explained that if the whales don't approach, people don't bother them. But if they come and you don't stroke them, they leave. Whatever their motivation or reason, they are seeking contact with humans. Is it just egotistical—as usual—to believe that other species have some special affinity for us?

From antiquity to recent times, stories recounting dolphins pushing distressed swimmers to the surface are too numerous to track. But for millions of years dolphins lived and died on a planet with no human beings. Dolphins have an instinctive urge to support their own babies and their ailing companions. When they do help humans, perhaps it's just misdirected instinct. Maybe just something to do. They don't *care* about us. Right?

My editor Jack Macrae was sea kayaking beyond a long barrier island off the Georgia coast when the wind and tide changed and conditions became challenging. He didn't know the area well and was beginning to grow worried. Soon dolphins appeared, flanking him, seemingly piloting him. He went with them, and they brought him to an inlet where he could get to safety. When a researcher swimming in the waters of the Bahamas got tired and needed to be towed by a swimming crew member, an

Atlantic spotted dolphin suddenly stopped what she was doing and imme-diately escorted them to their boat. When researchers there swam more than about a hundred yards from the boat, the dolphins "rapidly brought us back to the mother ship. . . . When we allowed the dolphins to lead the encounter they still swam us in circles or brought us back." Researcher Denise Herzing also says, "It is not unusual for the dolphins to surround us when a shark is present, or even escort us back to the boat with great determination."

In 2007, when a great white shark seriously bit a surfer named Todd Endris, a group of bottlenose dolphins formed a protective ring around him. Endris got to shore and survived. On a sailboat off Venezuela in 1997, the crew could not find a sailor who had fallen overboard. About an hour later, searchers in a powerboat saw two dolphins approach and quickly turn away, approach and quickly turn away, several times. The captain had already searched in that direction. But he decided to follow. They found the sailor, alive—attended by dolphins. Elián Gonzáles, a six-year-old ref-ugee from Cuba who in 2000 became a cause célèbre after his mother and others drowned when their boat sank, survived for two days on a floating inner tube. His human rescuers saw dolphins attending the stricken boy. Elián reported that whenever his strength failed and he began to lose his grip, the dolphins pushed him back onto the tube. He said that the only time he felt safe was when the dolphins were in sight.

This could all be nothing more than instinctive reflexive responses to a mammal in distress, reflexes evolved to aid other dolphins, misdirected at humans. But sometimes dolphins do things with humans that they never do with one another—things wholly unnatural to them and com-pletely human-oriented. "I've often observed that dolphins come up to our anchored vessel and tail-slap before a squall or strong storm," says Denise Herzing. If implying that dolphins warn and guard researchers seems like wishful misinterpretation, consider this: after Herzing's anchor line broke and the vessel drifted away, a dolphin named Blaze "headed over to the anchor and circled it until we turned our vessel around, launched the Zodiac, and retrieved our lost anchor. It was a nice interspecies gesture."

. . .

The problem with those stories is that they are casually documented, inconsistent, prone to subjective misinterpretation, and, thus, easy to discount.

But try to discount this: One foggy day, the biologist Maddalena Bearzi was taking notes on a familiar party of nine bottlenose dolphins who'd cleverly encircled a school of sardines near the Malibu pier. "Just after they began feeding," she writes, "one of the dolphins in the group suddenly left the circle, swimming offshore at a high speed. In less than an instant, the other dolphins left their prey to follow." To abruptly stop feeding—that was pretty odd. Bearzi followed, too. "We were at least three miles offshore when the dolphins stopped suddenly, forming a large ring without exhibiting any specific behavior." That's when Bearzi and her assistants spotted an inert human body with long, blond hair floating in the center of the dolphin ring. "Her face was pale and her lips were blue as I pulled her fully dressed and motionless body from the water." Warmed with blankets and the researchers' bodies, she began to respond. Later, in the hospital, Bearzi learned that the eighteen-year-old had swum offshore to commit suicide. She survived.

Such things are profound.

When breakthroughs happen, they don't come as confirmation of what we already know. They come as something unexpected, hard to fathom, something producing puzzlement, demanding new explanations. They come as things that many people dismiss or scorn. Until they turn out to be true. So while I am wary of believing, I'm also wary of dismissing. The many stories have pushed me into the "I just don't know" category. And it's pretty hard to get me there.

When someone has spent decades devoted to observing certain creatures, their observations are not to be taken lightly. Dolphins solemnly accompanied a boat with a dead man aboard, other dolphins left their food to surround a suicidal woman miles at sea—. Exactly what that *means,* that's more difficult for humans to understand.

How *do* we explain the facts of so unexpected a truce, so unilateral a peace? It seems to me that it is, yes, a big leap to go from the fact of no aggression to the idea that killer whales have chosen to be a benevolent presence and occasional protectors of lost humans. But what do the whales think? How is it that all the world's free-living killer whales have settled upon this one-way relationship of peacefulness with us? Before I encountered these stories, I was dismissive. Now I feel shaken out of certainty. I've suspended disbelief. It's an unexpected feeling for me. The stories have forced open doors I had shut, doors to that greatest of all mental feats: the simple sense of wonder, and of feeling open to the possibility of being changed.

Do Not Disturb

———•———

Back in his home office, Ken plugs his camera into his computer. During Ken's time, the technology has advanced from black-and-white film to digital photography. What else has changed?

Dave chimes in: "We're boring to them now. They're past the point of wanting to interact with every boat."

"And if they wanted to come to us," Ken adds, "the cops would come." In the early days, Ken would often whistle in a specific way, "kinda giving them my own signature call," he says, to help the whales recognize him. Now—he cannot.

Where once whales could be shot at will or chased and captured without even a permit, now it's illegal to whistle at a whale. These days you're not allowed to do anything that "might alter their behavior."

When jazz and world-music innovator (and mutual friend) Paul Winter played Johann Sebastian Bach on his saxophone into a steel tube taped to the side of Alexandra Morton's inflatable boat, the huge male named Top Notch veered from his passing pod, sculled over, and floated nearby until Paul finished. "When the song was over," Morton wrote, "Top Notch let loose a long sweeping call, exhaled, and vanished." This would now be illegal.

Agreed, you don't want bachelor party boatloads following the whales around and yelling while throwing beer cans at them. But sometimes the protections seem excessive, alienating—and targeted at the easiest people for police to monitor: the researchers.

"It's unfortunate," Ken says, "because we're entertaining to them. The limits of that entertainment might be beyond anything we've known so far."

If they chose to interact on their own terms and at their own times, was it still, in a way, disturbing them?

"I can tell you this categorically," asserts Ken, a little pointedly, "I've *never* felt that I ever *disturbed* a whale." I'm firmly on his side.

We share the world with creatures whose curious brains peacefully seek us, and we do it like this: We put up a firewall to protect them, while we destroy their food—and their ears. It would seem diabolical, but that isn't the thinking behind it. There is no thinking behind it. Our human brain doesn't reach.

In Baja, Mexico, the ecotourism business based on close encounters with gray whales has been key to protecting their birthing lagoons from industrial development. Instead of a firewall, there's an invitation, sent by the whales themselves. Most of the lagoon is off-limits to boats. The remainder can be visited for only a few hours each day. The whales have plenty of privacy if they prefer it. Some, though, choose to approach boats with their babies beside them. In the United States or Canada, stroking a whale could land you a conviction. But in Baja, if you *don't* stroke the whales, they'll leave you, looking for more interesting and interactive humans. Having been there, I like that system better. Certainly, it's much better for human understanding of the whales—and for that reason, it's been better for the whales. For elephants, wolves, whales, and many others, getting closer has replaced fear and loathing with more profound understanding that's been better for all. Laws making it illegal to play music or whistle to whales do nothing to prevent humans from crowding them out of existence. In fact, in this strange new time when animals need a human political constituency in order to survive, such enforced alienation may only hasten their demise.

Nowadays the killer whales are far more dispersed and less frequent around the San Juan Islands than in the past. Ken laments, "We're not going to have the good old days again."

He means the 1980s. He was younger, the salmon populations seemed adequate, and whales were recovering instead of declining. But for the killer whales, the *really* good old days were much further back in time. Since at least the mid-twentieth century, humans have killed them as competitors, captured them for entertainment, and depleted their food by degrading salmons' spawning rivers and by overfishing.

In 1874, the whaler Captain Charles Scammon wrote of killer whales, "In whatever quarter of the world they are found, they seem always intent upon seeking something to destroy or devour." You'd almost have thought he was writing about his own whaling fleet. Killer whales sometimes eat larger whales, but after millions of years of killers, there were still millions of large whales. In contrast, by the time Scammon's companions were just about finished—so were the whales.

Within the lifetime of the older whales still swimming here, humans widely feared and hated them. With the name "killer," who would trust them to forgo any opportunity to attack a human? A 1973 U.S. Navy diving manual asserted that killer whales "will attack human beings at every opportunity." A 1969 book titled *Man Is the Prey* called killer whales "the biggest confirmed man-eater." The only problem with these pronouncements is their total disconnect from reality.

Sperm whales are another species whose early reputation for blood lust eventually got dialed back to reality. "We might be led to believe that there is no animal in the creation more monstrously ferocious," wrote Thomas Beale in his 1838 book *The Natural History of the Sperm Whale*. "But not only does the sperm whale in reality happen to be a most timid and inoffensive animal . . . , readily endeavouring to escape from the slightest thing which bears an unusual appearance, but he is also quite incapable of being guilty of the acts of which he is so strongly accused."

The Pacific Northwest natives' more mystical view was more developed. In a real way, it was more objective. The logic of their observations more accurately reflects the reality of the high-finned whales. At intimate proximity, they saw a giant creature of vast killing power who, mysteriously, never harmed them. And so the whales evoked, quite reasonably, awe. Awe was the raw material from which the people shaped respect for their intelligence, appreciation for their judgment, gratitude for their forebearance. The people viewed the black-and-white swimmers who penetrated the seas and so capably commanded their otherworldly realm as spirit beings. The Tlingit of what is now southeast Alaska believed killer whales would aid them with gifts of strength, health, and food, all of which these whales knew how to leverage from the dark, frigid waters. To native peoples of British Columbia, too, *kakawin,* the killer whale, is a respected spiritual presence of supernatural powers. *Kakawin* is the ocean counterpart of *qwayac'iik,* the wolf. Thus *kakawin,* the sea wolf, is associated with truth and justice.

Most European and Japanese people knew nothing, and cared even less, about killer whales. To fishermen, they were pests and competitors, demonized by mariners and stoned by children. As a child, Graeme Ellis— who later spent his working life with killer whales, first training and then studying them in their free state—threw rocks at them. "That's what you did; and when you got older, you shot at them."

Between the 1950s and about 1980, Norway, Japan, and the Soviet Union slaughtered some six thousand killer whales, no doubt causing wide disruption to their societies. Various other countries contributed to the mortality as they could.

In 1956 the Icelandic government, panicked over the fact that killer whales eat herring and had damaged fishing nets, blamed them for "costing the herring industry" $250,000 (an astonishingly puny amount even considering inflation and, of course, heedless of what the herring industry costs herring-eating mammals, seabirds, and fishes). Iceland called America for help. In October 1956, *Naval Aviation News* bragged that U.S. Navy planes had "completed another successful mission against killer whales . . . hundreds were destroyed with machine guns, rockets, and depth charges." The pain and havoc in the sea must have been horrific.

When owners of sport fishing lodges around Vancouver Island's Campbell River area complained about competition for salmon, Canada's Department of Fisheries responded on a July day in 1960 by hatching this enlightened plan for preventing killer whales from approaching a fishing area called Seymour Narrows: "It is recommended that one .50 calibre machine gun with tripod mounting be used . . . to open fire when they approach." But after the gun was set up, the whales mysteriously shifted their foraging pattern, staying away from the area. Another one of those crazy stories; how could the whales know?

Better than killing them would be to see what they're like alive. In captivity. Right?

Captivity did not get off to a tidy start. In 1962, two employees of California's Marineland of the Pacific lassoed a killer whale from a forty-foot boat in Puget Sound. Her screams brought a male's help. The men panicked and started shooting. The male disappeared; six shots killed the roped female. She became dog food. In 1964, the Vancouver Aquarium not only commissioned a thirty-eight-year-old sculptor to create a life-sized replica of a killer whale—they sent him to kill one as a model. He harpooned a small one, not much more than a baby, who went into shock and started to sink; two pod members rushed to the stunned youngster, pushing him to the surface so he could breathe. When the little one began to breathe again, the artist took out a rifle and started shooting. The harpooned whale began whistling so loudly that people a hundred yards away heard it. Then the artist decided to tow him back alive. To lessen the pain, the little harpooned whale swam alongside, as if leashed. The event made international news. No killer whale had ever before been held captive. The public was riveted. The injured young whale refused food for fifty-five days. After breaking his fast, he survived for another month. The Victoria *Times* opined that the young whale—who had been named Moby Doll—had "died a miserable death." People felt bad. But not everyone. "I worry about this sentimentalizing," the aquarium's director told a reporter. "It was a nice whale, but . . . it could swallow you alive."

That tormented young whale marked a tragic but pivotal point. His gentle, curious, cooperative nature—so unlike the ferocious beast of false repute—surprised people. Inevitably, aquariums spawned the idea of displaying killer whale captives to a paying public.

On a late July day in 1965, a killer whale that had been accidentally caught in a fishing net arrived at the Seattle Aquarium. For over a year, Namu, as he was known, proved wildly attractive to ticket buyers. Then he died. He was the first of many.

The aquarium and several other marine-themed parks wanted more. The first live-capture operation was mounted jointly by SeaWorld and the Seattle Aquarium in October 1965. By 1973, catchers were getting about

$70,000 per whale. Using helicopters, speedboats, and explosives, they would harass and chase a group of whales into a bay, where a fishing boat would wrap a net around them. The catchers wanted weaned babies. It didn't always go smoothly.

One night in 1969, catchers corralled four out of a group of twelve whales that included the well-known Top Notch. In the morning, the free whales had not left their trapped family members. So the catchers encircled them, too, leaving a harbor crisscrossed with nets. After one of the captives escaped, he repeatedly crashed back into the mesh, making holes. Most of the family—disoriented and perhaps in shock—failed to immediately follow. One female came to the nets as if looking for a way out, but she didn't find one; meanwhile, the fishermen were repairing the breaks as fast as they could. The male eventually stopped slamming the nets but waited around for a few days. Then, perhaps in hunger, perhaps in defeat, he left.

The captors, pleased to be fielding offers from American and European bidders, auctioned seven young whales. They released four elders. Those released whales, too, hung around for a day or so before leaving.

Then, for many years, no whales returned to that place.

Two pregnant whales were caught in British Columbia in 1968. After they had not eaten for a month, they were sold to a place named as though it had an identity disorder: Marine World Africa U.S.A. One gave birth to a stillborn baby; then she died, too. Workers kept training the other, making her jump. Her baby was also stillborn. She herself survived that initial ordeal.

The catchers were free to take as many young whales as they wanted. No one understood anything about their social structures or population sizes. Everyone wanted to believe that whales were randomly coming and going to these inside waters from an essentially unlimited population of killer whales wandering the whole Pacific. What was the harm in snagging a few for the tanks?

Ken thought in traditional fisheries terms back then, too; but he wanted to know what the "sustainable yield" of whales might be. He reasoned that it could not be unlimited. The brilliant Canadian researcher Mike Bigg realized that he could consistently identify individual whales and that the groups were stable—and *much* smaller in number than anyone had imagined. He correctly perceived that "residents" and "transients" swam the same waters with differing diets, calls, and social habits and never mixed. This had been completely unknown—and seemed inexplicable. For his extraordinary insights, he was ridiculed and marginalized. Not just the capture people dismissed him; officials treated Bigg, Ken says, "like a loony." Ken got caught in that same net of official chronic harassment from U.S. government officials and on-the-water enforcers. It made for tense times.

Between 1962 and the mid-1970s, many individual killer whales got netted repeatedly by catchers intent on taking their young ones from them. A quarter of the live-captured whales had bullet wounds from random shootings. This was the relationship between humans and the Northwest's whales.

The whales began avoiding some of their favorite, most food-rich places, which had turned so dangerous. Then public sentiment began souring on the captures. In 1976, more than a thousand people descended in protest on the scene of one capture.

Ultimately the researchers documented—beyond doubt—that fewer than 150 southern resident whales swam these waters. Their work probably prevented the group's extinction. Counting whales taken alive and others killed during netting activities, the captures removed about 40 percent of the population—roughly 60 whales. Of 53 whales taken live to the tanks, 16 (about one out of three) died before one year had passed. During the catching heyday, ocean theme parks took about 95 killer whales from the Pacific Northwest and Iceland. In 1975 and 1976, Canada and Washington, at least, finally banned killer whale captures.

In the summer of 1977, in Victoria, Canada, and fresh out of college, I bought a ticket and found a seat in the bleachers to see my first killer whales. (It would be another fifteen years before I would glimpse free-living killer whales in the real world.) And there they were, gently taking fish from pretty girls yet doing full-body leaps that seemed impossibly powerful.

I was so astonished by what I was watching these "killer" whales do with their human friends that I was moved to tears. They were not mindless killers; they were sensitive, interactive, careful gentle giants. Magnificent. The show seemed filled with compassion, with the generosity of spirit of people willing to reach across the species barrier—and with *hope* that we would learn to love the whales. It never crossed my mind to look behind the curtain.

In the minds and on the lips of many who saw what I saw, killer whales were exonerated. Having served their time as killers, they were sprung from a reputation they'd never deserved and graduated to "orca."

The whales had not changed. It's just that we, for the first time, got a world-altering glimpse of them. In those days, whale watching didn't exist. Wildlife documentary filmmakers hardly dared dream of what they've since achieved. The first captive whales sacrificed their lives for a just cause they could not comprehend. So the question is: Was the sacrifice of those performing whales worth the value of changed public sentiment?

Different answers are possible now. But on that day in 1977, as I wiped my eyes and left the stadium feeling awed just to share the world with such creatures, there was no question. No question at all. As far as I could see, the whales were obviously having fun.

To Have and to Hold

———•———

In the 1860s, aquariums in Great Britain and the United States began displaying beluga whales and bottlenose dolphins. P. T. Barnum's beluga was probably the first cetacean trained to perform tricks, and in 1914, New York Aquarium director Charles Townsend was amazed that his dolphins' play resembled "the tussling of puppies." But for decades, poor care meant captured dolphins didn't survive long.

In the 1930s, several motion picture producers built a big underwater movie set in Florida. Marine Studios quickly became Marineland of Florida, welcoming a paying public. Until Marineland, dolphins' social, emotional, and cognitive capacities were completely unknown. When Marineland's curator Arthur McBride reunited two male dolphins who'd been captured together but then separated for several weeks, McBride wrote with amazement that they showed "the greatest amount of excitement. . . . No doubt could exist that the two recognized each other." Moved and fascinated, McBride wrote that the dolphins in his charge represented "our most 'human' deep sea relatives . . . an appealing and playful water mammal who remembers his friends." Scientists could now watch bottlenose dolphins at close range. Before this, people thought of them— if they thought of them—as sources of meat, oil, and leather. Aquariums brought dolphins and whales to the public's attention as remarkable mammals with family lives. They provided literally the first windows onto dolphin social life.

One evening at Marineland in the early 1950s, a night watchman noticed that one of the dolphins seemed to be tossing a pelican feather toward him.

Soon they were tossing balls and toys back and forth. Marineland began featuring the world's first "educated porpoise." Dolphin shows followed. But the dolphin had started the interaction, and the watchman and the public had gotten the education. For the next thirty years, the world's first and only dolphin studies involved captives.

Captivity shifted into higher gear. It became bigger business, with bigger numbers and higher stakes. And killer whales were the biggest game.

In the gripping film *Blackfish*, Howard Garrett, an advocate for the whales, recalls one particular chase during the 1970s. Speedboats were hurling explosives to frighten a group of whales toward the net boats. But these orcas had been caught before, he explains, "and they knew what was going on, and they knew their young ones would be taken from them. So the adults without young went east, into a cul-de-sac. And the boats followed them, thinking they were all going that way." But the adults with babies had split off, shepherding their young ones around the far side of an island. The ones without young made themselves obvious; the ones with the babies stealthily slipped away. It seemed a tactically brilliant strategy, confronting us with a question we've faced before: *How might they have communicated such thinking?*

But as Garrett reminds us, "they have to come up for air eventually." And when they did, the catchers' aircraft spotted them. So the speedboats caught them there. After they had the young ones penned, the catchers slacked the main net so the older ones could swim off.

They didn't leave.

"As the catchers began lassoing the babies," Ken tells me, "mothers would vigorously try to prevent their babies from being taken. The mom would get in between and try to push the baby away. There'd be a lot of squealing." As Ken recalls it, catchers afraid for their safety sometimes simply killed resisting adults.

Diver John Crowe picks up the narrative in the film. While they were maneuvering a baby into a stretcher for removal, he recalls, "the whole fam-damily is twenty-five yards away in a big line, communicating back and forth. Well, you understand then what you're doing. I lost it. I just started crying. . . . Just like kidnapping a little kid away from its mother. . . . I can't think of anything worse than that." He finished the job, though: "Everybody's watching; what can you do?" When it was all over, the net held three dead whales. Crowe and two others were directed to "cut the whales open, fill 'em with rocks, put anchors on their tails, and sink 'em." Crowe remembers the whole operation with these words: "the worst thing I've ever done."

It's impossible to imagine the mental experience of a social mammal with a brain comparable to ours who has just tried her best to prevent her child from being taken, has failed, and is swimming away from the chaos bereft of her small one, with whom, for the last few years, she has been in constant touch. For the baby, isolated, suddenly cut off from her family's voices, going from the limitless ocean to the confinement of a concrete teacup, the terror and confusion—

When the United States and Canada stopped permitting the capture of killer whales, aquariums moved their catching operations to Iceland. In 1983 a two-year-old, twelve-foot-long whale caught in Iceland arrived at Sealand of the Pacific in Victoria, Canada, right across Haro Strait from Ken's home. The staff named him Tilikum. Eric Walters, a former trainer at Sealand, remembers Tilikum as "the one you really loved to work with . . . very well behaved, and he was always eager to please. . . . Tilikum was the one you trusted."

But early on, Tilikum had a trainer who teamed him up with a pre-trained killer whale and used punishment. If the trained whale performed the behavior the trainer wanted but Tilikum did not perform it, the trainer punished *both* whales, depriving both of food. This caused the trained whale to become frustrated enough to rake Tilikum head to toe with bleeding tooth marks. Nothing like that has ever been documented for free-living killer whales.

Sealand was just a big net pen surrounded by bleachers, floating in the bay like a small marina. Because management was afraid that someone sympathetic to their three whales might cut the net, at night they "stored" the killer whales in a dark, twenty-by-thirty-foot floating steel container. For creatures who travel seventy-five miles a day and whose body length is more than half the width of their cell, spending nearly two-thirds of their hours immobile and sensory-deprived "was just wrong," admits former Sealand director Steve Huxter. On many mornings, Tilikum—now sixteen feet long and spending most of his time jammed into that steel can with two hostile companions not of his tribe—appeared with freshly bleeding bites. Tilikum thus found himself subjected to a wholly unnatural level of violence, from which there was no escape.

Ken tells me that locking Tilikum in the box for fourteen hours a day with other whales who were ill-disposed to him and bored out of their minds "probably led to psychosis."

As early as 1981, in the first book focused on killer whales, Erich Hoyt wrote, "Captive orcas at Sea World and Marineland have held trainers underwater, nearly drowning them. There have been a number of bitings. These incidents generally occur after an individual whale has been in captivity for several years. Due to a change in routine or sometimes due to boredom, the whale suddenly becomes frustrated or disturbed. Fortunately, there is usually some warning to the trainer. To date, no captive has killed its trainer."

One day in 1991, Tilikum and two other whales drowned a trainer named Keltie Byrne after she accidentally slipped into the water. Trainers there didn't normally enter the water. One colleague, Colin Baird, thinks that the whales, surprised to suddenly find a human in the pool with them for the first time, were just playing. "You know, they couldn't conceptualize," he said, ". . . that she can't hold her breath for twenty minutes." Regardless, the publicity forced Sealand's closure. Tilikum was sold to the SeaWorld theme park in Orlando, Florida. As a producer of sperm, he was worth millions.

Arriving at SeaWorld weighing twelve thousand pounds, he was put in with females who continually attacked him. Simple tensions of close quarters likely aren't even the whole story. Think of the differing acoustic clans, the different, nonsocializing resident communities, the culturally and genetically distinct transients and residents whose ranges actually overlap in the Pacific Northwest but who shun all contact. Penning an Icelandic whale with Pacific Northwest residents might be the killer whale equivalent of putting a Neanderthal mammoth hunter in a cell with three Japanese waitresses. Even by the unnatural standards of orca captivity, Tilikum was the orca from another realm, possibly even another species. And he immediately suffered abuses.

SeaWorld eventually succeeded in getting babies out of its captive whales. But instead of leaving the mothers and their surviving children together, as is normal for them, SeaWorld's management removed the young ones soon after weaning, like cattle farmers. Corporate management shipped them among their chain of theme parks like any commodity, as dictated by financial calculations.

Former SeaWorld trainer Carol Ray tells her interviewer in *Blackfish* that after the SeaWorld staff took Katina's baby, Katina "stayed in the corner of the pool, literally shaking and screaming, screeching, crying. I'd never seen her do anything like that. . . . There is nothing that you could call that besides grief." Former SeaWorld trainer John Hargrove remembers Kasatka and her baby as "very close . . . inseparable." After the baby had been taken to the airport, Kasatka "continued to make vocalizations that had never been heard before." A research scientist who analyzed the sounds concluded that Kasatka was making long-range calls, trying to establish contact with her missing child.

Howard Garrett reminds us in the film that when killer whales were first brought into captivity, we knew less than nothing; they were considered vicious killers. But we've learned that "they're amazingly friendly and understanding and intuitively want to be your companion. And to this day there's no record of an orca doing any harm to any human in the wild."

Though no free-living killer whale has ever killed a human, captivity causes violence among killer whales. Violence that is never seen in normal killer whale society. Violence seemingly stemming from the frustrations of so unnatural an existence. In 1999, a man who'd snuck into SeaWorld Orlando was found dead in Tilikum's pool, his body very roughed up. In 2010, Tilikum killed trainer Dawn Brancheau. By all accounts, Dawn was a sensitive, enormously motivated trainer.

Tilikum had long been subjected to bizarre treatment. He had already been involved in the death of two humans. Yet he was still made to continue his moneymaking dance for the company. Just before his attack on Brancheau, he seemed to have missed a cue from her; it appears that he thought he'd done what she'd asked, then became frustrated when she did not reward him. Only between two beings capable of understanding can so deep a misunderstanding arise.

In captivity, other dolphins sometimes act frustrated or angry when given negative feedback. When a captive bottlenose dolphin in an artificial language study in Hawaii did not respond as required and got no reward, she grabbed a large floating plastic pipe and hurled it at the trainer, narrowly missing her head. Another annoyed dolphin deliberately threw the spiny part of a fish. Turnabout isn't just fair play; it's mind play. But the size and strength and mind of a killer whale raises the response—and the stakes—to a new level.

It hardly matters whether Tilikum did not initially intend harm but acted from frustration, or boredom, or just felt aggravated and then got carried away. He and the trainers would never have gotten their lives intertwined had it not been for the fundamental injustice of taking him from his family and his world. SeaWorld is just an amusement business. The sea is a real *world*. When we trifle with the creatures from that world instead of meeting them in their realm, a certain logic of consequences goes into motion.

When I left that stadium in 1977, it never occurred to me to imagine how the whales had been caught. It never occurred to me to imagine captivity in reverse, that a young killer whale growing up among humans is like a young human growing up among killer whales. No matter how lovingly, whales could never provide the full physical and emotional context in which a child could be normal. Imagine yourself captured around age four, raised by whales who find you fascinating. Your language acquisition would end; normal socialization would end. The known world would shrink to a single room surrounded by whales looking in at you. Your memories of the wider world and your family would fade. You would get your meals by putting your head underwater to take handouts from fascinated keepers who'd never seen humans living in human families. They'd learn a little something from almost everything you did. Your own education, in any meaningful sense, would have been terminated. You would no longer be part of the world. You'd be only an amusing little part of their world. As a youngster, you'd find them interesting. Anyway, interacting with them would be almost all the stimulation you'd ever get. You'd certainly need stimulation. The whales would fill some of your loneliness. You would not exactly understand what you were missing, but your basic needs for human fulfillment would be going unmet. The routine would get boring. Inevitably, you wouldn't be quite right.

Whales are born and built for a complex world of long-distance sound and long-distance travel. They remain with their mothers and siblings their entire lives. They maintain long-distance relationships, too, with occasional reunions with dozens of other individuals whom they know for their whole long lives. We put them in concrete pools that function as both isolation quarters and echo chambers. What does life in a hard little tureen do to a whale's growing mind? Imagine a life spent in a circular room with blank walls. Round and round you go.

The theme parks and aquariums that describe their captives as "ambassadors" have a point. And a bottom line. What they could use, though, is a heart. During an earlier era, captive Native Americans and Pacific Islanders were taken on ships to Europe as specimen examples. In 1906, a generation after slavery was outlawed in the United States, an Mbuti Pygmy man named Ota Benga was exhibited at the Bronx Zoo monkey house. We later outgrew things like that. Though his handlers tried to be nice, he eventually killed himself. He wasn't where he belonged.

SeaWorld's killer whales perform under the stage name Shamu. Ken says it stands for "shame on you." The whales are in show business. After half a century of killer whale leaps and tricks, is our knowledge mounting? I know our losses are. Some wild captures continue, for instance in Russian waters, with new marine parks in China becoming a main source of demand. I hope that when the shows are finally ended and the era of killer captivity passes, what we've come to understand about killer whales will, eventually, outlive the damage done.

I'm not saying we've learned nothing from whale captures. Quite the opposite; by holding them close, by challenging the normalcy of their lives and watching them cope, we began seeing them for the first time. And they astounded us. Like learning about the depth and reach of the human spirit by watching human prisoners doing magnificent things to help one another stay alive, we confronted the relational capacities of whales. We learned the most basic thing about them: that they are somebody.

Ken is telling me that during the 1970s, a mother and son who'd been captured and held in a large net pen had both refused food for three weeks. Their captors didn't even realize that they were mammal eaters, "transients" whose normal prey is seals, sea lions, dolphins, and whales. The captors were trying to feed them herring. The whales must have gotten very hungry. "They were wasting away," Ken says.

They were moved to nearby Sealand. When they arrived, a trained whale named Haida—who was from a fish-eating "resident" pod (either J or L pod) and had been brought into captivity in 1968—dove down to inspect them along the netting that separated them. Haida swam back to a trainer who'd been scratching him, took a herring, and pushed it through the netting for the new whales. Sharing food with strangers; we thought only humans do that.

Because free-living residents and transients never mingle, Haida's gesture becomes, in human terms, transcendent. At first the newcomers did not take the fish. Haida pressed a fish against one of the others' mouth, and repeated this several times with both newcomers. The new whales soon began eating. You might call it—what? If a human did such a thing, the word applied would be "mercy." "Transcendent mercy." Let us be at least generous enough not to deprive so generous a whale of two mere words.

Caught with those two had been three other transients, who were still in the net pen in the bay where they'd been captured. By the time they'd not eaten for seventy-five days, their bodies had shrunk over their rib cages, a state of emaciation unheard of for a whale. One of the whales started slowly swimming, bumping into things as if in a delirium; then at five in the afternoon she charged the net full force, punching through heavy polypropylene netting up to her dorsal fin. Stuck, exhausted, starved, she went backward out of the net, opening her mouth to allow air bubbles to escape, and sank, dead. It was almost as if the failure of that final desperate dash took what remained of her will to live and she'd intentionally let go of life. Immediately after that whale died, one of the other whales, dubbed Charlie Chin, looked over at the human attendants. He grabbed the net and started yanking on it. Was he asking for help, for release? The humans started hitting him on the head, but he hung on for a while. Then he let go.

On day seventy-eight, Charlie Chin took a salmon from an attendant's hand and, starving, swam with it to his surviving comrade. The two of them vocalized. He dropped the salmon right in front of her nose. She grabbed it by the tail. He took hold of the head. With each whale holding one end of the fish, they made one circuit of the pool, vocalizing back and forth. Then they pulled the fish apart. Each whale ate half. A few minutes later, he got another fish and again presented it. She ate it whole. He went and got another for himself.

Soon they were each eating 450 pounds of fish daily.

And soon, too, they were sold to a Texas aquarium.

But before Sealand shipped them out, someone, one night, weighed down a section of the netting. The whales left. (Though the perpetrator was never caught, I and lots of other people would like to thank them. It says much about us that people could catch and sell the whales into captivity and get wealthy, and that people could simply liberate the whales and get arrested. As Bob Dylan observed, "Steal a little and they throw you in jail. Steal a lot and they make you king.")

A few years later, both of the whales that were sprung that night were photographed together, along with a new baby. "We saw them occasionally for about twenty-five years," Ken says. Charlie Chin lived until 1992. "They didn't want *anything* to do with people."

~

Graeme Ellis has spent decades studying free-living killer whales. But fresh out of high school, he got a job with the Vancouver Aquarium. His assignment: convince a new whale who wouldn't eat to start taking food. One month passed; the whale took no food. One day Ellis was just sitting idly when he began splashing the whale. The whale, unexpectedly, splashed back, disappeared, then suddenly leapt clear of the water. Within hours he was coming to get scratched and rubbed; the next day he was eating. A social creature, he'd just needed to establish a little relationship first. Some scientists believe that killer whales have social needs as strong or stronger than humans'. Needs more important to them, sometimes, than food.

Ellis has said, "It's not how many tricks you can train them to do . . . it's how long you can maintain a whale's sanity." You have to know how a whale's mind works, he says. Juvenile orcas are eager for at least a year. But after a couple of years in captivity, the novelty wears off and a whale's mental health starts declining. "Some get bored, lethargic. Others turn neurotic and perhaps dangerous." After a few years in captivity, he says, "they all start to get a bit nutty."

Expect Personality

John Ford, a leading Canadian researcher of free-living killer whales, started out working aquarium shows, where he found killer whales to be "incredibly perceptive," each responding differently to different people. Even while he was walking along the back of a stadium behind as many as five hundred people gathered to see a show, the whales could recognize and follow him with their eyes. Because they "make a game of changing things," he found them quite challenging. In subtle ways that he did not sense at first, he eventually realized that his *own* behavior "was being modified by them." Another thing he hadn't counted on: each whale has a "strikingly different" personality.

Personality is probably the most underrecognized aspect of free-living creatures. Dolphins have personality galore. They're born with personalities. Shy. Bold. Rambunctious. Bullying.

We see stereotypes when we see "elephants" or "wolves" or "killer whales" or "chimps" or "ravens." But the instant we focus on individuals, we see that individuals differ. We see an elephant named Echo with exceptional leadership qualities; we see wolf Seven Fifty-five struggling to survive the death of his mate and exile from his own family; we see a lost whale who is lonely but humorous and stunningly gentle. It's not *person*ality; it's *individua*lity. And it's a fact of life. And it runs deep. *Very* deep.

Professor Joanna Burger has a small pond in her yard. We walk to the pond's edge and stand. I see nothing. Then she calls, and I am astonished when several turtles come to be fed. I did not think turtles capable of being so responsive, so alert, of coming out when called! I had thought turtles were "just" turtles. Several frogs appear, too, and unlike every frog I've ever seen, they hop *out* of the water *onto* rocks, anticipating our insect treats. It's so surprising to watch them gather round.

But why am I surprised? Why do we continue to expect living things to be so incapable? Before we existed, they were already on the job. We so vastly underestimate them. We impose a self-isolation that deprives ourselves of experiencing so much of the world's persona. People used to think turtles were deaf. I am beginning to realize how blind we've been. It's been known for a while that turtles hear, and that some make sounds. But only in 2014 did scientists announce their discovery that hatchlings and adults of a species of river turtle vocalize to one another, using eleven types of calls. The scientists observed that the calls functioned "to congregate hatchlings with adults for mass migration." Had you asked me before I read that, I (and most turtle experts) would have told you—wrongly—that no turtles provide parental care, at all. As my neighbor J. P. Badkin wryly says, "If you're not careful, you can learn something every day."

I'm not going to tell you what creatures my friend Darrel Frost is talking about. Try to guess. (He gets to it at the end.) Darrel is a curator at the American Museum of Natural History, in New York City. He's able to keep his pets with him while he works. I'm in his office for the first time, and he's introducing me and saying, "Mud is the larger one with the undershot jaw. Hermes is the one with the broken back and epilepsy. When Mud is really excited, he will almost dance side to side. Before our secretary, Iris, retired a year ago, they would run down to her office to get goodies from her. Mud would bite at Iris's pant cuffs to get her attention. She visited yesterday, and even though they hadn't seen her in months, they still get really excited when she comes into the room. Likewise when our volunteer, Denny, visits to pamper them—they just light up. Denny and Iris talk to them, and they really seem to appreciate that contact and the socializing.

"I'm the one who feeds them, so you'd think they would respond to me—but I never get that kind of reaction. My care is a lot more matter-of-fact, I fear. Iris and Denny lecture me that I don't talk to them enough. As for personality, Mud is like a little kid, incredibly curious when people are in my office. He wants to come in to see if people are having fun without him. He will scrape at the door until he is let in. Hermes may come in but has always been more shy around strangers. Mud loves Mexican music; it gets him running around. When Mud would start getting out of hand, Iris would just touch his nose with the eraser end of a pencil and he would get very upset, stop what he was doing, and sulk. A soft touch, but he knows who is in charge. He could easily have pushed her out of the room, but her disapproval was clearly hard on him.

"The funniest thing is that they know their names, but if you catch them doing something they shouldn't do and you call their name, they will look away to avoid eye contact. One day Mud *extremely* quietly came in, and very quietly opened the door of the small refrigerator where I kept their greens, and was quietly working on a head of lettuce. After I noticed, I watched him for a moment. It was the *quietest* I had ever seen him. He *knew* that if he got busted he would have his lettuce taken away, so he was trying to keep from attracting my attention. And, jeez, when I closed the fridge door, was he mad! He had a little tantrum right there, jerking back and forth—and then he ran back into Iris's office so he could be with her.

"One day I was sitting in my office and Iris passed by my doorway sitting in her office chair, which has wheels. Mud was pushing the chair, with her on it, down the hallway. She was loving it. And so was he. She had been behind her desk and he had gone in and pushed her chair, with her in it, out of the office. Over and over again, both Mud and Hermes present jealousy, sneakiness, venality, excitement, wanting to belong—behaviors that I associate with two- to three-year-old humans. They have dominance hierarchies and, like big dogs, they develop strong attachments to their 'masters.'"

The whole time Darrel is talking, we're both looking straight at Mud and Hermes. "Sometimes they're buttheads," Darrel adds with a warm smile, "but they are usually a real joy." I ask what they weigh. Regarding them with a look both affectionate and appraising, Darrel says, "Mud is right at one hundred pounds, and Hermes, because of his health problems I think, is at eighty-five pounds. They're still young. The species' maximum size is around two hundred and fifty pounds, making spur-thighed the largest mainland tortoise; only some of the Galápagos and the Aldabra

Island tortoises get bigger." No wonder reptiles have been Darrel's life; *seeing* relationships is his reward for *building* them.

It's easier to imagine that highly social, mentally well-endowed apes and elephants, wolves and dolphins have individual personalities. Of course, dogs have personalities, from neurotic to almost sublime. What's surprising—until you make individual acquaintances—is how deep and widespread the phenomenon of personality is. When you work with hawks, say, you see that each responds a little differently, each hunts a bit differently. No two quite alike. Theodore Roosevelt, who brought a scientific mind (if not a compassionate heart) to his love of hunting, wrote, "Bears differ individually in courage and ferocity precisely as men do." Researchers have also published findings on the individual personalities of monkeys, rats, mice, lemurs, finches and other songbirds, bluegill and pumpkinseed sunfish, stickleback fish, killifish, bighorn sheep, domestic goats, blue crabs, rainbow trout, jumping spiders, house crickets, social insects. . . . In other words, pretty much everywhere they've looked, they've found that individuals differ. Some are more aggressive, bolder, shier, some more active; some fear the new, while others are explorers.

At the Stazione Zoologica, in Italy, researchers presented a crab in a jar to each of two octopuses. The first octopus embraced the jar, popped off the top, and devoured part of its prize. "Then it replaced the cap on the jar as if to save the rest for later," say my friends the professors Peter and Judy Weis of Rutgers University, who were there. "That *floored* us!" The researchers put the second octopus in the same setup. This octopus had been slithering back and forth across the glass tank like a hungrily pacing leopard, so the scientists expected an instant performance. But this time when the jar splashed in, Octopus Two, apparently much shier or more easily frightened, darted behind a rock—and wouldn't budge from hiding. "It didn't care what was in the jar." Peter said. "We thought the first one showed us 'what octopuses do.' But the second one didn't do anything." Judy elaborated: "We really don't appreciate how much personality most animals have. Even as scientists, we've hardly ever thought about that."

The previously mentioned killer whales Orky and Corky had been captured in British Columbia in 1968 and 1969 and shipped to a place called

Marineland of the Pacific, near Los Angeles. In the late 1970s, a young Alexandra Morton began to study their vocalizations and document their behavior. She watched them invent their own complex swimming routines. Once they perfected a routine, they worked on inventing another.

They also had a morning routine. Or perhaps the word is "ritual." In the hour or so between dawn and the time the sun finally burst over the stadium rim, they "diligently squirted water at a particular spot on the tank wall, right at the waterline. They licked that spot with their thick pink tongues." When the first shaft of sun struck the wall, it crept down to touch the waterline "at the *exact* spot the whales had marked. No one, I thought, was going to believe me." She added, "Through the months the spot moved in response to the earth's rotation, but the whales always knew just where the first shaft of light would hit the water." A killer whale Stonehenge? Early killer whale astronomers?

Sun observation was a morning activity, but "Orky was less of a morning whale" and often tried to resume resting. When this happened, Corky sometimes went into action. "Corky ran the tip of her pectoral fin from the tip of his jaw, down his belly, and over his genital slit. If this didn't cause an immediate bulge in the smooth pocket that housed his penis, Corky escalated her tactics. She swam beneath him and pushed him into the air like a forklift picking up a rolled carpet. . . . What Corky wanted was sex, and whale sex is a turbulent affair." With Corky's genital area "flushed with rosy excitement," foreplay took a while. Water splashed out of the tank as the whales entwined and spiraled. Then mating was quick. When Corky was pregnant, Orky would go through all the foreplay but not copulate. That, Morton says, "drove Corky wild." But how did Orky know? Had he been scanning her body with his sonar, his own ultrasound?

In 1978, Corky gave birth. She'd given birth a few years earlier; her first baby had lived a few weeks, then died. The small tank required tight circling, but the baby couldn't make the maneuver, so Corky kept preventing her baby from bumping into the wall. This continually put Corky's face next to her baby; the baby was never in the position of following alongside that would properly present the mother's teats for nursing. After a week of difficult force-feeding by handlers, the baby was looking thin. Management thought they might feed the baby better if it was in a shallower pool. Handlers put the baby in a sling and a crane pulled the sling into the air. Alexandra Morton was there: "As her baby's voice left the water and entered the air, the mother threw her enormous body against the tank walls, again and again, causing the entire stadium to shake. I burst into tears. Corky slammed her body for about an hour."

Morton, an expert on whale sound, recalled that the night Corky's baby was taken, she kept repeating a new and different sound. This sound was "strident, guttural, and urgent." After each breath, Corky returned to the bottom of the tank. There she resumed her lament. The baby's father, Orky, circled, occasionally uttering staccato, gunshot-like echolocation sounds. Morton listened to this for three days, as "Corky's calls grew hoarse." At dawn on the fourth day, Corky grew silent, rose, took a breath, and called, *Pituuuuuuuu*. Her mate returned the same call, and the whales began moving and breathing in unison. When the trainers arrived, Corky ate for the first time since her baby was removed. Grief, mourning, recovering—but not forgetting. After that, Corky began lying by a window with a view of gift-shop merchandise. For hours she'd stay there—next to a stack of toy stuffed orcas. Did the toys remind her of her lost children? Did she think that somewhere in there was her lost baby?

Corky got pregnant again. Then one day, she, whose exquisite sonar allowed her to avoid any obstacle, shattered a three-quarters-of-an-inch-thick glass window of her tank. The window that she burst was the one adjacent to the stacks of stuffed-toy killer whales. Was she trying to take her unborn baby out of the tank from which her babies disappeared? Toward the place where baby orcas rested undisturbed? The most certain thing we can say is: she knew the tank; she didn't shatter the glass by accident. A few weeks later her stillborn baby arrived, seven months premature.

Years after Corky shattered the window, a film crew at SeaWorld (where Corky and Orky had been moved after Marineland closed) let Corky hear a recording of whales from her remaining free-living pod, her family members. "While her Icelandic pen mates ignored the sounds," wrote Alexandra Morton, "Corky's whole body began shuddering terribly. If she wasn't 'crying,' she was doing something terribly similar."

Ken says that after Keiko—the famously captive *Free Willy* killer whale—was moved to a facility in Oregon prior to his eventual release, one of the rehab exercises was to play him killer whale movies. "He'd watch them,"

Ken says, anticipating my obvious question. Ken's son Kelley—an accomplished artist whose work graces some of Ken's walls—used to take drawings of killer whales to the Vancouver Aquarium and hold them up to the glass for a killer whale named Hyak. Hyak would come and just look the drawings over and over. And, Ken adds, "You could go and open up our ID guide of photos of killer whale fins, and he'd be like"—Ken mimics a whale looking from one photo to another—"just like that. For minutes on end, just looking from photo to photo." Ken emphasizes his amazement, saying, "They know that these little black-and-white photos of fins are *depictions* of whales. They have a self-aware concept of *abstractions* of themselves." Ken winds up to a point, and the point is: "These are characteristics of creatures who've reached the supreme-being stage, who have a lot of time and brainpower to spend beyond the requirements of mere survival."

Paul Spong, a psychologist who'd worked at the Vancouver Aquarium, has written, "Eventually my respect verged on awe. I concluded that *Orcinus orca* is an incredibly powerful and capable creature, exquisitely self-controlled and aware of the world around it, a being possessed of a zest for life and a healthy sense of humour and, moreover, a remarkable fondness for and interest in humans."

If that seems a little, well, anthropomorphic—that's the point.

A Vision True and Mighty

It was the story of a mighty vision given to a man too weak to use it; of a holy tree that should have flourished in a people's heart with flowers and singing birds, and now is withered; and of a people's dream. . . . But if the vision was true and mighty, as I know, it is true and mighty yet; for such things are of the spirit, and it is in the darkness of their eyes that men get lost.

—Black Elk

"The captures in the 1960s and '70s—especially of young whales—*really* mattered," Ken is saying emphatically. "It caused a long-term problem." In round numbers, remember, the southern resident community totaled about 120 whales before the captures; after the captures, it was down to around 70. It started rebuilding, managing to hit 99 whales in the 1990s. But when the whales captured and removed as babies would have been the maturing generation of new breeders, the reproductive rate felt their absence. The rebuild hit a pause. Forty years later, the population—around 80 whales—is declining. They're losing one or two a year.

Now there's another, deeper, longer-term problem. Food. Not enough. Canada's northern residents, numbering about 260, were increasing during the last decade. Recently their growth has slowed, perhaps stopped.

"No reproduction—almost none—is what's the bummer," Ken laments. "In the beginning of the study, I took special interest in the new whales that were born. I wanted to see what they experienced as they grew up. But then they started dying very young."

"You can see one bizarre thing here," Ken explains as he pulls up the identification catalog to all whales of the southern resident population. "The whole southern resident population now has just two dozen females of reproductive age."

Still, if each gave birth even once every five years, they'd be having five newborns per year. So they should—

"Yes—and last year we had just *one*. And this year, too, we've had only *one*, born to J-28. It washed up, *dead*." Poor physical condition.

First we took their children, then we destroyed their food supply. Long-term, whales' fortunes follow their foods' fortunes. The Northwest's mammal-eating "transients" have *more* food now than they did forty years ago—and they've been showing up increasingly often. That's because of the decades-long recovery of seals, sea lions, and whales, thanks to legal safeguards including the U.S. Marine Mammal Protection Act of 1972, the international whaling ban enacted in 1986, and the United Nations' high-seas driftnet ban of 1991. By the 1960s, harbor seals in British Columbia were down to 10 percent of normal and many Steller's sea lion colonies were gone, largely because fishermen shot everything that seemed like "competition." That's improved too.

But for the Northwest's fish-eating whales, life's been increasingly difficult. There's been no salmon protection act. So after decades of abuse, salmon struggle along at a fraction of their former abundance here. Consequently, these salmon-catching "resident" whales have been struggling, too. They've long lived below the waterline. Now they live below the poverty line.

Alarmingly, you can see by scrolling through the ID guide that various resident families have *no* living females of reproductive age. For instance, in the family that Ken is displaying, he's pointing out that it's all males except for its matriarch, and she's past menopause. He looks at me while it sinks in: this whole family is doomed.

In fact, there's so much trouble in so many familes now that the only viable southern resident pod left is J pod. Their local intimacy with these interior waters probably helps the J-pod whales. Ls and Ks more widely range the outer coast from the central coast of California up through British Columbia. Ken flips to L pod's roster of births and deaths. "I mean," he says almost plaintively, "look at all these tombstones." The icons show whales who've died. Many died young. Some, *very* young.

Over 40 percent of babies are dying before they're a year old. But all ages and both sexes are perishing at relatively high rates. Looking at the makeup of each family in L pod and K pod is like slowly realizing you're checkmated in chess. No way out. Present trends will erase these pods in a few decades.

King (chinook) salmon declines appear to be pretty tightly linked with whales dying off. That's not surprising; the residents' diet is 65 percent chinook salmon.

Formerly, southern residents made appearances here in every month of the year. Summer and fall was always their time of strength, when they'd frequently come together in superpod aggregations, and they'd keep those festivities going much longer than they do anymore.

"There were really incredible numbers of fish around," Ken vividly recalls. "You'd have maybe a million and a half sockeye and pink salmon, and several hundred thousand kings swimming by. A lot of kings weighed twenty pounds or more, and the whales would only need about ten fish a day. They'd all hang out together and, I mean, *party down!* They'd push a salmon around with their nose or maybe drape one over their back. All that playful, social stuff would happen right in front of my window."

While I look out into the open space of the strait, Ken is seeing back in time, and a little bit of him seems to vanish into memory. His voice changed, he adds wistfully, "This was a way, *way* more productive system. During May to October, we had enough fish in these straits to support a hundred killer whales for the whole damn summer. And enough for human fishing. Then we had the massive overfishing, and river destruction from all the dams and clear-cut logging, and the *major* decline in the region's great iconic fish. And the whales started a slow decline, too."

The party atmosphere has wound down. Nowadays, after briefer, more subdued get-togethers, the pods soon split up again. J pod might check what's over at the Fraser River, and L pod will go back out the mouth of the strait; K pod will head around another island.

In winter, when the fish are usually more spread out to begin with, food finding requires more of the whales' time. The whales become, Ken says, "more businesslike. More serious. Not much play." Pods remain separate from one another; then each *pod* comes apart as families go their separate ways. Individual pod members might spread over an area, say, twelve miles long and three miles wide, their voices filling that volume. And they roam prodigiously. Searching for existence.

Visualize how spread out: all the southern residents—all three pods combined—total at this moment eighty-one whales. Picture eighty-one individuals ranging from around the middle of Canada's Vancouver Island down to California's Monterey Bay. Eighty-one. Imagine a little community of eighty-one people, and imagine that those eighty-one are the only people between Boston and the Florida border—or between Chicago and Houston, or between Montana's southern border and the border patrol at Juárez, Mexico, or between Milan and Madrid—and you get an idea of what "endangered" means.

From forever ago until just yesterday in this region, two million king salmon were just a small kickback the whales could easily rake off between partying, a little silver they could pocket without anyone noticing, the world's payment in exchange for the honor of their presence. Or, more scientifically, the ease of finding a few million king salmon is the reason a fifteen-thousand-pound fish-eating dolphin could both evolve and so thoroughly specialize as to largely ignore most other salmon species, most other fish, and every single seal they came across. Put it this way: The population is only eighty-one whales. Even if a whale ate thirty salmon a day (triple what they probably need), the Columbia River system alone—which saw five to ten million returning adult salmon per year before dammers and loggers and fishermen broke it—could have supported five hundred killer whales. That's not to mention central California's Sacramento–San Joaquin system, British Columbia's Fraser, and the millions of fish that annually issued from and returned to the hundreds of salmon-raising rivers in between. There might have been thousands of killer whales along the coast.

Not helping: toxic chemicals. Being at the top of the food chain doesn't just mean getting all the ocean's drifting nutrients collected in the packets of living flesh that come swimming up to you in a miracle called, in English, "salmon." Nowadays, toxic chemicals also concentrate as they move up in the food pyramid from plankton to small fish to big fish to whale—toxic chemicals that did not exist in the world in the first half of the 1900s when the oldest living whales here were born. The southern resident fish-eating killer whales bear five times the toxic load of harbor seals living nearby in their range. Mammal-eating transients—who further concentrate what the seals they eat have already concentrated—might have as much as fifteen times the seals' toxic load. When mammals metabolize fat to make milk, toxins take the ride. Babies are born with a toxic heirloom, then their moms' milk continues endowing them with a further toxic burden from day one. This is as as true for seal-eating killer whales as for seal-eating Arctic peoples. Banned chemicals like DDT and PCBs— which in the 1970s caused birth defects in Puget Sound seals—are declining. But in ascendance are flame retardants and other new, gender-bending, estrogen-mimicking chemicals. These chemicals weaken immune systems and can disrupt reproductive systems.

After forty years of work, Ken carries this shadowing worry: that the whales he's devoted his life to getting close to and protecting might be doomed. Ken is a cheerful man. He loves the whales. Whenever he sees them, he gets an obvious kick out of where they are, their antics, the joy of them. But behind the crinkle around his eyes, there's a chronic twinge of longing. Here in his heart's abode, from his eagle's perch, surrounded by mountains and moving waters and this wondrous strait full of magic— right exactly where he wants to be—Ken can never go home again.

"The whales often live forty to fifty years," Ken's saying, "but if there's almost no reproduction—" He thinks for a moment, as if trying to remember something. He tells me for the second time that he wants to be positive but that the one thing that would most help—letting the salmon recover—doesn't look likely. Fishermen are too committed to squeezing what they can out of the fish; agency people are too locked into policy process and political relationships; there's stream-killing logging; too many dams; toxic chemicals; disease-incubating salmon farms. That would *all* be too much. But—

—We're not done.

On the monitor, Ken displays photos of three-year-old female L-112, a.k.a. Victoria—a "sweet little whale," says Ken. "A favorite of whale watchers here, very playful. Jumping all the time. Very outgoing and vivacious. A real charismatic whale. Just a sweetie."

Found dead. Look at these photos. Her young corpse looks battered to death. Hemorrhages all over her head, blood in her eyes and ear canals. These next images show her ear bones actually blown right off their attachments. I'm trying to assimilate the images while Ken is saying, "We had whales on the hydrophones. It was night. Then we heard the navy sonar. And then, an explosion. Based on my navy experience, I'd estimate it was about a hundred miles away from us. You get the whole burst of frequencies right at the explosion, but the longer wavelengths take a different path and arrive at a distant sensor ahead of the shorter ones; so if you're far away, you hear an upsweeping sound. That's what we heard. Then K and L pods basically just ran for cover, heading toward Discovery Bay behind Protection Island off the Olympic Peninsula, so they'd be acoustically isolated from all the noise.

"A warship had transitted from Canadian waters into U.S. waters near Neah Bay, and then crossed back to the Canadian side near Constance Bank off Victoria, where a final explosive device was detonated. The Canadian forces admitted to several explosive detonations. And the U.S. Navy had to be involved."

I look at him.

Ken adds, "Yes, it is hard to understand why live bombs are dropped in the Olympic Coast National Marine Sanctuary. The Canadians said they looked for whales prior to the detonations. Well, how come *we* heard whales at Folger Deep and Neah Bay during the exercise, but the forces' acoustic monitoring didn't detect them? My simple request was that the detonation of live bombs be done off the continental shelf. Nothing changed."

I look back at the photos of L-112 as Ken continues, "So, I think a bomb dropped from a training plane killed this little whale. To blow her ear bones right off their pedestals, it would have to explode within about one kilometer." Ken explains, "When the shock wave hits, rapid compression of air in internal spaces such as the ears creates enough of a vacuum to make the adjacent blood vessels—which are pressurized—burst *inward*. Once burst, that's it; they just continue bleeding. That's the hemorrhage. At less than a few hundred yards, by the way, military sonar *alone* can also create fatal hemorrhaging."

If the hemorrhage isn't immediately lethal and the ears fill with blood,

Ken says, "Well—between the headache and an inability to hear anything, or if you're knocked unconscious underwater, either way you're screwed.

"Here in this photo of her swimming behind her mom, you see that she's in good health, good body condition—" Ken shakes his head. "We were really looking forward to having a little female who'd grow up and add some badly needed reproductive potential."

Another female, L-60, age thirty, also washed up on the beach with bruising on her throat and head indicating a pressure trauma. The shot I see of her corpse also looks like a police photo of someone who's been fatally beaten. So much for being "protected" with an endangered species listing. A submarine base and a destroyer base and an antisubmarine aircraft base are all near here, pumping billions in Department of Defense contracts into Washington State. And the navy is determined to do its thing.

Here's a photo of a beaked whale with a blood-soaked eye. Twenty or thirty years ago, hundreds of hemorrhaged seals washed up not far from here. Porpoises have also died near here after navy exercises.

This week while I'm at Ken's, I read an e-mail: "The U.S. Navy says it will ignore a unanimous recommendation by the California Coastal Commission to reduce the harmful effects of naval sonar on the state's marine mammals. The Navy is planning to dramatically increase its use of dangerous sonar and high-powered explosives off the coast of Southern California during training and testing. It predicts that such operations will kill hundreds of marine mammals—and injure thousands of others—over the next five years. New research shows that . . ." The Natural Resources Defense Council is working to stop this, or to get the plan modified, or something.

The navy runs such operations on both coasts. For years they bombed Vieques Island, off Puerto Rico—where people live—until they finally killed someone and got thrown out.

They do it worldwide. And it's not just militaries. An oil company's high-intensity sonar caused a mass stranding of whales in northwest Madagascar in 2008. Always there is increasing pressure to explore for more oil, train for more bombing.

In 1996, NATO forces practicing off Greece drove a group of beaked whales onto the beach. That was the first documented whale-killing military sonar incident. Beaked whales are particularly deep divers. Normally, they come up, breathe, then do several shallower dives that allow them to avoid the "bends," or decompression sickness, while safely ridding their blood of excess dissolved nitrogen. Running at the surface to flee intolerably loud sonar may cause nitrogen to bubble out of their blood. Whether that's exactly what happened is not clear. Clear: navy sonar kills healthy whales. Killer whales. Beaked whales. Minke whales. Pygmy sperm whales. Dolphins.

"If you put several sonar transducers in phase to create a beam, you can form a tremendous pressure wave that will travel thirty miles at high intensity," Ken tells me. "That's become the standard for antisubmarine detection. Many navies in the world now have it." Ken guesses that we find less than 1 percent of the whales that get killed. He believes that thousands get killed each year.

"If they practice-drop a live bomb, everything within a kilometer that has an air space in its body is going to die. Out at ten kilometers, you'll only get bruising, and maybe a hemorrhage in the brain. When we see sonar practice here, and then we see distress and disturbance in all the whales, and suddenly a dozen porpoises wash in dead, we let the navy know we think they're at fault. But they control the examination and the reports. Then they say, 'Well, it's inconclusive.' Basically, they're not gonna admit responsibility."

Throughout the ocean, our secret war games speak of how thoroughly we feel we cannot trust ourselves with our own kind. In the Bahamas in March 2000, several whales of different species washed up right in front of a house where Ken was staying. British and American ships were there. On TV in Miami, and for the news show *60 Minutes*, Ken said he believed the navy had caused their deaths. "They denied it for about a month. Tied themselves into tighter and tighter knots. We had photos." Finally, they confessed. "My navy buddies seem to see me as an enemy," Ken says, sounding a little disappointed. "That's unfortunate, because I'm a patriot. I served in the military. But I'm the one who blew the whistle on the sonar, so—"

Whales are vocal, but they lack a political voice. They, too, are like tribal people, like peasants, natives, like the poor and most of us: underrepresented, rolled by the big money of strong-armed, weak-minded people who can never grasp that they already have too much, who are politically connected yet so lethally out of touch with themselves and the world.

What would it be like to be joy-stricken? To labor through the days inconsolably shadowed by delight; pierced by overwhelming, paralyzing beauty; immobilized with wonder; felled by curiosity; unable to get past appreciation; unable to function except to ask over and over, giddily, "Why me? Why such luck?" That would be nice.

⊸

Our immediate objective is to find and ID some whales we've been hearing about via the radio chatter. In Ken's boat, our propeller drills us into Haro Strait under a heavy, fast-moving weather system that alternates between the rain of autumn and the sunshine of a lingering summer. Two or three gulls are keeping an eye on the whales from the air.

Soon, only about a mile from shore and directly off Ken's house, we're streaming along with big two-toned whales moving in a two-toned world. The water is slate blue and the hills look slate blue, and the whales are slate black and cloud white.

Members of both L pod and K pod are here. This is good. So Ken is good. He smiles mischievously and says, "If I didn't have to live ashore, I'd live with them. Go with the flow. The fish, the family—" The old joke. He laughs. He's not entirely joking.

As many as fifty whales are moving through a much wider area than I'd first realized. They're pacing along at an even clip, southbound, breathing evenly, surfacing with a slight blow, slipping back down, then easing back up.

But despite their seeming effortlessness, the most striking thing about them is their momentum. Even though they are graceful and easy about it, the sheer bulk of them makes their every movement seem like a surging lunge. It strikes me as nearly impossible that they, real and ancient as they are, commanding as they are, needing so much of what we've taken, remain. I can hardly believe that we have overlapped in time and place. I so avidly hope they last.

Soon we're at one of the whales' favorite local salmon-hunting spots, Pile Point. Tidal currents pile up and then shoot rapidly around the point, creating a consistent gathering place for foraging salmon and for whales foraging *for* salmon. Fishermen know it, too.

Several whales bow their backs and dive steeply. Below, the fish have their attention. A couple of other whales slice rapidly through the surface, quickly switching directions, a maneuver Ken calls "sharking." They're in determined pursuit. The closest whale, right behind us, is L-92. This big one over here with the high, wavy dorsal fin is K-25. He begins a series of high-arcing lunges, with lots of splashing and commotion. He's after one large, isolated fish. He dives away. When he suddenly bursts through the surface, his mass and momentum startle me wide-eyed.

"See them working toward the shore there?" Ken lays out the scene for me. They're corraling salmon toward the shoreline, concentrating them a bit. "Very leisurely. They might have, say, a hundred fish. The whales will slowly work the salmon, trying not to panic them, pushing them into bunches while looking for one that might be lagging, or individuals that stray from the group. Just push them. That's what they do. Every once in a while, a fish will get a little behind or too far from its school. They'll nail it." We make the rounds so Ken can complete today's cataloging.

It's so extraordinary to be doing our task among these whales who are so actively working and feeding. I think about how Ken often says that he'd be with them if he could. Watching him, I realize that in a real sense, and more than anyone, he is. With them he is diving into his deep store of knowledge, his unique lifetime of knowing these whales and their network. Here we have, he tells me, K-22, K-25, K-37, L-83, L-116. . . . He knows *who* they are. He knows *where* they have been. He knows their lives because their lives have been his life. They *are* his life at this very moment. As for being among them in a small boat while they are so energetically hunting, Ken and I and the whales all agree that there is nothing at all for us to fear. So I don't. The only worry I have is about my camera under this heavy-lidded sky, which has just released a light smattering of raindrops. Being amid lunging killer whales—*that's* nothing to worry about.

Ken checks his bazooka lens and keeps skillfully wielding it. Ebullient among his whales, he is again—as he is every time—the young man with the camera, yearning to know them well.

More lunging and massive splashes. Somewhere down below, where their lives occur, a lot is going on. Into a realm where we cannot follow, they so easily slip away. *That* is my fear. Not that they will come for me but that they will vanish.

"Okay, ready now," Ken says to me. "The fish-in-the-mouth photo is what you want."

We continue recording frame after frame. Much of this work is repetitive. Endless identifying, cataloging, keeping tabs and keeping track. The work, though, is beautiful, and urgent, an almost holy quest for deeper intimacy. Not just with the whales. With the world. Who has been here with us in our time? This question stokes a continual remembering, a never-forgetting. *Who is here, now?* For forty years, Ken has asked that question like a sacred meditation. And answers *have* come, and even wisdom. But not perfect enlightenment. We know only surfaces. Ken can photograph their backs and tally their life spans and spend his days devoted to theirs. But *they* remain in control, the true fullness of their lives as effortlessly mysterious as a withheld breath. We *need* the deeper intimacy. We *need* to seize our one brief lifetime opportunity to know these wondrous neighbors.

The sky begins flecking us with raindrops that crowd to a steady drizzle, sizzling the surrounding water. Reluctantly Ken says, "That's a wrap. I've ruined enough cameras. Tomorrow's another day."

But, cameras stowed, we linger. In the rain, we watch. For a while, everywhere in the near and medium distance, black fins continue urgently scribbling their stories on the slate of the sea. I read them as intently as I can, knowing that the sea will soon erase what they have written, and that we don't have a backup on file.

Final Scratch

Anyone who studies a wild animal faces the challenge of, in effect, making a case for its life on earth. I pray that mine is strong enough.

—Alexandra Morton

When my experiences with dogs and other animals—and people—were fewer, I used to think it silly for people to speak of dogs as "family" or other animals as "friends." Now I feel it's silly not to. I'd overestimated the loyalty and staying power of humans and underestimated the intelligence and sensitivity of other animals. I think I understand both better. Their gifts overlap, though they are different gifts.

Just as all humans are the same and each human differs, all species are the same and each species differs, and within that, each creature, too, is an individual. It is a matter of mystery and delight compounded that so many species can bridge that boundary between us, so that the hawk looks for the falconer, the dog seeks its human companion, the elephant stands vigil for the lost woman, and the killer whale playfully shoves a sailboat but gives a kayak the gentlest nudge.

The different species are like people who knew each other in high school but have since gone on to different lives and livelihoods. Lots in common. Common roots. A bond, perhaps neglected. We are all so similar under the skin. Four limbs, the same bones, the same organs, the same origins, and lots of shared history. And between first breath and final gasp, we endeavor toward a common quest: to live, to raise our young, to find space enough for our lives, to survive the confronting dangers, to do what it takes, to the best of our abilities, to live out the mystery and opportunity of finding ourselves somehow in existence.

Almost all people who study the behavior of other animals justify their interest by saying that it helps us understand ourselves. It does. But much more important, it helps us understand other animals. We hear status reports about "nature" in statistics like: 60 percent of the habitat gone, 15 percent of a population remaining, 3,000 endangered individuals left. In that telling, the disappearance of the world clocks in as a mere series of numerals.

Anyone can read about how *much* we are losing. All the animals that human parents paint on nursery room walls, all the creatures depicted in paintings of Noah's ark, are actually in mortal trouble now. Their flood is us. What I've tried to show is how other animals experience the lives they so energetically and so determinedly cling to. I wanted to know *who* these creatures are. Now we may feel, beneath our ribs, why they must live.

Understanding other animals is not a boutique endeavor. Failure will speed their end and the bankrupting of our world. And if we treated animals as they deserve, human inhumanity to humans would stand out all the more appallingly. We might then turn our attention to the next step beyond human civilization: *humane* civilization. Justice for all.

Some of my best friends are human. The trouble is that for every ballerina there are thousands of soldiers. Creative, compassionate—yes. Destructive, cruel—also yes. It clues us: we're not doing our best. Our species best understands the world yet has the worst relationship with it.

It remains to be seen whether human intelligence will continue to succeed or become a catastrophe. The most beautiful thing about our minds might be the occasional triumphal moment when we see ourselves *not* in a mirror but from a distance. We see the whole universe through a human lens. The harder step is to get outside ourselves, look back at where and how we live.

There is no better prayer to morning than to feel glad to know: the greatest story is that all life is one.

NOTES

PART ONE: TRUMPETS OF ELEPHANTS

THE BIG QUESTION

10 *area roughly twenty times larger:* Moss et al., *Amboseli Elephants*, p. 89.
11 *elephants and joy:* Moss, *Elephant Memories*, p. 125.
14 *elephants can pick up an egg:* Moss et al., *Amboseli Elephants*, p. 174.
14 *"It has double hoses":* Douglas-Hamilton and Douglas-Hamilton, *Among the Elephants.*
14 *"what a person would rely on":* Nicol, C. 2013. "Do Elephants Have Souls?" *New Atlantis*, no. 38: 10–70.
14 *"Imagine having a nose":* Yoshihito Niimura quoted in R. Feltman. 2014. "New Study Finds That Elephants Evolved the Most Discerning Nose of Any Mammal." *Washington Post*, July 22.

THE SAME BASIC BRAIN

18 *"understanding third-party relationships":* Oliveira et al. 1998, as cited in Moss et al., *Amboseli Elephants*, p. 179.
18 *so do wolves hyenas, dolphins:* Paz-y-Miño, G. C., et al. 2004. "Pinyon Jays Use Transitive Inference to Predict Social Dominance." *Nature*, no. 430: 778–81. See also Engh, A. L. et al. 2000. "Mechanisms of Maternal Rank 'Inheritance' in the Spotted Hyaena, *Crocuta crocuta*." *Animal Behaviour* 60(3): 323–32. See also Palagi, E., and Cordoni, G. 2009. "Postconflict Third-Party Affiliation in *Canis lupus*: Do Wolves Share Similarities with the Great Apes?" *Animal Behaviour* 78(4): 979–86.
18 *A parrot can act jealous:* Burger, *Parrot Who Owns Me.*
18 *when vervet monkeys hear:* Bearzi and Stanford, *Beautiful Minds*, p. 188.
18 *when dolphin mothers want* and *dawdling youngsters:* Herzing, *Dolphin Diaries*, pp. 38, 101, 160.
21 the thing that feels like something: Koch, C. 2014. "Ubiquitous Minds." *Scientific American Mind* 25(1): 26–29.

21   *"One's mind neither controls"*: Ferris, Tim. 1995. "The Mind's Sky." In *The New Science Journalists*, edited by Ted Anton and Rick McCourt, pp. 32–33, New York: Ballantine.

22   *"Our mind"*: Kandel, E. R. 2013. "The New Science of Mind." *New York Times Sunday Review*, September 8, p. 12.

22   *"show superb expertise"*: Sacks, O. 2014. "The Mental Life of Plants and Worms, Among Others." *New York Review of Books* 61(7).

22   *Honeybees will interrupt*: Nieh, J. C. 2010. "A Negative Feedback Signal That Is Triggered by Peril Curbs Honeybee Recruitment." *Current Biology* 20(4): 310–15.

22   *pessimistic bees*: Bateson, M., et al. 2011. "Agitated Honeybees Exhibit Pessimistic Cognitive Biases." *Current Biology* 21(12): 1070–73.

22   *bees' thrill-seeking hormone*: Zhengzheng, L., et al. 2012. "Molecular Determinants of Scouting Behavior in Honey Bees." *Science* 335(6073): 1225–28.

22   *wasps recognize faces*: Sheehan, M. J., and M. J. Tibbetts. 2011. "Specialized Face Learning Is Associated with Individual Recognition in Paper Wasps." *Science* 334(6060): 1272–75.

22   *Roger lost about 95 percent*: Philippi, C. L., et al. 2012. "Preserved Self-Awareness Following Extensive Bilateral Brain Damage to the Insula, Anterior Cingulate, and Medial Prefrontal Cortices." *PLoS ONE* 7(8): 1.

23   *"Whatever consciousness is"*: Koch, *Consciousness*, p. 151.

23   *plants and quotes about them*: Pollan, M. 2013. "The Intelligent Plant." *New Yorker*, December 23–30, pp. 92–105. (He notes that the experiment involving the recording of the sound of a munching caterpillar was done by chemical ecologist Heidi Appel at the University of Missouri.)

DISTINCTLY HUMAN?

26   *elephant communication expert*: Poole, *Coming of Age*.

27   *"isn't a project I'd recommend"*: Yoerg, S. I. 1992. "Mentalist Imputations," review of *Animal Minds*, by Donald Griffin. *Science* 258: 830–31.

28   *"It was a bit shocking"*: Goodall quoted in Quammen, D. 2014. "Gombe Family Album." *National Geographic*, August, p. 54.

29   *"The dilemma remains"*: Nicol. 2013. "Do Elephants Have Souls?," 10–70.

DEEP AND ANCIENT CIRCUITS

31   *"deep and very ancient circuits"*: Panksepp, J. 2005. "Affective Consciousness: Core Emotional Feelings in Animals and Humans." *Consciousness and Cognition* 14(1): 30–80.

31   *rats craving addictive drugs*: Ibid.

31   *dogs with compulsive behaviors*: Tufts University. 2013. "Dogs, Humans Affected by OCD Have Similar Brain Abnormalities." *Tufts Now*, June 4. See also Ogata, N., et al. 2013. "Brain Structural Abnormalities in Doberman Pinschers with Canine Compulsive Disorder." *Progress in Neuro-Psychopharmacology and Biological Psychiatry*, no. 45: 1–6.

31   *crayfish anxiety*: Fossat, P., et al. 2014. "Anxiety-Like Behavior in Crayfish Is Controlled by Serotonin." *Science* 344: 1293–97. See also Vignieri, S. N. 2014. "The Crayfish That Was Afraid of the Light." *Science* 344(6189): 1238.

32   *at least seven hundred million years*: Beets, I., et al. 2012. "Vasopressin/Oxytocin-Related Signaling Regulates Gustatory Associative Learning in C. elegans." *Science* 338: 543–45.

32   "*deserve to be called intelligent*": Darwin, C. 1881. *Formation of Vegetable Mould, Through the Action of Worms.* London: John Murray.

32   *oxytocin and vasopressin source* and "*Just as today's major roads*": Emmons, S. W. 2012. "The Mood of a Worm." *Science* 338: 475–76. See also Garrison, J., et al. 2012. "Oxytocin/Vasopressin-Related Peptides Have an Ancient Role in Reproductive Behavior." *Science* 338: 540–43.

32   *Oxytocin drives bonding*: Klatt, J. D., and J. L. Goodson. 2013. "Oxytocin-Like Receptors Mediate Pair Bonding in a Socially Monogamous Songbird." *Proceedings of the Royal Society of London, Series B* 280(1750).

WE ARE FAMILY

36   "*It's more like wisdom*": Jacobsen, R. 2013. "The Homeless Herd." *Harper's,* August, pp. 64–69.

36   *The family is the foundation*: Moss et al., *Amboseli Elephants*, p. 190.

36   *The matriarch makes decisions*: Ibid., p. 105.

36   *While a matriarch is alive*: Douglas-Hamilton and Douglas-Hamilton, *Among the Elephants*, p. 221.

36   *Relationships radiate into a wide*: Moss, *Elephant Memories*, p. 125.

37   *elephant weight*: Moss et al., *Amboseli Elephants*, p. 192.

38   *Each elephant in Amboseli probably knows*: Ibid., p. 211.

38   *When researchers played the recorded call*: Ibid., p. 165.

38   "*Intelligent, social, emotional, personable*": Ibid., p. 318.

38   "*Even in times of distress*": Douglas-Hamilton and Douglas-Hamilton, *Among the Elephants*, p. 265.

38   *Even during hard times*: Moss et al., *Amboseli Elephants*, pp. 229, 245.

39   *Slit Ear was so aggressive*: Moss, *Elephant Memories*, p. 132.

39   *old females' extensive knowledge of calls*: Moss et al., *Amboseli Elephants*, p. 179.

39   *Desert-living elephants visit water sources*: Ibid., p. 175.

39   *desert elephants arrive at water*: Blake et al. 2003, cited in Moss et al., *Amboseli Elephants*, p. 175.

40   *experienced matriarchs, larger families*: Ibid., p. 191.

40   *oldest Amboseli female to have given birth*: Moss et al., *Amboseli Elephants*, p. 201.

40   *grandmothering wise-elders*: Moss, *Elephant Memories*, p. 171.

40   *Eventually their teeth wear down*: Ibid., p. 245.

40   *devastating psychological consequences* and *extraordinarily close care bonds*: Ibid., p. 322.

40   *Older orphans sometimes wander*: Moss et al., *Amboseli Elephants*, p. 320.

MOTHERHOOD HAPPENS

42   *five gallons of milk daily*: Moss et al., *Amboseli Elephants*, p. 53.

42   *Tallulah and Deborah*: Moss, *Elephant Memories*, pp. 152–55.

43   *elephant brains*: Ibid., p. 265.

44   *researchers get the impression*: Ibid., pp. 161–64.

44   *they suck their trunk for comfort*: Ibid., pp. 161–62.

44   *trunk mastering* and *babies reach into the mouths*: Ibid., pp. 164–65.

45   *quadrupled testosterone*: Moss and Colbeck, *Echo of the Elephants*, p. 166.

48   *two evenly matched males in musth*: Ibid., p. 184.

DO ELEPHANTS LOVE THEIR BABIES?

49   *Lucy Bates collected some urine:* Moss et al., *Amboseli Elephants,* p. 176.

50   *loose and "floppy" way:* Ibid., p. 122.

53   *Tom and Tao:* Moss, *Elephant Memories,* p. 163.

53   *when wondering whether a mother ape:* Moussaieff and McCarthy, *When Elephants Weep,* p. 73.

55   *chimpanzees gazing at sunset:* Teleki, G. 1994. "They Are Us." In *The Great Ape Project,* edited by Paola Cavalieri and Peter Singer, pp. 296–302. New York: St. Martin's. See also Kortlandt, A. 1962. "Chimpanzees in the Wild." *Scientific American* 206(5): 128–38. Both as described in Moussaieff and McCarthy, *When Elephants Weep,* pp. 192–93.

56   *bowerbirds:* Diamond, *Third Chimpanzee,* p. 155.

56   *"not singing just for aesthetic":* Ibid., p. 153.

ELEPHANT EMPATHY

59   *They sometimes stand on either side:* Moss et al., *Amboseli Elephants,* p. 179.

59   *Cherie pursued her:* Douglas-Hamilton, I., S. Bhalla, G. Wittemyer, and F. Vollrath. 2006. "Behavioural Reactions of Elephants Towards a Dying and Deceased Matriarch." *Applied Animal Behaviour Science* 100(1–2): 87–102.

59   *J. H. Williams in Burma:* Walker, *Ivory's Ghosts,* pp. 26–42. Quoting from: Williams, J. H. 2001. *Elephant Bill.* Long Riders' Guild Press, p. 227.

59   *baby who could not straighten:* Moss and Colbeck, *Echo of the Elephants,* pp. 64–74.

60   *Suddenly he panicked:* Ibid., p. 37.

61   *"Elephants show empathy":* Moss et al., *Amboseli Elephants,* p. 182.

61   *half-blind Turkana woman:* Douglas-Hamilton and Douglas-Hamilton, *Among the Elephants,* p. 240.

62   *one-year-old children, dogs, and cats:* de Waal, F. 2012. "The Antiquity of Empathy." *Science* 336(6083): 874–76.

63   *play requires empathy:* Panksepp, J., and J. B. Panksepp. 2013. "Toward a Cross-Species Understanding of Empathy." *Trends in Neurosciences* 36(8): 489–96.

64   *after a moat was drained:* de Waal. 2012. "Antiquity of Empathy," 874–76.

64   *Rats will free cagemates:* Inbal, B. B., et al. 2011. "Empathy and Pro-Social Behavior in Rats." *Science* 334(6061): 1427–30. See also Panksepp, J. 2011. "Empathy and the Laws of Affect." *Science* 334(6061): 1358–59.

64   *bonobo captured a starling:* de Waal, *Primates and Philosophers,* p. 30.

GOOD GRIEF

66   *Cynthia Moss was there as the family:* Moss, *Elephant Memories,* p. 84.

67   *The wounds went septic:* Ibid., p. 264.

67   *"There were many bright-green":* Ibid., p. 265.

67   *an elephant's chance of being killed by a human:* Ibid., p. 267.

67   *recording of an elephant who had died:* Vicki Fishlock, resident scientist at the Amboseli Elephant Research Project (AERP), personal communication, July 2013.

67   *"probably the strangest thing about them":* Moss, *Elephant Memories,* p. 270.

67   *"It is their silence that is most unsettling"*: Poole, *Coming of Age.*

68   *the parts that would have been most familiar*: Moss, *Elephant Memories,* p. 270. See also Moss and Colbeck, *Echo of the Elephants,* p. 61.

68   *"a strange habit of removing"*: Sheldrick quoted in Douglas-Hamilton and Douglas-Hamilton, *Among the Elephants,* p. 237.

68   *Iain Douglas-Hamilton once moved*: Ibid., p. 238.

68   *elephants returned a shoulder blade*: Ibid., p. 240.

69   *plastered his large head wound*: Ibid., pp. 240–41.

69   *Eleanor's death*: Douglas-Hamilton, I., et al. 2006. "Behavioural Reactions of Elephants." *Applied Animal Behaviour Science*: 87–102.

69   *prematurely born, dying baby*: Moss and Colbeck, *Echo of the Elephants,* p. 124.

69   *killer whale pushing a dead newborn*: Calloway-Whiting, C. 2010. "Mother Orca and Her Dead Calf: A Mother's Grief?" *Seattlepi.com*, September 11.

70   *Atlantic spotted dolphin named Luna*: Herzing, *Dolphin Diaries,* p. 230.

70   *dolphin named Spock*: Reiss, *Dolphin in the Mirror,* p. 202.

70   *"A grieving dolphin mother"*: Bearzi, M. 2012. *Dolphin Confidential: Confessions of a Field Biologist.* Chicago: University of Chicago Press, p. 172.

70   *definition of grief*: King, B. J. 2013. "When Animals Mourn." *Scientific American* 309(1). See also her book *How Animals Grieve.*

70   *In a zoo in Philadelphia*: Brown, A. E. 1879. "Grief in the Chimpanzee." *American Naturalist*, March, 173–75.

71   *More than a century later*: de Waal, F. 2013. "Bonobo Bliss: Evidence That Doing Good Feels Good." *Natural History,* August 8. Excerpted from: de Waal, *Bonobo and Atheist.*

71   *Two male chimpanzees in Uganda*: Zimmer, C. 2012. "Friends with Benefits." *Time.* February 20.

71   *Patricia Wright studies*: Dr. Patricia Wright, American primatologist, anthropologist, and conservationist, personal conversation, September 2014. See also Radin, D. 2014. "The Amazing Emotional Intelligence of Our Primate Cousins." *Ecologist,* June 24.

73   *The two brothers spent days*: Simmonds, M. P. 2006. "Into the Brains of Whales." *Applied Animal Behaviour Science* 100(1–2): 103–16.

74   *two years after Teresia's death*: Moss, *Elephant Memories,* p. 323.

I DON'T KNOW HOW YOU SAY GOOD-BYE

75   *"If someone in the family"*: Moss et al., *Amboseli Elephants,* pp. 116, 155.

76   *"members of a supportive unit"*: Ibid., p. 153.

76   *During high social excitement*: Ibid., p. 115.

76   *Elephants use well over one hundred*: Ibid., p. 109. See also ElephantVoices.org.

76   *larynx for some calls, trunk for others*: Ibid., p. 126.

76   *they may reconcile*: Ibid., p. 113.

78   *Elephant song spans ten octaves*: Ibid., p. 130.

78   *communication through the ground*: Ibid., p. 127. See especially: O'Connell, C. 2008. *The Elephant's Secret Sense: The Hidden Life of the Wild Herds of Africa.* Chicago: University of Chicago Press.

78   *Rumbles during tense encounters*: Moss et al., *Amboseli Elephants,* p. 127.

79   *"The reason animals"*: Descartes, R. 1646 letter to the Marquess of Newcastle. Retrieved from http://pubpages.unh.edu/~jel/Descartes.html.

79   *"What a pitiful"*: Voltaire. 1924. *The Philosophical Dictionary.* Translated by H. I.

Woolf. New York: Knopf. Retrieved from http://history.hanover.edu/texts /voltaire/volanima.html.

80   *"Animals, whom we have made our slaves"*: Darwin, C. 1837–38. *Notebook B: Transmutation of Species.* Darwin-online.org.uk/.

80   *"I am in terror!"*: Based on Moussaieff and McCarthy, *When Elephants Weep,* p. 229.

82   *human brain gets active several seconds*: Roose, Steven P. 2012. "Neuroscience vs. Philosophy: Taking Aim at Free Will." *Journal of the American Psychoanalytic Association* 60: 393–94.

83   *Dr. Poole discusses elephant rumble*: Moss et al., *Amboseli Elephants,* pp. 134, 140, 146, 153, 158.

I SAY HELLO

86   *their word for "Bees!"*: King, L. E., I. Douglas-Hamilton, and F. Vollrath. 2007. "African Elephants Run from the Sound of Disturbed Bees." *Current Biology* 17(19): R832–33. See also Bouché, P., et al. 2011. "Will Elephants Soon Disappear from West African Savannahs?" *PLoS ONE* 6(6): e20619.

86   *Aauurrrr, Some rumbles by mothers,* and *Meaning often depends*: Moss et al., *Amboseli Elephants,* pp. 147, 148, 149, and 158.

87   *Vervet monkey calls with distinct meanings*: Diamond, *Third Chimpanzee.*

87   *Titi, putty-nosed, and colobus monkeys*: Zuberbühler, K. 2002. "A Syntactic Rule in Forest Monkey Communication." *Animal Behaviour* 63(2): 293–99.

88   *Campbell's monkeys have three*: Altenmüller, E., et al. *Evolution of Emotional Intelligence,* p. 35.

88   *Gibbons*: Clarke, E., U. H. Reichard, and K. Zuberbühler. 2006. "The Syntax and Meaning of Wild Gibbon Songs." *PLoS ONE* 1(1): e73.

88   *Chimpanzees use nearly ninety*: Crockford, C., and C. Boesch. 2005. "Call Combinations in Wild Chimpanzees." *Behaviour* 142(4): 397–421.

88   *"tend to exaggerate"*: Altenmüller et al., *Evolution of Emotional Intelligence,* p. 35.

88   *"Hello, it's good to be near you again"*: Moss et al., *Amboseli Elephants,* p. 151.

89   *"Syntax is what tells us"*: Reiss, *Dolphin in the Mirror,* p. 196.

90   *"simple form of syntax"*: J. Poole, as cited in Moss et al., *Amboseli Elephants,* p. 153.

91   *sudden, abrupt lift of her head* through *their vocabulary changes*: Moss et al., *Amboseli Elephants,* p. 154.

92   *rumble frequency and loudness* through *they know very well*: Moss, *Elephant Memories,* pp. 314, 315–16.

92   *"Elephants are able to detect"*: Moss et al., *Amboseli Elephants,* p. 326.

92   *"elephant whisperer"*: Martin, D. 2012. "Lawrence Anthony, Baghdad Zoo Savior, Dies at 61." *New York Times,* March 11, A19. See also Zimmerman, J. 2012. "Elephants Hold Vigil for Human Friend." *Grist.org.,* May 14.

HOLDING BACK, LETTING GO

95   *"The sensation I was feeling"*: Watson, L. 2003. *Elephantoms: Tracking the Elephant.* New York: Norton, p. 207.

97   *Tito broke a leg*: Moss, *Elephant Memories,* p. 329.

97   *attempting to feed a dead elephant*: Moss et al., *Amboseli Elephants,* p. 123.

98   *left deep skid marks:* Moss, *Elephant Memories,* p. 186.

98   *Nim:* Terrace, H. S. 1979. *Nim: A Chimpanzee Who Learned Sign Language.* New York: Knopf, pp. 150–52.

98   *Tuskless and Tania and their family:* Moss, *Elephant Memories,* p. 188.

99   *"It hurts":* Ibid., pp. 335–36.

TROUBLED MINDS

100   *In camp this morning:* Wittemyer, G., et al. 2014. "Illegal Killing for Ivory Drives Global Decline in African Elephants." *Current Biology* 111: 13117–21. See also Scriber, B. 2014. "100,000 Elephants Killed by Poachers in Just Three Years, Landmark Analysis Finds." *National Geographic News,* August 14.

101   *survivors have elevated stress hormones:* Gobush, K., et al. 2008. "Long-Term Impacts of Poaching on Relatedness, Stress Physiology, and Reproductive Output of Adult Female African Elephants." *Conservation Biology* 22: 1590–99.

101   *"genocide going on":* Joyce, C. 2013. "Elephant Poaching Pushes Species to Brink of Extinction." *Morning Edition,* NPR, March 6.

102   *The Maasai once occupied:* Moss et al., *Amboseli Elephants,* pp. 32–33.

104   *They will panic and run:* Moss, *Elephant Memories,* p. 222.

105   *When elephants heard recorded voices:* Moss et al., *Amboseli Elephants,* p. 314.

105   *elephant brains larger than expected:* Ibid., p. 52.

EBONY AND IVORY

109   *In the 1960s:* Douglas-Hamilton and Douglas-Hamilton, *Among the Elephants,* p. 226.

109   *Tiny three-foot-high elephants:* Moss et al., *Amboseli Elephants,* p. 53.

109   *komodo dragon evolved:* Diamond, J. 1987. "Did Komodo Dragons Evolve to Eat Pygmy Elephants?" *Nature* 326: 832.

109   *Czechoslovakian mammoth hunters:* Douglas-Hamilton and Douglas-Hamilton, *Among the Elephants,* p. 246.

110   *The last mammoths died out:* Vartanyan, S. L. 1995. "Radiocarbon Dating Evidence for Mammoths on Wrangel Island, Arctic Ocean, until 2000 BC." *Radiocarbon* 37(1): 1–6.

110   *Syria's final elephants* and *China's near extirpation:* Walker, *Ivory's Ghosts,* pp. 26–42.

110   *twenty-six million elephants:* "The History of the Ivory Trade: History Has Been Tragic for Africa's Elephants." Online video. *National Geographic.*

110   *Pliny:* Douglas-Hamilton and Douglas-Hamilton, *Among the Elephants,* p. 248.

110   *hundreds of miles inland* and *killed millions:* Walker, *Ivory's Ghosts,* pp. 5, 64, 84, 91, 96, 134.

111   *Reaching a village of any size:* Conniff, R. 1987. "When the Music in Our Parlors Brought Death to Darkest Africa." *Audubon,* July, p. 86.

111   *the ivory was more valuable* and *In a photo:* Walker, *Ivory's Ghosts,* p. 120.

111   *"It is custom to buy":* Conniff, 1987. "When the Music in Our Parlors," p. 89.

111   *tusks often weighed over eighty pounds:* Walker, *Ivory's Ghosts,* p. 134.

111   *tusks' average weight now:* Wasser, S. K., et al. 2007. "Using DNA to Track the Origin of the Largest Ivory Seizure Since the 1989 Trade Ban." *PNAS* 104(10): 4228–33.

111   *over 440 pounds:* Moss et al., *Amboseli Elephants,* p. 27.

112   "We spear the child": Swann, A. J. 2012. *Fighting the Slave Hunters in Central Africa.* 3rd ed. New York: Routledge, pp. 49–50.

112   *"discharged in the same manner":* Shepard quoted in Conniff, "When the Music in Our Parlors," p. 81.

112   *hunting had already exterminated elephants:* Spinage, 1973, as cited in Moss et al., *Amboseli Elephants,* p. 320.

118   *From an estimated ten million elephants:* Bradshaw, G. A., et al. 2005. "Elephant Breakdown." *Nature* 433: 807.

118   *elephant number losses by nation:* Moss, *Elephant Memories,* p. 294. See also Nowak, K., et al. 2013. "Elephants Are Not Diamonds." *Ecologist,* February 8.

121   *30,000 to 40,000:* Dell'Amore, C. 2014. "Beloved African Elephant Killed for Ivory." *National Geographic News.*

122   *in Kenya, humans quadrupled:* Moss et al., *Amboseli Elephants,* p. 329.

122   *"Dear Elephant, Sir":* Gary, R. 1967. "Dear Elephant, Sir." *Life,* December 22, p. 126.

PART TWO: HOWLS OF WOLVES

INTO THE PLEISTOCENE

140   *Jane Goodall's first scientific paper:* Bekoff, M., and C. Allen. 1997. "Cognitive Ethology: Slayers, Skeptics and Proponents." In *Anthropomorphism, Anecdotes and Animals: The Emperor's New Clothes?,* edited by R. W. Mitchess, N. Thompson, and L. Miles, 313–34. New York: State University Press of New York State.

A PERFECT WOLF

143   *Even from a distance* and *"remarkably gentle":* Smith and Ferguson, *Decade of the Wolf,* p. 43.

145   *When packs fight:* Ibid., pp. 72, 87.

146   *"handicap principle":* Zahavi, A. 2007. "Sexual Selection, Signal Selection, and the Handicap Principle." In *Reproductive Biology and Phylogeny of Birds,* edited by B.G.M. Jamieson. Enfield, N.H.: Science Publishers.

PACKING AND UNPACKING

151   *wolf pack facts:* Smith and Ferguson, *Decade of the Wolf,* pp. 88–92.

151   *Extended child care:* Ibid., p. 41.

152   *large "acclimation pens":* Ibid., p. 54.

152   *jaws exert twelve hundred pounds:* Ibid., p. 55.

153   *The Druids traveled:* Ibid., p. 66.

153   *"tough, supersized behemoths":* Ibid., p. 68.

154   *bottlenose dolphins' division of labor:* R. C. Connor in Mann et al., *Cetacean Societies,* p. 212. See also Simmonds, M. P. 2006. "Into the Brains of Whales." *Applied Animal Behaviour Science.* 100(1–2): 103–16. (Simmonds reviews and cites other sources.)

154   *Humpback bubble-netting:* Ibid., pp. 211–12.

157   *wolf matriarchs and wolves Seven, Forty, and Cinderella:* Doug Smith, interview with the author, March 2013, and Smith and Ferguson, *Decade of the Wolf,* pp. 78–79.

A SHATTERING OF PROMISES

168   *In 1806, when Lewis and Clark*: Whittlesey, L., and P. Schullery. 2011. "How Many Wolves Were in the Yellowstone Area in the 1870s?" *Yellowstone Science*, no. 19: 23–28.

168   *"Greater Yellowstone Ecosystem"*: Goldman, J. G. 2014. "Reintroducing Wolves Is Only Effective at Large Scales." *Conservation*, June 18.

169   *researchers estimate that 380,000*: Leonard, J. A., et al. 2005. "Legacy Lost: Genetic Variability and Population Size of Extirpated US Grey Wolves." *Molecular Ecology* 14: 9–17.

169   *wiped wolves off 95 percent*: Smith and Ferguson, *Decade of the Wolf*, pp. 7–8.

170   *more than 500 wolf skins*: Whittlesey and Schullery, "How Many Wolves," pp. 23–28.

170   *no license, no limit*: "Wolves in Wyoming: WGFD Notifies That Gray Wolf Take Is Suspended." 2014. *Wyoming Game and Fish Department*. http://wgfd.wyo.gov/wtest/wildlife-1000380.aspx.

171   *"the devil's dog," lower jaws cut off, "a vengeance applied,"* and *"killing for fun"*: Smith and Ferguson, *Decade of the Wolf*, pp. 30–31.

171   *"Gut-shoot every goddamn last one"*: Ketcham, C. 2014. "How to Kill a Wolf." *Vice*, March 13.

171   *"a society to match the scenery"*: Egan, T. 2009. "Stegner's Complaint." *New York Times*, February 18.

171   *"The country was always better"*: Hemingway, E. 1935. *The Green Hills of Africa*. New York: Scribner, p. 73.

172   *Rangers pursued eradication* and *elk populations irrupted*: Doug Smith, interview with the author, March 2013.

173   *Aldo Leopold observed*: Leopold, A. 1949. *A Sand County Almanac*. Oxford: Oxford University Press, pp. 129–32.

174   *wolves liberated the willows*: Ripple, W. J., and R. L. Beschta. 2012. "Trophic Cascades in Yellowstone: The First 15 Years After Wolf Reintroduction." *Biological Conservation* 145(1): 205–13.

174   *"In the time it takes to drink a cup of coffee"*: Poole, O. 2002. "Success Brings Death Sentence for US Wolves." *Telegraph*, Dec. 22.

174   *killed more than 550 wolves*: Black, J. 2013. "Protected No Longer, More Than 550 Gray Wolves Killed This Season by Hunters and Trappers." *NBC News*, March 6.

175   *people account for 80 percent*: Doug Smith, interview with the author, March 2013.

175   *The irony is*: Johnson, K. 2014. "Study Faults Efforts at Wolf Management." *New York Times*, December 3.

175   *"If you have the capability to scan"*: Hull, J. 2013. "Out of Bounds: The Death of 832F, Yellowstone's Most Famous Wolf." *Outside Online*, February 13.

175   *"It's a huge blow"* and *Nathan Varley*: Schweber, N. 2012. "Research Animals Lost in Wolf Hunts Near Yellowstone." *New York Times*, November 28.

175   *"approximately 94,000 visitors"*: Duffield, J. W., et al. 2008. "Wolf Recovery in Yellowstone: Park Visitor Attitudes, Expenditures, and Economic Impacts." *Yellowstone Science* 16: 20–25.

IN A TIME OF TRUCE

177   *Native American groups have tried*: Pember, M.A. 2012. "Wisconsin Tribes Struggle to Save Their Brothers the Wolves from Sanctioned Hunt." *Indian Country Today Media Network*, August 14.

178   *"I do not deny"*: Spinoza, B. de. 1677. *Ethics,* Part 4, Prop. 37, Note 1. Online.

178   *William Westmoreland:* Davis, P., director and producer. 1974. *Hearts and Minds.* DVD. BBS Productions and Rainbow Releasing.

178   *"face-to-face"*: Garcia, C. 2010. "'Wolf Man' Doug Smith Studies Yellowstone's Restored Predators." *Christian Science Monitor,* July 20.

178   *don't view people as potential prey:* Smith and Ferguson, *Decade of the Wolf,* p. 105.

179   *People long accustomed to living with Amur tigers:* Vaillant, *Tiger,* p. 110.

179   *"these carefully managed agreements"*: Ibid., p. 141.

179   *"the Amur tiger's capacity"*: Ibid., pp. 137–39.

180   *One particular tiger certainly did:* Ibid., p. 15.

180   *lions and the San:* Thomas, E. M. 1990. "The Old Way." *New Yorker,* October 15, p. 78.

MAGNIFICENT OUTCASTS

186   *Old Blue and Fourteen:* Smith and Ferguson, *Decade of the Wolf,* p. 11.

WHERE THE WOLF BIRDS LEAD US

192   *Ravens don't trust humans:* Heinrich, B. 1999. *Mind of the Raven.* New York: Ecco, p. 356.

192   *Odin:* Ibid., p. 355.

192   *ravens' tool kit of reasoning and insight* and *"primate-like intelligence"*: Emery, N. J., and N. S. Clayton. 2004. "The Mentality of Crows: Convergent Evolution of Intelligence in Corvids and Apes." *Science* 306(5703): 1903–7.

193   *raven rapidly solving a puzzle that stumped poodles and child: Inside the Animal Mind: The Problem Solvers.* Video. BBC. (Scene occurs 20 minutes in.)

193   *crows' intelligence* and *a crow named Betty:* Emery and Clayton, "Mentality of Crows," 1903–7.

193   *crow shaping wire into a hook:* Klein, J. 2008. "The Intelligence of Crows." *TED Talk.* Online.

193   *crow solving an eight-step puzzle:* Packham, C., presenter. 2014. "Are Crows the Ultimate Problem Solvers?" Episode 2 of *Inside the Animal Mind.* BBC Two.

193   *rook experiments with tubes:* Bird C. D., and N. J. Emery. 2009. "Insightful Problem Solving and Creative Tool Modification by Captive Non-Tool-Using Rooks." *PNAS* 106(25): 10370–75.

193   *cockatoos use insight:* Warwicker, M. 2012. *Cockatoos Show Tool-Making Skills.* BBC Nature.

193   *crows remember faces for years:* Nijhuis, M. 2008. "Friend or Foe? Crows Never Forget a Face, It Seems." *New York Times,* August 25.

194   *"crows and now rooks"*: Bird and Emery, "Insightful Problem Solving," 10370–75.

194   *"display similar intelligent behavior"*: Emery and Clayton, "Mentality of Crows," 1903–7.

194   *In 1844, a missionary to Liberia:* Savage, T. S., and J. Wyman. 1844. "Observations on the External Characters and Habits of the *Troglodytes niger.*" *Boston Journal of Natural History* 4(4): 362–86. As cited in Wrangham, R. W. 2006. "Chimpanzees: The Culture-Zone Concept Becomes Untidy." *Current Biology* 16(16): R634–35.

194   *in 1887 another observer:* Carpenter, A. 1887. "Monkeys Opening Oysters." *Nature* 36: 53.

195   *Cracking nuts occupies:* Wrangham, "Culture-Zone Concept," R634–35.

195 *club-and-anvil technique:* Sundaram, A. 2005. "Scientists Study Gorilla Who Uses Tools." *Environmental News Network,* October 19.

195 *Capuchin monkeys transport stones:* Byrne, R. W., and L. A. Bates. 2010. "Primate Social Cognition: Uniquely Primate, Uniquely Social, or Just Unique?" *Neuron* 65: 815–30.

195 *rooks in experiments with food in tubes:* Bird and Emery, "Insightful Problem Solving," 10370–75.

195 *Eurasian jays in experiments with food in tubes:* "Clever Corvids: The Eurasian Jay." 2012. Episode 1 of *Super Smart Animals.* BBC. http://www.bbc.co.uk/programmes/p00nltf1.

196 *Elephants make at least six:* Moss et al., *Amboseli Elephants,* p. 176.

196 *might make a back scratcher:* Poole, *Coming of Age,* p. 36.

196 *crows using automobiles as nutcrackers:* Reiss, *Dolphin in the Mirror,* p. 61.

197 *"It was one of the most amazing things":* Herzing, *Dolphin Diaries,* p. 28.

197 *cockatoo named Figaro* and *blue jays:* Auersperg, A.M.I., et al. 2012. "Spontaneous Innovation in Tool Manufacture and Use in a Goffin's Cockatoo." *Current Biology* 22(21): R903–4. (Online, with excellent video.)

197 *fish tool use:* Brown, C. 2014. "Fish Intelligence, Sentience and Ethics." *Animal Cognition,* June 19.

197 *insect tool use:* Pierce, J. D. 1986. "A Review of Tool Use in Insects." *Florida Entomologist* 69(1): 95–104.

WOLF MUSIC

201 *Triangle:* McIntyre, R. 2013. "The Story of Triangle." Unpublished manuscript. (Rick credits Laurie Lyman with first spotting the wolves that day.)

202 *music, prosody, pigeon experiments:* Altenmüller, et al., *Evolution of Emotional Intelligence,* pp. 116–17.

204 *tamarins and music:* Ibid., pp. 144–48.

205 *"music is one of the best forms":* Ibid., p. 134.

A WILL TO LIVE

217 *The black wolf grabs the elk:* I thank Laurie Lyman for private correspondence and for her contributions to *Yellowstone Reports* describing some of these incidents.

DOMESTIC SERVANTS

223 *elephants can follow pointing:* Smet, A. F., and R. W. Byrne. 2013. "African Elephants Can Use Human Pointing Cues to Find Hidden Food." *Current Biology* 23(20): 2033–37.

223 *wolves can follow pointing:* Udell, M.A.R., et al. 2008. "Wolves Outperform Dogs in Following Human Social Cues." *Animal Behaviour* 76(6): 1767–73.

224 *"In the midst of the struggle":* Gwynne, S. C. 2011. *Empire of the Summer Moon.* New York: Scribner, p. 176.

224 *"Get the dax!":* Hare, B., and M. Tomasello. 2005. "Human-like Social Skills in Dogs?" *Trends in Cognitive Sciences* 9(9): 439–44.

225 *"overlap extensively"* and *"Our best friend in the animal kingdom":* Wang, Guodong, et al. 2013. "The Genomics of Selection in Dogs and the Parallel Evolution Between Dogs and Humans." *Nature Communications* 4, article no. 1860.

225   *"Humans have had to tame":* Zimmer, C. 2013. "From Fearsome Predator to Man's Best Friend." *New York Times,* May 16.

226   *Darwin on drooping ears and correlation:* Darwin, C. 1859. *On the Origin of Species.* London: Mentor, pp. 34–35.

227   *Russian fox experiment:* Hare and Tomasello, "Human-like Social Skills," 439–44.

228   *domestication syndrome in foxes and others:* Hare, B., et al. 2012. "The Self-Domestication Hypothesis: Evolution of Bonobo Psychology Is Due to Selection Against Aggression." *Animal Behaviour* 83(3): 573–85.

TWO ENDS OF THE SAME LEASH

229   *Chimpanzees will not cooperate* and *food-sharing experiments:* de Waal, "Bonobo Bliss."

230   *self-domestication in bonobos:* Wobber, V., R. Wrangham, and B. Hare. 2010. "Bonobos Exhibit Delayed Development of Social Behavior and Cognition Relative to Chimpanzees." *Current Biology* 20(3): 226–30.

230   *"performed at the level of juvenile chimpanzees":* Hare et al., "Self-Domestication Hypothesis," 573–85.

231   *Females prefer belly-to-belly* and *comparing skulls of bonobos and chimps* and *differences in foraging time, area, and group size:* Blount, B. G. 1990. "Issues in Bonobo (*Pan paniscus*) Sexual Behavior." *American Anthropologist* 92(3): 702–14.

231   *Compared to chimpanzees, bonobo brains:* de Waal, F. 2012. "The Antiquity of Empathy." *Science* 336(6083): 874–76.

231   *Bonobo gray matter and brain:* Rilling, J., et al. 2011. "Differences Between Chimpanzees and Bonobos in Neural Systems Supporting Social Cognition." *Social Cognitive and Affective Neuroscience,* April 5.

231   *labia majora:* Dahl, J. F. 1985. "The External Genitalia of the Female Pygmy Chimpanzee." *Anatomical Record* 211(1): 24–28.

232   *Bonobos as "chimpanzees with a threefold path to peace"* and *"everything is peaceful":* de Waal, "Bonobo Bliss."

232   *"Following this line of reasoning":* Hare and Tomasello, "Human-like Social Skills," 439–44.

233   *"If I wished to express":* Bolk, L. 1926. *Das Problem der Menschwerdung* [The Problem of Human Development]. Jena: Gustav Fischer. Quoted in Fuerle, R. D. 2008. *Erectus Walks Amongst Us.* New York: Spooner Press.

233   *relative brain sizes:* Ruff, C. B., et al. 1997. "Body Mass and Encephalization in Pleistocene *Homo.*" *Nature* 387(6629): 173–76.

234   *changes suggesting that humans self-domesticated* and *"had much smaller faces":* Quoted in Leach, H. M. 2003. "Human Domestication Reconsidered." *Current Anthropology* 44(3): 349–68.

234   *modern versus Neanderthal brain volume:* Roth, G., and U. Dicke. 2005. "Evolution of the Brain and Intelligence." *Trends in Cognitive Science* 9(5): 250–57.

235   *summary of Allman's views:* Leach, "Human Domestication," 349–68.

235   *Colin Groves:* quoted in Leach, "Human Domestication," 349–68.

PART THREE: WHINES AND PET PEEVES

NEVER MIND THEORY

243   *wolves did as well:* Udell, "Wolves Outperform Dogs," 1767–73.

244   *"another can have thoughts that differ":* Personal conversation with autism expert Naomi Angoff Chedd, 2014.

244   *"I have an idea of what's on your mind":* Reiss, *Dolphin in the Mirror*, p. 185.

244   *"to read the minds of others":* Call, J., and M. Tomasello. 2008. "Does the Chimpanzee Have a Theory of Mind? 30 Years Later." *Trends in Cognitive Sciences* 12(5): 187–92. See also Whiten, A. 1996. "When Does Smart Behaviour-Reading Become Mind-Reading?" In *Theories of Theories of Mind,* edited by P. Carruthers and P. K. Smith. New York: Cambridge University Press, pp. 277–92.

244   *"our sophisticated mind-reading":* Gallese, V. 2007. "Before and Below 'Theory of Mind': Embodied Simulation and the Neural Correlates of Social Cognition." *Philosophical Transactions of the Royal Society B* 362(1480): 659–69.

244   *"Theory of mind" was coined:* Premack, D., and G. Woodruff. "Does the Chimpanzee Have a Theory of Mind?" *Behavioral and Brain Sciences* 1(4): 515–26.

245   *"In most animal species":* Harmon, K. 2012. "The Social Genius of Animals." *Scientific American Mind* 23: 66–71.

245   *"a complex, and familiar, inner life":* de Waal, *Primates and Philosophers,* p. 67.

SEX, LIES, AND HUMILIATED SEABIRDS

252   *"Dogs Are No Mind Readers":* "Dogs Are No Mind Readers." 2009. *Science Now,* August 17.

253   *"offer no support for the idea":* Pettera, M., et al. 2009. "Can Dogs (*Canis familiaris*) Detect Human Deception?" *Behavioural Processes* 82(2): 109–18.

254   *tigers and masks:* Simons, M. 1989. "Face Masks Fool the Bengal Tigers." *New York Times,* September 5.

CONCEIT AND DECEIT

258   *detect the difference between the humor:* Brüne, M., and U. Brüne–Cohrs. 2006. "Theory of Mind: Evolution, Ontogeny, Brain Mechanisms and Psychopathology." *Neuroscience & Biobehavioral Reviews* 30(4): 437–55.

259   *bonobos use gestures:* Veà, J. J., and J. Sabater-Pi. 1998. "Spontaneous Pointing Behaviour in the Wild Pygmy Chimpanzee (*Pan paniscus*)." *Folia Primatologica* 69(5): 289–90.

259   *groupers hunting collaboratively:* Vail, A. L., et al. 2013. "Referential Gestures in Fish Collaborative Hunting." *Nature Communications* 4, article no. 1765.

259   *"nearly identical to that of chimpanzees":* Vail, A. L., et al. 2014. "Fish Choose Appropriately When and with Whom to Collaborate." *Current Biology* 24(17): R791–93.

260   *dolphins and fishermen in Brazil:* Bearzi and Stanford, *Beautiful Minds,* p. 230. See also Mann et al., *Cetacean Societies;* and Simões-Lopes, P. C., M. E. Fabian, and J. O. Menegheti. 1998 "Dolphin Interactions with the Mullet Artisanal Fishing on Southern Brazil: A Qualitative and Quantitative Approach." *Revista Brasileira de Zoologia* 15(3): 709–26; and Daura-Jorge, F. G., et al. 2012. "The Structure of a Bottlenose Dolphin Society Is Coupled to a Unique Foraging Cooperation with Artisanal Fishermen." *Biology Letters* 8(5): 702–5.

260   *Caroba and Scooby:* Strain, D. 2012. "Clues to an Unusual Alliance Between Dolphins and Fishers." *Science Now,* May 1.

260   *killer whales were hunting partners:* Mead, T. 2002. *Killers of Eden: The Killer Whales of Twofold Bay.* Oatley, NSW, Australia: Dolphin Books.

260   *stone-gathering chimp:* Osvath, M. 2009. "Spontaneous Planning for Future Stone Throwing by a Male Chimpanzee." *Current Biology* 19(5): R190–91.

261   *an orangutan figured out:* Radiolab. January 25, 2010. "Fu Manchu." NPR. Retrieved from http://www.radiolab.org/story/91939-fu-manchu/.

261   *drongos:* Flower, T. 2010. "Fork-tailed Drongos Use Deceptive Mimicked Alarm Calls to Steal Food." *Proceedings of the Royal Society of London, Series B.* Online.

261   *Vervet monkeys sometimes cry "Leopard":* Diamond, *Third Chimpanzee.* See also Bearzi and Stanford, *Beautiful Minds,* p. 188.

261   *chimpanzees in Gombe:* Linden, E. 1993. "Can Animals Think?" *Time,* March 22, p. 60.

262   *rhesus monkeys and grapes:* Flombaum, J. I., and L. R. Santos. 2005. "Rhesus Monkeys Attribute Perceptions to Others." *Current Biology* 15(5): 447–52.

262   *Similarly, monkeys prefer to take:* Santos, L. R., et al. 2006. "Rhesus Monkeys, *Macaca mulatta,* Know What Others Can and Cannot Hear." *Animal Behaviour* 71(5): 1175–81.

262   *dogs less likely to snatch forbidden food:* Udell, "Wolves Outperform Dogs," 1767–73.

262   *smart food-hiding jays:* Emery and Clayton, "Mentality of Crows," 1903–7. See also Clayton, N. S., J. M. Dally, and N. J. Emery. 2007. "Social Cognition by Food-Caching Corvids: The Western Scrub-Jay as a Natural Psychologist." *Philosophical Transactions of the Royal Society B* 362(1480), 507–22.

262   *capuchin experiment with cucumbers and grapes:* de Waal, F. April 4, 2013. "Two Monkeys Were Paid Unequally: Excerpt from Frans de Waal's TED Talk." *TED Blog Video.* Retrieved from http://www.youtube.com/watch?v=meiU6TxysCg. See also de Waal, F., et al. 2008. "Giving Is Self-Rewarding for Monkeys." *PNAS* 105(36): 13685–89. See also Takimoto, A., and K. Fujita. 2011. "I Acknowledge Your Help: Capuchin Monkeys' Sensitivity to Others' Labor." *Animal Cognition* 14(5): 715–25.

262   *ravens, crows, and dogs sensitive to fair payment:* Wascher, C.A.F., and T. Bugnyar. 2013. "Behavioral Responses to Inequity in Reward Distribution and Working Effort in Crows and Ravens." *PLoS ONE* 8(2): e56885.

263   *gorillas dismantling snares:* Than, K. 2012. "Gorilla Youngsters Seen Dismantling Poachers' Traps—a First." *National Geographic News,* July 19. See also Andrews, C. G. 2013. "Gorillas Thwart Poachers." *Good Nature Travel,* August 27.

263   *hyenas:* Holekamp, K. E., et al. 2007. "Social Intelligence in the Spotted Hyena (*Crocuta crocuta*)." *Transactions of the Royal Society B—Biological Sciences* 362(1480): 523–38.

264   *sneak a little sex:* Bearzi and Stanford, *Beautiful Minds,* p. 190.

264   *"Chimpanzees understand both the goals":* Call and Tomasello, "Does the Chimpanzee Have a Theory of Mind?," 187–92.

264   *Chimpanzees pursue power:* de Waal, *Primates and Philosophers,* p. 76.

CHUCKLES AND WACKY IDEAS

266   *"They seem to be reacting to distinct":* Harmon, K. 2012. "The Social Genius of Animals." *Scientific American Mind* 23: 66–71. See also Horowitz, A. 2011. "Theory of Mind in Dogs?" *Learning and Behavior* 39(4): 314–17.

267 *"Theory Theory" (TT):* Nichols, S., and S. Stich. 2005. "Reading One's Own Mind: A Cognitive Theory of Self-Awareness." In *New Essays in Philosophy of Language and Mind,* edited by M. Ezcurdia, R. Stainton, and C. Viger, pp. 297–339. Canada: University of Calgary Press.

267 *Gauguin, Lucretius, Yeats, Locke, and Valéry:* quoted in Humphrey, N. 2007. "The Society of Selves." *Philosophical Transactions of the Royal Society B* 362: 745–54.

269 *discern human faces:* Barrett, L., P. Henzi, and D. Rendall. 2007. "Social Brains, Simple Minds: Does Social Complexity Really Require Cognitive Complexity?" *Philosophical Transactions of the Royal Society B* 362: 561–75.

269 *Park rangers have asked visitors to stop:* Associated Press. 2007. "Hawaii Aims to Deter Volcano Offerings." *Washington Post,* April 21.

269 *Christine M. Korsgaard:* "Morality and the Distinctiveness of Human Action" in de Waal, *Primates and Philosophers,* p. 114.

MIRROR, MIRROR

273 *Gordon Gallup:* quoted in Tennesen, M. 2003. "Do Dolphins Have a Sense of Self?" *National Wildlife Federation,* February 1.

276 *New Guinea tribesmen and mirror:* Byrne, R. W., and L. A. Bates. 2010. "Primate Social Cognition: Uniquely Primate, Uniquely Social, or Just Unique?" *Neuron* 65(6): 815–30. See also Rochat, P., and D. Zahavi. 2011. "The Uncanny Mirror: A Re-Framing of Mirror Self-Experience." *Consciousness and Cognition* 20: 204–13.

277 *dogs can recognize images:* Somppi, S. 2014. "How Dogs Scan Familiar and Inverted Faces: An Eye Movement Study." *Animal Cognition* 17(3): 793–803.

277 *dogs recognize photographs of dogs:* Autier-Derian, D., et al. 2013. "Visual Discrimination of Species in Dogs (*Canis familiaris*)." *Animal Cognition* 16(4): 637–51.

277 *Zookeepers had been watching apes:* Reiss, *Dolphin in the Mirror,* p. 139.

277 *"first experimental demonstration":* Gallup, G. G. 1970. "Chimpanzees: Self-recognition." *Science* 167(3914): 86–87.

278 *look at places that are hard to see:* Vance, E. 2011. "It's Complicated: The Lives of Dolphins & Scientists." *Discover Magazine,* September 7.

278 *like a ballet dancer:* Reiss, *Dolphin in the Mirror,* p. 148.

278 *they'll back up until it can again see:* Ibid., pp. 143, 149.

279 *magpies in mirrors:* Prior, H., A. Schwarz, and O. Güntürkün. 2008. "Mirror-Induced Behavior in the Magpie (*Pica pica*): Evidence of Self-Recognition." *PLoS Biol.* 6(8): e202. See also "Mirror Test Shows Magpies Aren't So Bird-Brained." 2008. *New Scientist.* http://www.youtube.com/watch?v=HRVGA9zxXzk.

AND SPEAKING OF NEURONS

280 *parrots sometimes get crazy jealous:* Burger, *Parrot Who Owns Me.*

281 *"great evolutionary leap," tool use, fire, shelter, language, and "the sudden emergence":* Ramachandran, V. November 2009. "The Neurons That Shaped Civilization." TED.com.

281 *a teeny-tiny bit exaggerated?:* Jarrett, C. 2013. "A Calm Look at the Most Hyped Concept in Neuroscience: Mirror Neurons." *Wired Science,* December 13.

281 *"I don't think they're being exaggerated":* Marsh, J. 2012. "Do Mirror Neurons Give Us Empathy?" *Greater Good,* March 29. Online.

282   *"The functional role(s) of mirror neurons":* Kilner, J. M., and R. N. Lemon. 2013. "What We Know Currently About Mirror Neurons." *Current Biology* 23(23): R1057–62.

282   *"I myself am partly responsible":* Marsh, "Do Mirror Neurons Give Us Empathy?"

285   *Ludwig Wittgenstein:* quoted in Reiss, *Dolphin in the Mirror*, p. 171.

PEOPLE OF AN ANCIENT NATION

288   *tickling rats:* Panksepp, J. 2005. "Affective Consciousness: Core Emotional Feelings in Animals and Humans." *Consciousness and Cognition* 14(1): 30–80.

288   *Frans de Waal and bonobos:* de Waal, *Primates and Philosophers*, p. 72.

289   *In a sense, the primate vocal tract:* Altenmüller et al., *Evolution of Emotional Intelligence*, p. 31.

290   *Some signing chimpanzees' sentences:* Bearzi and Stanford, *Beautiful Minds*, p. 173.

290   *Chimpanzees remember the locations:* Ibid., p. 256.

290   *"the crudest shadow":* Diamond, *Third Chimpanzee*, p. 155.

290   *ape gestures:* Moore, R. 2014. "Ape Gestures: Interpreting Chimpanzee and Bonobo Minds." *Current Biology* 24(14): R645–47. See also Hobaiter, C., and R. W. Byrne. 2014. "The Meanings of Chimpanzee Gestures." *Current Biology* 24(14): 1596–1600.

290   *gorilla gestures:* Genty, E., et al. 2009. "Gestural Communication of the Gorilla (*Gorilla gorilla*): Repertoire, Intentionality and Possible Origins." *Animal Cognition* 12(3): 527–46.

290   *bonobos use a human-like wave:* Genty, E., and K. Zuberbuehler. 2014. "Spatial Reference in a Bonobo Gesture." *Current Biology* 24(14): 1601–5.

291   *"If there is a difference":* Bearzi and Stanford, *Beautiful Minds*, pp. 176–77.

291   *Dawn Prince-Hughes:* Brown, J. 2010. *Writers on the Spectrum: How Autism and Asperger Syndrome Have Influenced Literary Writing.* London: Jessica Kingsley. See also Prince-Hughes, D. 1987. *Songs of the Gorilla Nation: My Journey Through Autism.* New York: Harmony, p. 135.

291   *Washoe:* Fouts, R. 1997. *Next of Kin: My Conversations with Chimpanzees.* New York: Avon, p. 291.

292   *"I thinked":* Pinker, S. 1994. *The Language Instinct.* New York: William Morrow. As cited by Tyack, *Biology of Marine Mammals*, p. 312.

292   *dolphins and chimpanzees form abstract concepts:* Tyack et al., *Biology of Marine Mammals*, p. 313.

292   *"When we ask things":* Thomas, E. M., "The Old Way," p. 78.

292   *Orangutans evaluate humans:* Cartmill, E. A., and R. W. Byrne. 2007. "Orangutans Modify Their Gestural Signalling According to Their Audience's Comprehension." *Current Biology* 17(15): 1345–48.

PART FOUR: KILLER WAILS

SEA REX

297   *intelligent, maternal, long-lived, cooperative:* Pitman, R. 2011. "An Introduction to the World's Premier Predator." *Whalewatcher* 40(1): 2–5.

299   *transients follow no routines:* Ford and Ellis, *Transients*, p. 13.

300   *killer whales frequently share food:* Ford, J.K.B., and G. M. Ellis. 2005. "Prey Selection and Food Sharing by Fish-Eating 'Resident' Killer Whales (*Orcinus orca*) in British-Columbia." Fisheries and Oceans Canada. Research Document 2005/041.

300   *vampire bats:* Wilkinson, G. S. 1986. "Social Grooming in the Vampire Bat, *Desmodus rotundus.*" *Animal Behaviour* 34(6): 1880–89.

300   *Some monkeys share:* Yamamoto, S., et al. 2012. "Chimpanzees' Flexible Targeted Helping Based on an Understanding of Conspecifics' Goals." *PNAS* 109(9): 3588–92.

300   *bonobos:* Hare, B., and S. Kwetuenda. 2010. "Bonobos Voluntarily Share Their Own Food with Others." *Current Biology* 20(5): R230–31.

300   *video of horses sharing hay:* "Horse Feeds Another Horse." June 9, 2014. https://www.youtube.com/watch?v=p4jhtJC25EQ.

300   *killer whale named Magga:* Hoelzel, A. R. 1991. "Killer Whale Predation on Marine Mammals at Punta Norte, Argentina: Food Sharing, Provisioning and Foraging Strategy." *Behavioral Ecology and Sociobiology* 29(3): 197–204.

300   *different names for killer whales:* Ford et al., *Killer Whales*, p. 68.

301   *transients sometimes disappear for years:* Ford and Ellis, *Transients*, p. 61.

302   *dolphins can generate something over 220 decibels:* Herzing, *Dolphin Diaries*, p. 153.

302   *transients' calls differ:* Bigg et al., *Killer Whales*, p. 12.

302   *J pod chasing transients:* Ford and Ellis, *Transients*.

303   *moving swiftly, no splashing :* Morton, *Listening to Whales*, p. 226.

A MORE COMPLEX KILLER

304   *a far simpler killer whale:* Pitman, R. 2011. "An Introduction to the World's Premier Predator." *Whalewatcher* 40(1): 2–5.

304   *offshores' existence wasn't suspected:* Ford, J.K.B. 2011. "Killer Whales of the Pacific Northwest Coast." *Whalewatcher* 40(1): 15–23.

305   *One seen off Mexico:* Dahlheim, M., et al. 2008. "Eastern Temperate North Pacific Offshore Killer Whales (*Orcinus orca*): Occurrence, Movements, and Insights into Feeding Ecology." *Marine Mammal Science* 24(3): 719–29. (Some information originates in references cited by these authors.)

305   *types of Antarctic killers, their hunting methods,* and *Bob Pitman quotes:* Pitman, R. L. 2011. "Antarctic Killer Whales." *Whalewatcher* 40(1): 39–45.

307   *"For transmitting large quantities of acoustic information":* Pabst et al. 1999. In *Biology of Marine Mammals,* edited by J. E. Reynolds III and S. A. Rommel, p. 61.

307   *The big whales make sounds:* Tyack, 1999, In *Biology of Marine Mammals*, p. 293.

JUST VERY SEXUAL

309   *Pan and Delphi:* Reiss, *Dolphin in the Mirror,* p. 136.

309   *same-sex enjoyment:* Herzing, *Dolphin Diaries*, p. 44.

309   *"Dolphins love to have sex":* Herzing, *Dolphin Diaries,* p. 53.

310   *Each whale in a pod has exactly the same call repertoire:* Ford et al., *Killer Whales*, p. 75.

311   *"no parallel outside humans":* Rendell, L., and H. Whitehead. 2001. "Culture in Whales and Dolphins." *Journal of Behavioral and Brain Science* 24(2): 309–82.

311   *pilot whales:* Connor et al., in Mann et al., *Cetacean Societies*, pp. 260–61.

311   *sperm whales:* Rendell, L. E., and H. Whitehead. 2003. "Vocal Clans in Sperm

Whales (*Physeter macrocephalus*)." *Proceedings of the Royal Society B* 270(1512): 225–31.

312 *"acceptance, approval, and peace":* Morton, *Listening to Whales,* p. 105.

312 *I envision them rapidly closing a circle:* As described in Hoyt, *Orca,* pp. 143–44.

313 *"Touch the Frisbee":* de Rohan, A. 2003. "Deep Thinkers." *Guardian,* July 2.

313 *dolphins ignore nonsense:* Bearzi and Stanford, *Beautiful Minds,* pp. 164–66.

313 *dolphins can learn several dozen human words:* Simmonds, M. P. 2006. "Into the Brains of Whales." *Applied Animal Behaviour Science* 100(1–2): 103–16. (Simmonds reviews and cites other sources.)

313 *Dolphins who hear their own signature whistle:* King, S. L., and V. M. Janik. 2013. "Bottlenose Dolphins Can Use Learned Vocal Labels to Address Each Other." *PNAS* 110(32): 13216–21. See also Tyack in *Biology of Marine Mammals,* p. 304, and Janik, V. M. 2013. "Cognitive Skills in Bottlenose Dolphin Communication." *Trends in Cognitive Sciences* 17(4): 157–59.

313 *dolphins calling each other by name:* "Dolphins May Call Each Other by Name." *Science News,* March 8, 2013.

313 *Dolphins more than ten miles:* Janik, V. 2000. "Source Levels and the Estimated Active Space of Bottlenose Dolphin (*Tursiops truncatus*) Whistles in the Moray Firth, Scotland." *Journal of Comparative Physiology A* 186(7–8): 673–80.

313 *Atlantic spotted dolphins seemingly use:* Herzing, *Dolphin Diaries,* p. 103.

313 *When groups meet at sea:* Quick, N. J., and V. M. Janik. 2012. "Bottlenose Dolphins Exchange Signature Whistles When Meeting at Sea." *Proceedings of the Royal Society B* 279(1738): 2539–45.

314 *bat song:* Morell, V. 2014. "When the Bat Sings." *Science* 344(6190): 1334–37.

314 *parrot species and calls* and *"an intriguing parallel":* Berg, K. S., et al. 2011. "Vertical Transmission of Learned Signatures in a Wild Parrot." *Proceedings of the Royal Society B* 279: 585–91.

314 *fairy wrens:* Morell, V. 2014. "A Rare Observation of Teaching in the Wild." *Science,* June 11.

314 *Dolphins remember and recognize:* Bruck, J. N. 2013. "Decades-long Social Memory in Bottlenose Dolphins." *Proceedings of the Royal Society B* 280(1768): 1726.

INNER VISIONS

316 *dolphins' whistles convey information:* Samuels and Tyack in Mann et al., *Cetacean Societies.*

316 *humpback song:* Tyack et al. in *Biology of Marine Mammals,* pp. 297–98.

317 *Australian humpbacks' song:* Noad, M. J., et al. 2000. "Cultural Revolution in Whale Songs." *Nature* 408: 537.

318 *Pituuu and* Wee-oo-uuo: Morton, *Listening to Whales,* p. 117.

318 *ping-pong ball:* Tyack et al. in *Biology of Marine Mammals,* pp. 291–92.

318 *four hundred clicks per second* and *click trains:* Ford and Ellis, *Transients,* p. 78.

319 *sonar discovery:* Au, *Sonar of Dolphins,* pp. 3–4.

320 *when sonar signals are slowed:* Ibid., p. 209.

321 *infrared and ultraviolet sensing:* "Infrared Detection in Animals." November 10, 2014. MapofLife.org. See also Lewis, T. 2014. "Cats and Dogs May See in Ultraviolet." *Livescience,* February 18.

322 *Daniel Kish:* " 'Bat Man' Navigates Primarily by Using Echolocation." *National Geographic,* n.d.

323   *one-third are usually caressing*: Tyack et al., *Biology of Marine Mammals*, p. 289.

323   *"sonic hedgehog"*: Bearzi and Stanford, *Beautiful Minds*, p. 248.

DIVERSE MINDS

325   *"the carousel"*: Similä, T., and F. Ugarte. 1993. "Surface and Underwater Observations of Cooperatively Feeding Killer Whales in Northern Norway." *Canadian Journal of Zoology* 71(8): 1494–99.

325   *A fifth of the transients' diet*: Ford and Ellis, *Transients*, p. 26.

326   *"a wall of white water erupted"*: Morton, *Listening to Whales*, p. 192.

326   *team of killer whales may pursue*: Pitman, R. L. 2011. "Antarctic Killer Whales." *Whalewatcher* 40(1): 39–45.

326   *minke pursuit*: Ford, J.K.B., et al. 2005. "Killer Whale Attacks on Minke Whales: Prey Capture and Antipredator Tactics." *Marine Mammal Science* 21(4): 603–18.

327   *Often grays will lessen*: Matkin, C., and J. Durban. 2011. "Killer Whales in Alaskan Waters." *Whalewatcher* 40(1): 24–29.

327   *killer whales attacking sperm whales*: Pitman, R. L., et al. 2001. "Killer Whale Predation on Sperm Whales: Observations and Implications." *Marine Mammal Science* 17(3): 494–507.

329   *Stealth's dolphin hunting*: Visser, I. 2005. *Swimming with Orca*. New York: Penguin, pp. 94–95.

330   *short-finned pilot whale menopause*: Connor, R. C., et al. 1988. "Social Evolution in Toothed Whales." *Trends in Ecology & Evolution* 13(6): 228–32.

330   *killer whale grandmothers*: Ward, E. J., et al. 2009. "The Role of Menopause and Reproductive Senescence in a Long-Lived Social Mammal." *Frontiers in Zoology* 6: 4.

330   *postmenopause lifespan and offspring mortality*: Foster, E. A., et al. 2012. "Adaptive Prolonged Postreproductive Lifespan in Killer Whales." *Science* 337(6100): 1313.

331   *produce milk for up to fifteen years*: Connor, "Social Evolution," 228–32.

331   *White Patches*: Herzing, *Dolphin Diaries*, p. 51.

331   *sperm whale females nursing*: Gero, S., et al. 2009. "Who Cares? Between-Group Variation in Alloparental Caregiving in Sperm Whales." *Behavioral Ecology* 20(4): 838–43.

331   *Nootka and Tweak*: Parfit and Chisholm, *Lost Whale*, p. 13.

332   *"There were so many females"* and *balancing a newborn*: Morton, *Listening to Whales*, p. 139.

333   *When young dolphins test*: Herzing, *Dolphin Diaries*, p. 42.

333   *"Play is a hallmark of intelligence"*: Bunnell, S. 1974. In *Mind in the Waters*, edited by Joan McIntyre. New York: Scribner.

333   *Young bottlenose dolphins sometimes*: Paulos, R. D., M. Trone, and S. A. Kuczaj II. 2010. "Play in Wild and Captive Cetaceans." *International Journal of Comparative Psychology*. 23(4): 701–22.

333   *bubble play* and *Etch A Sketch concept*: Reiss, *Dolphin in the Mirror*, pp. 112–18.

334   *"seemed the courteous thing"*: Herzing, *Dolphin Diaries*, p. 28.

INTELLIGENT IN WHAT WAY?

336   *"There is someone in there"*: Vance, E. 2011. "It's Complicated: The Lives of Dolphins and Scientists." *Discover Magazine*, September 7.

336   *The seas are home to:* Hof, P. R., and E. Van Der Gucht. 2007. "Structure of the Cerebral Cortex of the Humpback Whale, *Megaptera novaeangliae.*" *Anatomical Record* 290(1): 1–31.

339   *"truly godlike" mind:* Lilly quoted by Tyack in *Biology of Marine Mammals*, p. 287.

338   *Akeakamai:* Reiss, *Dolphin in the Mirror*, p. 196.

338   *Kelly:* de Rohan, A. 2003. "Deep Thinkers." *Guardian*, July 2.

338   *Spock:* Reiss, *Dolphin in the Mirror*, p. 129.

338   *A young killer whale at Marineland:* Associated Press, September 7, 2005. "Whale Uses Fish as Bait to Catch Seagulls Then Shares Strategy with Fellow Orcas." *Mongabay.com.*

338   *Circe* and *Pan:* Reiss, *Dolphin in the Mirror*, pp. 75, 100–103.

339   *Delphi:* Ibid., p. 132.

340   *"I personally do not believe":* Tyack in *Biology of Marine Mammals*, p. 287.

341   *Max Delbrück:* quoted in Reiss, *Dolphin in the Mirror*, p. 176.

341   *brain weights:* Bearzi and Stanford, *Beautiful Minds*, pp. 140, 251.

341   *honeybee language:* Tyack in *Biology of Marine Mammals*, p. 288.

342   *"primate-like intelligence":* Pearson and Shelton in *Dusky Dolphin*, pp. 333–53.

342   *EQ numbers:* Ibid.

342   *human EQ of 7.6:* Roth, G., and U. Dicke. 2005. "Evolution of the Brain and Intelligence." *Trends in Cognitive Science.* 9(5): 250–57.

342   *capuchin EQ compared to chimpanzees* and *shrews:* Ibid.

342   *whales' neocortex:* Pearson and Shelton in *Dusky Dolphin*, pp. 333–53.

343   *number of processing units:* Byrne, 1996, as cited in Moss et al., *Amboseli Elephants*, p. 174.

343   *"Humans have more cortical neurons"* and *birds have much smaller cells:* Roth and Dicke, "Evolution of the Brain," 250–57.

343   *16 billion cortical neurons:* Koch, *Consciousness.* Online.

344   *A person's individual brain neurons:* Ibid.

THE SOCIAL BRAIN

345   *nearly 20:* Tyack in *Biology of Marine Mammals*, pp. 316–17.

346   *male alliances:* R. C. Connor et al. in Mann et al., *Cetacean Societies*, p. 266.

346   *alliances sometimes merge:* Simmonds, M. P. 2006. "Into the Brains of Whales." *Applied Animal Behaviour Science* 100(1–2): 103–16. (Simmonds cites R. C. Connor, M. R. Heithaus, and L.M. Barre. 2001. "Complex Social Structure, Alliance, Stability and Mating Access in a Bottlenose Dolphin 'Super-Alliance.'" *Proceedings of the Royal Society of London, Series B* 268([1464]: 263–67.)

346   *Janet Mann saw:* Bearzi and Stanford, *Beautiful Minds*, p. 188.

346   *"Male chimpanzees have political careers"* and *fathers the most babies:* Ibid., pp. 197–99.

347   *the social brain:* Tyack in *Biology of Marine Mammals*, pp. 316–17.

347   *"our kind of intelligence":* Coghlan, A. 2006. "Whales Boast the Brain Cells That 'Make Us Human.'" *New Scientist*, November.

347   *von Economo neurons:* Hakeem et al. 2009, as cited in Moss et al., *Amboseli Elephants*, p. 175.

347   *spindle cells in whales and dolphins:* Butti, C., et al. 2009. "Total Number and Volume of von Economo Neurons in the Cerebral Cortex of Cetaceans." *Journal of Comparative Neurology* 515(2): 243–59.

347   *hippos, manatees, and walruses:* Nieuwenhuys, R. 2012. "The Insular Cortex: A Review." *Progress in Brain Research* 195: 123–63.

347   *"express trains of the nervous system":* Coghlan, A. 2006. "Whales Boast the Brain Cells That 'Make Us Human.'" *New Scientist,* November.

348   *Alzheimer's disease, autism, and schizophrenia:* Hof, P. R., and E. Van Der Gucht. 2007. "Structure of the Cerebral Cortex of the Humpback Whale, *Megaptera novaeangliae." Anatomical Record* 290(1): 1–31.

348   *spindle cell damage in dementia:* Hakeem, A. Y., et al. 2009. "Von Economo Neurons in the Elephant Brain." *Anatomical Record* 292(2): 242–48.

348   *Patrick Hof:* quoted in Coghlan, "Whales Boast the Brain Cells." See also Hof and Van Der Gucht, "Structure of the Cerebral Cortex of the Humpback Whale," 1–31.

348   *When a young chimpanzee watches:* de Waal, F. 2013. "Animal Conformists." *Science* 340(6131): 437–38.

348   *Same with certain ants:* University of Bristol. 2006. "First Demonstration of 'Teaching' in Non-human Animals: Ants Teach by Running in Tandem." *Science Daily,* January 13.

348   *Crozet Islands:* Guinet, C., and J. Bouvier. 1995. "Development of Intentional Stranding Hunting Techniques in Killer Whale (*Orcinus orca*) Calves at Crozet Archipelago." *Canadian Journal of Zoology* 73(1): 27–33.

349   *two killer whales teaching:* Matkin, C., and J. Durban. 2011. "Killer Whales in Alaskan Waters." *Whalewatcher* 40(1): 24–29.

349   *Atlantic spotted dolphin mothers:* Bender, C., D. Herzing, and D. Bjorklund. 2009. "Evidence of Teaching in Atlantic Spotted Dolphins (*Stenella frontalis*) by Mother Dolphins Foraging in the Presence of Their Calves." *Animal Cognition* 12(1): 43–53.

349   *bottlenose dolphins wearing snout sponges:* Krützen, M., et al. 2005. "Cultural Transmission of Tool Use in Bottlenose Dolphins." *PNAS* 102(25): 8939–43.

349   *teaching examples:* Hoppitt, W. J., et al. 2008. "Lessons from Animal Teaching." *Trends in Ecology & Evolution.* 23(9): 486–93.

350   *Daan cleaning the window:* Taylor, C. K., and G. Saayman. 1973. "Imitative Behavior by Indian Ocean Bottlenose Dolphins (*Tursiops aduncus*) in Captivity." *Behaviour* 44(3–4): 286–98. See also Reiss, *Dolphin in the Mirror,* p. 168.

350   *dolphin named Haig:* Reiss, *Dolphin in the Mirror,* p. 126.

350   *bottlenose named Dolly:* Ibid., p. 169.

350   *Dolly* came up with the idea: Tyack in *Biology of Marine Mammals,* p. 315.

350   *Also about Dolly:* Taylor, C. K., and G. Saayman. 1973. "Imitative Behavior by Indian Ocean Bottlenose Dolphins (*Tursiops aduncus*) in Captivity." *Behaviour* 44(3–4): 286–98.

WOO-WOO

352   *enveloped by fog* and *One September day in 1986:* Morton, *Listening to Whales,* pp. 113–15, 210.

355   *"Those whales saved my dog":* Ibid., pp. 93, 121.

356   *"Sometimes I don't know what to believe"* and *"They can read your mind":* Ibid., pp. 237–39, 97–98.

357   *Howard Garrett recalled:* Garrett, H. 2014. "SeaWorld's Orcas Deserve a Retirement Plan," *The Dodo.* November 14.

358   *"When I die, I am going to come back"* and *"to wash away hurt":* Parfit and Chisholm, *Lost Whale,* pp. 31, 280.

358   *People quoted about Luna:* Ibid., pp. 36, 66, 186–87.

359   *"look through your otherness":* Ibid., pp. 170–71.

360   *if a person remained aboard sleeping:* Ibid., p. 300.

360   *Michelle Kehler and Erin Hobbs:* Ibid., pp. 82–83, 119.

361   *"I could feel"* and *Luna was playing:* Ibid., pp. 99, 141, 143, 301. (See also the other Parfit quotes pp. 286, 313.)

362   *dolphins shook their* tails: Reiss, *Dolphin in the Mirror,* p. 198.

363   *Karen Pryor* and *"Do something new":* Samuels and Tyack in Mann, *Cetacean Societies,* p. 26. See also Reiss, *Dolphin in the Mirror,* p. 199.

363   *" 'Joyous' is probably"* and *"The dolphins seemed to know":* Herzing, *Dolphin Diaries,* pp. 29, 64.

364   *one of the people aboard:* Ibid., pp. 31–32.

366   *Photographer Bryant Austin:* Austin, B. 2013. *Beautiful Whales.* New York: Abrams. See also "Photographer Gets Up Close with Whales." 2013. *Here & Now,* June 3. http://hereandnow.wbur.org/2013/06/03/photographer-beautiful-whale.

HELPING IN MIND

367   *"The cow and the bull":* Ford et al., *Killer Whales,* p. 83.

367   *pilot whales supporting a harpooned comrade:* Reiss, *Dolphin in the Mirror,* p. 205.

368   *"Just as the seal":* Pitman, R. L., and J. W. Durban. 2009. "Save the Seal!" *Natural History,* November.

368   *Zigzag:* Herzing, *Dolphin Diaries,* p. 106.

368   *humpback whales off San Francisco:* Fimrite, P. 2005. "Daring Rescue of Whale off Farallones." *San Francisco Chronicle,* December 14.

369   *riveting amateur video:* Lewis, R. 2013. "Injured Wild Dolphin Swims to Nearby Divers for Help." *Yahoo News,* January 22.

369   *Dash:* Herzing, *Dolphin Diaries,* p. 184.

369   *Jeff Wolkart:* Safina, C. 2011. *A Sea in Flames: The Deepwater Horizon Oil Blowout.* New York: Crown, p. 193.

370   *"I would have let him go":* Lopez, B. H. 1978. *Of Wolves and Men.* New York: Scribner, p. 98.

370   *wild raven in Nova Scotia:* J. Heimbuch. 2013. "Raven with a Face Full of Porcupine Quills Gets Help from Human Neighbors." *Grist,* July 17.

370   *"It was odd how many":* Tomkies, M. 1985. *Out of the Wild.* UK: Jonathan Cape, p. 197.

370   *Don Pachico:* Don Pachico's interview can be viewed online in the "Destination Baja" episode of the PBS series *Saving the Ocean with Carl Safina,* available at PBS.org.

371   *researcher in the Bahamas:* Herzing, *Dolphin Diaries,* p. 28.

372   *When researchers there swam:* Ibid., pp. 55–56.

372   *It is not unusual:* Ibid., p. 193.

372   *Todd Endris:* Celizic, M. 2007. "Dolphins Save Surfer from Becoming Shark's Bait." *Today,* November 8.

372   *On a sailboat off Venezuela:* Reiss, *Dolphin in the Mirror,* p. 207.

372   *Elián Gonzáles:* Ibid., p. 206.

372   *dolphins tail-slap:* Herzing, *Dolphin Diaries,* p. 50.

372   *"headed over to the anchor":* Ibid., p. 32.

373   *"We were at least three miles":* Bearzi and Stanford, *Beautiful Minds,* pp. 25–26.

DO NOT DISTURB

375   *"Top Notch let loose"*: Morton, *Listening to Whales,* p. 94.

377   *Within the lifetime of the older whales:* Ford, J.K.B. 2011. "Killer Whales of the Pacific Northwest Coast." *Whalewatcher* 40(1): 15–23.

377   *"will attack human beings"*: quoted in Ford et al., *Killer Whales,* p. 11.

378   *Tlingit of southeast Alaska believed:* Ford et al., *Killer Whales,* p. 11.

378   *"That's what you did"* and *Between the 1950s and about 1980:* Hoyt, *Orca,* pp. 37, 228.

378   *six thousand killer whales:* Bigg et al., *Killer Whales,* p. 15.

378   *"completed another successful mission"*: Hoyt, *Orca,* p. 93.

378   *"It is recommended that one"*: Ford et al., *Killer Whales,* p. 12.

379   *people a hundred yards away:* Parfit and Chisholm, *Lost Whale,* p. 108.

379   *history of capture* and *"It was a nice whale, but"*: Hoyt, *Orca,* pp. 15–19.

380   *$70,000 per whale:* Ford, "Killer Whales of the Pacific Northwest Coast," 15–23.

380   *One night in 1969:* Hoyt, *Orca,* p. 70.

380   *Two pregnant whales:* Ibid., p. 147.

381   *Between 1962 and the mid-1970s:* Ford et al., *Killer Whales,* p. 12.

381   *In 1976, more than a thousand:* Hoyt, *Orca,* p. 203.

381   *Of 53 whales taken:* Ibid., p. 20.

TO HAVE AND TO HOLD

383   *In the 1860s* through *One evening at Marineland:* Samuels and Tyack, in Mann, *Cetacean Societies,* pp. 22–25.

384   *Quotes for Garret, Crowe, Walters, Huxter, Ray, and Hargrove and some of the information on Tilikum and SeaWorld are from:* Cowperthwaite, G., director and producer. 2013. *Blackfish.* DVD. Manny O Productions.

386   *"Captive orcas at"*: Hoyt, *Orca,* p. 19.

386   *Colin Baird:* Kuo, V. 2013. "Orca Trainer Saw Best of Keiko, Worst of Tilikum." *CNN.com,* October 28.

387   *other dolphins sometimes act frustrated:* Simmonds, M. P. 2006. "Into the Brains of Whales." *Applied Animal Behaviour Science* 100(1–2): 103–16.

388   *hurled it at the trainer:* Schusterman, 2000, as cited in Simmonds, "Into the Brains of Whales," 103–16.

390   *Haida and Charlie Chin and the fasting whales:* Hoyt, *Orca,* pp. 118–20.

391   *Charlie Chin lived until 1992:* Ford and Ellis, *Transients,* p. 21.

391   *One day Ellis was just sitting* and *"They all start to get a bit nutty"*: Hoyt, *Orca,* pp. 37, 126.

EXPECT PERSONALITY

392   *John Ford:* Parfit and Chisholm, *Lost Whale,* p. 39.

393   *turtles call their young:* Ferrara, C. R., et al. 2012. "Turtle Vocalizations as the First Evidence of Posthatching Parental Care in Chelonians." *Journal of Comparative Psychology* 127(1): 24–32. See also Ferrara, C. R., et al. 2014. "Sound Communication and Social Behavior in an Amazonian River Turtle (*Podocnemis Expansa*)." *Herpetologica* 70(2): 149–56.

395   *"Bears differ individually"*: Roosevelt, T. 1903. *The Works of Theodore Roosevelt, the Wilderness Hunter.* New York: Scribner, p. 96.

395   *Researchers have also published:* Verdolin, J. L., and J. Harper. 2013. "Are Shy Individuals Less Behaviorally Variable? Insights from a Captive Population of Mouse Lemurs." *Primates* 54(4): 309–14.

395   *individual personalities:* Sih, A., et al. 2004. "Behavioral Syndromes: An Integrative Overview." *Quarterly Review of Biology* 79(3): 241–77. See also Sweeney, K., et al. 2013. "Predator and Prey Activity Levels Jointly Influence the Outcome of Long-Term Foraging Bouts." *Behavioral Ecology* 24(5): 1205. See also Brown, G. E., et al. 2012. "Retention of Acquired Predator Recognition Among Shy Versus Bold Juvenile Rainbow Trout." *Behavioral Ecology and Sociobiology* 67(1): 43–51.

395   *Peter and Judy Weis:* Personal conversation with Rutgers professors Peter and Judith Weis, 2014.

395   *Corky and Orky:* Morton, *Listening to Whales,* pp. 53–55.

396   *Corky and her baby* and *Corky shattering glass:* Ibid., pp. 49–50, 100.

397   *"If she wasn't 'crying'":* Ibid., p. 97.

398   *Paul Spong:* Hoyt, *Orca,* p. 44.

A VISION TRUE AND MIGHTY

399   *"It was the story":* Neihardt, J. G. 1972. *Black Elk Speaks.* New York: Washington Square, p. 238.

400   *harbor seals in British Columbia:* Ford and Ellis, *Transients,* p. 81.

401   *residents' diet is 65 percent:* Ibid., p. 26.

402   *Columbia River salmon production:* NOAA Southern Resident Recovery Plan, online.

403   *contaminants in transients compared to residents:* John Durban conversation with author; and Ford and Ellis, *Transients,* p. 87.

405   *Madagascar:* 2013. "Sonar Used by Oil Company Caused Mass Whale Stranding in Madagascar." September 25. *Mongabay.com.*

EPILOGUE: FINAL SCRATCH

410   *"Anyone who studies a wild animal":* Morton, *Listening to Whales,* p. 5.

SELECTED BIBLIOGRAPHY

Altenmüller, E., S. Schmidt, and E. Zimmermann. 2013. *The Evolution of Emotional Communication*. Oxford: Oxford University Press.

Au, W.W.L. 1993. *The Sonar of Dolphins*. New York: Springer.

Bearzi, M., and C. B. Stanford. 2008. *Beautiful Minds: The Parallel Lives of Great Apes and Dolphins*. Cambridge, MA: Harvard University Press.

Bigg, M. A., et al. 1987. *Killer Whales: A Study of Their Identification, Genealogy, and Natural History in British Columbia and Washington State*. Nanaimo, BC: Phantom Press.

Burger, J. 2002. *The Parrot Who Owns Me: The Story of a Relationship*. New York: Villard Books.

de Waal, F. 2013. *The Bonobo and the Atheist: In Search of Humanism Among the Primates*. New York: Norton.

de Waal, F. 2006. *Primates and Philosophers: How Morality Evolved*. New Jersey: Princeton University Press.

Diamond, J. 1991. *The Rise and Fall of the Third Chimpanzee: How Our Animal Heritage Affects the Way We Live*. New York: Vintage Books.

Douglas-Hamilton, I., and O. Douglas-Hamilton. 1975. *Among the Elephants*. New York: Viking Books.

Ford, J.K.B., and G. M. Ellis. 1999. *Transients: Mammal-Hunting Killer Whales of British Columbia, Washington, and Southeastern Alaska*. Seattle: University of Washington Press.

Ford, J.K.B., G. M. Ellis, and K. C. Balcomb. 1994. *Killer Whales*. UBC Press and University of Washington Press.

Herzing, Denise L. 2011. *Dolphin Diaries: My Twenty-five Years with Spotted Dolphins in the Bahamas*. New York: St. Martin's.

Hoyt, Erich. 1981. *Orca: The Whale Called Killer*. New York: Dutton.

Koch, C. 2012. *Consciousness: Confessions of a Romantic Reductionist*. Cambridge, MA: MIT Press.

Mann, J., R. C. Connor, P. L. Tyack, and H. Whitehead. 2000. *Cetacean Societies: Field Studies of Dolphins and Whales*. Chicago: University of Chicago Press.

Morton, Alexandra. 2004. *Listening to Whales*. New York: Ballantine Books.

Moss, C., and M. Colbeck. 1993. *Echo of the Elephants: The Story of an Elephant Family*. New York: William Morrow.

Moss, C. J. 2000. *Elephant Memories: Thirteen Years in the Life of an Elephant Family.* Chicago: University of Chicago Press.

Moss, C. J., H. Croze, and P. Lee, eds. 2011. *The Amboseli Elephants: A Long-Term Perspective on a Long-Lived Mammal.* Chicago: University of Chicago Press.

Moussaieff Masson, J., and S. McCarthy. 1996. *When Elephants Weep: The Emotional Lives of Animals.* New York: Delta.

Parfit, M., and S. Chisholm. 2013. *The Lost Whale: The True Story of an Orca Named Luna.* New York: St. Martin's Press.

Pearson, H. C., and D. E. Shelton. 2010. "A Large-Brained Social Animal." In *The Dusky Dolphin*, edited by B. Würsig and M. Würsig. London: Elsevier.

Poole, J. 1997. *Coming of Age with Elephants: A Memoir.* New York: Voyageur Press.

Reiss, D. 2011. *The Dolphin in the Mirror: Exploring Dolphin Minds and Saving Dolphin Lives.* Boston: Houghton Mifflin Harcourt.

Smith, D. W., and G. Ferguson. 2005. *Decade of the Wolf: Returning the Wild to Yellowstone.* Guilford, CT: Lyons Press.

Tyack, P. L. 1999. In *Biology of Marine Mammals,* edited by J. E. Reynolds III and S. A. Rommel. Washington, DC: Smithsonian.

Vaillant, J. 2011. *The Tiger: A True Story of Vengeance and Survival.* New York: Vintage Departures.

Walker, J. F. 2009. *Ivory's Ghosts: The White Gold of History and the Fate of Elephants.* New York: Atlantic Monthly Press.

ACKNOWLEDGMENTS

Any recounting of kindnesses that went into helping me create this book will be inadequate and incomplete. But let me try: Reading about traumatized elephants while I was surrounded by dolphins in the Gulf of California made me ask myself a penetrating question whose answer formed the central concept for this book. For that fertile combination I thank author Gay Bradshaw and Brett Jenks of RARE Conservation. For exceptional help in understanding elephants, I owe Cynthia Moss, Iain Douglas-Hamilton, and Vicki Fishlock especially, along with Katito Sayialel, David Dallaben, Daphne Sheldrick, Edwin Lusichi, Julius Shivegha, Gilbert Sabinga, Frank Pope, Shifra Goldenberg, George Wittemyer, Lucy King, Ike Leonard, Soila Sayialel, and Joseph Soltis. I thank also Andrew Dobson and Katarzyna Nowak and John Heminway for helping alert us all. And for wide perspectives, Jeff Andrews, Otto Fad, Diane Donohue, Judy St. Ledger, and Ray Ryan. For crucial logistics that made my trip to Kenya click, Jean Hartley. In Yellowstone, I thank the singular Rick McIntyre and the amazingly dedicated Laurie Lyman, Doug McLaughlin, and Doug Smith for observations, insights, and stories that made the wolf section possible. I also thank Sian Jones for good spotting, and the underfunded U.S. National Park Service for doing its best. For my killer whale immersion, I am deeply grateful to Ken Balcomb, Dave Ellifrit, Kathy Babiak, Bob Pitman, John Durban, Nancy Black, and Alexandra Morton. For expertise and insight, I thank Diana Reiss, Heidi C.

Pearson, Diane Doran-Sheehy, Kyle Hanson, whose injured crow put out food for free-living crows, Crystal Possehl, whose bearded dragon seemed to mourn, and ravenologist Derek Craighead.

Please consider contributing to Save the Elephants, the Amboseli Trust for Elephants, Big Life Foundation, the David Sheldrick Wildlife Trust, the Yellowstone Park Foundation, or the Center for Whale Research, which work on the front lines to keep these creatures with us.

On the editorial side, I thank the incomparable Jack Macrae, Jean Naggar, Jennifer Weltz, and Bonnie Thompson, skilled and faithful partners all. For reading all or part of earlier troubled drafts and pointing out weaknesses, I thank John Angier, Patricia Wright, Cynthia Tuthill, Joanna Burger, Mike Gochfeld, Margaret Conover, Rachel Gruzen, Tom Mittak, and the ever-insightful Paul Greenberg. In memoriam, I'd like to humbly acknowledge the inspiration and encouragement I received for many years from Peter Matthiessen.

For material support, I thank especially Julie Packard, the Gilchrist Family, Andrew Sabin, Ann Hunter-Welborn and family, Susan O'Connor, Roy O'Connor, Robert Campbell, Beto Bedolfe, Glenda Menges, Sylvie Chantecaille, and others who prefer anonymity. I offer my appreciation to Eric Graham, Sven Olof Lindblad, Jeff Rizzo, Richard Reagan, Rainer Judd, Howard Ferren, Andrew Revkin, and Paul Winter. On the home campus, I thank Howie Schneider, Elizabeth Bass, Minghua Zhang, Stefanie Massucci, Deborah Lowen-Klein, Dexter Bailey, and David Conover. For keeping us in business, Jesse Bruschini, Mayra Mariño, reference wrangler Megan Smith, and Elizabeth Brown. For clueing me in to choice tidbits of animal information, John Todaro, John and Nancy DeBellas, Peter Osswald, Danielle Gustafson, and my daughter Alexandra Srp.

For sharing life, spotting falcons, saving horseshoe crabs, closing in the chickens at night, and feeding everybody, I thank my wife, Patricia Paladines, in whom I've long recognized a deep reflection. What she sees in me, well; as you know, I'm not a mind reader.

Not least, of course, I thank Chula, Jude, Rosebud, Kane, Velcro, Emi, Maddox, Kenzie, and so many others, great and little, free-living, domesticated, and in between—who have opened my eyes. From doggies and furry orphans of our living room and yard to the great seabird colonies of remotest shores; the great fishes, turtles, and whales of deep, wide oceans;

the hawks of autumn skies and the warblers of the springtime woods—to those in these pages and all the rest, I offer my delighted gratitude for bringing so much beauty, grace, love, joy, richness, heartache, dirt, mess, and mud into my life. In other words, for making it real.

Thanks, everybody.

INDEX

Page numbers in *italics* refer to maps.

ABOUT THE AUTHOR

CARL SAFINA's work has been recognized with MacArthur, Pew, and Guggenheim Fellowships, and his writing has won Orion, Lannan, and National Academics literary awards and the John Burroughs, James Beard, and George Raab medals. He has a PhD in ecology from Rutgers University. Safina is the inaugural holder of the endowed chair for nature and humanity at Stony Brook University, where he co-chairs the steering committee of the Alan Alda Center for Communicating Science and is the founding president of the not-for-profit Safina Center. He hosted the ten-part PBS series *Saving the Ocean with Carl Safina*. His writing appears in the *New York Times, National Geographic, Audubon,* and other periodicals, and on the Web at National Geographic News, the Huffington Post, and CNN.com. This is Carl's seventh book. He lives on Long Island, New York.